P9-ARS-940

THE THESSALONIAN EPISTLES

EPISTLES

A Call to Readiness

THE THESSALONIAN EPISTLES

A Call to Readiness

A Commentary by
D. EDMOND HIEBERT

MOODY PRESS
CHICAGO

To
my students
who have joined me
in the study of these epistles
in the original or in translation

© 1971 by
THE MOODY BIBLE INSTITUTE
OF CHICAGO

All rights reserved. No part of this book may be reproduced
in any manner whatsoever without written permission except
in the case of brief quotations embodied in critical articles or
brief reviews.

ISBN: 0-8024-8640-1

Library of Congress Catalog Card Number: 76-143478

Moody Paperback Edition, 1982

6 7 8 9 10 11 12 Printing/EB/Year 87 86 85 84 83 82

Moody Press, a ministry of the Moody Bible Institute, is
designed for education, evangelization and edification.
If we may assist you in knowing more about Christ and
the Christian life, please write us without obligation to:
Moody Press, c/o MLM, Chicago, Illinois 60610.

Printed in the United States of America

CONTENTS

Part 2   SECOND THESSALONIANS

PREFACE

THE TITLE INDICATES the nature and scope of this volume. This interpretation of the Thessalonian epistles is built around a detailed outline which is inserted into the discussion of the contents in order to keep the course of thought in the epistles clearly before the reader.

The scripture quotations are taken from the American Standard Version (1901). The interpretation however is based upon a study of the Greek text. All Greek words, whenever they are used, are translated in the context and transliterated.* The transliterations are supplied to aid the student not acquainted with that language. The author remembers his own feelings of frustration with untransliterated Greek words—and especially with untranslated Greek words—in books on the New Testament before he had opportunity to study that language.

This interpretation seeks to bring out something of the truths of the biblical text which a study of the original conveys to the careful student. It is intended for the diligent student of Scripture who has little or no personal knowledge of the Greek, yet desires to delve into the riches of the inspired Word of God.

My indebtedness to the labors of many others will readily be evident from the footnotes and bibliography.

---

*In transliterating Greek words I have used the usually adopted equivalents for the Greek letters, except in the case of *upsilon* where instead of the more usual *y* I have consistently used *u* instead.

Part 1

FIRST THESSALONIANS

1

AN INTRODUCTION TO
1 THESSALONIANS

FIRST THESSALONIANS has aptly been stamped as "a classic of Christian friendship."[1] It is a genuine letter called forth by the warm spiritual ties that bound the writers to the readers. For its proper interpretation it must be read in the light of the historical circumstances which evoked its composition. In the study of no other form of literature is it more important to know something of the life-situation amid which it was produced than in the study of a letter.

THE CITY OF THESSALONICA

Location

The city of Thessalonica enjoyed the advantages of a strategic location. The famous *Via Egnatia* (Egnatian Way), spanning Macedonia from east to west, passed through the walls of the city. This important Roman highway facilitated brisk travel and commerce and put Thessalonica into ready contact with the important inland districts on either side of it. It was the principal artery of communication between Rome and her eastern provinces.

Situated in a declivity at the northeastern corner of the Thermaic Gulf, Thessalonica had the further advantage of a splendid harbor. Its busy waterfront formed Macedonia's chief outlet to the sea. It stood in ready maritime contact with the rest of the Mediterranean world. Its only commercial rivals on the Aegean Sea were Corinth to the south and Ephesus on its eastern shores. Ships from all parts of the Roman world might be seen in the comparatively sheltered harbor at Thessalonica.

Due to its location, Thessalonica might well be called "the key to the whole of Macedonia."[2] The dictum of Meletius concerning it was, "So long as nature does not change, Thessalonica will remain wealthy and fortunate."[3] One of its native poets proudly called it the "mother of all Macedon."

11

Inhabitants

The teeming metropolis of Thessalonica was the largest city of Macedonia. Harrison estimates that during the time of Paul its population may have been as high as 200,000.[4]

The majority of its inhabitants were native Greeks, but it contained a considerable mixture of Romans, Asiatics, or Orientals of various backgrounds, including a sizable group of Jews. The Jewish colony maintained an influential synagogue where the Jewish religion and its forms of worship were furthered. It exerted a strong proselyting influence upon a considerable number of Gentiles in the city.

Like every large city, among its citizens were the very wealthy as well as the poor. Wealthy Romans often resided in the city, and its leading merchants were able to amass considerable wealth. The majority of the inhabitants supported themselves by their daily toil, by trade and manual labor.

The moral standards of the Thessalonians, the majority of whom were idolaters, were certainly no higher than those in any ordinary Greek city. Thessalonica never acquired a reputation for immorality like Corinth, yet immoral practices were frightfully common in its idolatrous society. The effects of the paganism that clutched its inhabitants were truly degrading. Immorality was fostered under the protective shield of religion in the wanton rites connected with the worship of the Cabiri, deities of Samothrace.[5]

History

It was about 315 B.C. when Cassander, the son-in-law of Philip of Macedon, collected the inhabitants of a number of villages in the area and resettled them in his new city of Thessalonica. He named it in honor of his wife, the half-sister of Alexander the Great.

When after the battle of Pydna in 168 B.C. the Romans divided the conquered territory into four districts, Thessalonica was named the capital of the second district. In 146 B.C. Macedonia was united into one Roman province with Thessalonica as the natural choice for its capital. In 42 B.C. Thessalonica was made a "free city" by Anthony and Octavian, the future Augustus, as a reward for the help given in the struggle against Brutus and Cassius.

The Roman proconsul, the governor of Macedonia, had his residence in Thessalonica, but because it was a "free city" he did not control its internal affairs. No Roman garrison was stationed there, and in spirit and atmosphere it was a Greek rather than a Roman city. Enjoying local autonomy, the city was governed by a board of magistrates, whose number of members apparently varied. According to Moulton and Milligan, "there were 5 politarchs in the time of Augustus, and 6 in the time of Antonius and Marcus Aurelius." Lightfoot holds that their number was seven rather than six.[6] They bore the rather unusual title of "politarchs" (*politarchai*, Ac 17:6), a title not found in any classical author. This fact was once made a basis for assailing the reliability of Luke, but inscriptional evidence has triumphantly vindicated his accuracy. Some five or six inscriptions bearing this title have been recovered from Thessalonica itself; a number of others have been found in different Macedonian cities, proving that the title was not restricted to Thessalonica. It has also been found in a papyrus document from Egypt.[7] The city apparently also had a senate and a public assembly.

Thessalonica has continued its existence, with fluctuating fortunes, down through the centuries. Today it is an important Greek city with a population of over 300,000. It is one of few important New Testament centers that have maintained an unbroken continuity from the first century to the present.

THE MISSIONARIES IN THESSALONICA

The preaching of the gospel in Thessalonica was but a further carrying out of the commission received by Paul at Troas to work in Macedonia (Ac 16:8-10). In recounting the story of the apostle's second missionary journey Luke gives a concise account of the mission in Thessalonica in Acts 17:1-10.

Arrival

Their successful work at Philippi was suddenly terminated when Paul and Silas received a shameful beating and imprisonment because their work had touched the sensitive nerve of vested financial interests (Ac 16; 1 Th 2:2). Events had made it clear that it was no longer expedient to remain there. Luke thus records the trip of the missionaries to Thessalonica: "Now when they had passed through Amphipolis and Apollonia, they came to Thessalonica" (Ac 17:1). The trip was made along the Egnatian Way and was a journey of about a hundred miles. There is no indication that any preaching was done in the two cities through which they passed. Apparently this was because these cities had no Jewish synagogues. Also it seems that Paul recognized the strategic importance of Thessalonica as the key to the evangelization of the whole of Macedonia and was eager to begin preaching there.

The passing by of these cities does not mean that the gospel was not to be preached there. Rather, as Roland Allen has pointed out, it was part of Paul's missionary strategy to seek to plant Christian churches in the important centers of a province with the confidence that from there the gospel would spread to the surrounding areas.[8] Thessalonica was of crucial importance in carrying out this strategy.

It is not certain who all were in the missionary party that entered Thessalonica. Who is included in Luke's *they*? The sudden dropping of the *we*, whereby Luke has shown his presence with the party from Troas to Philippi (Ac 16:10; 17:15), indicates that he remained behind at Philippi. Was Timothy also left at Philippi for some time? Acts is silent about the presence of Timothy at Thessalonica; he is next mentioned as being with Paul at Berea. Does this mean that Timothy did not journey to Thessalonica with Paul and Silas and only rejoined the missionary party at Berea? This is the view of Zahn who holds that Timothy would naturally stop to visit the new converts at Thessalonica on his way to Berea.[9] Lenski thinks that this explains why Timothy could be sent back to Thessalonica from Athens while Paul and Silas could not return; they "had been driven out of Thessalonica, while Timothy had not been. Timothy would encounter fewer difficulties."[10]

Since the name of Timothy is included in the salutation of 1 Thessalonians, others think that Timothy must also have had a share in the founding of the church. It is generally assumed that Timothy was in the weary party that concluded the hundred mile trip from Philippi to Thessalonica. Commentators point out that Luke's interest is in recording the spread of the gospel and this did not require naming the subordinate members in the party there.

That Timothy's name is included in the salutation does not prove that he had a share in the initial work at Thessalonica; it does prove that he too stood in close contact with the Thessalonian believers. If he was not at Thessalonica during the initial preaching there, he may well have formed the acquaintance of the brethren when on his way to Berea to rejoin Paul. But from 1 Thessalonians 3:5-6 it is clear that Timothy had just completed an assignment which had brought him into close contact with the suffering saints there.

Synagogue Ministry

Luke at once records that there "was a synagogue of the Jews" at Thessalonica (Ac 17:1). Paul's synagogue ministry is described as follows:

> And Paul, as his custom was, went in unto them, and for three sabbath days reasoned with them from the scriptures, opening and alleging that it behooved the Christ to suffer, and to rise again from the dead; and that this Jesus, whom, *said he,* I proclaim unto you, is the Christ. And some of them were persuaded, and consorted with Paul and Silas; and of the devout Greeks a great multitude, and of the chief women not a few (vv. 2-4).

In saying "as his custom was" Luke underlines the fact that it was Paul's practice in beginning work in a new center to start preaching in the Jewish synagogue if possible. Not only was this in harmony with his principle "to the Jew first" (Ro 1:16) but it was also the most advantageous place to begin. There he found "an audience provided for him which understood the underlying principles of his religion, and was familiar with the texts on which he based his argument."[11]

Paul's synagogue message centered around two points. He used the Old Testament Scriptures to set before his hearers the great facts concerning the promised Messiah. These Scriptures proved that it was necessary for the Messiah "to suffer, and to rise again from the dead." This emphasis upon the suffering and death of the expected Messiah would be a strange new note for Paul's audience. The traditional teaching in the synagogue did not associate suffering with the Messiah but rather proclaimed His coming as the champion and deliverer of Israel. On the basis of the talmudic teaching, Bruce concludes that there is little or no evidence to think that the Old Testament references to His sufferings were attributed to the Messiah Himself before the coming of Christ.[12]

Having established this teaching concerning the Messiah by his skillful expounding and comparing of the scriptural teaching on the subject, Paul next recounted to his synagogue audience the story of the sufferings, death, and resurrection of Jesus in exact fulfillment of these prophecies to prove that He "is the Christ." The fact that He is the Christ of course implies that He will also fulfill the prophecies concerning His coming reign. This naturally led on to the teaching concerning the return of Christ as the expected King.

Paul's synagogue audience was composed mainly of two classes of hearers, Jews and "devout Greeks." The latter class, as usual, proved to be the most responsive to his message. They may have included some "heathens honestly in search of truth,"[13] but the usual meaning of the term points to Gentiles who, disillusioned with their pagan gods and pagan morality, had been drawn to the purer ethical teachings of the Jews. They had become informal adherents of the synagogue as worshipers of Jehovah without accepting the rigorous, ritualistic demands of Judaism. While accepting the monotheism of the Old Testament and the hope of a coming deliverer, they

> had found themselves dissatisfied with the narrow nationalism and ritual requirements of Judaism, and the advent of Christianity supplied their demand for an adequate and even greater conception of God than that which Judaism provided, a nobler ethic centred in the remarkable personal example of Jesus, and a universal outlook which came as a breath of liberation after the tightness of Jewish exclusivism.[14]

The result of this synagogue ministry was the conversion of a few Jews and a large number of these God-fearers, including a number of the wives of the first men of the city.

Length of Stay

Acts speaks only of a ministry in the synagogue extending over three Sabbath days. This account is immediately followed by the story of the Jewish-led attack which forced the abrupt departure of Paul and Silas from Thessalonica. Was the stay of the missionary party limited to these three weeks, or did they spend a longer time there?

If we had only the account in Acts, we should naturally conclude that the work was confined to some twenty-one days, that the mission was limited to the circle of the synagogue, and that the pagan population of the city was not directly touched. One the other hand, 1 Thessalonians seems clearly to indicate that many of the Thessalonian converts were won directly from heathenism (1:9; 2:14). Apparently Acts does not tell the whole story.

Interpreters like Zahn, Frame, and Lenski hold that the work in Thessalonica cannot have extended much beyond these three weeks which Luke mentions. Zahn points out that meetings were also held in the synagogue on Monday and Thursday, and that the synagogue "was open at other times, and served as a meeting-place for unusual gatherings."[15] This would give the work at Thessalonica the nature of a short, intensive campaign. Frame feels that there is nothing incredible in the results attained in these three weeks "if the intensity of the religious life and the relative smallness of the group are once admitted."[16] Advocates of this short ministry point out that the Gentile converts who composed the majority of the church had already been conditioned for receiving the gospel and that Paul's powerful preaching of that gospel would achieve large results in a short time. It is further pointed out that here, like at Athens, Paul doubtless took advantage of opportunities during the week to reach Gentiles outside the synagogue.[17] Thus he may well have won some of the members directly from paganism. On the other hand, Lenski insists that 1 Thessalonians 1:9 and 2:14 "apply to Greek proselytes, and do not demand only converts from paganism."[18] Thus these advocates hold that the facts can be fitted into a ministry of three weeks.

Others think that there is good ground for holding that the stay lasted considerably beyond the three weeks mentioned in Acts. Rackham believes that "the definite mention of the three weeks' preaching in the synagogue seems to imply a turning to the Gentiles at its end, as at the Pisidian Antioch."[19] That Paul should turn directly to the Gentiles in Thessalonica when the synagogue was closed to him is very probable.

In Ephesus his work in the synagogue was followed by a two-year ministry directly to the Gentiles (Ac 19:8-10). The devout Gentiles won in the synagogue would form a natural bridge to the Gentile masses of the city.

Beare holds that "the pastoral care with which the apostles had followed up their evangelism [see especially 2:9-12] and the strength of the affection which they had developed toward their converts [2:8; 3:6-10] would suggest, if not absolutely require, a period of months rather than weeks."[20] He is also impressed with the strong Gentile complexion of the church as revealed in the epistles. He concludes that from a reading of 1 Thessalonians alone one would never learn "that there was a Jewish community in Thessalonica at all, much less that it had been the center of the mission and had provided the apostle with the nucleus of the church."[21] Beare's comment well underlines the Gentile features of the church, but it overlooks the true reason for Paul's strong words against the Jews in 2:14-16.

Advocates of a longer stay also point to the fact that Paul supported himself by manual labor while at Thessalonica (1 Th 2:9; 2 Th 3:8). Gloag thinks that "it was his custom to do so only when his residence in any city was prolonged."[22] It may simply mean that he was low on funds when he arrived and was settling down for an anticipated longer stay. The practice of self-support was necessary to keep his ministry free from any suspicion of being merely a money-making activity.

More substantial evidence for a longer stay is found in the fact that the Philippian church sent Paul an offering twice while he was working at Thessalonica (Phil 4:16). While it is possible that such a gift "once and again" was received during the short period of three weeks, it is not probable. Since he was working, it is not likely that the Philippian brethren felt that he was in such urgent need for support, nor is it likely that they would be able to afford it. "Once and again" naturally means twice, but Frame seeks to break the force of this argument by rendering it "(when I was) in Thessalonica and repeatedly (when I was in other places)."[23] While this is a possible interpretation of the original, the other is simpler.

We cannot specify with certainty how long Paul and Silas remained in Thessalonica. It seems preferable to hold that the stay was longer than three weeks and that the subsequent period was used to work directly with the Gentiles of the city. The length of this period can only be conjectured. Ramsay was willing to allow six months for the work at Thessalonica.[24] In view of the fact that Paul felt he was prematurely torn away from his converts, the suggestion of Moffatt that "two or three months possibly may be allowed for this fruitful mission at Thessalonica" seems more probable.[25]

Departure

Luke gives a vivid account of the Jewish plot that succeeded in forcing the missionaries out of Thessalonica.

> But the Jews, being moved with jealousy, took unto them certain vile fellows of the rabble, and gathering a crowd, set the city on an uproar; and assaulting the house of Jason, they sought to bring them forth to the people. And when they found them not, they dragged Jason and certain brethren before the rulers of the city, crying, These that have turned the world upside down are come hither also; whom Jason hath received: and these all act contrary to the decrees of Caesar, saying that there is another king, *one* Jesus. And they troubled the multitude and the rulers of the city, when they heard these things. And when they had taken security from Jason and the rest, they let them go. And the brethren immediately sent away Paul and Silas by night unto Berea (Ac 17:5-10*a*).

Luke's account of the Thessalonian mission leaves the impression that this riot may well have occurred almost immediately after the third week of synagogue ministry by the missionaries. But the account is equally intelligible if there was a period of ministry to the Gentiles before the Jews staged their riot. The Jews had closed the synagogue to Paul but they continued to watch with jealous eyes the success of his work in the city. Since the work was now completely beyond their jurisdiction, they could only watch with helpless wrath unless they took violent action to expel the missionaries from the city.

Their base motive for their action is perfectly understandable. For years they had been wooing receptive Gentiles with the hope that they would be led fully to embrace the Jewish faith. But these hopes had been shattered by the work of the missionaries. Not only had large numbers of these God-fearing Gentiles been won by the apostolic company, but their continued success among the Gentiles in the city ruined all further Jewish hopes of reaching any of them with their rigid legal requirements. Regarding the work of the missionaries as a perversion of the Jewish faith, they resolutely took strong measures to suppress it.

Unable to act alone against the missionaries, the Jews resorted to vile strategy. From among the numerous market-loungers, men loitering around in the marketplace and eager for some excitement, the Jews enlisted those who were known for their trouble-making. With their aid they gathered a crowd and set the city into a loud and boisterous commotion. When a sufficient following had been secured, they assaulted the house of Jason with the intention of seizing the missionaries. Jason's house apparently served not only as the place of residence for the missionaries but also as the place of assembly for the Christians.

The mob, led by the Jews, burst in on the home of Jason and searched for Paul and Silas, intending to haul them before "the people," apparently the Thessalonian assembly. Since Paul and Silas could not be located, they dragged Jason and certain other Christians before the city rulers, the politarchs, and charged them with being parties to a revolutionary movement. They were sheltering revolutionaries, men who "have turned the world upside down." More specifically they were charged with treasonable activity, for they were all acting "contrary to the decrees of Caesar, saying that there is another king, one Jesus."

The charge was cleverly planned and clearly shows the Jewish prompting behind it. Since it was easy to pervert Paul's teaching concerning the return of Christ as judge and coming ruler, it had a semblance of truth. His spiritual teaching concerning the expected return of the Messianic King was easily misinterpreted to mean that he was disloyal to Caesar by advocating adherence to another king.

It was a dangerous charge, one to which the politarchs would be very sensitive. It was the charge most likely to arouse the antagonism of the politarchs against the Christians. But in spite of the agitation of the crowd, the magistrates refused to be panicked into violent action. Instead, they took security of Jason and his associates and released them. Perhaps they saw through the plot, suspecting that these Jews were acting out of hostility rather than loyalty to the government. Ramsay calls the action of the politarchs "the mildest that was prudent in the circumstances."[26] By their action the magistrates guarded themselves against any charge of condoning treason, the Christians were not unjustly hurt, and the agitators could feel that action had been taken against their enemies.

The exact significance of the security or pledge taken from Jason and his associates is not certain. Ramsay thought that it was a monetary security or bail which required them "to prevent the cause of disturbance, Paul, from coming to Thessalonica."[27] But Acts does not say that Jason was required to guarantee the withdrawal of Paul from Thessalonica. Paul's statement that he twice tried to return to Thessalonica (1 Th 2:17-18) seems against this conclusion. The probable meaning is that Jason and the brethren were forced to give bond that the peace of the city would not be further disturbed. This demand in effect made it impossible for Paul and Silas to continue work in the city. Were they to risk any further preaching there the Jews would undoubtedly stage another riot. This would involve Jason and his fellow Christians in serious financial loss and would arouse the active hostility of the magistrates against the church.

Under the circumstances the missionaries agreed to the view of the brethren that it was expedient for Paul and Silas to leave at once. This forced departure, due to vicious circumstances beyond their control, prematurely tore the missionaries from their young converts. It deprived the young church of the needed personal guidance of the missionaries. It also unleashed the outbreak of persecution against believers, which continued long after the missionaries had departed.* That the instigators of the persecution were Jews is clear from the Acts account as well as Paul's statement in 1 Thessalonians 2:14-16. But clearly the antagonism and persecution started by the Jews were caught up and continued by their pagan neighbors (1 Th 2:14).

THE OCCASION AND PURPOSE OF 1 THESSALONIANS

Occasion

Leaving Thessalonica that night under cover of darkness, Paul and Silas traveled some forty miles westward to Berea. Timothy, whether or not he had worked with them at Thessalonica, joined them there. An effective ministry in the synagogue at Berea was again disrupted by the trouble-making Jews from Thessalonica. This outbreak of hostilities compelled Paul, the main target of their hatred, to leave Berea quickly and quietly.

Silas and Timothy remained on in Berea. Some of the Berean brethren conducted Paul safely to Athens. Upon returning they delivered an urgent summons to Silas and Timothy to come to Athens as soon as possible (Ac 17:10-15).

Acts records that Silas and Timothy did rejoin Paul after he had moved on to Corinth (18:1, 5). Had we only the condensed account of Acts we would conclude that they had not been able to comply with Paul's request until then. But from 1 Thessalonians 3:1-5 it is clear that at least Timothy, apparently also Silas, did come to Athens as requested.

Ever since Paul had been torn away from his Thessalonian converts his pastoral heart had been deeply concerned about them. He was well aware that he had left them a heritage of suffering. He had indeed warned them that suffering awaited them in becoming believers (1 Th 3:4), but would they endure when subjected to the fiery test? His own experience of the implacable hatred of the Thessalonian Jews, even at Berea, only increased his concern for his new converts. If the Jews had hounded him all the way to Berea, what would they do to his followers at home? He could well imagine the bitter attacks to which they would be subjected. Apparently Timothy and Silas brought unfavorable news which further increased Paul's anxiety.

The uncertainty concerning the effect on the Thessalonians of the storm of persecution raging around them produced an unbearable strain on

*From 2 Th 1:4 we learn that the persecution against the church was still continuing, or had broken out anew, when that epistle was written.

Paul. Unable to endure the suspense, he decided that Timothy should return to Thessalonica to encourage the brethren and to bring back a report concerning them. Timothy would have no great difficulty in going back to Thessalonica since he had not been publicly identified with the disturbance there. Apparently Silas was also dispatched on a mission to Macedonia, perhaps Philippi. Paul may well have feared that the bitter hatred of the Thessalonian Jews might also lash out against the believers at Philippi.

The immediate occasion for writing 1 Thessalonians was the return of Timothy from Thessalonica with his report (1 Th 3:6-7; Ac 18:5). The report was largely favorable. It relieved Paul's anxiety and filled him with praise and exultation. In response he sat down and dictated this letter, full of personal affection and thoughtful instructions. Since he was unable to return personally, a letter was the best substitute for his presence with them.

Was the letter also written in response to a letter which Timothy had brought along from the Thessalonian church? This was suggested by J. Rendel Harris and more recently has been advocated by Chalmer E. Faw.[28] Faw suggested that the first three chapters echo Timothy's oral report while the last two chapters are a point-by-point reply to the questions sent by the Thessalonians. He pointed out that the introductory phrase "but concerning" (*peri de*) in 4:9 and 5:1 occurs in several passages in 1 Corinthians where Paul makes a direct reply to the letter of the Corinthians to him. But I Thessalonians does not offer an exact parallel to 1 Corinthians. There Paul explicitly informs us that he is replying to a letter (7:1), but 1 Thessalonians contains no hint that he is answering a letter. Harrison well remarks that Paul's failure to recognize such a communication from the Thessalonians would have been a discourtesy on his part.[29] The phrase to which Faw appealed occurs elsewhere in the New Testament in circumstances which clearly do not reflect a reply to a letter (Mk 12:26; 13:32; Jn 16:11). The details which Faw thought pointed to an oral report in the first part and a letter in the last part are quite indistinguishable.

The hypothesis of a letter from the Thessalonians is in itself quite tenable, but the evidence for it is elusive. If the hypothesis is accepted, it is not difficult to construct a series of questions to which reply is being made. That such a supposed list of questions can be reconstructed offers little proof that such a letter was actually written. A similar letter of inquiry might also be constructed for the letter to the Philippians. The hypothesis lacks a valid foundation. Hendriksen concludes, "A memorandum carefully prepared by Timothy himself or even a systematic oral report fills all the requirements."[30]

Purpose

The content of 1 Thessalonians indicates quite adequately the purpose of the letter. It was written to record the reactions of the writers and meet the needs of the readers.

The first purpose of the letter was to record the writers' joy at the good news concerning the steadfastness of the readers in the face of the affliction to which they were subjected. This report evoked a veritable torrent of thanksgiving to God for the readers, as found in chapter 1.

A further purpose of the letter was to refute certain false charges and slanderous insinuations being circulated in Thessalonica against the missionaries. This campaign of slander, directed especially against Paul, was apparently promoted by the Jews. It was aimed at detaching the converts from their loyalty to the missionaries. For the Thessalonians to believe these charges would be fatal to the work of the gospel in Macedonia. They must be refuted. But Paul's answer to these charges, contained in chapters 2 and 3, was not evoked by a feeling of wounded personal pride; he was motivated by a passionate concern to safeguard the faith of his converts.

The attacks being made were of a personal nature. It was an attempt to strike at the faith of the Thessalonian believers through an effort to discredit the messengers from whom they had received their new faith. The missionaries were the first Christians the Thessalonian believers had known. From them they had learned the nature of Christian life and character. If therefore the enemies could shake the faith of the converts in the moral integrity and trustworthiness of these men, their faith would be practically destroyed.

The attacks assailed the motives of the missionaries in carrying on their work in Thessalonica. The attempt was being made to class them with the wandering, mercenary, religious teachers of that day who plied their skills on the gullible people for personal benefit. Was not the fact that Paul's "dupes" at Philippi had twice sent him money even while he was at Thessalonica, ample evidence that his preaching was really a money-making business? Were not all their smooth words and persuasive professions of interest in the welfare of their followers a cover-up for their own self-seeking?

Paul countered these slanderous charges of self-seeking by asking the readers simply to recall the nature of their own experiences with the missionaries while they were working there. A clear recollection of the facts will refute the charges (2:1-12).

Paul was further charged with cowardice in connection with his hurried departure and continued absence from Thessalonica. When charges of seditious teaching were made against him before the rulers of the city Paul did not dare to meet them. When dangers arose because of his teachings he quickly assured his own safety by flight, leaving his converts to suffer the consequences. If he was so interested in them as he claimed, why did he not come back?

Paul refuted these accusations by recounting his deep yearnings for them and his repeated efforts to return to them. His efforts to return had been hindered. Evidence of his sincere concern for them and desire to reestablish contact with them was seen in the fact that he had willingly sacrificed the help of Timothy to send him back to them. Timothy's assignment had been to further the spiritual welfare of the readers as well as to relieve his own anxiety concerning them (2:17-3:5).

A further purpose of the letter was to meet the definite needs in the church, which Timothy had reported. Certain defects and problems needed to be dealt with. Had Paul been able to return personally he would have dealt with these matters directly. What he would have preferred to do in a face-to-face encounter he must now do by letter. The last two chapters are devoted to these matters.

On the basis of Timothy's report he feels it necessary to put them on guard against their former heathen vices by reminding them of the superiority of Christian morality over paganism, and to exhort them to continued love of the brethren and to honest work (4:1-12). He comforts and reassures them concerning their loved ones who have died, by explaining the nature of events at the return of the Lord for His own (4:13-18). He urges them to personal watchfulness in view of the uncertainty of the time of the Lord's return (5:1-6). He appeals to them to show proper respect for their leaders, to unite in securing the needed church order and discipline, and to live a life of holiness (5:12-22). His answers and instructions were further proof of his unselfish interest in the spiritual welfare of the readers.

THE PLACE AND DATE OF 1 THESSALONIANS

Place

It is clear from Acts that this epistle was written during the second missionary journey. The place of writing is almost certainly Corinth. Silas was Paul's co-worker on this journey, but he is not again mentioned in Acts following the termination of the work at Corinth. Paul had sent Timothy back to Thessalonica from Athens (1 Th 3:1-2), and this epistle was written upon his return from Thessalonica (3:6-7). From Acts 18:1 and 5 we learn that Silas and Timothy rejoined Paul at Corinth upon returning from Macedonia. It was shortly after Paul had moved on from Athens to Corinth. Only a few months at most had elapsed since Paul left Thessalonica. Their presence together now at Corinth meets all the requirements as to the place of writing.

A few manuscripts carry a subscription which reads "Written from Athens." This subscription, which of course was not a part of the original, embodies a scribal conclusion concerning the place of writing. It is evidently an error. It apparently arose out of a misunderstanding of Paul's words, "we thought it good to be left at Athens alone" (3:1). Paul's remark refers to a past event "and indirectly implies that the apostle was not at Athens when he wrote these words."[31]

Date

There are few events in the life of Paul that can be fixed with any chronological precision. The work of Paul at Corinth offers one of the most certain contacts with secular chronology in that it was partly parallel with the proconsulate of Gallio (Ac 18:12). Proconsuls usually held office for a year, seldom for two.

An imperfectly preserved inscription of a letter from the Emperor Claudius was discovered at Delphi in the present century which named Gallio as proconsul. Claudius dated the letter as "in the 12th year of his tribunicial power, acclaimed Emperor for the 26th time."[32] The twelfth year of his tribunicial power extended from January 25, A.D. 52 to January 24, 53, while his twenty-seventh acclamation as emperor took place before August 1, 52. The inscription therefore definitely locates Gallio in Corinth between January 25 and August 1, 52.

But at what time of the year did Gallio take office? It is generally assumed that he arrived in Corinth about July 1. The mutilated inscription apparently indicates that Gallio had been in office long enough to give the Emperor some information of importance concerning the Delphians. This leads to the natural conclusion that Gallio must have entered upon his proconsulship at Corinth in midsummer of A.D. 51. This date is widely accepted today.[33]

Other scholars, however, insist that this date is about a year too early. Lenski points out that "Imperial orders designated the time when the appointed proconsul was to leave Rome for his province as April 1, later April 15."[34] He therefore holds that Gallio did not begin his office in midsummer but rather in May, and that the date was May 1, 52, rather than 51. Harrop says that it is "virtually certain that he was proconsul of Achaia in A.D. 52-53."[35] This view places Gallio's coming to Corinth about ten months later.

The narrative in Acts does not indicate when Paul was hauled before Gallio by the Corinthian Jews, but it seems clear that it was shortly after his arrival. The Jews would be eager to have Paul silenced as soon as possible. Paul's encounter with Gallio must then be dated either in July 51 or May 52.

It is not certain how long Paul had already been in Corinth when Gallio arrived. Estimates differ. Lenski thinks Paul had been there six months.[36] On the other hand Kümmel says that "Paul had already been in Corinth one and a half years."[37] Clearly Paul had already exercised a powerful ministry in Corinth by that time, but Luke's mention that Paul still remained there "many days" after the encounter indicates that it was not at the very end of his work at Corinth, which lasted eighteen months (Ac 18:11). It seems most probable that he had been at Corinth a year at the time. Thus Paul arrived in Corinth in midsummer of 50 or in early summer of 51.

Since 1 Thessalonians was written within a short time after his arrival, the epistle may be dated in late summer or early fall of either 50 or 51. In either case we see that it was written within twenty or twenty-one years after the crucifixion of Christ and seems to be the earliest of the Pauline epistles.

Who took the letter to Thessalonica we do not know, but it is certain that a private courier was employed. The Emperor Augustus had established an imperial postal system, but its use was strictly limited to state and official communications. Ordinary correspondence had to be sent by a special messenger or taken by a friend or passing traveler. Paul generally sent his letters by one of his co-workers. The very nature of his letters made it desirable that its transmission be entrusted to someone who was in sympathy with Paul's work.

THE AUTHENTICITY OF 1 THESSALONIANS

The Pauline authorship of 1 Thessalonians is no longer seriously challenged. A hundred years ago many scholars felt serious difficulties regarding its authenticity, owing largely to the influence of the Tübingen School. F. C. Baur, its leading spirit, accepted as genuinely Pauline only the four *Hauptbriefe* (Romans, 1 and 2 Corinthians, and Galatians) and denied that Paul was the author of the remainder of the epistles ascribed to him. The radical Dutch school of Van Manen even made a clean sweep of all the Pauline epistles.

It is recognized today that the objections that were advanced against the authenticity of 1 Thessalonians are inadequate or even baseless, and may in fact be arguments in favor of its genuineness. The objections that have been raised are "more than counterbalanced by the tone and character of the Epistle as a whole."[38] An impartial reading of the letter reveals an unmistakable ring of reality which no imitator could ever have attained. No convincing explanation for its appearance has yet been produced if it was a forgery. The historical situation, as presented above, offers a logical and rational explanation for this letter purporting to be from the hand of Paul. Modern scholarship has reached practical unanimity concerning its Pauline authorship. Thus Robert and Feuillet can say, "There is no longer any dispute about the authenticity of I Thes, for at the present time it is accepted by all the critics as a work of St. Paul."[39]

2

AN INTERPRETATION OF THE TITLE

THE TITLE obviously is not from Paul. It is an appropriate scribal super-scription designating the nature, authorship, and destination of the document in hand.

The scribal addition was an obvious convenience. A papyrus roll, inscribed with a copy of this letter, would usually have affixed to the outside of the rolled up scroll some such designation as a means of easy identification. When the epistles of Paul were brought together as a definite collection, such an identifying superscription was logically placed at the head of the text of each letter in order to distinguish it readily from the others.

In the oldest manuscripts of the Pauline epistles the titles are brief and to the point. Thus this epistle is simply designated "Unto Thessalonians 1" (*Pros Thessalonikeis A*). But later scribes were not content with these bare designations and they generally expanded and amplified them. To the name of the recipients there was added the name of the writer, "of Paul," or sometimes, "of Paul the Apostle," as well as the indication that the writing was an "epistle." Since there was a second letter to the Thessalonians this one was naturally designated as the "first."

The designation of the writing as an epistle correctly indicates its nature. The Greek word *epistolē*, from which our English term *epistle* is derived, meant something sent by a messenger, a message; then a written communication to a person or group of people. The word occurs twenty-four times in the New Testament and in our common English versions it is rendered "epistle" or "letter" with almost equal frequency.* It might be applied to an official as well as a private communication. All the extant Pauline epistles are communications from Paul in his official character.

Some writers insist upon a rigid distinction between a letter and an epistle and maintain that the Pauline writings should be called letters rather than epistles. Adolf Deissmann defined a "letter" as a private com-

---

*The KJV renders *epistolē* "letter" 9 times and "epistle" 15 times; the ASV uses "epistle" 17 times; the RSV uses "letter" only.

munication intended for a particular individual or group, while an "epistle" he defined as a literary production more impersonal and general in aim and intended for the general public.[1] Under these definitions the writings of Paul must be classified as "letters." It is certain that Paul did not compose theological dissertations intended for Christians everywhere under the guise of a letter to a particular group. All the writings of Paul are marked by that intimacy and spontaneity which characterize genuine letters. His writings arose out of a definite life situation and were intended to meet a definite need.

But the suggested distinction between *letter* and *epistle* cannot be sharply maintained in regard to the writings of Paul. While they clearly reveal the characteristics of genuine correspondence, they contain literary elements which far transcend the merely local and temporal characteristics of a letter. His letters were directed to the needs of the readers to whom they were addressed; yet in the providence of God, Paul and the other New Testament epistolary writers so wrote that their writings possessed abiding value and authority for the universal church. Because of their unique nature there need be no objection to the common practice of applying both designations to the Pauline writings.

The Pauline epistles stand forever distinguished from the ordinary letters of that day. The contemporary letters, evoked by the affairs of everyday life, passed into oblivion with their composition; but these letters have retained their significance and value through the centuries. The secular letters of the day, temporal in their aims and import, perished with the occasion; the letters of Paul, characterized by a dynamic nature and permanent worth, are ageless treasures. Their enduring significance, their spiritual vitality, and their transforming power forever stamp these epistles as unique. Thus Moule observes, "There had been nothing quite like the Christian epistle previously—still less, before or since, has anything quite like the Pauline epistle appeared."[2] Vitalized by that divine element usually defined as inspiration, the Pauline epistles challenge us to a rich and rewarding study.

3

AN OUTLINE OF 1 THESSALONIANS

I. Salutation 1:1
   A. Writers
   B. Readers
   C. Greeting

II. Personal: Relations to the Thessalonians, 1:2-3:13
   A. Thanksgiving for them, 1:2-10
      1. Character of the thanksgiving, v. 2
      2. Grounds for the thanksgiving, vv. 3-10
         a) Because of their Christian virtues, v. 3
         b) Because of their divine election, vv. 4-7
            (1) Assurance of their election, v. 4
            (2) Reasons for the assurance, vv. 5-7
               (a) Preaching to them, v. 5
               (b) Response by them, vv. 6-7
                  (i) External manifestation, v. 6a
                  (ii) Accompanying experiences, v. 6b
                  (iii) Widespread result, v. 7
         c) Because of reports concerning them, vv. 8-10
            (1) Facts behind the reports, v. 8
            (2) Contents of the reports, vv. 9-10
               (a) Success among them, v. 9a
               (b) Change in them, vv. 9b-10
                  (i) Turning to God, v. 9b
                  (ii) Serving God, v. 9c
                  (iii) Awaiting His Son, v. 10
   B. Relationship while with them, 2:1-16
      1. Ministry at Thessalonica, vv. 1-12
         a) Circumstances of the ministry, vv. 1-2
            (1) Their knowledge of it, v. 1a

(2) Description of it, vv. 1b-2
    (a) Negative assertion, v. 1b
    (b) Positive delineation, v. 2
b) Motives of the ministers, vv. 3-4
    (1) Denial of impure motives, v. 3
    (2) Work under God's approval, v. 4
c) Conduct of the messengers, vv. 5-12
    (1) Description of their conduct, vv. 5-8
        (a) What their conduct was not like, vv. 5-6
        (b) What their conduct was like, vv. 7-8
            (i) Nature of the conduct, v. 7
            (ii) Expression of the conduct, v. 8
    (2) Memories of their conduct, vv. 9-12
        (a) Memory of the work among them, v. 9
        (b) Witness to the work among them, vv. 10-12
            (i) Character of their conduct, v. 10
            (ii) Work with their converts, vv. 11-12
                [a] Its nature, v. 11a
                [b] Its elements, v. 11b
                [c] Its aim, v. 12

2. Renewed thanksgiving for the converts, vv. 13-16
  a) Reception of the Word of God, v. 13
    (1) Thanksgiving for the reception, v. 13a
    (2) Nature of the reception, v. 13b
  b) Suffering because of the Word of God, v. 14
    (1) Sufferers imitated, v. 14a
    (2) Suffering experienced, v. 14b
  c) Jews' opposition to God's Word, vv. 15-16
    (1) Its violent manifestations, v. 15a
    (2) Its sad evaluation, vv. 15b-16a
    (3) Its fatal outcome, v. 16b

C. Relations since separated from them, 2:17-3:13
  1. Desire to revisit them hindered, 2:17-20
    a) Frustrated efforts to return to them, vv. 17-18
      (1) Nature of the separation, v. 17a
      (2) Endeavor to return, vv. 17b-18a
      (3) Hindrance by Satan, v. 18b
    b) Deep affection for them, vv. 19-20
      (1) Question asked, v. 19a
      (2) Answer suggested, v. 19b
      (3) Answer asserted, v. 20

   2. Sending of Timothy to them, 3:1-5
       a) Circumstances behind the sending, v. 1
       b) Designation of the one sent, v. 2*a*
       c) Purpose in sending, vv. 2*b*-5
            (1) In relation to the Thessalonians, vv. 2*b*-4
                (*a*) Designated task, vv. 2*b*-3*a*
                (*b*) Supporting reminder, vv. 3*b*-4
            (2) In relation to Paul, v. 5
   3. Effect of Timothy's report about them, 3:6-13
       a) Report brought by Timothy, v. 6
            (1) His coming from them, v. 6*a*
            (2) His report concerning them, v. 6*b*
       b) Reaction to Timothy's report, vv. 7-10
            (1) Experience of encouragement, vv. 7-8
            (2) Thanksgiving and prayer, vv. 9-10
                (*a*) Thanksgiving because of them, v. 9
                (*b*) Prayer in regard to them, v. 10
       c) Prayer in view of the report, vv. 11-13
            (1) Petition concerning the writers, v. 11
            (2) Petition concerning the readers, vv. 12-13
                (*a*) Petition formulated, v. 12
                (*b*) Aim indicated, v. 13

III. Practical: Instructions in Doctrine and Life, 4:1-5:24
   A. Exhortations concerning Christian living, 4:1-12
      1. Exhortation to advance in God-pleasing conduct, vv. 1-2
          a) Attitude in making the exhortation, v. 1*a*
          b) Content of the exhortation, v. 1*b*
          c) Reminder of the past charges, v. 2
      2. Exhortation to sanctification, vv. 3-8
          a) Basis for the exhortation, v. 3*a*
          b) Application of sanctification, vv. 3*b*-6*a*
              (1) To abstain from fornication, v. 3*b*
              (2) To know how to possess himself of his own vessel,
                  vv. 4-5
                  (*a*) Positive duty, v. 4
                  (*b*) Negative description, v. 5
              (3) To avoid wronging the brother, v. 6*a*
          c) Reasons for the exhortation, vv. 6*b*-8
              (1) Its violation will bring God's vengeance, v. 6*b*
              (2) Its harmony with the divine will, v. 7
              (3) Its rejection is a rejection of God, v. 8

   3. Exhortation to brotherly love and industry, vv. 9-12
     a) Commendation of their love, vv. 9-10*a*
       (1) Commendatory statement, v. 9*a*
       (2) Confirmatory evidence, vv. 9*b*-10*a*
     b) Exhortations to those loving, vv. 10*b*-12
       (1) Exhortation to abound in love, v. 10*b*
       (2) Exhortation to be industrious, vv. 11-12
         (*a*) Contents of the exhortation, v. 11*a*
         (*b*) Reminder of past charges, v. 11*b*
         (*c*) Purpose in the exhortation, v. 12

B. Instructions concerning the dead in Christ, 4:13-18
   1. Character of the instructions, v. 13
   2. Contents of the instructions, vv. 14-17
     a) Assurance concerning their dead, v. 14
     b) Revelation concerning the two groups, v. 15
       (1) Character of the revelation, v. 15*a*
       (2) Corrective in the revelation, v. 15*b*
     c) Portrayal of Christ's return, vv. 16-17
       (1) Manner of His return, v. 16*a*
       (2) Events at His return, vv. 16*b*-17*a*
       (3) Consequence of His return, v. 17*b*
   3. Comfort in the instructions, v. 18

C. Exhortation to personal watchfulness, 5:1-11
   1. Uncertainty of the time of Christ's coming, vv. 1-2
     a) Their information concerning the times and the seasons, v. 1
     b) Their knowledge concerning the day of the Lord, v. 2
   2. Result of the uncertainty for the unprepared, v. 3
   3. Life of believers as sons of the day, vv. 4-11
     a) Characterization of believers, vv. 4-5
     b) Exhortation to preparedness, vv. 6-8
       (1) Exhortation to watchfulness, vv. 6-7
         (*a*) Statement of the exhortation, v. 6
         (*b*) Confirmation of the exhortation, v. 7
       (2) Exhortation to be armored, v. 8
     c) Salvation appointed for believers, vv. 9-10
       (1) Nature of salvation, v. 9*a*
       (2) Agent of salvation, vv. 9*b*-10*a*
       (3) Goal of salvation, v. 10*b*
     d) Exhortation to mutual edification, v. 11

D. Instructions concerning assembly relations, 5:12-15
  1. Instructions concerning their leaders, vv. 12-13
    a) Attitude toward their leaders, vv. 12-13*a*
      (1) To know them, v. 12
      (2) To esteem them, v. 13*a*
    b) Preservation of peaceful relations, v. 13*b*
  2. Instructions concerning faulty members, vv. 14-15
    a) Work with various individuals, v. 14
    b) Promotion of proper relations with others, v. 15
E. Instructions for holy living, 5:16-24
  1. Principles for holy living, vv. 16-22
    a) Principles for the inner life, vv. 16-18
      (1) Triplet of commands, vv. 16-18*a*
      (2) Justification for the commands, v. 18*b*
    b) Principles for corporate spiritual life, vv. 19-22
      (1) Negative commands, vv. 19-20
      (2) Positive commands, vv. 21-22
  2. Prayer for their entire sanctification, vv. 23-24
    a) Statement of the request, v. 23*a*
    b) Elaboration of the request, v. 23*b*
    c) Assurance concerning the answer, v. 24

IV. Conclusion, 5:25-28
  A. Request for their prayers, v. 25
  B. Greeting in mutual love, v. 26
  C. Letter to be read to all, v. 27
  D. Benediction of Christ's grace, v. 28

4

SALUTATION

1:1 Paul, and Silvanus, and Timothy, unto the church of the Thessalonians in God the Father and the Lord Jesus Christ: Grace to you and peace.

THE STRUCTURE of this brief salutation conforms to the prevailing epistolary practice of that day. The opening salutation of a letter commonly followed a basic three-point formula: A to B, greeting. This formula was adhered to by Christians and non-Christians alike (cf. Ac 15:23; 23:26). Thus for a writer to begin his letter with his own name was accepted procedure and entirely devoid of any egotistical implication. It was certainly more logical than the modern practice of appending our signature at the close, for who ever reads a letter without first turning to its close to identify the writer?

Each of these three points of a salutation might be expanded at will. In his various epistles Paul's expansion of any one or all of these points is always in harmony with the genius of Christianity and the needs of the occasion. Here only the second member receives any expansion. Any special stress in the salutation is thus placed on the readers. Paul felt no strain between himself and his readers when he wrote. The relations between himself and the Thessalonians were normal. They were ready for instruction and admonition.

A. WRITERS

Any communication coming from Paul, and Silvanus, and Timothy would at once evoke eager interest on the part of its recipients. The very names stirred memories of men who had intimate contacts with the addressees.

The union of their names in the salutation indicates that, after having parted at Athens (3:1), the three men were together again in Corinth at the time of writing. Following Paul's departure from Corinth on the second missionary journey we have no evidence that the three ever worked together again.

34

Paul's name naturally stands first as the leading spirit of the group and as the real author of the epistle (cf. 2:18; 3:5; 5:27). But he gladly associates with his own the names of these co-workers who have labored with him in the work of the gospel at Thessalonica. Fergusson called them "the joint asserters and approvers of the truth contained in it."[1] They are represented as joint authors not only because they fully endorsed all that Paul wrote but because they stood very much in the same position to the Thessalonians as Paul himself, as devoted messengers to them who might claim the respect and obedience of these young believers. Thus, as Lenski asserts, "this letter is the voice of the three,"[2] although Paul himself formulated and dictated its contents. Thus his consistent use of *we* retains its natural meaning and need not be explained away as an editorial *we*. Who acted as Paul's amanuensis we do not know, although some have conjectured that it was Timothy.

The apostle's Jewish name was Saul (*Saulos*), the Grecianized form of the Hebrew *Shaoul*. It means "asked for." He is always called Saul in Acts until his clash with Bar-Jesus at Paphos, when Luke suddenly writes, "Saul, the one also Paul" (*Saulos ho kai Paulos*, Ac 13:9). Thereafter he is always called Paul in the Acts as well as in the epistles. This change to the use of his Roman name is peculiarly appropriate at the time he was entering upon his position of leadership in the evangelization of the Gentiles. As a Jew who was born a Roman citizen (Ac 22:28), he doubtless carried both names from birth. Apparently the two names were chosen by his parents because of their resemblance in sound. It was a common practice for Jews of the dispersion to have a Jewish as well as a Roman name.

The name Paul means "little." But there is no evidence in the New Testament that either Paul or any of his contemporaries attached any personal significance to the meaning of his name. Certainly his reference to himself in Ephesians 3:8 as "less than the least of all saints" cannot be claimed as a playful reference to the meaning of his name. But later expositors did attempt to draw spiritual significance from the name.*

Silvanus is a Roman proper name, originally the name of the god of the woods, and hence signifies "woodland." As the man whom Paul chose as his associate for the second missionary journey (Ac 15:40), his name naturally stands second. Luke always calls him Silas, but Paul always uses Silvanus. A comparison of Acts 18:5 with 2 Corinthians 1:19 establishes that the Silvanus of the Pauline epistles is the Silas of Acts. Silvanus was

---

*Hendriksen raises the question why Paul did not continue to use his Jewish name in its Grecianized form, *Saulos*, while working among the Greeks. He aptly replies, "This, however, would not have been pleasant. Who likes to be called *loose, wanton, straddling, waddling* (saulos)?" (William Hendriksen, "Exposition of I and II Thessalonians," in *New Testament Commentary*, p. 38, note).

apparently his adopted name of Roman citizenship (cf. Ac 16:37-38), presumably chosen because of the resemblance in sound.

We first hear of Silas in Acts at the time of the Jerusalem Conference; he was then an esteemed member of the Jerusalem church and regarded as one of the "chief men among the brethren" (15:22). He was also a "prophet" (15:32). He doubtless was a Jew by birth, otherwise it is difficult to account for the esteem in which he was held in the mother church. That he belonged to the Hellenistic section of the Jerusalem church is implied from the fact that he was a Roman citizen (16:37) as well as his hearty agreement with the decision of the conference upholding the liberty of Gentile believers (15:22-32). Thus his background and sympathies well fitted him to be a co-worker with Paul among the Gentiles.

Silas worked aggressively with Paul during the stirring events of the second missionary journey (Ac 15:40-18:6). But we hear no more of him in connection with Paul after the apostle left Corinth. He simply disappears. There is no further mention of him in Acts, nor do the Pauline epistles refer to him in connection with any subsequent event. It is probable that he is the Silvanus mentioned in 1 Peter 5:12, but since the name is common the identity cannot be insisted on.

Paul naturally named Silvanus before Timothy, for he was an older and more experienced man. But Timothy is rightly included in this triumvirate because he too had close connections with the addressees. He is not specifically mentioned in Acts in connection with the founding of the Thessalonian church. This may be due to the subordinate position of Timothy in the missionary party. A probable suggestion is that Timothy had remained at Philippi when Paul and Silas left for Thessalonica and that Timothy rejoined them at Berea (Ac 17:14). But Timothy had just returned from Thessalonica; Paul had sent him there with the assignment to further the stability of the believers in Thessalonica (1 Th 3:1-2, 6). Even if Timothy was not with Paul and Silas during the initial mission there, he had close and valued contact with the church.

Timothy was half Greek, reared in a pagan community (Ac 16:1). There is no indication that he too, like the others named, bore a double name. This name is uniformly given as Timothy (*Timotheos*), meaning "honoring God."† Doubtless his Jewish mother gave her son the name in the sincere hope that he would live to fulfill its meaning; her aspiration for her son was abundantly fulfilled.

The relationship between Paul and his affectionate young co-worker was deep and abiding. Beyond the Thessalonian epistles, Paul associates

---

†His name is mentioned 24 times. Seven times the KJV used the Grecianized form *Timotheus*, elsewhere the common English form Timothy. The ASV and RSV uniformly use the familiar English form.

the name of Timothy with that of his own in the salutation of four other epistles,‡ while he is the further recipient of two letters from the pen of Paul. None of Paul's younger companions more fully caught and reflected the life and spirit of Paul than Timothy. Paul sent Timothy to Corinth in order that the Corinthian believers might have a visual reminder of how their father lived (1 Co 4:17).

Thus three men of varied background unite in sending a letter to the Gentile believers at Thessalonica. It is an illustration of the mixed national backgrounds of the early Christians. Findlay well remarks,

> These three names—*Paul, Silas, Timothy*—are typical of the mixed state of society in Apostolic times, and the varied material of which the Church was at first composed. It was built on a Jewish basis, with a Graeco-Roman super-structure. Paul and Silvanus were *Jews*, with *Roman* name and citizenship. Timotheous had a *Greek* name and father, with a *Jewish* mother (Ac xvi:1-3).[3]

Only in the Thessalonian epistles does Paul name the writers without any additional word of identification. Lünemann sees in this "a mark of the very early composition of the Epistle, and consequently of its authenticity."[4] A later forger would have added Paul's customary designation of himself as an "apostle."

In simply enumerating the three names without any further comment Paul makes no distinction between them and clearly intends that none shall be made. All three were men whom the Thessalonians knew and loved, and that was sufficient. It indicates the particularly friendly relations between writers and readers. No official status is insisted on.

That Paul does not claim to be an apostle indicates that the question of his apostolic authority was not involved in the writing of the letter. Calvin saw in the omission "a proof that those to whom he is writing had had no reluctance in recognizing him for what he was."[5] It is clear that the enemies at Thessalonica have sought to undermine the converts' confidence in Paul, but the attack had not been launched against his apostolic authority. It was rather an attack upon his person, an attempt to destroy the validity of his message by discrediting his character. Thus Paul feels no need to approach the Thessalonians in his official capacity as an apostle; he rather recalls to their memory the facts concerning his character and conduct.

B. READERS

The letter is addressed "unto the church of the Thessalonians in God the Father and the Lord Jesus Christ." The word rendered "church" (*ekklēsia*) was a familiar nonreligious term among the Greeks. Composed

‡2 Corinthians, Philippians, Colossians, Philemon.

of the preposition *ek* (out of) and the substantive form of the verb *kaleō* (to call) the term quite literally means "a called out company." It was a political term denoting the town assembly, the citizens called out from their homes to assemble and transact public business.

For the Jews of the dispersion and the devout pagans who frequented the synagogues, the term also had a religious connotation. In their Greek Bible (the Septuagint) the term was used of the Israelites assembled for religious purposes. For them it meant the assembled people of God. This religious connotation naturally led to its distinctively Christian usage as the assembly of the believers in Jesus Christ.

When the Jewish nation forfeited its prerogative of being the distinctive people of God, through its rejection of the Messiah, the believers in Jesus Christ carried on the claim to be the true *ekklēsia*, the Christian church. With the multiplication of Gentile converts the term *church* lost its Jewish implications and became the distinctive designation of a spiritual fellowship that transcended all racial distinctions. Barclay observes, "In the New Testament the Church is always a company of worshipping people who have given their hearts and pledged their lives to Jesus Christ."[6] In the New Testament the word *church* never means a building.

In this salutation the word clearly refers to a *local* church. The thought of the *church* as the whole company of the redeemed of this age, the universal church, is not developed in the Thessalonian letters. The epistle is addressed to the "congregation"[7] or "assembly"[8] located in the city of Thessalonica. It is addressed to the entire local membership there, not just to its presbyters or teachers.

The church is given a twofold description. It is first the congregation "of Thessalonians." The article is omitted in the original; properly it was not the assembly of *the* Thessalonians, for comparatively few of the residents of Thessalonica were members. It was an assembly composed of a select number of Thessalonians. Only in the salutation of the Thessalonian epistles does Paul express the local designation by the civic identification of the readers.§ Elsewhere Paul always expresses the local limitation by naming the place of residence.

But for a true identification of this *church* more was needed. The added delineation, "in God the Father and the Lord Jesus Christ," gives its distinctive spiritual nature. It is uniquely a Christian assembly, to be distinguished from all that is pagan or Jewish. "In God the Father" distinguishes it from any pagan assembly or association, whether political or religious, while "and the Lord Jesus Christ" distinguishes it from Jewish assemblies. The whole statement identifying the addressees is made without a repeated article, thus stressing the close unity of the entire descrip-

§A parallel expression is used in Col 4:16, "in the church of Laodiceans" (Gr.).

tion. For the true picture of the recipients the local and the spiritual should not be severed. The experiences they were undergoing as Christians had a definite relation to their local environment.

Paul's indication of the character of the readers gives an incisive indication of the essential nature of the Christian church. Its members are people who have received and accepted the call of God and Christ unto eternal life and thus have been separated from the world in its spiritual alienation and death. They have been brought into a new sphere of life, into vital union with God the Father and the Lord Jesus Christ. Their faith and experience center in these two names.

Paul's construction, which unites the two under the government of the one preposition in (*en*), places the two names side by side on a basis of equality. It is a clear witness to his conviction concerning the deity of Jesus Christ. Thus to unite the name of a mere man, however exalted, with the eternal God would have been unthinkable for a strong monotheist like Paul. "Paul could never think of God without seeing the face of Jesus, and he could never commune with Jesus without feeling the presence of God."[9]

It is this double union that is the distinctive of the Christian life. Christians have a vital experiential relation to God the Father who stands in opposition to the pagan gods they once served; their union with the Lord Jesus Christ sets them in contrast to the Christ-rejecting Jews. Their new life as an assembly is the development of the communion that flows from this new relationship.

God, the eternal all-pervading omnipotence, they have come to know as Father, the source and sustainer of the new life they have received. Their knowledge of Him as Father has been brought to them through the revelation of the Lord Jesus Christ. Him they have enthroned as their sovereign Lord, the one to whom they owe their supreme allegiance. In the Septagint the name *Lord* (*kurios*) was the translation for *Jehovah*, the God of Israel.|| And this divine Lord is none other than the incarnate *Jesus*, the Saviour, whom Christians accept and confess as the *Christ*, the Anointed One, the promised Messiah, the expected Deliverer awaited by God's people. The combination of all three of these designations in one person is necessary to set forth the true character of the new Master they love and serve.

C. GREETING

The form of the greeting "Grace to you and peace," is distinctly Pauline. The formula probably was Paul's own inspired coinage, an expression of

---

|| The title "Lord," with all the consequent implications, was applied to Jesus in the Christian community from the very beginning—Ac 2:36; 7:59.

his own deep spiritual experience. Findlay remarks that Paul's "whole gospel is enfolded in the wish" of grace and peace, just as "the whole faith of his readers" was embodied in the definitive "in God the Father and the Lord Jesus Christ."[10]

The common greeting among the Greeks was *chairein* (to rejoice, greetings).# The Hebrew greeting was *shalom* (peace, prosperity and well-being). It has been asserted that Paul simply combined the Greek and Hebrew forms of greeting. This is doubtful; the similarity between these old greetings and Paul's usage is only superficial. But if so, Paul deepened and spiritualized both concepts. Christianity took these every-day words of greeting and transformed them into vehicles able to convey the distinctive truths of the gospel.

Grace is the free and unmerited favor of God bestowed upon guilty man in and through Christ; peace is the result of receiving the grace of God, that precious sense of inner tranquility and well-being that comes to those who have been reconciled to God through Christ. "To you" marks the writers' desire that both the grace and peace are to be theirs in personal experience. In reality they already know both in their lives, but the desire is that they may know both in increasing measure. The order in the New Testament is always "grace and peace," never the reverse. No one can experience this peace without first receiving the grace.

The familiar words "from God our Father, and the Lord Jesus Christ," are lacking in some of the oldest Greek manuscripts and are properly omitted here. (They are unquestionably genuine in 2 Thessalonians.) This then is the only epistle where Paul writes nothing concerning the source of the grace and peace. The very uniqueness of this short form of the greeting would lead the scribes to assimilate the reading here to the common formula. If they appeared in the original the scribes would have no reason for leaving them out, but if they were lacking in the original they would be strongly tempted to insert them here as elsewhere.**

#This is the form used by James (1:1), as well as in the letter of the Jerusalem council (Ac 15:23). It is also the form used by the Roman chiliarch in Ac 23:26.

**The shorter reading in Col 1:2, "from God our Father," was likewise enlarged to the full formula by the scribes.

5

PERSONAL: THANKSGIVING

IT HAS BEEN COMMONLY RECOGNIZED that this epistle divides into two main parts, the division coming at the end of chapter three. Some of the ancient scribes sought to mark this division by adding an "amen" at the close of the third chapter. The contents of the first three chapters are personal in nature, where Paul sets out his feelings and relations to the Thessalonian believers; the remaining two chapters are practical in purpose, devoted to imparting needed instructions and admonitions to the readers.

The first division of the epistle readily falls into three parts. Chapter 1 is Paul's heartfelt outburst of thanksgiving for the Thessalonians because of the good news concerning them. In 2:1-16 he recalls the nature of the missionaries' work at Thessalonica and again expresses his thanksgiving for the way they received the gospel. The remainder of the division (2:17-3:13) is given to an account of the writers' relations to the Thessalonians since being forcibly separated from them. (It would have been better if chapter 3 had been made to commence at 2:17).

A. THANKSGIVING FOR THEM

1:2-10 We give thanks to God always for you all, making mention *of you* in our prayers; (3) remembering without ceasing your work of faith and labor of love and patience of hope in our Lord Jesus Christ, before our God and Father; (4) knowing, brethren beloved of God, your election, (5) how that our gospel came not unto you in word only, but also in power, and in the Holy Spirit, and *in* much assurance; even as ye know what manner of men we showed ourselves toward you for your sake. (6) And ye became imitators of us, and of the Lord, having received the word in much affliction, with joy of the Holy Spirit; (7) so that ye became an ensample to all that believe in Macedonia and in Achaia. (8) For from you hath sounded forth the word of the Lord, not only in Macedonia and Achaia, but in every place your faith to God-ward is gone forth; so that we need not to speak anything. (9) For they themselves report concerning us what manner of entering in we had unto you; and how ye turned unto God from idols, to serve a living and true God, (10) and to wait for his Son from heaven, whom he raised from the dead, *even* Jesus, who delivereth us from the wrath to come.

In thus commencing his first extant epistle* with a fervent and emphatic note of thanksgiving, the apostle launched a characteristically Pauline practice. Paul begins with an expression of thanksgiving to God in each of his letters addressed to churches,† except in that to the Galatians where he feels it necessary to let the readers feel the lash of his amazement and indignation at their fickleness. But the variety in his expressions of thanksgiving proves it was no conventional form, but a true expression of his personal gratitude. And this feeling found ready expression in sincere verbal utterance.

A reading of the Pauline epistles makes it clear that Paul assigned a very high place to thanksgiving in the Christian life. Bicknell makes bold to assert, "He seems to have made a rule never to offer a petition for himself or others without first giving thanks for blessings previously received."[1] In this rich paragraph of thanksgiving, Paul first sketches the character of the thanksgiving (v. 2) and then elaborates three grounds for the thanksgiving (vv. 3-10).

1. Character of the Thanksgiving (v. 2)

"We give thanks" asserts that the thanksgiving was united. But the question at once arises as to the force of *we*. Some expositors[2] and modern versions[3] seek to make this an editorial we simply referring to Paul himself. Thus Conybeare contends that "his true meaning" is really "the first person *singular*."[4]

That the literary plural was used by writers of that day is clear from evidence in the papyri and the inscriptions.[5] That Paul on occasion did use the literary plural as the equivalent of the singular is very probable. But no hard and fast rule can be laid down concerning his employment of the plural as an editorial we. Each instance of the plural must be studied in its context and decided on its own merits.

It seems most natural here to take Paul's plural as a reference to the three men he has just named together in the salutation (v. 1). To make this an editorial we and thus sever this plural from the plural designation of the writers just before seems arbitrary. It is more natural to assume that as the three men united in writing to the Thessalonians, so they also united in their thanksgiving for them.

That Paul should thus include his two co-workers in the thanksgiving is consistent with the fact that all three stood in the same close relations to the Thessalonians. It is further in accord with the consistent use of

---

*Some scholars think Galatians is earlier. For our dating of these epistles see Hiebert, *An Introduction to the Pauline Epistles*, pp. 42-43, 84-90.

†Paul's thanksgiving is usually for the recipients of the letter. In 2 Co it is rather for his own experience of divine comfort, and in Eph it is a general hymn of praise for Christian salvation.

the plural in this epistle. In 2 Corinthians and Colossians Paul names Timothy in the salutation, but his opening "we" is soon displaced with "I." In 1 Corinthians, Philippians, and Philemon, Paul names someone else with himself in the salutation but at once proceeds with "I thank." In the Thessalonian epistles his consistent use of "we" is most naturally intended to include Silvanus and Timothy. His occasional use of the singular (2:18; 3:5; 5:27) can be sufficiently explained from the context as Paul's effort to distinguish himself from his helpers on those occasions.

The thanksgiving is also Godward, for it is expressly directed "to God." Deissmann quotes some papyrus letters to indicate that Paul was "adhering to a beautiful secular custom when he so frequently began his letters with thanks to God."[6] That there were pious pagans who did make it a practice to thank their gods is obvious. But Paul's thanksgiving is not offered to whatever gods there may be. It is explicitly addressed to "the God" (*tō theō*), the one true God already identified in the salutation. He stands in contrast to the many false gods the Thessalonians served before they came to know the true God.

Paul's heart is full of praise because of the good news concerning the Thessalonians, but he does not simply congratulate them on the success that has been achieved. He is well aware that the spiritual results evoking his gratitude are due ultimately neither to the preachers nor the converts. God Himself is the real cause of it all. To Him belonged the thanks for what had been wrought.

This expression of his thanks to God is an illustration of Paul's practice of taking his various experiences, whether sad or glad, into the presence of God. All experiences were viewed in relation to Him. Thus he practiced the presence of God in life. But this expression of thanks also serves to remind the Thessalonians that the blessings which they have received are God's gifts to them toward the fulfillment of His gracious purposes with them.

Further, the thanksgiving is continual. In describing the thanksgiving as being *always*, or at all times, he assures them that the thanksgiving is not sporadic or occasional but regularly repeated. The regularly recurring nature of the thanksgiving is also implied in the use of the present tense of the verb. It is their practice to give thanks to God "continually, never skipping a single day."[7]

The thanksgiving is also inclusive, for he assures them that it is "for you all." It included without exception all the Thessalonian believers; none were excluded in their thinking. Paul was well aware of the imperfections that still existed in the Thessalonian church (3:10). And Neil adds a further comment, "There is no reason to suppose that the Thessalonian church consisted of any less odd a collection of characters

than the average congregation to-day."[8]   However, Paul's nonselective
gratitude saw sufficient cause for thanks to God in each of them. In the
words of Hogg and Vine, "Christians differ in attainments, but there is
always something of Christ in each, and hence always something for
which to thank God, since Christ is the oil that feeds the lamp of praise."[9]
When viewed in contrast to their pagan neighbors, there was solid ground
for thanksgiving for the change that had taken place in these Thessalonians. Further, the Thessalonian church did not manifest any marked
moral aberrations, such as Paul had later to rebuke in the Corinthian
church.

Supplementing his assertion with a participial clause, Paul informs
them that their thanksgiving is accompanied by prayer. The missionaries'
thanksgiving for the Thessalonians is expressed as they engage in united
prayer; it is then that they are "making mention of" them "in our prayers."
The word rendered "prayers" (*proseuchē*) is a general word for prayer,
including the various elements in communion with God. Upon each occasion of their united devotions (*epi tōn proseuchōn hēmōn*), specific mention was made of the Thessalonians. The thanksgiving is mingled with
their prayer and intercession.

Here we get a glimpse of the unified prayer life of the missionaries.
Not only do they unite in preaching and in discussing the needs of their
converts; they also unite in praying for them. The Thessalonians had a
definite place on their prayer list. This need not mean that Paul kept a
formal prayer list which was mechanically read during their devotions;
rather their praying for the people was free and Spirit-prompted. The use
of the middle voice (*poioumenoi*) indicates that they had a personal
interest in doing so.

2. Grounds for the Thanksgiving (vv. 3-10)

Three grounds for thanksgiving are developed. Thanksgiving to God
for the Thessalonian believers is prompted by their Christian virtues (v.
3), their divine election (vv. 4-7), and the reports of others concerning
the nature and results of the mission at Thessalonica (vv. 8-10). This
elaboration of their grounds for thanksgiving forms an adequate background for the remainder of the epistle.

A problem of punctuation and consequent interpretation arises at the
beginning of v. 3 because of the position in the original of the adverb
rendered "without ceasing" (*adialeiptōs*). Does it go with what precedes
or with what follows? If the former, it connects with the making mention
of the readers in prayer and emphasizes (by position) that this is without
ceasing. If the latter, it properly describes the missionaries' remembrance
of the Christian virtues of the readers as unfailing.

Advocates of the former connection point out that the term, as an adverb‡ or adjective,§ is used only by Paul in the New Testament and that elsewhere he always uses it, directly or indirectly, in connection with prayer. Findlay also feels that "the rhythm and balance of the participial clauses seem to speak for the attachment of the adverb to v. 2."[10] Then each of the participles stands alone at the beginning of the successive clauses in verses 2, 3, and 4. Milligan finds further support for this connection from "the position of corresponding phrases in the papyri."[11] Accepting this connection, Moffatt renders, "when we mention you constantly in our prayers."‖

Proponents of its connection with verse 3 insist that the adverb is properly connected with the nearer participle according to general usage. Then the word order is "unceasingly remembering," the adverb thus emphatically beginning the new clause. Lünemann insists that if connected with verse 2 "as an addition inserted afterward, it would drag."[12] Ellicott holds that it "far more naturally" goes with verse 3, thereby "each new clause serving to enhance and expand what had preceded."[13] Calvin remarks that the adverb "may be taken in conjunction with the previous words, but it makes more sense as it stands."[14] Since the Thessalonians have already been assured that the missionaries are always thanking God for them, it is less significant to add that they are continually praying for them than to assure them that they have continual remembrance of their Christian character and its fruits.

Views will doubtless continue to differ. Frame concludes that the problem "cannot be determined."[15] We are quite willing to take it with what follows.

a) BECAUSE OF THEIR CHRISTIAN VIRTUES (v. 3). Their vivid memory of the spiritual excellence of the Thessalonian converts was the immediate cause for the thanksgiving by the missionaries at their joint prayer sessions. They continue *remembering*, calling to mind, their observance of the development of these excellencies in the lives of the Thessalonian believers while still with them. The meaning is not that this memory occupies them to the exclusion of everything else, but rather that their remembrance of it constantly recurs.

The apostle's statement of the spiritual excellence of the Thessalonian believers constitutes a satisfactory portrayal of the nature and scope of the Christian life. His words are high praise for the Thessalonians, but

‡*Adialeiptōs* occurs in Ro 1:19; 1 Th 1:3; 2:13; 5:17.
§*Adialeiptos* occurs in Ro 9:2 and 2 Ti 1:3.
‖This connection is also accepted in the versions of Conybeare, Montgomery, Lattery, the RSV and the NEB. See Bibliography.

he felt they were deserved. Paul knew the value of sincere appreciation and encouragement.

The excellence being remembered is set forth in a triple delineation, "your work of faith and labor of love and patience of hope." The possessive *your* stands emphatically at the head of the whole statement and relates all three ideas directly to the Thessalonians. The three objects of the participle *remembering#* are *work, labor,* and *patience.* Each noun in turn has a modifier in the genitive, "of faith," "of love," and "of hope." Each of these genitives is to be construed alike as a descriptive or subjective genitive.

"Work of faith" is the work or activity that faith inspires, that springs from and is motivated by faith. The emphasis is on the work that faith produces. If there were no faith there would have been no work. The faith of the Thessalonians was no mere speculative belief; it was energetic and productive. Paul fully agreed with James that "faith apart from works is dead" (Ja 2:26). Paul's reference is not to the initial work of saving faith but rather relates to the whole Christian life as it is ruled and energized by faith.

"Labor of love" is the toilsome, laborious activity that is prompted and sustained by love when the going gets hard. The stress in the word *labor* (*kopos*) is on the cost, the exertion, fatigue, and exhaustion that it entails. Work (*ergon*) may be pleasant and stimulating, but *labor* implies toil that is strenuous and sweat-producing. Had there been no *love* (*agapē*) they would not have persisted in carrying on the hard and difficult activities now being performed. This love is not romantic love (*eros*), nor the love of personal affection and warmth drawn forth by the attractiveness and desirableness of the object of love (*philia*), but distinctively Christian love, the love which springs from an unconquerable good will and persistent desire for the welfare of the one loved.[16] Such love found its supreme expression on Calvary. Such a divinely imparted and sacrificial love prompted the toil of the Thessalonians.

Just what form this love-prompted toil took is not indicated. Alford thinks it was "probably towards the sick and needy strangers."[17] Certainly conditions in the persecuted church at Thessalonica offered opportunities for such activities. But Hendriksen, in the light of verses 6-10, holds that Paul is "thinking especially of the work of making propaganda for the gospel, and doing this even in the midst of bitter persecution."[18] That the toil, whatever its precise form, was ultimately Godward is certain from verse 9.

"Patience of hope" is the steadfast endurance that is inspired by true

#Construed with the genitive case, according to the usual usage of the verb in the New Testament.

hope. The connotation of the word rendered "patience" (*hupomonē*) is larger than our English word *patience*. It is not a quiet resignation which passively endures the burdens heaped upon it, but rather it is that combination of heroic endurance and manly constancy that courageously faces the various obstacles, trials, and persecutions which may befall the believer in his conflict with the inward and outward world. The persecution heaped upon the Thessalonian believers gave ample opportunity for the exercise of this steadfast endurance inspired by the hope that the gospel had brought to them. This inspiring hope is a central feature of the Christian life. It stands in striking contrast to their former hopelessness as pagans. Hope relates to anticipations for the future, but biblical hope is always something that is completely certain. It is not a mere personal aspiration or yearning for something to come; it is something certain because it is based on what God has said He will yet do.

Here for the first time, chronologically, in Paul's writings we have this famous triad: *faith, love, hope.* But Paul's stress is not on these virtues alone, but rather upon what they produce. They are the active ingredients of the Christian life, finding expression in active work, patient toil, and enduring constancy. Thus Paul does not link these basic virtues with that which is beautiful, poetic, and ethereal, but rather with that which is toilsome and difficult. They are seen to their best advantage amid the rugged demands of daily life.

Faith, love, hope are here named in their logical order. As Lightfoot remarks, "Faith rests on the past; love works in the present; hope looks to the future."[19] In the Christian life faith comes first as the source of all Christian virtues; love is the sustaining power which enables the believer to persevere in the face of opposition and suffering for the faith; and hope looks to the future, serving as the beacon-star which guides the saint to his heavenly haven. It has been summed up by saying "Faith looks *back* to a Crucified Saviour. Love looks *up* to a Crowned Saviour. Hope looks *on* to a Coming Saviour."[20] While none of the members of this triad can truly exist apart from the others, each may be prominent at a given time. In the Thessalonian epistles hope stands forth as receiving the chief emphasis.

Paul might have completed his sentence with *hope.* But the rich flow of his thoughts causes his sentence to run on with two further clauses. Both clauses create some uncertainty as to their precise connection with what has gone before.

The words "in our Lord Jesus Christ" (*tou kuriou hēmōn Iēsou Christou*)** may be regarded as connecting with all three members of

** The phrase must be construed as an objective genitive.

the triad just mentioned or only with hope, the last mentioned. Under the former view not only our hope but also our faith and our love have Christ as their object. All of them center in Him and cannot exist apart from Him. Under the latter connection the phrase is a fuller delineation of the object of our hope. Christian hope has Him as its personal object; it relates to what He will yet do.

From the context it seems more natural to take this phrase in close connection with the noun nearest to it, that is, hope. This expansion of hope is in accord with the strong eschatological emphasis in these epistles. Any objection that such an addition unduly draws out the third member of the triad and destroys the symmetry of the construction has little weight. Paul was not primarily concerned with such rhetorical symmetry; it is not unusual for Paul to draw out or vary the last member of a series.

He who is the object of all Christian hope is fully identified as "our Lord Jesus Christ." (See comments on v. 1 above). The possessive *our* testifies that the writers join the readers in thus claiming Him as their own. This full title, which is never applied to Jesus in the gospels, is His majestic title since His ascension to the right hand of God (Ac 2:36; Phil 2:9-11). Christian hope eagerly awaits His triumphant return.

The precise connection of the last phrase, "before our God and Father," has also been differently understood. Some would connect it with *remembering* at the beginning of verse 3. Conybeare adopts this connection and renders, "remembering, in the presence of our God and Father, the working of your faith, etc."†† Thus connected, the phrase relates to the devotional life of the missionaries; their prayers are offered in their conscious sense of the presence of God. It would then serve to stress the solemn circumstances under which the writers express their evaluation of the Christian character of the readers, assuring them of its sincerity and earnestness.[21]

The difficulty with this suggested connection is the remoteness of the participle; if the phrase is to be connected with *remembering* at the beginning of the verse, its position at the very end of the verse tends to make it drag. To make clear this connection calls for the transposition to which Conybeare resorts. More natural is a connection with the part of the verse just preceding. Then it somehow relates to what is said about the readers rather than the writers. But is it to be taken with all three of the elements characterizing their Christian life, or is it to be restricted to the last only?

Under the former view the entire life of the Thessalonians is placed in the presence of "our God and Father." Their working faith, toiling love, and steadfast hope are all maintained in the consciousness of His

††This transposition of the phrase is also found in the versions of Goodspeed, Williams, 20th Cent., RSV, and the NEB.

presence. However difficult their circumstances may be, they are living their life "before Him, who is not only our Supreme Ruler, but has also all the tenderness and affection of a father towards us, who watches all our actions with a fatherly solicitude."²²

If the phrase is restricted to *hope*, then the meaning is that their hope is centered in the Lord Jesus Christ whose coming they await, but that their hope now gives them a standing before the Father, and He, rather than men, is the central factor in their lives. They are now living in the sense of His presence, but they will one day be brought to see Him face to face. That will be the ultimate fruition of their hope, the consummation of their salvation.

It is difficult to decide between these two views; we incline toward the former. Whatever the connection adopted, the verse well illustrates the fertility of Paul's mind. As he writes (or dictates) one thought comes crowding in on the other clamoring for expression. As Jowett remarks, Paul's sentences "seem to grow under his hand."²³

b) Because of their divine election (vv. 4-7). Beyond their Christian virtues, the ultimate reason for thanksgiving for the Thessalonians was their divine election. After recording their remembrance of what the writers had seen with their own eyes (v. 3), reference is now made to the conviction that the readers are God's elect. Since this is not a matter of direct observation, being supersensible, the ground for this conviction is immediately added. The assured knowledge of their election (v. 4) is grounded in a double reason (vv. 5-7).

(1) *Assurance of their election* (v. 4). "Knowing, brethren beloved of God, your election." This participial clause is parallel to that in verse 3; the participle is masculine plural and relates back to the plural subject of the verb "we give thanks" in verse 2.‡‡ To seek to refer this asserted knowledge to the Thessalonians themselves is inconsistent with the grammatical structure of the passage.

The subjects of the missionaries' assured knowledge are warmly addressed as "brethren beloved of God." The expression indicates both a manward and a Godward relationship. Manward, Paul gladly accepts them as *brethren*. This is a common term of address in the letters of Paul. He uses it around sixty times in all. It occurs fourteen times in this epistle and seven times in 2 Thessalonians. The frequent use of this form of address in these letters, which Milligan calls one of their "most noticeable features,"²⁴ accentuates Paul's strong attachment to the Thessalonians. It is his happy acknowledgment that with him they have been born into the

‡‡Since they regard Paul's "we" as an editorial plural, the versions of Conybeare, Way, and Montgomery here render the plural participle by a finite verb in the singular, "I know."

same family through faith in Christ; they are now members of the same spiritual brotherhood. This common spiritual experience caused the once proud Pharisee to welcome affectionately these once despised Gentiles as his beloved brethren. Insurmountable barriers between different groups have been effectively removed in Christ. Here is the true secret for effective brotherhood among men.

The sense of the brotherhood of the redeemed was strong in the early church. It was a familiar concept. Papyrus usage shows that the term "brethren" was frequently used in secular circles to refer to members of the same guild or to those closely associated in some form of organized activity. It was also common in Jewish usage as a term of address for fellow Jews. But because of the rich nature of the brotherhood experienced in the church, the term developed a warm and vital connotation for believers. It testified to their sense of vital oneness which they found through their common faith in Christ.

Paul's address to the Thessalonians as brethren is enriched by the unique addition, "beloved of God." The closest parallel in the New Testament is in 2 Th 2:13. Membership in the Christian brotherhood also involves a Godward relationship. As brethren they are also the objects of God's abiding love. The term here rendered "beloved" (*ēgapēmenoi*) is a perfect passive participle and denotes a love which existed in the past but continues into the present with unabated force. This participial form as a term of address occurs only three times in the New Testament, each time by Paul (Col 3:12; 1 Th 1:4; 2 Th 2:13). This participial construction is richer than the verbal (*agapētos*) ordinarily used (as in Ro 12:19; 1 Co 10:14; Phil 2:12).

The Thessalonian believers are being abidingly loved "of God." God Himself is thus loving them. Those who are assuredly the permanent objects of divine love are also loved by the missionaries.

The King James Version is quite alone in connecting the words *of God* with *election* rather than with *beloved*. The punctuation in Young's version apparently assumes this connection also: "having known, brethren beloved, by God, your election." Barnes thinks that "the common version may be regarded as giving the true meaning,"[25] but that is not the consensus of modern scholarship. Lightfoot tags the connection as "quite inadmissible," but he concedes that it is "supported by some respectable commentators ancient and modern."[26] It is not in harmony with the natural meaning of the original arrangement of the words; it also requires the assumed omission of an infinitive in the original. Milligan points out that in Paul's sense of the term any other election "than by God is inconceivable,"[27] hence this connection is quite pointless. Findlay insists that the parallel construction in 2 Thessalonians 2:13, in context, proves that the words *of God* should not be here connected with *election*.[28]

The writers express their assurance concerning the *election* of the beloved Thessalonians. That Paul thus uses the term without any further word of explanation indicates that the Thessalonians would readily understand the significance of the assertion. It seems obvious that doctrinal instruction had been given them on the point. The truth of election was a basic element in Paul's view of the church (Eph 1:4). Paul here assumes a doctrine of election but says nothing further as to the time and scope of God's electing grace. The use of the possessive, *your* election, focuses this concept on the readers directly.

The noun *election* (*eklogē*) denotes the act of picking out or choosing someone; it implies a selection of some from among others who are not selected. The term occurs six times in the New Testament (Ro 9:11; 11:5, 7, 28; 1 Th 1:4; 2 Pe 1:10), and always "appears to denote an act of Divine selection taking effect upon human objects so as to bring them into special and saving relations with God."[29] It is always the independent act of God. Thus a number of the modern versions render "that he has chosen you."§§

In the Old Testament the concept of election was applied to the nation of Israel as a chosen people of God; the divine choice selected and separated them from the other nations. In the New Testament the election is individual and spiritual (Jn 13:18; 15:16; Ac 9:15; 1 Co 27-28; Ja 2:5; 2 Pe 1:10). The election of the Thessalonian believers was not done collectively as a body but as individuals.

The definite article with the noun (*tēn eklogēn*) points to a particular election when God selected the Thessalonian believers. Some scholars hold that Paul here refers to the Thessalonians' "gracious admission into religious privilege in *this* life,"[30] that is, "to their being chosen to *Church membership* and *Christian privilege*."[31] This view apparently lies behind the rendering of Way, "how you were chosen out of the world." But if Paul was referring to an act in time which enrolled them among the members of the church, he would rather have spoken of "your calling" (*klēsis*), their effective and successful call. The reference is rather to God's gracious act of selecting them unto salvation which took place in the council chambers of God in eternity past (Eph 1:4). Lenski insists that "Paul knows of no twofold act of election"[32] such as the former view requires.

In this age "the election of grace" (Ro 11:5) includes all those who are saved. It assumes that there are those who remain unchosen. But the truth of election must not be turned into a harsh and arbitrary doc-

§§Weymouth, Montgomery, Goodspeed, Williams, 20th Century, RSV, NEB. Cf. also Moffatt, Conybeare, NASB.

trine. That it presents some unfathomed mysteries is unquestioned. "Why God should choose one continent, one nation, one town, one man rather than another is the unsolved mystery of the doctrine of election."[33] The sovereign God has revealed Himself as infinitely righteous and holy and motivated by infinite love; this assures us that He is not an unprincipled tyrant in His selection. The truth of divine election has been revealed for the benefit of believers; it is a family doctrine which they only can truly appreciate. Morris remarks, "It is not a device for sentencing men to eternal torment, but for rescuing them from it. Election protects us from thinking of salvation as depending on human whims, and roots it squarely in the will of God."[34]

Paul's assertion that he knows that the Thessalonians are the subjects of divine election does not mean that Paul sat in on the divine council when that choice was made. Nor does he mean that he has received a direct revelation from God in the matter. The participle here rendered "knowing" is not from the verb *ginōskō* which denotes "a knowledge grounded in personal experience," but rather from *oida* which signifies "a clear and purely mental perception,"[35] a certainty intuitively realized. The knowledge of their election was an intuitive conviction based upon known and observed facts.

(2) *Reasons for the assurance* (vv. 5-7). The evidence that the Thessalonians are God's elect is at once presented. It is two-sided. It is based upon the experience of the preachers in proclaiming the gospel in Thessalonica (v. 5) as well as the response by the believers to the gospel (vv. 6-7).

(a) *Preaching to them* (v. 5). God works out His electing purposes through the preaching of the gospel. The way the missionaries were enabled to present the saving gospel at Thessalonica assured Paul that the Thessalonians were the subjects of God's efficacious grace. As John Trapp quaintly remarks, "A husbandman would not send his servant with his sickle to reap thistles and nettles only."[36] Verse 5 presents the evidence from the side of the preachers.

The force of the conjunction *hoti* has been differently understood. The rendering "how that" (ASV and Rotherham) or "that" (Westminster Version by Lattey) might suggest that Paul is now analyzing their election to show wherein it consisted. Rather he is setting forth the evidence or grounds for the assurance that they are elect. Its causal force has been indicated by such renderings as *because* (Young and 20th Cent), *since* (Weymouth), and *for* (KJV, Darby, Conybeare, Way, Montgomery, Moffatt, Goodspeed, Williams, Phillips, RSV, NASB). It thus indicates why they believe the readers are God's elect. Lenski insists that the force of the conjunction is "best rendered by 'seeing that.' In consequence of the fact now stated the writers have come to know of the election of the Thessalonians."[37]

The writers' assurance is intimately connected with the way "our gospel came" to the Thessalonians. The designation of their message as *our* gospel indicates their personal commitment to this message. There is no suggestion that the message originated with them or that it differed from that of the other gospel preachers. Rather it is a message which they have personally accepted as a trust and are now proclaiming to others.

The simple identification of their message as "our gospel" expresses Paul's deep conviction that the message of Christianity was truly a message of "good news" (Young, Goodspeed, Williams, 20th Cent) or "glad tidings" (Darby, Conybeare, Way). The very heart of that message is the offer of God's free salvation through faith in Christ Jesus. The word *gospel* embodies the essential nature of the message as good news. Had Paul instead used the term *kērugma*, "proclamation," the emphasis would rather have been that the message was something committed to them to be officially proclaimed or heralded to others. Thus Paul's thought centers on the nature of the message itself rather than the manner of its communication.

Paul's emphasis upon the gospel itself, not the messengers, is further evident from the fact that he says "our gospel came . . . unto you," rather than "we came to you with the gospel." God's elective purpose for the Thessalonians was realized through the message rather than the messengers. The messengers apart from the message would have been totally powerless to achieve such a result.

The verb rendered "came" (*egenēthē*) is more literally "became, came to be." As it was presented to the hearers that message revealed itself as a vital operative force working through the messengers. The gospel is indeed the power of God unto salvation (Ro 1:16).

How the gospel worked through the preachers is explicitly stated both negatively and positively. As a dynamic power it came "not unto you in word only." As the adverb *only* indicates, the gospel certainly was made known to the Thessalonians through the instrumentality of human words. The Christian message cannot be transmitted through mere forms or rituals. It is an intelligent message that must be made known through well-chosen and appropriate terminology. In making known to men His saving grace, God uses men, not angels, "recipients themselves of the same grace; who can give testimony with their lives as with their lips."[38]

But the gospel is not transformingly communicated through mere words, however brilliant, eloquent, or imposing they may be. Mere rhetorical skill apart from the spiritual dynamic of the message can never achieve such a result.

With a strongly contrasting *but* (*alla*) three positive features of the preaching at Thessalonica are next enumerated. Words were used, but the message they conveyed came "also in power, and in the Holy Spirit and in much assurance." Each successive term is needed to give the whole picture.

The objective fact is that the message came "in power," with a spiritual dynamic which proved that divine power was operative. As they spoke the preachers were keenly conscious of the presence of this supernatural power behind their words, producing spiritual persuasiveness and penetrating conviction. Paul delights in this contrast between mere words and the dynamic of the gospel (1 Co 1:18; 2:1-4; 4:20).

Power does not mean that it came "with *miraculous* manifestations,"[39] for that would require the plural form of the noun. Paul's term neither requires nor expressly excludes the presence of special miracles during the ministry at Thessalonica. Paul seldom makes reference to the miracles that did accompany his ministry.

The missionaries keenly felt as they preached that the message was in the Holy Spirit, and in much assurance. They well knew that only a power beyond themselves could accomplish the task of transforming spiritually benighted souls, and they knew that the Spirit was working through them to that end.

Denney remarks that in preaching at Thessalonica, Paul was "aglow with Christian passion.[40] It was manifested in him by the Holy Spirit. He knew that this was a good omen concerning God's saving purpose toward the Thessalonians. Before coming to Thessalonica Paul had known the restraint of the Holy Spirit upon his effort to preach (Ac 16:6-7). But now he was deeply conscious that the Spirit was making the message powerful and effective.

The missionaries delivered their message in "much assurance" (*plērophoria pollē*). Cremer defined the term translated *assurance* as "perfect certitude, full conviction."[41] Milligan asserts that "full assurance" or "confidence" is "its characteristic N.T. sense."[42] Way renders the expression "with ample assurance of success," while Moffatt has "with ample conviction on our part." The literal meaning of the term is "complete carrying or bearing." Some hold that its meaning here is rather "fulness, abundance," as denoting the rich effect that is produced. But this meaning is not suitable here unless the reference is to the Thessalonian converts themselves.

Since the preposition "in" (*en*) is not repeated before "much assurance," the concept is closely connected with the Holy Spirit. Named between the power and the assurance, the Holy Spirit was the agent who empowered the message and worked the assurance in the messengers. They worked in a Spirit-wrought conviction and certainty as to the validity of their message and had unshaken confidence in its ultimate triumph. Denny points out that "'much assurance' is the counterpart of misgiving or doubt. . . . Doubt paralyses; God cannot work through a man in whose soul there are misgivings about the truth."[43]

Some interpreters insist the mentioned assurance must be taken to refer to the experience of the Thessalonians rather than the missionaries. Thus De Boer holds that "it is more to the point to understand Paul as referring to the way the gospel entered into the Thessalonians than to the way that it issued forth from him."[44] No one questions that the Thessalonians had assurance concerning the gospel which they accepted; yet the context seems clearly to indicate that the primary reference is to the missionaries. Paul is speaking about the way the missionaries came to know the election of the Thessalonians; the reference is still to the character of the message rather than to its reception. Thus viewed, verse 5 describes the *preaching* and verse 6 the *reception* of the gospel at Thessalonica. Swete feels that "the passage will certainly gain in logical clearness by this interpretation."[45] Ellicott holds that the effort to refer the assurance to the Thessalonians "seems to mar the correct sequence of thought, and to introduce notices of the state of the recipients which only come first into view in ver. 6."[46]

The view referring the assurance to the missionaries seems required by the last part of verse 5. Paul's appeal to the knowledge of the Thessalonians clearly restricts the foregoing remarks to the preachers. Alford says, "This interpretation is fixed by the term *even as*, referring back to the whole previous description."[47]

Having described his preaching while at Thessalonica, Paul turns directly to the Thessalonians, who personally knew the nature of that original work, to confirm the claim just made. This sudden appeal to the personal knowledge of the readers is the first hint that attempts have been made by opponents at Thessalonica to bring the work and character of the missionaries under suspicion. This note of self-defense is elaborated in 2:1-12.

In saying, "even as ye know" Paul indicates his assurance that the knowledge of the Thessalonians will fully substantiate the claim he has made. But his appeal is not merely that they will confirm the facts concerning the preaching; rather, he asks them to recall the character of the preachers: "what manner of men we showed ourselves toward you." Let them recall not only his preaching but the whole manner of his conduct while with them. Paul was fully aware that the message of the gospel could not truly be separated from the character of the messengers. As Auberlen remarked, "The whole man preached."[48] The character of the messengers provided no occasion to cast doubt on the message which they delivered.

A clear recollection of the character of the missionaries will confirm the unselfish nature of their work. Their activities among them were carried out "for your sake." The nature of their work made evident the motives of the workmen. Their work was done not in the interest of the preachers but in the interest of the hearers. They worked to give rather than to get. Their unselfish service had given the Thessalonians a worthy example.

(b) Response by them (vv. 6-7). The way the Thessalonians responded to the gospel constituted the other side of the evidence which assured Paul that they were God's elect. In setting forth that evidence, Paul notes the external manifestation demonstrating their reception of the gospel (v. 6*a*), indicates the experiences accompanying that reception (v. 6*b*), and informs the readers of the widespread result (v. 7). Each feature bears a dual aspect.

(i) *External manifestation* (v. 6*a*). Paul's *And* indicates that additional evidence is now being presented, while the emphatic *ye* (*humeis*) marks the change of subject from the writers to the readers. Paul does not begin with their personal acceptance of the gospel, but with the external manifestation demonstrating that reception. "And ye became imitators of us, and of the Lord." The point action indicated by the verb (*egenēthēte*) marks the fact that a definite, observable change became evident in their lives. That change consisted in the hearers becoming *imitators* (*mimētai*) of the missionaries. They did not simply become their "followers" (KJV) in the sense of being adherents to their teaching. Rather, as believers in their message they began to pattern their lives after the example set by the missionaries. It was his observance of this fact that rejoiced the heart of Paul; it was open evidence of the reality of their conversion, and therefore of their divine election.

Paul's description of the converts as *mimētai* (from which we get our English word "mimic") does not imply that their conversion was artificial or insincere. It does not have the belittling connotation of our English derivative. It was no superficial or slavish copying of merely external resemblances. As De Boer well remarks,

> It was an imitation in the deep and basic sense of the word; it was a bringing to expression in their own lives of what they had seen and detected outside of themselves. It was a capturing of something they had witnessed around them and making it a part of themselves.[49]

Clearly their conversion went beyond mere verbal profession. They actively began to express in their own lives the characteristics of this new life as they observed it in the lives of the missionaries. It was an imitation perfectly consistent with the development of their own selfhood under the inspiration of the new life which they had received. Such imitation demands moral effort.

The object of their imitation proved to be twofold. They became imitators "of us, and of the Lord." The order may at first strike us as startling, but it is the logical order. Way's reversal of this order, "You, also, took my Lord and me for your examples," is quite unwarranted. It is the natural order in the experience of converts on a new mission field. Even before the message of a missionary is fully understood or personally accepted, the hearers will observe the outworking of that message in the life of the missionary. And when the Spirit leads them to a personal acceptance of the message, the new converts naturally look to the missionary to learn how to live the Christian life. To reflect their message in their own lives is part of the work of missionaries. "In so far as they are truly Christian, they represent not simply Christ's teaching but Christ's life (cp. I Cor. xi. 1)."[50]

Paul knew the value of his own personal example. He was keenly aware that he represented Christ not only by what he taught but also by what he did (1 Co 11:1). He was deeply conscious of the integrity of his own life (1 Co 4:1-4) because of the power of the indwelling Christ (Gal 2:20; Phil 4:13). He therefore was bold to appeal to the value and importance of his example (1 Co 4:16; Phil 3:17; 4:9; 2 Th 3:7-9). He did so because he was conscious that his own example pointed back to Christ. If his converts would truly imitate his example they would go on to imitate his Master.

The order of the wording in the original forms a climax and separates the two objects of imitation as far as possible: "and ye, imitators of us ye became, and of the Lord" (*kai humeis mimētai hēmōn egenēthēte kai tou kuriou*). Young's rendering most nearly preserves the exact force of the original, "and ye—ye did become imitators of us, and of the Lord." Paul is not seeking to minimize the impact of the missionaries' example on the Thessalonians. He is rather stressing the true nature of their imitation by indicating that it goes beyond the visible example given them. The roots of the Thessalonians' conduct were broader and went deeper than the example which the missionaries had provided. The ultimate pattern for their Christian conduct was "the Lord." In Him they have "the living power in which alone this 'imitation' could be accomplished, and man's highest end successfully reached."[51]

Because of its frequent occurrence Milligan calls "the Lord" "the distinctive Name of these epistles."[52] It points not only to Christ's authority but also "sums up His Divine attributes; v. 8, iii. 8, 12, iv. 6, 15, 16, 17, v. 2, 12, etc. To Him faith, obedience, and worship are due."[53]

This reference to "the Lord" as an object of imitation seems clearly to imply that the Thessalonian believers had received some instruction from the missionaries concerning the life, sufferings, and death of the Lord Jesus. Bailey remarks that this implication is "of value in understanding just what Paul had brought into his message at Thessalonica."[54] Barnes thinks that the reference makes it "evident that the manner in which the Saviour lived was a prominent topic of their preaching, and also that it was one of the means of the conversion of the Thessalonians."[55]

In his writings Paul seldom mentions details of our Lord's earthly life, but he does display a knowledge of details sufficient to show that he knew more than he says. While Paul's chief interest was to set forth the inner content of the Christian faith which centers in the exalted Christ, he never loses sight of the historical Jesus. That he does not lay greater stress on the historical facts in the life and ministry of Jesus does not prove that he gave his converts no information concerning them, much less that he was himself uninformed concerning them. His epistles were not written for the purpose of giving an account of the earthly life of Jesus.[56]

(ii) *Accompanying experiences* (v. 6*b*). Their life of imitation arose out of their personal acceptance of the gospel. Paul indicates this causal relationship by immediately adding "having received the word" (*dexo-menoi ton logon*). Williams brings out the causal force of the participle by rendering "because you welcomed our message." The aorist tense points to a definite act of reception on their part. The time of that reception was of course prior to their becoming imitators, but no long interval is implied or possible. The consequences of that reception for the Thessalonians became rapidly apparent.

The verb rendered "received" (*dechomai*) indicates that the reception was a voluntary and willing act on their part. The term is used of receiving or welcoming guests (Lk 10:8, 10; Heb 11:31). Having heard the preaching of the missionaries, they personally welcomed and appropriated "the word."‖ ‖ Used without any further description, it is indeed "the word" par excellence. It is a common designation for the Christian message. It may be used with various modifiers according to the desired emphasis of the context.##

Grundmann points out that *receiving the word* when used in connection with the gospel is "an equivalent of faith."[57] By a personal act of faith the Thessalonians accepted the message offered them. It entered their hearts

---

‖ ‖ "The word" is not Christ the personal Word, the *Logos*, a meaning found only in John's prologues; nor is it the *written* word, for it was the oral preaching of the gospel that was received.
For a list see Hogg and Vine, p. 39.

as well as their ears. This response of faith is man's part in the work of salvation, but it is not a meritorious act; it is merely the condition under which God's salvation becomes operative.

Their acceptance of the gospel produced a twofold effect for the Thessalonian believers. The word was received "in much affliction, with joy of the Holy Spirit." It was in this double experience that the Thessalonians became imitators of the missionaries and of the Lord. (That the imitation does not include the "receiving of the word" is clear from the fact that in that area no analogy could be found in Christ's life.) In both areas Paul and Silas could point to a vivid example in their own experiences at Philippi (Ac 16:23-24). Our Lord also manifested deep joy in the midst of tribulation (Lk 10:21; Jn 12:20-36; 15:11; 16:33).

The external effect, *in much affliction,* dated back to the very beginning of their Christian life (Ac 17:5-6). The Thessalonian church was at once plunged into severe difficulty. The term rendered "affliction" (*thlipsis*) denotes "not mild discomfort, but great and sore difficulty."[58] Greek writers used the word only in a literal sense of "pressure," and that of a severe kind; in the Septuagint and the New Testament it is used in a figurative sense to denote the trials and pressures which afflict the believer in this world.

The history of the primitive church shows that such affliction and suffering were almost invariably the lot of those who accepted the gospel. The experience of the Thessalonian converts proved to be no exception. That they were aware of this prospect when they welcomed the gospel seems clear. They were aware that the missionaries had experienced a cruel beating and unjust imprisonment at Philippi on account of the gospel (Ac 16:23-24; 1 Th 2:2). While Luke does not give details concerning the initial antagonism to the gospel by the unbelieving Jews, it is clear that the gospel preaching at Thessalonica produced heated controversy and sharp antagonism. To become an adherent openly of that gospel was a courageous act; it was to court not only derision but open violence. It demanded vigorous self-denial and a willingness to surrender personal comfort, honor, property, and perhaps life itself. Neil remarks,

> We simply cannot appreciate to-day what it must have cost in terms of family, friends, society, to become a follower of the Way. The nearest parallel is perhaps the Hindu Christian today.[59]

This adverse outer effect was counterbalanced by an amazing inner effect, "with joy of the Holy Spirit." While enduring tribulation because of their faith, they were experiencing a joy which the Holy Spirit worked in them. "The same Spirit Who enabled the apostles to preach with *power* in spite of all opposition, enabled the Thessalonians to believe with *joy* in spite of all persecution."[60] The Spirit was not only the external giver but also the internal source of their joy. No other explanation for their deep joy under the circumstances was possible. A joy arising out of a spurious religious excitement will fail under such circumstances.

This experience of "affliction with joy" was an anomaly to the non-Christian world; it was completely baffling. Neil calls it "the perennial Christian paradox."[61] It was indeed a new phenomenon. "This combination of affliction and spiritual joy, this original, paradoxical experience, is the token of election."[62]

The early Christians found in their new faith not an avenue of escape from the unpleasant and trying experiences of life but a power which enabled them joyously to endure their sufferings. They found that their sufferings for their faith did not break their spirit or embitter them; they found it an experience which changed evil into something that worked for their spiritual good. Their joy amid suffering drew the attention of the world and was one of the causes for the rapid spread of Christianity.

The depth of a disciple's joy in the Lord may well be measured by the degree of his participation in the sufferings of the Lord. It is still true that those who pay a great price in suffering to remain true to Christ know a deep measure of this Spirit-wrought joy in their lives. Perhaps our Christian lives are so lacking in this joy because our Christian profession costs us so little.

Paul's references to the Holy Spirit (vv. 5, 6) indicate that the readers were instructed concerning the person of the Spirit and were well acquainted with His active presence in their hearts. In these first few verses of this epistle, touching upon the experience of the early believers, the doctrine of the Trinity is clearly implied.

(iii) *Widespread result* (v. 7). This paradoxical experience of the Thessalonian believers made a deep impact and produced a widespread result. "So that ye became an ensample to all that believe in Macedonia and in Achaia." The words *so that ye became* (*hōste genesthai humas*) point to a definite result which was achieved by the readers in consequence of their manner of life. The plural *ye* points to the various individuals composing the Thessalonian church as the ones who have produced this effect. Collectively they have become "an ensample" to those in the various areas where their experience has become known.

The word rendered *ensample* (*tupon*) meant originally the "mark" left by a blow, as when a die strikes the image on a coin; then it came to be used of the figure formed by blows; and hence more generally of any image, model, or pattern. It is most frequently used in the New Testament in the sense of an example or pattern in the moral life (Phil 3:17; 1 Th 1:7; 2 Th 3:9; 1 Ti 4:12; Titus 2:7; 1 Pe 5:3). Thus these Thessalonian believers, who began by being themselves imitators, have become examples in character and Christian living to others. It is proof of a healthy Christian life when those who begin by following the example of other Christians themselves develop into worthy and attractive examples for others. Such an achievement is not a matter of the mere length of life as a professed Christian, but the outcome of a vital inner experience consistently expressed in consecrated Christian conduct.

There is textual uncertainty as to whether the word for *ensample* was originally plural or singular. This uncertainty is reflected in our modern English versions.*** If the term is plural, the meaning is that each member of the Thessalonian church was a living witness of the truth and a personal example to other believers. If the singular is adopted, the meaning is that the Thessalonian church as a whole served as a model church to others.

Those advocating the plural as the original reading, point to the fact that the balance of the manuscript evidence, which is divided, is for the plural. (But the ancient versions favor the singular). It is further pointed out that the readers are not viewed "as *one* abstract *collective body*" to which the singular *tupos* might properly be applied.[63] Calvin remarks,

> The plural number in my opinion expresses somewhat more than if he had said that that Church as a whole has been set forth as an object of imitation, for the meaning is that there were as many examples as there were individuals.[64]

Advocates of the singular insist that the plural "is an obvious correction to agree with the plural 'you.'"[65] They hold that it is more likely that the singular in the original would be changed to the plural than vice versa. It is further urged that since the Thessalonians are examples to those at a distance the meaning cannot be that each individual member is known to be such an example but rather that it is the church collectively.[66]

We accept the singular as the original reading. In either case Paul's words bear clear witness to the mighty impact that the mission at Thessalonica has produced. Its reputation as an exemplary church is high praise for the Thessalonian believers. No other church does Paul thus designate as "the model church" (Way).

The Thessalonians have become shining examples "to all that believe," not merely to their pagan neighbors or to inquirers or potential believers, but what is more difficult, to their fellow Christians elsewhere. Thus to become a worthy example to other believers requires a higher degree of

---

***Thus, "ensamples"—KJV; "examples"—Williams, Phillips; "models"—Darby; "patterns"—Young, Conybeare. The singular: "ensample"—Rotherham; "example"—Goodspeed, RSV, NASB; "pattern"—Lattey, Montgomery, Moffatt, Weymouth; 20th Cent; "model"—NEB; "the model church"—Way.

spiritual excellence than to be a pattern to an unregenerated world. The addition of *all* augments the praise being bestowed on the Thessalonians. Since they are said to be an example to those who are already believers it is clear that the example lies not in their reception of the gospel but in their suffering for it.

The participial construction *pasin tois pisteuousin*, "to all those believing," is the practical equivalent of a substantitive, "to all believers." It is a common designation for Christians in the New Testament. The present tense, denoting continuing action, points to faith as the abiding characteristic, the root essence of the Christian life. For Paul faith was central and he uses it as more or less synonymous with Christianity. The object of that faith is not here indicated but it centered in Jesus Christ to whom these early believers were passionately devoted as their divine Saviour and Lord.

The widespread impact of their exemplary suffering for the gospel is indicated in the dual statement "in Macedonia and in Achaia" (*en tē Makedonia kai en tē Achaia*). The repetition of the preposition (*en*) and the definite article with each name emphasizes the distinctness of the two provinces where their example has exerted its influence. Macedonia and Achaia were the northern and southern provinces into which the Romans had divided the ancient land of the Greeks. Thessalonica was in Macedonia, while Paul was in Achaia at the time of writing. The statement is quite in harmony with Paul's penchant for talking in terms of Roman provinces. He planned his missionary strategy in terms of Roman provinces. While as yet the gospel was established only in the main centers in these provinces, Paul thought of the gospel as spreading along the highways and byways into all parts of the provinces from these city centers.

c) BECAUSE OF REPORTS CONCERNING THEM (vv. 8-10). The precise relation of these verses to the preceding may be differently understood. Impressed by the unity of this outpouring of thanksgiving for the Thessalonians, many interpreters regard these verses as simply an explanation and enlargement of verse 7. That they are closely connected with the preceding is clear from Paul's confirmatory *for* (*gar*). But the contents of these verses seem clearly to indicate that Paul's thought goes much beyond the mere confirmation of the fact of the exemplariness of the Thessalonians. That exemplariness is the bridge whereby he passes to a further ground for thanksgiving, namely, the good reports about the Thessalonians which continue to reach him. In this third ground for thanksgiving, Paul again closely associates himself with his beloved converts.

In verse 8 Paul sets forth the facts behind the good reports concerning the Thessalonians, while verses 9-10 summarize the contents of those reports.

(1) *Facts behind the reports* (v. 8). Paul first states the widespread impact of the Thessalonians' exemplary conduct and then indicates its effect upon his own work.

While the import of verse 8 is clear, with the usual punctuation there is some irregularity in the construction of the sentence. The opening *For* indicates that proof of the statement in verse 7 is being introduced, but the proof runs beyond the thing to be proved. If grammatically regular, the sentence should properly have terminated with the words "in every place." By position the words "not only" belong to "in Macedonia and Achaia" as forming the natural contrast to "in every place." However, they are followed by a new subject and predicate with the adversative *but* to which no exact parallel is forthcoming. Due to this irregularity some commentators and versions put a strong punctuation after *Lord*, thus making two sentences. Rotherham places a dash after the word *Lord;* Way reads: "From you pealed forth the trumpet-call of that message of our Lord; and not through Macedonia and Achaia only, but in every land"; New English Bible: "From Thessalonica the word of the Lord rang out; and not in Macedonia and Achaia alone, but everywhere"; and Lattey: "For from you the word of the Lord hath been noised abroad; not only in Macedonia and Achaia, but in every place." This smoothing out of the construction is attractive, but Findlay objects to this punctuation in that it "makes an awkward asyndeton [the absence of a connecting particle], out of keeping in a paragraph so smoothly continuous as this."[67] But asyndeton is not uncommon in explanatory clauses. Although the usual punctuation leaves the sentence somewhat irregular, it is yet perfectly intelligible as another example of Paul's "impetuous style"[68] (Compare v. 3). Instead of limiting himself to the thought of the places where they have become examples, Paul's thought rushes on to indicate not only the method of the spreading of the reports about them but also its result for his own work.

Verse 8 offers proof of the praise in verse 7. Paul's statement concerning the widespread impact of their joyous suffering may have surprised the Thessalonians. But the explanation in this verse must have been a greater surprise to them.

"For from you" implies that the action in the verb emanated from them as the starting point, rather than having been accomplished by them as its agent. The verb "hath sounded forth" (*exēchētai*) denotes the resounding reverberations of a loud noise. Usually the picture is taken to be that of a mighty trumpet blast, although Lightfoot suggests thunder.[69] The perfect tense indicates the abiding effect of the blast; "the blast hangs on the air as the result of the trumpet having been blown."[70] The word forcibly indicates the clear and pervasive nature of the sound that has issued forth.

Paul designates that which has been sounded forth as "the word of the Lord." This is a standard phrase in the Old Testament to denote a prophet's utterance setting forth the revealed will of God. But here the Lord is Jesus Christ and the expression is a synonym for the gospel. The expression stresses the authoritative nature of the gospel message. It is a message which comes from Him and is delivered by His messengers under His authority. "Of the Lord" (*tou kuriou*) is not the objective genitive, "a word which tells about the Lord," but is subjective, "a word which comes from the Lord." Since the gospel has a divine source it can be proclaimed without apology or alteration. "If men think of the gospel only as another philosophy, as the result of the reflection of certain, admittedly profound, first-century thinkers on religious topics, they will never have the burning zeal which sent the first Christian preachers through the world to proclaim what God had done for man."[71]

The spread of the gospel from Thessalonica was the result of vital Christian living rather than aggressive missionary propaganda. Paul's picture is not that of an organized missionary campaign on the part of the Thessalonians aimed at spreading the gospel to the regions beyond. The picture is rather that of a trumpet or sounding board amplifying the sound. The amazing joy of the Thessalonian believers under affliction has amplified the message of the gospel, causing the reports to spread in all directions. A trumpet or sounding board does not itself create the sound but receives, amplifies, and sends it out. Barnes surmises that the Thessalonian believers also took advantage of their position to send out messengers of salvation to other parts of Greece.[72] While that is quite possible, it is not the natural meaning of Paul's words. The verb is passive, "has been sounded forth," and indicates that the message has been disseminated from them by the reports of others. Conybeare and Montgomery translate it thus; Lattey renders "hath been noised abroad;" Moffatt has it, "has resounded from you."

The strategic position of Thessalonica did much to further this rapid spread of the reports. The city was an important center on the famous Egnatian Way running across Macedonia; and because of its location at the head of the Thermaic Gulf, as an important seaport, it stood in constant ship communication with all parts of the Mediterranean world. Travelers coming to Thessalonica by land or sea soon heard about or came into personal contact with these believers, radiant amid suffering. What they learned was of such a striking nature that it became a ready topic of conversation wherever they went. Kelly suggests that this assembly was a subject of common discussion because they "renounced Zeus, Hera, Artemis, Apollo, and all the rest, without adopting circumcision or the institutions of Moses."[73]

That some of these travelers carrying the reports were themselves Christians is to be assumed, but there is no basis for restricting the reports to them. Pagans also would be sufficiently interested in this phenomenon at Thessalonica to spread the news along the way. Neil remarks that "travellers and merchants probably became the Church's best advertising agents, more so if some of them were Christians."[74]

Reports concerning this unique group at Thessalonica have gone out not only "in Macedonia and Achaia" (*en tē Makedonia kai Achaia*) but far beyond. By using only one preposition and article Paul unites both provinces as a unit in contrast to the other regions reached by the reports.†††

By means of a strong adversative *but* the provinces of Macedonia and Achaia are set over against "in every place." This is usually considered to be an understandable exaggeration as though Paul meant "in many places." Paul's statement of course is not intended to be strictly literal, but the fact that he wrote from Corinth, another important trading center where traffic converged from all parts of the Roman world, may offer factual ground for his statement. Aquila and Priscilla had recently arrived from Rome (Ac 18:2) and it may well be that they told Paul of reports heard at Rome concerning the Thessalonians. Neil further reminds us that it is "quite likely, for example, that the charge of treason levelled against the Thessalonian Christians (Acts xvii. 6-7) would be reported in Rome."[75] Its maritime connections would naturally place Thessalonica into possible contact with harbors located in practically all parts of the then-known world. At any rate the statement indicates the wide dissemination of the remarkable news concerning the Thessalonian Christians.

The statement "in every place your faith to God-ward is gone forth" is a practical parallel to the preceding assertion, yet the altered subject and verb change the picture. The verb "is gone forth," again in the perfect tense (*exelēluthen*), drops the preceding figure to suggest that reports concerning their faith have gone out in all directions like travelers. Instead of "the word of the Lord" the subject is now "your faith to God-ward." Auberlen remarks that the two expressions "describe Christianity on its two sides; the word on the Divine side, but offering itself to men; faith on the human, but turning to meet the approach of God."[76]

The faith of the Thessalonians, which is receiving such widespread publicity, is monotheistic, rightly characterized as "your faith to God-ward" (*hē pistis humōn hē pros ton theon*). The repeated article em-

†††The original reading is uncertain. There is good manuscript support for repeating the preposition and article with Achaia (*en tē Achaia*), thus conforming the reading to v. 7. Critical editors view the second preposition and article as an insertion, since it seems more likely to have been added to conform to v. 7 than to have been omitted if original.

phasizes the added prepositional phrase as a more exact definition of their faith. The preposition *pros*, which means "near" or "facing," indicates that their faith is directed toward and has as its object "the God," the one true God whom they have come to know and serve, in contrast to their former idols. Their faith has experienced a change of direction, bringing them into a face-to-face relation with the living God.

Paul adds the further fact that these reports concerning the Thessalonians have a direct relation to his own work. They have rendered a preparatory service for his ministry. Whenever he meets strangers from different places, before he has the opportunity to tell them about the work at Thessalonica, they are eager to tell him what they have heard concerning the Thessalonian believers. The result is, "so that we need not to speak anything," that is, about what has happened at Thessalonica. The infinitive *to speak* (*lalein*) indicates that these reports were being brought to Paul's ears through free, oral communications.

(2) *Contents of the reports* (vv. 9-10). In turning to summarize the contents of these reports, Paul's "For they themselves" again indicates that these reports are not being made by the missionaries but rather by travelers arriving at Corinth who had been deeply impressed by what they had learned about the Thessalonian believers. And the present tense of the verb *report* (*apanggellousin*) denotes that these reports are being received by the missionaries not in isolated instances but in repeated occurrences. And the good thing about these reports is that they state the facts quite accurately. Since the report is not formulated in terms that are characteristically Pauline, it seems clear that Paul is reproducing the essence of the reports as received. They relate both to the missionaries (v. 9a) and their converts (vv. 9b-10).

(a) *Success among them* (v. 9a). The first topic of the report was "concerning us," Paul and his colleagues. Silvanus and Timothy had recently joined Paul at Corinth from extended trips through Macedonia and they likewise could bring such reports.

Lünemann extended the meaning of *us* to include both the missionaries and the Thessalonians.[77] But Alford points out two objections to this interpretation. The emphatic position of the words "concerning us," which in the original stand before the verb *report* (*peri hēmōn apangellousin*), seems to necessitate that "us" keep its restricted meaning. Further, if "us" was intended to include the Thessalonians it would have been more natural for Paul to use the second person throughout, since the "entering in" was quite as much a matter happening to the Thessalonians as to the writers.[78]

Concerning the missionaries the reports recounted "what manner of entering in we had unto you." The "entering in" is not to be restricted to

the introduction or reception they received upon arrival but relates to
their whole approach to and dealings with the Thessalonians while with
them. The correlative pronoun "what manner of" (*hopoian*) stresses the
quality of the entrance. They gained "access not only to their friendship
but to their hearts and consciences."[79] "Unto you" (*pros humas*) indicates
that they carried on their ministry in a face-to-face relationship with the
Thessalonians. They were open and above-board in all their dealings with
them. It is a resumption of the thought already expressed in verse 5 above.

(b) *Change in them* (vv. 9b-10). The second topic in these reports dealt
with the change that had come into the lives of the readers. It was this
part that was the truly arresting part of the story. Clarke comments that
this report shows that the Thessalonians were walking "so conscientiously
before God and man, that their friends could speak of them without a
blush, and their adversaries could say nothing to their disgrace."[80]

(i) *Turning to God* (v. 9b). "How ye turned to God from idols" summarizes their conversion experience. The verb rendered "ye turned"
(*epestrepsate*) is the regular word for conversion in the New Testament
and marks the radical change that has come into the lives of the Thessalonian believers. In a physical sense the word means to turn around (Mk
5:30); in a spiritual sense it denotes the turning which has altered the
course of their lives so that they are now moving in the opposite direction.
The indicative mode records the fact that such a change has taken place,
while the aorist tense points to the definite crisis experience that has occurred. The active voice indicates that the conversion was the consequence of a deliberate choice on their part; it was not an act forced upon
them but was a voluntary turning on their part. Hogg and Vine point
out that "in no case is God, or Christ, or the Holy Spirit, said to turn, or
convert, anyone. Conversion is always the voluntary act of the individual
in response to the presentation of truth."[81]

This turning of the Thessalonians had a positive as well as a negative
aspect. Positively, it was a turning "unto God" (*pros ton theon*). The
preposition *pros* brings out the fact that their turning brought them into
a face-to-face relationship with "the God," the true God, previously unknown to them, who had been presented to them in the preaching of the
missionaries.

This positive turning unto God also involved the negative aspect of
turning "from idols" (*apo tōn eidōlōn*). The definite article with the word
idols, "the idols," makes the term generic and classifies all the idols that
they had known in their past lives. The preposition *apo* means "from" or
"away from," and indicates that in turning to God they turned their backs
on these idols, separating themselves from any further idol worship.

They recognized that the worship of the true God excluded the worship of idols. This truth formed part of Paul's preaching to idolaters (Ac 14:14-17; 17:22-25). He was keenly aware that the truth of God could not coexist with spurious and empty idolatry. The word *eidōlon* ("idol") in secular Greek meant "an appearance, a mere image, a shadow, a phantom." Paul was fully convinced of the nonexistence of the pagan gods the images were supposed to represent (1 Co 8:4), but he was fully aware of the evil, demonic powers that operated behind these idols (1 Co 10:19-20). Paul condemned the whole system of idolatry, root and branch, and insisted that Christians could not compromise with idolatry (1 Co 10:14).

The order in which Paul mentions these two aspects of conversion is significant. "Unto God from idols" sets forth the true order in genuine Christian conversion. The versions of Conybeare, Weymouth, Goodspeed, Williams, Phillips, and the New English Bible reverse this order and thus blur this significant truth. The Thessalonians did not turn to God because they had become disillusioned with idolatry and were repelled by the grossness and futility of their idols; it was the attractive character of the true God preached by the missionaries that drew them to Him.

> What has stript the seeming beauty
>   From the idols of the earth?
> Not the sense of right or duty,
>   But the sight of peerless worth.
>
> Not the crushing of the idols,
>   With its bitter void and smart,
> But the beaming of His beauty,
>   The unveiling of His heart.[82]

Salvation does not begin with giving up something but with receiving Someone. The coming of Christ into their hearts and lives effected their turning from their idols, causing these things to be no longer desirable.

Since idolatry was inseparably connected with all phases of pagan life, a conversion which led to the rejection and renunciation of idols was indeed a revolutionary experience. There seemed to be a solid basis for the charge of the enemies that the missionaries were men who "turned the world upside down" (Ac 17:6).

This description of their conversion clearly indicates that the majority of the Thessalonian believers were non-Jewish. Acts 17:4 records that Paul's synagogue ministry at Thessalonica led to the conversion of a few Jews and a large number of "devout Greeks." These devout or God-fearing Greeks may have included some heathen who were present as honest seekers after the truth, but the usual meaning of the term indicates Gentiles who had become adherents of the synagogue without accepting the rites of Judaism. Since Paul's expression would not be strictly applicable to such God-fearers who had already abandoned their idols, the reference to their turning "to God from idols" seems to imply their direct conversion from paganism. It seems to demand a ministry in Thessalonica directly to the pagan population.

This turning to God from idols was the beginning of a totally new life for the readers. It gave their lives a new orientation toward the present as well as the future.

(ii) *Serving God* (v. 9c). The aim of their present life is "to serve a living and true God." The present infinitive (*douleuein*) denotes that it is a life of continuous, complete, and wholehearted service to God. The literal connotation of the verb is "to serve as a slave," to discharge the duties of a bondservant. They had completely yielded their wills to carry out the will of their heavenly Master. Calvin remarks, "Only the man who has learned to put himself wholly in subjection to God is truly converted to Him."[83]

The Christian life is one of service. Frame comments that "the readers have exchanged a slavery to idols for a slavery to God."[84] Having been redeemed from the bondage of idolatry, their lives now belong to God to serve Him and further His cause. Yet to be the Lord's "bondsman" is perfectly consistent with true Christian liberty. Man's freedom consists in his liberty to choose his master, not to be without a master. As he voluntarily yields himself to God's service, the believer finds the power and the desire to do what he ought to do, so experiencing true liberty.

Moulton and Milligan point out that the verb *douleuō* (to serve) was apparently never used in a religious sense in pagan literature.[85] Paul's beautiful picture of the Thessalonians serving a living and true God by a life of voluntary obedience to His will was quite beyond pagan conception. Denney remarks,

> No Greek or Roman could take in the idea of "serving" a God. . . . There was no room for it in his religion; his conception of the gods did not admit of it. If life was to be a moral service rendered to God, it must be to a God quite different from any to whom he was introduced by his ancestral worship.[86]

Such a God, perfect and holy and worthy of their wholehearted love and service, the Thessalonians now knew.

The Master the Thessalonians have chosen to serve is characterized as "a living and true God" (*theō zōnti kai alēthinō*). The absence of the article with *theo* (God) draws attention to His character, which is the very opposite of the idols they have abandoned. Two characteristics are stressed. He is a *living* God, having life and power in Himself as "the author and preserver of life unto others."[87] He stands in contrast to the dead idols which are impotent to help their worshippers. He is also a *true*

God, genuine and real, as opposed to the counterfeit gods of idolatry which have no objective existence. This description, emphasizing the monotheistic character of the deity they are now serving, sharply distinguishes them from pagans.

(iii) *Awaiting His Son* (v. 10). Their conversion has also given the Thessalonians an attitude of expectancy concerning the future. While devoted to the service of God, they have set themselves "to wait for his Son from heaven." The infinitive rendered "to wait for" (*anamenein*) means "to await, expect, wait up for" and pictures them as people who are eagerly and expectantly looking forward to the coming of one whose arrival is anticipated at any time; the present tense gives this as their continuing attitude. Clearly the Thessalonians held the hope of the imminent return of Christ. The verb carries the further suggestion of being ready to receive the one whose coming is awaited.

This person is designated as "his Son," that is, the Son of the God whom they are serving. The term points to His inner relation to God and expresses Christ's deity. "First and foremost Paul believed and insisted that Jesus stood in a unique relationship with God."[88]

They are eagerly awaiting God's Son "from heaven" (*ek tōn ouranōn*), more literally, "out of the heavens" (Rotherham). The use of the plural "heavens" is not classical Greek but Hebrew, the Hebrew having no singular form. Auberlen thought that the plural was used to denote "the manifold, rich life of the super-terrestrial world."[89]

The New Testament distinguishes three heavens, the aerial (Mt 6:26), the sidereal (Mt 24:29), and "the third" (2 Co 12:2), the abode of God. In His ascension Christ "passed through the heavens" (Heb 4:14), entered "into heaven itself" (Heb 9:24), and "sat down on the right hand of the throne of the Majesty in the heavens" (Heb 8:1). From thence believers are eagerly expecting His return as Saviour (Phil 3:20-21). However, since the New Testament often used the plural and singular number for "heaven" without any marked difference in meaning, it would be unwise here to insist that Paul thinks of Christ's return as a dramatic passing through these different heavens. The fact of His expected return is the point of emphasis.

This anticipation of the return of Christ characterized the Christian church from its very beginning. Acts makes it clear that it was an essential part of the preaching of the gospel. That Paul laid considerable emphasis upon this hope in his preaching at Thessalonica seems clear from the perverted charge against the Christians in Acts 17:7 when read in the light of the Thessalonian epistles. This eschatological hope is the keynote of these epistles. This hope has taken a firm hold on the Thessalonian believers. If their serving a living and true God distinguished the Thessalonian believers from the Gentiles, this expectant hope for Christ's return distinguished them from the Jews.

Much of modern Christendom has lost this expectant waiting for the return of Christ, much to its own impoverishment. It is an essential part of a mature Christian life. Denney well says,

> That attitude of expectation is the bloom, as it were, of the Christian character. Without it there is something lacking; the Christian who does not look upward and onward wants one mark of perfection.[90]

Neil recognizes that this eschatological hope characterized the early Christians but he insists that today we cannot accept it as "an event in time at all."[91] He seeks to dissolve this hope of the literal return in a spiritualized eschatology by saying, "The Lord is always at hand and comes to every generation, and we pass the Judgment of Doomsday upon ourselves every living moment."[92] It is true that our present Christian life has eschatological implications, but this effort to dissolve the future in the ever changing experiences of present life is inconsistent with what the New Testament means when it speaks about the second coming. Paul here is thinking of an actual event in the future which will consummate this present age. A rational interpretation of Christian history demands the concept of a coming historical consummation of that history.

It is interesting to observe that Jesus is here not spoken of as the object of saving faith but rather as the object of Christian hope. Such faith is implied here, but the statement is in harmony with the life of the Thessalonian believers as it is being reported to Paul.

The one whose coming is awaited is none other than the historical Jesus. The human Jesus, who already lived on this earth during His first advent, is emphatically identified as the one "whom he raised from the dead." The Scriptures habitually attribute the resurrection of Jesus to the activity of the Father. The importance of the resurrection of Jesus is indicated by the fact that the assertion that He was raised is placed emphatically before the mention of His human name, "even Jesus." This reference to His resurrection takes us back to the first advent. It was the body of the human Jesus that was raised from the tomb. Any claim that His resurrection refers to His spirit rather than His body is spurious; the spirit cannot be embalmed and placed in a tomb. That the return of the risen Christ was being awaited by the Thessalonians implies the teaching concerning His ascension and present enthronement at the right hand of the Father.

Morris calls attention to the fact that an eschatological reference both precedes and follows this mention of Christ's resurrection.[93] Paul thus firmly ties the hope of the second advent to the crowning event of the first advent. His resurrection was the leading proof of the sonship and Godhood of Jesus Christ (Ro 1:4). It was an event that stands alone in history and confirms the validity of the gospel of salvation through Christ Jesus. It was the abiding evidence that the atoning work of Christ on the cross has been accepted by the just and holy God. The resurrection of Christ was decisive for the message that Paul preached in the Thessalonian synagogue (Ac 17:2-3). Findlay points out that it is this preaching of the resurrection of Jesus which "discloses the chasm parting the Church from the Synagogue."[94]

The resurrection of Christ is the ground and guarantee of His return. Had He not risen from the dead there could be no hope of His coming again. His work of redemption at the first advent, culminating in victory at the resurrection, forms the basis for His work as our rescuer at His return.

The Jesus whose coming the Thessalonians were awaiting is further identified as the one "who delivereth us from the wrath to come." The appositional articular participle rendered "who delivereth us" (*ton rhuomenon hēmas*) may be interpreted in two different ways. Those who stress the time element in the present participle would render "the one who is continually delivering us." (The past tense in the KJV, "delivered," has no foundation in the Greek. Its translators here followed the Vulgate. Phillips also uses the past tense.) They emphasize that the deliverance is already "going on—it commenced with his death, but will not be completed until his advent."[95] And certainly the present work of the inner transformation of the believer is intimately related to that future deliverance.

Others hold that the articular participle is timeless and has the force of a substantive, "our Deliverer" (Darby, Conybeare, Way, Montgomery, Weymouth, Goodspeed, 20th Cent, and NEB). Under this view it is "the *character* of the Saviour that is expressed."[96] The present tense indicates that it is His office and work to be our deliverer. It is His purpose and function to deliver or rescue as it is that of Satan to destroy. The eschatological mold of the context makes the latter view preferable.

The verb *delivereth* (*rhuomai*), having the meaning "to save, rescue, deliver," places the emphasis upon the greatness of the peril from which deliverance is given by a mighty act of power. It is just because believers await Christ's return as deliverer that the thought of His coming does not inspire terror but confidence. But He will not indiscriminately rescue everyone when He comes. The subjects of His deliverance, *us*, are Paul, Silvanus, Timothy, the Thessalonian believers, and all the elect.

The importance of this negative aspect of the Saviour's work at His return arises out of the great peril from the wrath that hangs over sinful men. At His coming Christ will rescue us "from the wrath to come" (*ek tēs orgēs tēs erchomonēs*). This wrath is not identified but it obviously is the divine wrath in the traditional sense of the coming day of judgment. Its eschatological character is stressed by the added definition as the wrath which is "to come." This emphatic appositional description of the wrath draws attention to its feature as still coming, while the present tense of the participle brings out the certainty, and possibly the nearness, of its future manifestation. Paul clearly teaches that there is a present manifestation of divine wrath against sin (Ro 1:18), but here the reference is to the future manifestation of His wrath "in the day of wrath and revelation of the righteous judgment of God" (Ro 2:5). This eschatological aspect of God's wrath is also stressed in 5:9 where Paul makes the experience of this wrath the opposite of obtaining salvation at the return of Christ.

This concise reference to "the wrath" implies that the readers would understand its significance and indicates that the preaching of divine wrath coming upon sin and idolatry was an essential part of the apostolic preaching to pagans. The peril of man as justly subject to the wrath of God because of his sinfulness in character and deed explains the need for the deliverance that the gospel proclaims. "To realize that we are under God's wrath and in dis-grace is the essential preliminary to the experience of His love and His grace."[97]

The fact of God's wrath against sin is declared in both the Old and New Testaments. His wrath against sin arises out of the holiness of His nature. "Wrath is the holy revulsion of God's being against that which is the contradiction of his holiness."[98] As the moral ruler of the universe, God must be totally opposed to sin and evil in every form. The concept of divine wrath roots in the fact of God's nature as holy and the nature of sin as rebellion against God. Without the truth of divine wrath the universe would sink into moral chaos. In the words of Rienecker,

> God would completely dissolve and deny himself as God if he would not prove himself as a "real and terrible wrath" against the sinning man. God cannot and will not favor sin. Therefore his wrath burns against everyone who opposes him. The wrath of God is not an illusion, but a reality.[99]

The wrath of God must not be interpreted in terms of uncontrolled or irrational human anger. It is not an arbitrary outburst of rage, nor is it a vindictive passion which lacks self-control. The word for *wrath* (*orgē*) comes from the verb *orgaō*, meaning "to teem, to swell," and thus implies that it is not a sudden outburst but rather His fixed, controlled passionate feeling against sin leading to its inevitable punishment. Hendriksen calls it *"the settled indignation* which by nature rests on the sinner."[100]

73

The manifestation of divine wrath is perfectly compatible with God's love. Anger had its proper place in the perfect human character of Christ (Mk 3:5).[101] God must be angry with sin because of the destructive character of sin. His love will not allow Him to be tolerant toward the devastating effects of sin. Hughes aptly remarks,

> For God to have permitted sin to flourish unchecked and unpunished, and passively to have watched the world degenerate into a dungheap of corruption and violence, would have been very far removed from an expression of love, apart from the fact that it would have argued the impotence of His purposes in creation and the incompetence of His hand to control the affairs of men, which would mean in turn that He was not God at all.[102]

The thought of the personal wrath of God against sin is an unwelcome concept to many today. Efforts are made to depersonalize the divine wrath by equating it with an impersonal process of retribution against sin. Thus Dodd asserts that Paul uses the term "not to describe the attitude of God to man, but to describe an inevitable process of cause and effect in a moral universe."[103] And Barclay seeks support for this depersonalization by remarking that "quite frequently Paul speaks about *the wrath*, without saying it is the wrath *of God*, and he speaks about it in a kind of impersonal way as if it ought to be spelled with capital letters—The Wrath—as if it was a kind of impersonal force at work in the world."[104]

The fact that Paul does at times speak about "the wrath" without saying that it is God's wrath does not prove that he conceived of it as an impersonal force operating in the world. That God does work through the divinely established laws of the universe does not eliminate His personal feeling of wrath against sin. Surely the biblical teaching concerning the divine wrath against sin "is not merely the consequences of lifeless laws, but the expression of the feeling of a living spirit."[105] Morris pointedly remarks,

> The God of the New Testament does not sit back and let 'natural' laws bring about the defeat of evil. He is actively opposed to evil in every shape and form. Where unpleasant consequences follow on evil-doing His hand is in it.[106]

The New Testament explicitly connects wrath with God in numerous passages (see for example Jn 3:36; Ro 1:18; 5:9; 9:22; Eph 5:6; Rev 14:10). Surely the eternal God, whose personal presence pervades all things, cannot remain merely passive to the active evils rampant in the world. The divine wrath is His personal reaction against sin. The striking expression "the wrath of the Lamb" (Rev 6:16) clearly associates wrath personally with a divine Being.

While believers fully recognize the seriousness of God's wrath against sin, they rest in the glorious truth of the gospel that Christ delivers His own *from* (*ek*), or "out of" the coming wrath. Milligan remarks that the preposition *ek* emphasizes the completeness of the deliverance and adds, "He brings us altogether out of the reach of future judgment."[107] Believers look forward to Christ's coming for they know that He "is to rescue us out of the anger that is coming" (Rotherham). The basis for His deliverance is not indicated here, but it is grounded in His atoning work on the cross.

In looking back over this summary statement of the remarkable testimony concerning the Thessalonians, one is impressed with the richness of its compressed theology about God, His Son, and the Christian life. Concerning God it indicates that He is a living person, is truly God, has a Son, raised Him from the dead, is the proper recipient of Christian service, and has wrath against sin. Concerning Jesus Christ it indicates His dual nature as the God-man, His death and resurrection, by implication His ascension, His expected return from heaven, and His delivering of believers from wrath. Concerning the Christian life it teaches the need for conversion as a definite break with past evil, that Christian living is characteristically a life of serving God, and that the Christian has the living hope of deliverance from the wrath of judgment through the returning Christ.

That the Thessalonians were expected to understand the significance of these compressed statements bears witness to the richness of Paul's preaching. Paul was concerned not merely to lead people to faith in Christ as Saviour but also to ground them in the truths of the gospel.

6

PERSONAL: RELATIONSHIP

B. RELATIONSHIP WHILE WITH THEM, 2:1-16

FOLLOWING THE THANKSGIVING for the readers in chapter 1, the thought now turns to the relationship of the missionaries with their converts while they were all together. This section falls into two parts. The first twelve verses recount the ministry among them, while verses 13-16 record a renewed thanksgiving for the readers' reception of the gospel which was preached to them.

1. Ministry at Thessalonica

2:1-12 For yourselves, brethren, know our entering in unto you, that it hath not been found vain: (2) but having suffered before and been shamefully treated, as ye know, at Philippi, we waxed bold in our God to speak unto you the gospel of God in much conflict. (3) For our exhortation *is* not of error, nor of uncleanness, nor in guile: (4) but even as we have been approved of God to be intrusted with the gospel, so we speak; not as pleasing men, but God who proveth our hearts. (5) For neither at any time were we found using words of flattery, as ye know, nor a cloak of covetousness, God is witness; (6) nor seeking glory of men, neither from you nor from others, when we might have claimed authority as apostles of Christ. (7) But we were gentle in the midst of you, as when a nurse cherisheth her own children: (8) even so, being affectionately desirous of you, we were well pleased to impart unto you, not the gospel of God only, but also our own souls, because ye were become very dear to us. (9) For ye remember, brethren, our labor and travail: working night and day, that we might not burden any of you, we preached unto you the gospel of God. (10) Ye are witnesses, and God *also*, how holily and righteously and unblamably we behaved ourselves toward you that believe: (11) as ye know how we *dealt with* each one of you, as a father with his own children, exhorting you, and encouraging *you*, and testifying, (12) to the end that ye should walk worthily of God, who calleth you into his own kingdom and glory.

In this paragraph Paul is clearly on the defensive. His detailed account of the ministry at Thessalonica is fully intelligible only on the supposition that Paul is vindicating his work and character against the attacks of local

Jews and pagans. Timothy, who has just returned from Thessalonica, has reported that the opponents of the gospel are circulating slanderous charges against Paul and his work. While Paul was still at Thessalonica his enemies twisted his preaching to extract from it a charge of treason (Ac 17:7). With the same subtlety they are now assailing his character and motives in an effort to destroy his message.

This passage is an *apologia* or "defense" of the life and labors of Paul and his colleagues. Clearly he is uneasy about the charges being flung at them. The view of some that Paul is merely reminiscing about their relationship with the readers with "the definite design of *strengthening and confirming*"[1] the Thessalonians in their newly adopted faith is inadequate. It does not sufficiently account for the strong assertions of the excellencies of the work among them, the solemn protestations being made (vv. 5, 10), nor the repeated appeals made to the personal recollections of the readers (vv. 1, 2, 5, 9, 10, 11). This self-revelation is not being made because the Thessalonian believers themselves were suspicious or doubtful about the missionaries. Paul is answering the insidious attacks being made by scandalmongers outside the church because of their hatred for him.

The enemies were attempting to destroy the faith of the Thessalonian Christians by undermining their confidence in the integrity of the men from whom they had received the gospel. They were attempting to stamp the missionaries as religious charlatans who used their propaganda of a free salvation as a pretext for securing personal honor and financial gain. Such a charge had a show of plausibility. The roads of that day were full of the missionaries of all sorts of new cults and strange creeds. Impostors were always at hand who traded on the gullibility of the people for personal advantage.

In refuting these enemy accusations Paul uses the method of simply letting the record speak for itself. The facts were still fresh in the memory of the readers. In thus repeatedly asking them to recall what they witnessed he is letting them judge if the evidence fits in with the charges being made against them. It was a masterly defense. It proved that the facts needed for their vindication were a matter of common knowledge. Nothing had been concealed from them. The readers needed no new and hitherto unknown information to bolster their new faith. When evaluated in the light of the known truth the malicious charges being made against them could not survive.

Such a defense is the best proof of the purity of a preacher's life. That Paul himself advocates this test is a strong witness to the integrity of his character and work. The missionaries had left their converts the memory of true Christian character and unselfish Christian service. To the consciousness of that fact they appealed as a safeguard to the readers.

The refutation of these attacks upon him was an unwelcome task for Paul. It was not undertaken because of wounded personal pride. Doubtless Paul found it distasteful thus to commend himself and his work before his converts, but the cause of the gospel demanded it. He knew well that the progress of the gospel would be undermined if the personal integrity of its chief exponents was successfully discredited.

The unsavory situation which evoked Paul's indignant protest and compelled him to make a frank revelation of his inner life and purposes has resulted in great gain for the Christian church. Without these attacks we would not have received these unveilings of the inner life of the apostle. Moffatt remarks that these insinuations "against Paul's character were like torches flung at an unpopular figure; they simply served to light up his grandeur."[2]

In this passage Paul recounts the circumstances of the ministry at Thessalonica (vv. 1-2), repudiates the false motives imputed to them as contrasted to their God-approved motive (vv. 3-4), and describes the conduct of the messengers with a reminder of the readers' personal knowledge of that ministry (vv. 5-12).

a) CIRCUMSTANCES OF THE MINISTRY (vv. 1-2). Paul reminds the readers of their own knowledge of the ministry to them (v. 1*a*) and then describes it negatively and positively (vv. 1*b*-2).

(1) *Their knowledge of it* (v. 1*a*). "For yourselves, brethren, know our entering in unto you." *For* is usually used to link a statement with what has immediately preceded, but here it obviously does not substantiate the reference to Christ's deliverance from coming wrath (1:10). It rather connects with 1:9 and finds its proper explanation "in the train of thought which was running in the Apostle's mind."[3] It resumes the reference to the work of the missionaries at Thessalonica in 1:9 and takes up explicitly the defense already hinted at in 1:5*b*. This entire section is in fact an elaboration of the two points mentioned in 1:9. Verses 1-12 are an expansion of "what manner of entering in we had unto you," while verses 13-16 renew the theme of "how ye turned unto God from idols, to serve a living and true God."

Paul has informed the readers about the reports from others he is continually receiving about the ministry at Thessalonica (1:9), but the Thessalonians are not dependent on such reports for their knowledge of it. No one has a better knowledge of that ministry in their midst than they themselves. *Yourselves* (*autoi*) is emphatic and contrasts their knowledge with that of others who report to Paul. Phillips brings out this emphasis by rendering, "You know from your own experience."

The readers are again affectionately addressed as *brethren* (cf. 1:4). It is in the interest of that relationship that this passage is written.

The Thessalonian brethren had a vivid personal knowledge of "our entering in unto you." The expression *our entering in* (*tōn eisodon hēmōn*) here has the same import that it had in 1:9. But now the former indefinite reference is made definite by the addition of the prepositional phrase *unto you* (*tēn pros humas*). The reference is not to the initial arrival at Thessalonica but rather to the whole period of work in Thessalonica, the "visit"* which they remember so well. That visit by the missionaries had brought them into a personal face-to-face relationship with *you*, the members of the Thessalonian church.

With his use of the plural pronoun *our*, Paul continues to associate himself with his colleagues in that ministry.†

(2) *Description of it* (verses 1b-2). The ministry at Thessalonica is first characterized by a single negative assertion (v. 1b) and then positively described as to its background and nature (v. 2).

a) NEGATIVE ASSERTION (v. 1b). Their knowledge concerning the ministry in their midst has a negative aspect, "that it hath not been found vain." The precise significance of this categorical negative has been differently understood, centering around the meaning of the word *vain* (*kenē*). Some view it as referring to the results of that ministry. This is implied in the renderings "was not barren of results" (Way), "was not fruitless" (Lattey, NEB), "was no failure" (Moffatt, Phillips). Against this view is the meaning of *kenē*, which means "empty, hollow," like a vessel with nothing in it. The thought of the ineffectiveness of the work would better have been expressed by the term *mataios*, which means "useless, ineffective, futile." The parallel with 1:9 indicates that the reference is to the character of the work rather than to its results. In this passage the result is not expanded on until verse 13. Besides, no one had denied that the work had produced striking results.

In view of its use in Mark 12:3 Hendriksen would interpret the meaning to be "empty-handed."[4] Then the significance is that the missionaries did not come with empty hands, eager to get something for themselves; rather, they came with filled hands, ready to impart the blessings of the gospel. It is then a denial of the charge that the preachers were selfishly motivated. Against this attractive interpretation Morris points out that "it is the 'entering in' rather than the preachers which is thus described."[5]

Barnes interprets *kenē* to mean empty in the sense of being without

*The rendering for *eisodon* used by Montgomery, Weymouth, Moffatt, Goodspeed, Williams, Phillips, RSV, and NEB.
†Conybeare, Way, and Montgomery again shrink Paul's plural into a singular on the assumption that he is using an editorial plural.

truth or reality, hence "false or fallacious."[6] This then amounts to a denial that the missionaries were deceivers. Here again the objection is that it applies the term to the missionaries themselves rather than to their work.

Morris would interpret the term in regard to the aim or purpose of the coming of the missionaries. He views the statement as "a strong repudiation of any thought that Paul had frittered his time away in aimless pursuits. He had come with a definite aim, and he had secured what he had aimed at."[7] But one wonders why such persistent preachers as Paul and his colleagues should be accused of being aimless or purposeless in their work.

It is perhaps best to interpret the negative assertion of the essential character of the visit; its positive character is set forth in verse 2. Their work at Thessalonica was known to be no hollow activity, "inconsequential in its intrinsic character."[8] It was not void of content and power. It is then parallel to the statement in 1:5 that their work was not "in word only." Paul can confidently assert that their entering in "hath not proved void" (Rotherham). The perfect tense (*gegonen*), "hath come to be," expresses this as an accomplished, unassailable fact.

b) POSITIVE DELINEATION (v. 2). Over against the negative assertion stands the strong positive picture of the character of their work. *But* (*alla*), the stronger of the two Greek adversatives, introduces the sharp contrast. Far from being empty and powerless, their work of preaching the gospel was carried on with boldness amid conflict.

They boldly proclaimed their message at Thessalonica in spite of the fact that they had just experienced cruel mistreatment at Philippi because of their preaching. "Having suffered before and been shamefully treated, as ye know, at Philippi" sets the background for their work at Thessalonica. The two aorist participles (*propathontes, hubristhentes*), expressing antecedent action, are best regarded as concurrent; "although we had just suffered and been insulted" (Williams). Although they had recently experienced this grievous mistreatment because of the work of the Lord, they did not hesitate to preach again at Thessalonica.

"Having suffered before" recalls the physical suffering they had just undergone at Philippi. Acts 16:23-24 records that the suffering included a public flogging and having their feet in stocks while confined in the city's inner prison. Such a Roman flogging was no light matter; it was an experience not soon forgotten.

Neil observes that judging from the Pauline epistles as a whole, and especially from the autobiographical passage in 2 Corinthians 11:23-25, "Paul was particularly sensitive to bodily pain, fearing it and remembering it, as here, with horror."[9] After having undergone such treatment for the preaching of the gospel, to face immediately the possibility of the same treatment for preaching in the next city required high courage. Paul's persistence in preaching in the face of such prospects and consequences can only be understood in the light of his consciousness of an inescapable commission.

But for Paul the physical suffering was not the worst part of the treatment received. Paul more strongly resented that they had "been shamefully treated," grievously insulted. Gross indignities had been heaped on them in the way they had been treated— arrested on a false charge, stripped of their clothes and publicly beaten without a trial, and thrown into the inner prison with their feet in the stocks as though they were the most dangerous criminals. They had suffered not only bitter cruelty but public humiliation. Paul was deeply conscious that his social status as a Roman citizen had been outraged. The treatment accorded them was contrary to Roman law. His desire to reverse this mistreatment caused Paul to demand that the Philippian magistrates come personally to conduct them out of prison (Ac 16:37).

Paul's insertion of the words "as ye know" within his statement of their suffering indicates his vivid feeling and strong desire to carry his readers fully with him in recalling the facts. His words, quite literally, "even as ye know," indicate that their memory will recall an exact correspondence between his assertion and the facts.

When the missionaries arrived in Thessalonica their lacerated backs were still far from fully healed. The painful movements of the new arrivals soon brought out the story of the suffering they had undergone at Philippi. It became immediately clear to their hearers that their work of preaching carried the possibilities of dangerous consequences. But the missionaries felt that they had nothing to hide. If any of his opponents charged that Paul had a police record and had been scourged by the officials at Philippi, he was quite willing to have the facts known. It was not Paul but the magistrates who had reasons to hide the truth.

Paul testified that upon their arrival in Thessalonica, "we waxed bold in our God to speak unto you the gospel of God." Their bold preaching after such experiences, when they were well aware of what could happen to them, was the best proof that it was not a self-seeking, mercenary endeavor. If they were mere time-servers they would have been cowed and discouraged by such painful experiences.

The rendering "we waxed bold" (*eparrēsiasametha*) regards the verb as an ingressive aorist. But surely Paul does not mean that they had lost their courage but regained it upon arrival at Thessalonica. It is better to regard the action as constative and render "we were bold" (KJV) to cover the whole time that they worked in Thessalonica.

The original verb is derived from two words (*pas rhēsis*) which mean literally "all speech." "It denotes the state of mind when the words flow freely, the attitude of feeling quite at home with no sense of stress or strain."[10] Included in the freedom of speech is the resultant confidence that comes from such freedom. The verb is always used in the New Testament of the preaching of the gospel (Ac 9:27, 29; 13:46; 14:3; 18:26; 19:8; 26:26; Eph 6:20). It indicates the free and confident manner in which the missionaries preached the gospel without a sense of restraint or restriction.

This boldness of the missionaries was no mere natural attribute. It had its source not in self but "in our God." It was imparted to them by virtue of their union with Him. It arose with their consciousness that their life had its sphere of existence in Him and all that happened to them was under His control. "Christian courage springs from the belief that 'this God is OUR God.'"[11] The possessive *our* reveals the consciousness of the missionaries that they stood in a personal relationship to the God whose message they delivered. But Paul may have intended to include his readers. He was the God whom the Thessalonian believers now knew as their own God as well (1:9).

The missionaries revealed their boldness as God's messengers in their eagerness "to speak unto you the gospel of God." "To speak" (*lalēsai*) is an explanatory infinitive, giving added stress to the oral nature of the boldness. They boldly uttered their message to the hearers with whom they stood in a face-to-face relationship (*pros humas*). That message was nothing less than "the gospel of God," the glad tidings of which God Himself was the author and sender. In 1:5 Paul spoke of that message as "our gospel," for they had made that message thoroughly their own. But their message was not their own invention; it was God's good news which He had committed to them to proclaim. Since God had put the message on their lips they knew a holy urge to proclaim it to others.

Their preaching at Thessalonica was "in much conflict." The word rendered *conflict* (*agōn*) contains a metaphor drawn from the athletic games or the arena. It means the place of contest, and then the contest itself—a race, a struggle, a battle. Such a conflict always involves intense exertion and strenuous, persistent effort to overcome the determined opponent or the dangerous antagonist. The struggle involved in the term may be either inward or outward. In Colossians 2:1 Paul uses it of his inner strivings and prayer battles, while in Philippians 1:30 he uses it of outward conflict with the enemies of believers. Views differ as to the meaning here.

Lenski advocates the view that the reference is to the inner struggle and straining which the missionaries, like athletes, underwent in order to win the coveted prize. He renders it "with much agonizing."[12] The translation of Moffatt follows this view: "in spite of all the strain." On the basis of this interpretation Neil suggests that the strain may refer to "the effects of the apostles' misfortunes at Philippi."[13] Frame thinks that the reference to internal struggle is possible and points out that in later Greek *agōn* tends to mean "anxiety."[14]

The majority of the commentators insist that the context points rather to the external dangers to which the missionaries had been subjected at Thessalonica. The Revised Standard Version follows this view in its rendering, "in the face of great opposition."‡ It is also the view of Phillips, "whatever the opposition might be," although his rendering blurs the fact that the opposition was actually experienced, not just potential.

That the primary reference is to the external opposition to the preaching of the gospel seems most in keeping with the context. Yet as Hogg and Vine point out, in actual experience "inward and outward conflict cannot be sharply divided one from the other."[15] The external opposition encountered would naturally produce deep inner concern and evoke "much earnest striving" (Darby) in an effort to overcome the opposition. Bailey concludes, "The context seems to suggest outer opposition as the basis of any inner conflict that might have arisen."[16]

b) MOTIVES OF THE MINISTERS (vv. 3-4). The preaching of the missionaries at Thessalonica must be evaluated in the light of their true motives. With his explanatory *for* Paul indicates what enabled and obligated the missionaries to preach with boldness in spite of suffering and opposition. He categorically denies three false motives imputed to them (v. 3) and asserts that their preaching is that of men who have been tested by God and divinely entrusted with the gospel (v. 4). Had they acted under the false motives attributed to them they would have been unable to preach as they did under the circumstances.

Paul's statement of defense falls into two parts, a negative and a positive. This manner of presentation is characteristically Pauline. Only rarely in his epistles does Paul put the positive before the negative. It is his practice first to sweep away the false, and then with the ground cleared to set forth the positive presentation of the truth.

In these two verses Paul is establishing the manner of their work at Thessalonica by an appeal to those qualities, negative and positive, which habitually characterize their work. It is not until verse 5 that he again speaks specifically of the work at Thessalonica. The original of verse 3

‡Similar are the renderings of Montgomery, Weymouth, Goodspeed, NASB; Way paraphrases, "amid storm and stress."

contains no verb, and *is* rather than *was* (used in KJV, 20th Cent, Darby, Way, and Montgomery) should be supplied. To insert *was* incorrectly limits the verse to the work at Thessalonica. These features of their preaching were true of them before they came to Thessalonica, were true while they worked there, and were now true of their work at Corinth. It should be noticed that in these two verses Paul makes no appeal to the knowledge of the Thessalonians. That which he asserts goes beyond the scope of their knowledge, hence he cannot ask them to confirm the claim from their own experience.

(1) *Denial of impure motives* (v. 3). "For our exhortation is not of error, nor of uncleanness, nor in guile." Paul's strong triple negative is obviously aimed at repudiating false motives attributed to them by enemies. The view of Stevens that Paul is simply indulging in "earnest, affectionate reminiscences" in an effort to interpret to his "new, ignorant converts" the nature of "his work, and the gospel method generally"[17] does not do justice to the force of the categorical denials. The context clearly implies that enemy insinuations are being contradicted. Bailey remarks, "It is very revealing of the character of the time (cf. Ro 1:18-32; 6:19, 'servants of uncleanness'), and of the defaming charges made against them, that the writers felt it necessary to enter such a disclaimer as is here recorded."[18]

Paul designates their preaching as "our exhortation" (*hē paraklēsis hēmōn*). The noun, which basically means "a calling to one's side," that is, for aid or comfort, is used with a wide variety of meanings according to the circumstances of those to whom it is directed. Alexander remarks, "As addressed to the careless, slothful, tempted, fallen, it is *exhortation*; as addressed to the sad and seeking it is *solace* and *comfort*."[19] Thus the term may signify entreaty, appeal, exhortation, encouragement, comfort, consolation.

Here the reference is to the outward appeal in preaching aimed at inducing the hearers to put away their sins and accept the gospel offer of salvation. The exhortation appeals to them to adopt a recommended course of action intended to benefit the recipients. The term relates not to the content of the preaching but rather to its aim to win and transform. It points to the power of persuasion and is "directed more to the feelings than the understanding."[20] Stevens remarks that the term indicates "something of the directness, personal force, and spiritually 'living' quality" of Paul's preaching "by which in the power of the Holy Paraclete himself he gained men for Christ."[21]

Concerning this exhortation Paul strongly asserts that it is "not of error" (*ouk ek planēs*). The preposition *ek* means "out of, from," and points to origin or source, while the negative *ouk* is used in the denial of an objective fact. So, Paul is categorically rejecting as not true the claim that their preaching originated in and sprang from *error*. This word may be used with an active or passive meaning. In the active sense it means "the leading astray, deceit," while in the passive it is "the being led astray, error, delusion." In the New Testament it is usually used in the passive sense. The passive suits the context better, for it thus retains a meaning distinct from "guile" just below. Paul repudiates any contention that their preaching has its source in objective doctrinal error or delusion, that their message was "the product of illusion or deception."[22] It was one of Paul's fundamental convictions that in preaching the gospel he was not the victim of a vast deception. He was unshakably convinced that his gospel was indeed the truth. Doubt on this point "would have taken the heart out of the Apostle, and made him incapable of braving anything for its sake."[23]

"Nor of uncleanness" passes to the denial of an evil subjective source for their exhortation. It rejects any claim that a false personal motive lay at the foundation of their preaching. But what is the nature of the *uncleanness* (*akatharsia*) which he denies? Is it fleshly impurity or uncleanness of spirit? Both views have their strong advocates.

Lightfoot and others hold that the reference is to sensuality, moral impurity.[24] The term, except for Matthew 23:27 where it is used of the corruption of a sepulchre, appears only in the epistles of Paul.§ Frame points out that it "regularly appears directly with *porneia* [fornication] or in contexts intimating sexual aberration."[25] In support of this interpretation it is further pointed out that ritualistic prostitution was common in many heathen temples of the ancient world. The concept would be familiar to Paul as well as his readers. "Corinth, from which the letter was probably written was notorious for sexual degeneracy; and at Thessalonica, the home of his readers, there was notably present the worship of the Dionysiacs and the Cabiri. The character of both of these is indicated by their phallic emblems."[26] The enemies of Paul, judging the spiritual excitement in the Christian assembly in the light of the known corrupt emotional practices in pagan religions, may well have subtly insinuated that the missionaries fostered such practices. Morris points out that the charge of immorality was later openly made against the Christians and that the Apologists continually had to refute such slanders.[27] Lightfoot remarks that Paul's "disclaimer, startling as it may seem, was not unneeded amidst the impurities consecrated by the religions of the day."[28]

Others insist that the uncleanness which Paul denied refers rather to impurity of spirit or sentiment. Findlay points out that "in classical Greek it denotes moral *foulness, dirty ways*, of any sort." He is also impressed with the fact that "there is no hint anywhere else in the Epistles that St.

§ Ro 1:24; 6:19; 2 Co 12:21; Gal 5:19; Eph 4:19; 5:3; Col 3:5; 1 Th 2:3; 4:7.

Paul was taxed with *fleshly* impurity."[29] Lenski insists that "sexual uncleanness does not lie in the present context," and Hendriksen agrees.[30]
They think the reference is rather to the impure desire to secure money
from their preaching (v. 5) or to gain honor from men (v. 6). Moffatt
accepts this view and points out that "both features were only too familiar
in the contemporary conduct of wandering sophists."[31]

It is difficult to decide which meaning Paul originally intended to convey. The context here seems to point to the latter meaning, while his
general usage of the term and the well-known corrupt moral practices of
that day support the former view. It is probably the intended meaning.
It may be noted that this association of immorality and doctrinal error
later became a sad fact among heretical teachers and drew sharp apostolic
condemnation (2 Pe 2:18; Jude 4; Rev 2:20).

The two denials concerning the source of their exhortation were followed by a denial of mode or method, "nor in guile." Paul denies that
their preaching was "conceived and cradled, living and moving, in a
congenial atmosphere of guile."[32] It did not clothe itself in deceit in order
to capture the audience. The word rendered *guile* (*dolō*) bears a connotation of trickery. The word properly signifies the catching of a fish
with bait, and so it came to mean any crafty method for deceiving or
catching the unwary. Paul denies that they had resorted to such manipu-
lated methods to ensnare converts. They were open and straightforward
in their preaching.

(2) *Work under God's approval* (v. 4). A strong adversative *but*
introduces the contrasting truth concerning their work. Although the
statement is not formulated as the direct antithesis to the three denials
just registered, the statement yet effectively counters all three charges.
The gospel which they preached was of God, hence they were not following a delusive error; they had been divinely commissioned to preach
this gospel, hence they could not be unclean in character or motive; their
aim was not to please men but God who tests their hearts, hence their
appeal was not meant to deceive.

The essential fact concerning their ministry is that "even as we have
been approved of God to be intrusted with the gospel, so we speak."
"Even as . . . so" emphasizes that there was an exact correspondence
between their commission and their performance. Their obligation motivated and directed their work.

They worked as men who "have been approved of God." The verb
rendered "have been approved" (*dedokimasmetha*) has the root meaning
of "putting to the test," like coins being tested for genuineness or for full
weight. But the verb further implies that the test is made with the
anticipation that it will be satisfactorily completed. Therefore the mean-

ing naturally glides into the thought of "approval," since that which
passes the test is accepted or approved. That which fails to pass the test
is disapproved, rejected (*adokimos*). Milligan notes that the term may
have a technical use "to describe the passing as fit for election to a public
office."[33] Just as Athenians were tested for their fitness before they were
allowed to assume public office, so the missionaries were tested before
they were commissioned as God's messengers. The perfect tense indicates
the abiding and restful result of the test which was applied "of God"
(*hupo tou theou*) under His personal agency. Trench points out that
this verb is never used of Satan, "seeing that he never proves that he may
approve, nor tests that he may accept."[34] The devil's activity is that of
tempting (*periazō*), putting to the test with the intention that the tested
will fail.

None of the missionary writers was a novice. They had all been tested
and approved in the actual work of the gospel locally before they were
called into the wider sphere of foreign missionary service. Each had been
a believer of some years standing and had gained the approval of the
church where he labored. Further, "each had been chosen as a colleague
by a worker of experience and standing superior to his own."[35] God still
demands that those whom He commissions for His service first prove
themselves before being assigned to a responsible sphere of evangelistic
activity.

"To be intrusted with the gospel" indicates the definite result of having
successfully passed the divine testing. The passive voice of the infinitive
(*pisteuthēnai*) indicates that their assignment was a trust committed to
them by God. Their ministry was not a self-chosen work. Thus to be
divinely entrusted with the precious message of the gospel is the highest
conceivable responsibility. The very form of the statement stresses the
subservient position of the missionaries and the transcendent value of the
gospel committed to them. Paul elsewhere speaks of the gospel as a
"stewardship" which had been entrusted to him (1 Co 9:17).

"So we speak" records the obedient response of the missionaries to
their commission. *So* indicates that they preach under the consciousness
that they are men who have been tested and commissioned. It is a simple yet confident claim that they are loyal to their assignment. The
present tense indicates that it is their normal practice to share the good
news with others.

The added description of their work, "not as pleasing men, but God,"
sets forth the true motive of these God-tested workers. It points out their
ruling aim and endeavor. They reject any thought of shaping their message in order to be "pleasing men," to gain the favorable reaction of the
people to whom they preach. The alternative involved is pleasing men

or pleasing God. When confronted with such a choice, their purpose is always to gain God's approval. For them to do otherwise would disqualify them as God's messengers (Gal 1:10). Paul resolutely refused to compromise his message to gain human favor, yet he was anxious to conduct himself to please men if he could (1 Co 9:20-22; Ro 15:2). Even this effort to please men was not selfish but was aimed at their welfare (1 Co 10:33).

Moulton and Milligan suggest that the verb translated "pleasing" (*areskō*) carries the underlying idea of service to those who are to be pleased. They point out that it is used "in monumental inscriptions to describe those who have proved themselves of use to the commonwealth."[36] Certainly Paul rendered his hearers an inestimable service in bringing them the message of eternal life, but this service was given in the spirit of "ourselves as your servants for Jesus' sake" (2 Co 4:5).

The missionaries are constantly aware that as God's messengers it is He "who proveth our hearts." The appositional participle construction (*theō tō dokimazonti*) describes God as continuing to test His commissioned workers. He is ever testing "our hearts." This testing of hearts is a divine attribute which psalmists, prophets, and apostles alike have acknowledged (Ps 17:3; Jer 11:20; Ac 1:24). Men are ever under the divine scrutiny, but here the reference is not to men generally but specifically the writers. This is shown by the insertion of the possessive *our* which would otherwise have been omitted, making "the hearts" quite general. Although God has approved them as His messengers, in carrying out their commission they stand under His continual testing. The consciousness of this fact makes any kind of impurity or deception impossible for them. It is the highest reason why they cannot be preaching from unworthy motives.

Paul stresses that God is testing their *hearts* (*kardias*), the very depths of their inner life. In the New Testament "the heart is the centre of the inner life of man and the source or seat of all the forces and functions of soul and spirit."[37] It is the seat not only of the feelings and emotions, but also of the understanding and the will. It lies at the very root of man's moral nature, determining moral conduct. In His testings God deals with His servants as moral, responsible beings.

c) CONDUCT OF THE MESSENGERS (vv. 5-12). Having set forth the habitual character of their ministry in verses 3-4, Paul now turns back to the work at Thessalonica for confirmation. His confirmatory *for* indicates that what was asserted of their ministry, generally was true also of their work at Thessalonica. Paul first describes the missionaries' conduct while among them as they knew it (vv. 5-8), and then appeals to the readers' vivid memories of their activities as further confirmation (vv. 9-12).

(1) *Description of their conduct* (vv. 5-8). The description of the missionaries' conduct at Thessalonica is again stated as an apologetic, intended to refute slanderous insinuations against them. The description is formulated in Paul's characteristic negative-positive manner. He first makes a triple denial concerning their conduct (vv. 5-6) and then gives a positive description (vv. 7-8).

(*a*) *What their conduct was not like* (vv. 5-6). The three denials are obviously repudiations of specific accusations. The charges seem somewhat closely related.

Paul first denies the charge of flattery. "For neither at any time were we found using words of flattery." Neither "at one time or another" (*pote*) did they resort to the use of flattering words. "Were we found using" is not the best rendering of the original (*egenēthēmen*). It must not be mistaken to mean "were not found out." There is no suggestion of successful concealment, but rather that flattery was never used. Preferable would be "used we," "resorted to," or "stooped to."|| The verb in the original means that as a definite fact they never entered into a state or condition where flattering words were employed.

Flattery does not simply mean complimentary words intended pleasurably to tickle the ears of the hearers. It is rather the smooth-tongued discourse of the orator aimed at making a favorable impression in order to gain influence over others for selfish advantage. Frame thinks that in the light of the reference to *guile* in verse 3 the meaning may be " 'cajolery,' a word that carries with it the additional notion of deception."[38]

Paul denies that they have used the preaching of the gospel as a foil for securing selfish advantage. That such a charge could easily be given a ring of plausibility is clear from the known conduct of the heathen rhetoricians of the day. Nor was the early church exempt from this evil. Barclay reminds us that the early Christian churches were plagued with "people who did attempt to cash in on their Christianity."[36] That ancient work, the *Didache*, written during the early part of the second century, gives some shrewd advice on how to get rid of pseudoprophets who attempted to gain a livelihood through their pretensions to be God's spokesmen.

"As ye know" is Paul's third appeal in this passage to the readers' knowledge of the truthfulness of his words (vv. 1, 2, 5). The force of the original (*kathōs oidate*), "even as ye know" (Rotherham), points out that the disclaimer is in exact agreement with their recollection of the missionaries' discourse.

The second denial, "nor a cloak of covetousness," rejects the charge

|| KJV; Montgomery, Moffatt, and Williams; Way renders, "Never did I stoop to flattery."

that their work was motivated by disguised greed. The word *prophasei,* translated "cloak," denotes something put forward for appearance to conceal what lies behind it. It is a pretext used to conceal the reality "of covetousness" (*pleonexias*), which quite literally means "a desire to have more," but of that to which one does not have a just right. The genitive "of covetousness" may be construed as an objective genitive, "a pretext *for* greed" (to cover up greed), or as subjective, "a pretext *of* greed" (used by greed as a cover-up). The resultant significance is essentially the same. Paul denies that the missionaries have ever used their preaching as a secret means of enriching themselves. Many of the Greek rhetoricians and peripatetic philosophers used their skills to mulct their followers, while the wandering Jewish magicians, such as Elymas whom Paul encountered at Paphos (Ac 13:6-11), were even more rapacious.

That men use a cloak or cover-up to conceal covetousness reveals that they instinctively feel that it is an unworthy motive, yet one to which they frequently yield. Whenever covetousness is working it is always concealed under some ideal end.

Paul assures the Thessalonian believers that "no secret avarice was hidden behind our zeal for your salvation."[40] The greed expressed by *pleonexia* is larger than covetousness. While it generally expresses itself in the desire for money, it includes that insatiableness which greedily grasps at anything desired for self-satisfaction. Beyond a desire for money, Paul's disclaimer rejects the thought of being motivated by a spirit of self-aggrandizement while pretending to be concerned for the spiritual interests of their followers.

Paul claims divine confirmation for this denial, "God is witness." This appeal shows how important Paul regarded it to be cleared of this charge of gain-seeking in his ministry. Since the Thessalonians could only judge the character of the missionaries' conduct but could not know the true motives behind it, Paul takes his appeal directly to God who fully knows the hidden matters of the heart. Paul resorts to this appeal only in cases where human testimony is inadequate.

The third denial concerns another form of self-seeking. "Nor seeking glory of men, neither from you nor from others." The negative (*oute*) with the present participle (*zētountes*) denies any practice or habit of seeking "glory of men" (*ex anthrōpōn doxan*).[41] "Of men," standing emphatically forward, denies that they are seeking human glory. There is a glory which believers rightly seek (Ro 2:7) but it is not a glory that originates with men. Further, Paul does not deny that he ever receives glory from men, or that he has no right to it, but he writes that he has sought it "neither from you" (*oute aph' humōn*), his Thessalonian converts, "nor from others," believers from a distance who have received reports of his work.

The missionaries have not used their preaching to gain for themselves human glory—the honor, recognition, and approval which men bestow. It is the repudiation of personal ambition, "that last infirmity of noble minds."[42] There is the constant possibility that the preacher may use his preaching ministry as a means of building up public esteem for himself rather than conveying God's message to men.

Hogg and Vine think that *glory*, or honor, is probably used here to denote "material gifts, honorarium, stipend."[43] In support of this view it might be argued that the glory of a man was measured by the amount of remuneration he received. But this meaning for *glory* (*doxa*) is improbable. That *doxa* ever means a monetary remuneration is questionable. Frame asserts, "There is no evidence that it is equivalent to *honor* in the later sense of honorarium."[44]

Paul at once safeguards the dignity of the missionaries by adding "when we might have claimed authority as apostles of Christ." The participial clause (*dunamenoi en barei einai*), subordinate to *seeking* (*zētountes*), is best regarded as concessive, "although we might have." This concessive clause qualifies the fact just asserted, although they have not sought honor from men, Paul yet makes it clear that he feels that they did have a right to do what follows.

The expression rendered "claimed authority" (*en barei einai*) is quite literally "to be in weight," which Findlay aptly calls "an ambiguous phrase."[45] The neuter noun (*to baros*) may be taken in its simple meaning of "weight, burden" and interpreted as a reference to the missionaries' right to financial support from their work. Or it may be understood in a derived sense of their importance, hence "authority, dignity," pointing to their assumption of authority and the demand for respect because of their office.

The former view derives support from Paul's remark in verse 9 that they had not been a financial *burden* to the Thessalonians. Also in its favor is the fact that Paul uses kindred expressions elsewhere in connection with the thought of financial support (2 Co 11:9; 12:16; 2 Th 3:8; 1 Ti 5:16). The Twentieth Century New Testament boldly adopts this view in rendering "we might have burdened you with our support." Under this view Paul is seeking to safeguard the right and lawful claim of the Christian worker to support from his work (1 Co 9:6-18), although he himself did not use this right.

In favor of the latter view is the close connection of the expression with "seeking glory of men" just before. It best expresses the evident antithesis of the sentence. There is no reference in the immediate context to financial support; it rather deals with the thought of receiving personal *glory*, outward honor and distinction. It also agrees better with the thought in the following verse. Moffatt accepts this view in his rendering, "we had the power of claiming to be men of weight." But being "men of weight" may mean men who claim to be recognized as weighty or important. Thus Williams has it, "we could have stood on our official dignity." Or the meaning may be men who assert their weight of power and influence. The New American Standard Bible reflects this thought, "we might have asserted our authority."

But it may well be that Paul's indefinite phrase, occurring only here in the New Testament, was intended to combine the thoughts of support and esteem. Findlay thinks the two views are quite "compatible; for official importance was measured *by stipend*, by the demand made for personal support (cf. 2 Cor. xi. 7)."[46] He holds that it is quite in Paul's style thus to play on the double meaning of the phrase. Moffatt likewise thinks that both ideas may be intended, the phrase thus catching up the thought of "a cloak of covetousness" and "seeking glory of men," namely, "self-interest in its mercenary shape and as the love of reputation."[47]

"As apostles of Christ" they could justly have claimed to be men of weight. The genitive "of Christ," placed emphatically forward, stresses that it is in virtue of their relationship to Him as His apostles that they can claim this dignity and authority. As the apostles of the Messiah, the Anointed King, they might have stepped forth with dignity and claimed esteem and support.

Apostles here includes Paul's colleagues, Silas and Timothy. It is used in the broader sense of a messenger or envoy (cf. 2 Co 8:23; Phil 2:25). The term denotes one who is commissioned and sent forth as the representative of another. It has the force of our word "missionary," which is the corresponding term from the Latin. Lattey renders the phrase "as missionaries of Christ."

It is unnecessary to interpret *apostles* in its restricted sense and limit it to Paul alone. This is contrary to his use of the plural as well as the inclusion of his colleagues in the context as seen from "our hearts" (v. 4) and "our souls" (v. 8).#

(*b*) *What their conduct was like* (vv. 7-8). *But* again introduces the positive side of the missionaries' conduct in contrast to the preceding negative characterization. Paul pictures the nature of their conduct (v. 7) and then indicates its affectionate expression (v. 8).

i) *Nature of the conduct* (v. 7). "We were gentle in the midst of you" succinctly depicts the nature of their conduct at Thessalonica. The words at once confront us with what Morris well calls "a first-class textual problem."[48]

#Conybeare, Way, and Montgomery again change the plural to a singular.

Instead of "gentle" (*ēpioi*) many manuscripts read "babes" (*nēpioi*). Since the preceding word (*egenēthēmen*) ends with the letter *n*, it is easy to see how these two readings, differing only by the absence or presence of an initial *n*, may have arisen. If *ēpioi* was the original reading, *nēpioi* may be accounted for as due to some scribe's accidental repetition of the *n* of the preceding word; if *nēpioi* was the original, the second *n* may have been omitted by an oversight. That either reading was produced by a deliberate change on the part of a scribe is possible but less probable.

In favor of the reading "babes" (*nēpioi*) is the fact that it is supported by the weight and diversity of the manuscript evidence, as well as a wide variety of versions and church Fathers. This reading has won the support of many scholars. In their Greek text Westcott and Hort use it without even indicating the alternative reading in the margin. Lattey quite literally renders, "but we became babes in the midst of you," while Williams has, "Instead we were little children among you." Way paraphrases, "Ah no! but I was unassuming—like one of yourselves."

Several considerations are urged in support of this striking reading. It is held that after the noun *apostles*, just before, the noun "babes" is more likely than an adjective; also that "babes" fits in better with "in the midst of you" immediately after. It is pointed out that the word for "babes" occurs fourteen times elsewhere in the New Testament, ten times in Paul's writings, while *gentle* occurs only once; thus *nēpioi* is held to be the more characteristic of Paul. Lightfoot contends that the sudden switching in metaphors from "babes" to a *nurse* "is quite in Paul's manner," since as usual he does not hesitate to mix his metaphors "that his image should cut clean."[49] It is held that this reading fits in with the preceding verse where Paul defends himself not against the charge of harshness but of self-seeking. Westcott and Hort defend their reading "babes" with the remark that "the change from the bold image to the tame and facile adjective is characteristic of the difference between St. Paul and the Syrian revisers."[50]

If "babes" is accepted as the original reading, the term must be understood as setting forth the absence of an authoritarian attitude, that the missionaries descended to the level of their spiritually immature children, becoming children among children. Thus Augustine spoke of it as "baby-language to those who were still babes in the faith."[51] Bicknell supports the reading with the remark, "The idea is the condescension of the true Christian pastor who is willing to put himself on the level of others, which is the essence of sympathy."[52]

But significant arguments are advanced in favor of the reading *gentle*. In the immediate context *gentle* is certainly the more appropriate antithesis to Paul's disclaimer concerning his apostolic authority and dignity

(v. 6*b*). This reading also forms the proper contrast to the slanders which Paul repudiates in verses 5-6. For Paul to speak of the writers in the same sentence as "babes" and a nursing-mother is confusion; "babes" is incongruous with *nurse,* for it exactly reverses the figure. Admittedly Paul is capable of changing his figures rapidly but he avoids inconsistency. While the juxtaposition of "babes" and a nursing-mother forms a jarring description of the writers, the term *gentle* is in full harmony with the maternal relationship which follows. In 2 Timothy 2:24 gentleness is posited as a mark of the true pastor.

The term "babes" does not really express the thought of condescension claimed for it here; Paul's use of the term elsewhere rather carries the uncomplimentary connotation of spiritual immaturity (Ro 2:20; 1 Co 3:1; Gal 4:1, 3; Eph 4:14). Certainly the writers are not here pointing out their own immaturity while with the Thessalonians. It should be noted that Paul never applies the term "babe" to himself, but rather to his converts who have not yet matured.

The term "babes" is certainly more common in Paul's writings than the adjective *gentle,* yet that fact does not prove that he wrote "babes" here. It may rather be argued that the known habit of scribes to change an unfamiliar word into a familiar word points rather to the unfamiliar adjective as the original reading here. In 2 Timothy 2:24 the correct reading is certainly *ēpioi* (gentle), yet Metzger points out that "more than one scribe succumbed to the temptation to substitute the more familiar word, *nēpioi,* for the true text *ēpioi.*"[53]

It is true that the preponderance of the manuscript evidence is for *nēpioi,* which, once introduced into the text, would be favored by subsequent scribes since it can be interpreted to make good sense. Adeney thinks that this is an instance "of how the best MSS. may sometimes be demonstrably wrong." Metzger, who makes a tentative decision in favor of *ēpioi,* sanctions the dictum of Daniel Mace that "no manuscript is so old as common sense."[54]

With the notable exception of Westcott and Hort, *ēpioi* (gentle) is favored by modern editors of the Greek text.** It is also the reading accepted by the majority of commentators and modern English versions. Admittedly the reading remains doubtful, but we accept this as more probably the original.

While at Thessalonica the missionaries had shown themselves gentle in dealing with their converts. They were mild and kind in their dealings, avoiding any harsh and high-handed assumption of authority. "All was

---

**Alexander Souter, *Novum Testamentum Graece*; Erwin Nestle and Kurt Aland, *Novum Testamentum Graece*; Kurt Aland, Matthew Black, Bruce M. Metzger, Allen Wikgren, *The Greek New Testament.*

tenderness and devotion, fostering and protecting care in their relations to these Thessalonian Christians who had won their hearts."[55] Riggenbach remarks that the added words "in the midst of you" point to the missionaries as "the centre of a group or society, drawing all eyes to itself."[56] The missionaries had held the position of a gentle teacher surrounded by his eager students. Far from ascending a lofty pinnacle and speaking down to their followers, the missionaries freely mingled with them.

The assertion concerning their gentle behavior is immediately followed by a figurative statement, "as when a nurse cherisheth her own children." This is indeed "a sudden change of metaphor"[57] if the original reading was "babes," but it forms a beautiful and appropriate amplification if the reading was "gentle." When the Thessalonians accepted the gospel they were indeed like children who were in need of the tender, loving care which the missionaries provided.

The *nurse* is the "nourisher" of the children; she is here apparently the mother herself, as the words "her own children" suggest. The term for *cherisheth* (*thalpē*) properly means "to warm;" it was used of birds covering their young with their feathers to warm and protect them (Deu 22:6 LXX). It thus suggests the mother's protecting care and tender love for her children. This lovely picture is a demonstration of the unselfish conduct of the missionaries in dealing with their converts. The nursing-mother cares for and protects her offspring, without seeking profit or honor for herself, but is intent upon bestowing; so the missionaries cared for their beloved converts with no thought of selfish gain.

Some interpreters suggest a different punctuation for verse 7. They propose to put a colon or period after the words "in the midst of you." Then the remainder of verse 7 may be closely connected with verse 8. So, to separate the verse into two parts is advantageous if "babes" is accepted as the true reading; it softens the sharp contrast between the two nouns. But if the adjective *gentle* is read it rather mars the force of the graphic supplement.

(ii) *Expression of the conduct* (v. 8). "Even so" (*houtōs*), "thus, in this manner," resumes the thought of the missionaries' conduct expressed in verse 7 but reemphasizes it by dropping the figure and stating the literal manner in which their conduct found expression. "Being affectionately desirous of you" indicates the strong attachment to the Thessalonians which prompted their self-giving.

The participle translated "being affectionately desirous" (*homeiromenoi*) is from an extremely rare verb of obscure origin. Wohlenberg conjectured that it was "a term of endearment derived from the language of the nursery."[58] Whatever its origin, it denotes the warm affection and tender yearning that the missionaries felt for their spiritual babes at

Thessalonica. The present tense marks the constant nature of the learning and affection they experienced.

Their affection expressed itself in giving to the Thessalonians. "We were well pleased to impart unto you, not the gospel of God only, but also our own souls." "Were well pleased" (*ēudokoumen*) indicates that this imparting was actually done as a free and deliberate choice. The imperfect tense testified that with continued hearty good will they acted "to impart" (*metadounai*) to them what they had to share. The preposition *meta* prefixed to the infinitive brings out the thought that the missionaries did not merely give a gift but rather imparted something which they desired to share with the Thessalonians. The aorist tense of the infinitive summarizes their work at Thessalonica as having this character.

Far from coming to get something from the people, the missionaries came to share with them the best possession they had, "the gospel of God." This good news, which has its origin and source in God, was indeed a priceless treasure which would enrich the Thessalonians for time and eternity. Paul, Silvanus, and Timothy's willingness to share this treasure was indeed an expression of genuine love. The sharing of the saving Gospel with others was the reason for their call and function as Christ's apostles.

But this sharing by the missionaries went beyond official duty. They freely imparted not only the gospel "but also our own souls." They gave not only their message but themselves. This giving of their own souls marks the climax of their giving. *Souls* (*psuchas*) denotes their inner being, their entire personality. Along with their preaching went an unstinting outpouring of their innermost self. "When soul goes out to soul, the Gospel so offered will be the more readily accepted."[59] It sets the true standard of pastoral service and is the key to a vital ministry. Such a ministry is costly but it is the antidote to the blight of professionalism.

Love was the inducement for this costly ministry, "because ye were become very dear to us." Their proclamation of the glad tidings of God's salvation was impelled by the energy of a passionate love. On having accepted the gospel, the Thessalonian believers won the tender love of the missionaries. "Ye were" (*egenēthēte*) is more literally "ye became" and points to the definite fact that a deep, affectionate relationship developed between the missionaries and their converts. "Very dear" renders the verbal adjective *agapētoi*; derived from the verb *agapaō*, it signifies that the Thessalonians were the objects of a high, persistent love which desired only their true welfare (cf. 1:3). As they now write, the missionaries have a vivid recollection of that love relationship which bound them together. The verse closes, as it began, with a reference to that love which the missionaries had experienced toward their readers.

(2) *Memories of their conduct* (vv. 9-12). The description of the conduct of the missionaries in verses 5-8 is now further amplified in an appeal to the memories of the Thessalonians concerning that conduct. In verse 9 the Thessalonians are asked to recall the facts concerning the labors of the missionaries while with them; in verses 10-12 appeal is made to the testimony of the readers concerning the missionaries' conduct and work with their converts.

The opening *for* of verse 9 confirms what has been said, but views differ as to precisely what is being confirmed. Some would relate it to what immediately precedes. Lünemann takes it with the last part of verse 8 as proof that the Thessalonians were very dear to the preachers. Ellicott regards the *for* as relating back to the assertion that the writers willingly imparted their very souls to their converts, while Lenski goes back to verse 7 and sees an amplification of what a nurse does for her children. It is perhaps better to regard the conjunction as introducing a general confirmation of the conduct just described in verses 5-8. Frame thinks that *for* resumes the *but* of verse 7 and further illustrates the denial of seeking glory from men made in verse 6.[60] The renewed picture of the workers' conduct in these verses is thus added to establish what has already been stated.

(a) *Memory of the work among them* (v. 9). "For ye remember, brethren" indicates that the writers are still solicitous to ground their assertions concerning their conduct in the consciences of the readers. This further unfolding of the nature of that conduct finds assured confirmation in the vivid recollections of the readers. The renewed address as *brethren* reminds their converts that the appeal to them is being made because they share common spiritual interests.

In 1:3 the readers were assured that the writers had continual remembrance of the Christian virtues of their converts; now reference is made to the readers' continual remembrance of the labors of the missionaries while at Thessalonica. "Our labor and travail" (*ton kopon hēmōn kai ton mochthon*) is an emphatic phrase employed only by Paul in the New Testament (2 Co 11:27; 2 Th 3:8). The repeated article gives emphasis to the nouns and enhances the climax in the second term. The first (*kopon*) indicates the weariness and fatigue arising from continued strenuous activity; the second (*mochthon*) points to the outward difficulties that must be overcome. The first relates to the active exertion required, the second to the exhausting effect. Ellicott remarks that "the former perhaps marks the toil on the side of the *suffering* it involves, the latter, on the side of the *magnitude* of the obstacles it has to overcome."[61]

The two Greek terms have a rhyming sound which Lightfoot seeks to reproduce with the suggested rendering "toil and moil."[62] The rendering

of Lattey is quite satisfactory, "our toil and trouble." Paul's expression
aptly stressed the reality and exhausting character of the work of the
missionaries. It certainly was no pleasant, self-chosen activity adopted
as an easy means of gaining a livelihood. In their own memories of the
toil of the missionaries the readers had proof of the self-sacrificing spirit
of the preachers.

The central purpose of the missionaries was to preach the gospel; but in
order to accomplish this, they found it necessary to be "working night and
day" (*nuktos kai hēmeras ergazomenoi*). The participial phrase depicts
the circumstances under which the preaching of the gospel was carried
out. The genitive "night and day," standing emphatically forward, stresses
that they worked long hours both during the night as well as the day.
Lünemann calls the expression "a concrete and proverbial circumlocution
of the abstract *adialeiptōs* [unceasingly]."[63] The present tense of the
participle points to the work as their continuing practice. Clearly the
labors they engaged in were not sporadic or occasional, but regular. Just
what hours Paul and his coworkers devoted to their preaching is not clear.
Ramsay concluded from Paul's expression that they began their work long
before dawn in order to be able to give part of the day to preaching.[64]

Paul always uses the order "night and day," both in his letters (1 Th
3:10; 2 Th 3:8; 1 Ti 5:5; 2 Ti 1:3) and his speeches (Ac 20:31; 26:7).
But the order is not due to the fact that the Jews, as well as the Athenians,
began the civil day with the evening. In the Septuagint the usual order
is "day and night" (eg. Jos 1:8; Ps 1:2). One order is as natural as the
other, and Jewish writers used both.

The word rendered "working" (*ergazomenoi*) denotes working for wages,
especially manual labor or working at a trade. From Acts 18:3 we learn
that by trade Paul was a tentmaker (*skēnopoios*). The precise nature of
Paul's handicraft is somewhat uncertain; did he weave the material out
of which tents were made, or did he cut and sew the actual tents? Proponents of the former view point out that the weaving of tent material,
called *cilicium*, made from the hair of a species of very shaggy goats, was
a flourishing occupation in Paul's native Tarsus. This material was in
great demand all over the East. Others point out that the word etymo-
logically means "tent-maker, tent-tailor" and see no need to depart from
the original import of the term. Since Paul found ready opportunity in
various cities to employ his skill, the latter seems the more probable.

During the first century the term was often given a wider connotation
to include the idea of a leather-worker, and tents were often made of
leather; therefore some modern scholars, like Bruce, follow the view of
Origen and Chrysostom that Paul was a worker in leather.[65] But since
Paul's father was a strict Pharisee (Ac 23:6) and contact with the skins

of dead animals was regarded as defiling, it seems improbable that he would have permitted his son to learn a defiling trade. However, when as a Christian Paul was freed from all such ceremonial scruples, he may at times have worked with leather in the manufacture of tents.

The Jews wisely insisted that every boy should be taught a manual trade. They had learned that every Jewish lad needed a means whereby he could earn his own living wherever the vicissitudes of life might place him. The Talmud required that every Jewish father must circumcise his son, instruct him in the Law, and teach him a trade. It was a saying of the rabbis that "he who teacheth not his son a trade doth the same as if he taught him to be a thief."

Doubtless, Saul's keen mind early marked him for rabbinical training, but he was taught a trade nevertheless. Nor does this imply any inferiority of social standing for his family. Since the Jews did not have salaried teachers, it was necessary for a rabbi to have some reliable source of income, apart from the occasional contributions he might receive from recipients of his instruction. As a Roman citizen (Ac 22:28) Paul's father apparently was a man of some means, for he was able to finance his son's schooling under Gamaliel, the famous rabbi at Jerusalem. The father may have been a textile merchant and Saul may have been apprenticed to his father's own business.

The trade Paul had learned as a youth proved to be of inestimable value to him during his missionary career. Having no mission board which provided for his material needs, Paul could support himself whenever he had to. But the work of tent-making was not highly remunerative employment and long hours were necessary to make ends meet. Even while he was working at Thessalonica his income from his work was supplemented by contributions from Philippi (Phil 4:15). Paul is also known to have worked at his trade at Corinth (Ac 18:3) and at Ephesus (Ac 20:34). No doubt Silas and Timothy also had trades of their own, but we have no information concerning them.

The expressed purpose of the missionaries in thus working at Thessalonica was "that we might not burden any of you." This costly personal concern of the missionaries not to be a financial burden on their converts proved that there was no greed behind their preaching. If they had been typical peripatetic philosophers the Thessalonian believers would not have been spared. It was a standard practice of the philosophers to demand pay for their instruction. Their action proved that the missionaries were motivated by an unselfish consideration for their flock.

It is often assumed that this refusal to ask money of them proved that the Thessalonians were poor. Most likely, the majority of the Thessalonian believers were common day laborers compelled to remain at their tasks to eke out a living (4:11). But apparently some of them, like Jason, may well have been able to give the missionaries financial assistance. Paul refused to take any support from the Corinthians although they were able to provide financially (1 Co 9:11-12). This practice of earning his own living enabled Paul to maintain a position of complete independence in dealing with his converts.

Paul was sensitive on this matter of remaining financially independent. It allowed him not only to maintain a dignified independence as a preacher of the gospel but also to refute any suspicion of mercenary motives for preaching. He had no trouble silencing the misrepresentations of his enemies and to "cut off occasion" to those who desired to turn the apostolic office into a money-getting profession (2 Co 11:7-12). It further enabled him to set a worthy example for his converts (2 Th 3:7-9) and thus to prove his unselfish love for them (2 Co 12:13-18). In earning his own livelihood Paul was also able to experience the personal joy of sharing his meager means with those in need (Ac 20:34-35).

Although the missionaries put in long hours at their work, the central fact regarding their stay at Thessalonica was that "we preached unto you the gospel of God." The verb rendered *preached* (*ekēruxamen*) means to proclaim a message as a herald, to proclaim loudly and publicly as an authorized messenger. It pictures the preachers as heralds of God, with formality, gravity, and authority proclaiming the message which has been entrusted to them. It marks the dignity of their function. A faithful herald accurately repeats the message which he has been given to proclaim; so the missionaries also had a message to proclaim without alteration or substitution, "the gospel of God." The designation stresses the divine origin and authority of their message and points to the greatness of the boon which they imparted to the Thessalonians. It was because the messengers were deeply convinced that their message was indeed God's gospel that they were willing to proclaim it freely while working for their own living. The aorist tense of the verb summarizes their preaching during their stay at Thessalonica.

"Unto you" marks the local recipients of the message which is here for the third time in this paragraph called "the gospel of God" (vv. 2, 8, 9). Hogg and Vine remark that at each occurrence of the expression the missionaries appear in a different capacity: "in v. 2 Paul refers to the work of the missionaries as evangelists among the as yet unconverted Thessalonians; in v. 8 he refers to their work as pastors, and in v. 9 as teachers, among their converts."[66] But the true herald, whether serving as evangelist, pastor, or teacher, always presents "the Glad-tidings of God" (Way).

(b) *Witness to the work among them* (vv. 10-12). Without any connecting particle Paul continues, "Ye are witnesses, and God also." In verse 5 Paul appealed to the human and the divine witnesses separately, but now he unites them in an appeal for confirmation of their whole ministry. This double appeal is stronger than his "ye remember" in verse 9. These verses conclude the review of their conduct. Verse 10 gives a summary statement of the ministry at Thessalonica as confirmed by the double witness, while in verses 11-12 we have a final picture of the workers' well-remembered relations to their converts.

i) *Character of their conduct* (v. 10). By the use of an emphatic *ye*, "Ye are witnesses," the writers make a direct appeal to the testimony concerning the missionaries' conduct which the Thessalonians apparently had personally expressed on occasion. Certainly the Thessalonians had witnessed the kind of life the missionaries had displayed among them and could personally testify to the manner in which they had conducted themselves. But since men cannot adequately judge the inward motives and dispositions, appeal is also made to the God who is constantly testing the hearts of His workers (2:4). Such an appeal shows that Paul could advance these claims concerning their conduct with a clear conscience. They worked under the consciousness that their ministry was subject both to human and divine observation.

"How holy and righteously and unblamably we behaved ourselves" forms a summary statement of what has previously been asserted in detail. Three adverbs are used to summarize the conduct. Adverbs rather than adjectives are employed because the emphasis is not on the character of the workers but on the manner of their conduct. *How* before the adverbs points to the degree of manner. There is no claim to perfection but rather to an eminent degree of attainment in the areas specified. The Thessalonian believers were able to judge this.

The first two adverbs, "holily and righteously," set forth the positive features of their conduct. *Holily* (*hosiōs*), which is not related to the ordinary word rendered "holy" (*hagios*) in the New Testament, means "devoutly, piously, religiously," and points to an inner disposition which gives regard to the sanctities of life. *Righteously* (*dikaiōs*) denotes the kind of conduct that comes up to the full standard of what is right or just and thus relates to the performance of the duties of life.

Lightfoot, following the usual classical distinction between the two terms, held that the former related to one's duties toward God, and the latter to one's duties toward men.[67] But this distinction is not rigidly maintained in the New Testament. In Luke 1:6 *dikaios*, "righteous before God," is used of life in relation to God. Nor can *hosios* as used in Acts 2:27 and Hebrews 7:26 be rigidly restricted to relations Godward. Any rigid distinction between duties Godward and manward on the basis of these terms is unwarranted, since Scripture "recognizes all righteousness as one, as growing out of a single root, and obedient to a single law."[68] It is best to take the two terms as describing all of Christian conduct whether toward God or men. The term *holily* relates to inward disposition, and points to the religious aspect of life; *righteously* covers the moral aspect, relating to that integrity and uprightness of conduct which must mark the Christian life.

Over against the two positive adverbs stands the negative *unblamably* (*amemptōs*), comprehending both. It claims an irreproachable conduct as a whole, indicating that no charges can be maintained, whatever charges might be made against them. It "affixes the seal of approval both by God and man."[69]

The lives of the messengers had demonstrated that they not only believed the gospel but also "behaved" it. They were deeply aware of the importance of living lives that commended the gospel if their preaching was to have abiding results. They had conducted themselves with the utmost fidelity in word and deed toward the readers, "you that believe" (*humin tois pisteuousin*). The appositional articular participle pictures them as characterized by their continuing faith. Faith is central in the Christian life, and a vital, saving faith is a continuing faith in Jesus Christ as Saviour. And it was that faith that enabled them to evaluate properly the conduct of the missionaries. Paul's appeal to their witness as confirmation of his claim proves the consciousness of his own integrity. "Paul and his evangelistic party were scrutinized, examined, and cross-examined, and their testimony held good."[70]

The verb rendered "we behaved ourselves" (*egenēthēmen*) has the basic meaning of "becoming" and implies that the conduct just depicted was not a matter of chance but the outcome of conscious obedience and effort. But the meaning is not that they first came to behave in this way while at Thessalonica. Rather, upon arrival there they came to be known as men whose conduct had these characteristics. Lightfoot suggests the rendering "we presented ourselves."[71] The aorist tense treats the entire time of their stay at Thessalonica as a unit.

(ii) *Work with their converts* (vv. 11-12). The general assertion concerning their conduct in verse 10 is now supported with specific evidence. This confirmatory statement of their work with their converts is presented as to its nature. v. 11a), its elements (v. 11b), and its aim (v. 12).

This evidence in confirmation of the virtuous life of the missionaries is in full harmony with the personal knowledge of the readers, "as ye know" (*kathaper oidate*). The strong comparative particle *kathaper* (composed of *katha*, "even as," and *per*, "thoroughly" and translated "even as, just as") indicates that the appended evidence can be taken in its fullest

extent. It is an appeal to their own experience concerning the efforts of
the missionaries to induce them to live virtuous lives. This concern of
the missionaries for the lives of their converts is evidence of their own
high aspirations. "For if any one can be truly desirous that *others* walk
virtuously, this presupposes the endeavor after virtue in himself."[72]

The sentence (vv. 11-12) is structurally defective because of the lack
of a finite verb. Different suggestions have been advanced to deal with
the irregularity: to regard the sentence as an example of the use of the
participle for an indicative; to insert some finite verb, as is done in the
American Standard Version, "dealt with;" or to resume the finite verb
egenēthēmen from verse 10 to form a paraphrastic construction with the
participles. This last seems simplest, making the sentence read quite
literally, "as ye know how each one of you, as a father with his own
children, (we were) exhorting you." In the rush of his dictation it would
be easy for Paul to forget to repeat the finite verb which he had just used.
The verb "dealt with," supplied in our version, is easily suggested from
"behaved ourselves" in verse 10, but it adds a concept which is not actually expressed in the original.

[a] *Its nature* (v. 11a). "Each one of you, as a father with his own
children" succinctly depicts the nature of their work with their converts.
It was both individual and fatherly. "Each one of you," standing emphatically forward, stresses the individual character of the work with their
converts. Way seeks to bring out the force of the double form (*hena
hekaston*) by saying "each of you, one by one." They exercised discrimi-
nation and care in dealing with each individual convert according to his
own needs. They used not only mass evangelism but also engaged in
personal work. Shepherd sees in the remark an indication "that the success of the apostles was not easily won, that converts were not made in
masses, but by the slow, toilsome affectionate application of the gospel
to individuals, one by one."[73] Neil thinks it implies that they engaged in
"house-to-house visitation."[74]

"As a father with his own children" indicates that the individual work
was devoted to the task of training and instruction. In verse 7 the picture
was that of a tender nursing-mother unselfishly pouring out her loving
care upon her babes; here the picture is that of the earnest father dealing
with his children in education and discipline. The former simile stresses
the tenderness of their dealings with their converts; the simile of the
father shows the sterner aspect of their love for their children. The
apostles dealt with them not with the severity of the taskmaster but the
earnest concern of the father intent upon training his children according
to their individual needs. The figure of a father was commonly used by
Jewish teachers to denote their relationship to their pupils. Converted

under their ministry, the Thessalonian believers were indeed their spiritual children who needed their instruction and guidance. The term *children* (*tekna*) expresses not only their endearment to the writers but also the immaturity of the converts. Hogg and Vine point out that in the Pauline epistles, figures based on the paternal relationship are found only in those letters where Paul had been instrumental in the conversion of the readers.[75]

They acted as a father not merely to the church as a whole but also to the individual members. Just as an earnest father keeps his children singly in view and trains each one according to his individual needs, so the missionaries dealt with the Thessalonian converts. Calvin remarks, "Instruction given to all is sometimes of little service, and some cannot be cured or corrected without particular medicine."[76]

[b] *Its elements* (v. 11b). Three elements are indicated in their fatherly work with their converts. In dealing with them as their children they were continually "exhorting you, and encouraging you, and testifying." The present tenses of the participles point to these activities as their continual practice. After emphasizing their work with them as individuals, Paul now adds the plural pronoun *you* to combine all of their converts as the objects of this fatherly oversight. Although dealing with them individually, they remembered that they constituted a distinct group.

The three participles unfold the nature of their pastoral dealings. The first, *exhorting* (*parakalountes*), is general and indicates the strong appeal made to their converts to adopt a suitable course of action (see explanation under 2:3). Findlay calls the verb "the general term for animating address."[77]

The following two participles are specific. *Encouraging* (*paramuthomenoi*) denotes the soothing and encouraging side of exhortation, inspiring them to continue the desired course of action; while *testifying* (*marturomenoi*) points to the solemnity and earnestness with which the appeal is made. The latter participle comes from a verb which basically means "to invoke witnesses," hence "to declare solemnly, to insist."

All three of these participles are in the plural, indicating that his colleagues joined Paul in this work. Their appeals carried three elements according to the need, "beseeching, or urging, the hesitant, encouraging the faint-hearted, and charging, or adjuring, the wavering."[78]

[c] *Its aim* (v. 12). All their efforts with their converts were directed toward one specific aim, "to the end that ye should walk worthily of God." This was their supreme desire for them. No worthier goal is conceivable.

There is disagreement as to whether the statement in the original was intended to express the aim or the substance of the exhortation. The preposition with the articular infinitive (*eis to peripatein*) may denote either. Moulton holds that the expression here indicates the contents of the entreaty and adds, "Purpose is so remote here as to be practically evanescent."[79] That Paul's expression does embody the substance of their exhortation is granted, but it is difficult to see how the thought of aim can be excluded. It seems best to conclude that the two thoughts here shade into each other. The missionaries did assert that the Thessalonian believers should walk worthily of God, but their aim in thus exhorting them was to teach them actually how to live.

Walk (*peripatein*) is a common New Testament figure of speech to denote moral conduct. The word is composed of the preposition *peri*, "around," and *pateō*, "to walk," hence "to walk around, to conduct one's self." The figure thus denotes the whole round of activities in one's life. The present tense marks the habitual conduct of daily life.

The adverb *worthily* (*axiōs*) has the root meaning of weight, speaking of a walk that is of equal worth or weight, befitting and suitable to, the God whom they have come to know as their Saviour. The task of training these converts from paganism how to live so that there would be true agreement between their new faith and their conduct, enlisted the utmost zeal and persistent efforts of the missionaries. For Paul there was a close connection between Christian faith and life. Acceptance of the gospel message carried with it the obligation to live a life consistent with that message. Paul was never content merely to gain large numbers of converts without seeking to induce them to walk worthily of the Lord they had professed. For a true believer the character of his daily life can never remain a matter of indifference.

The God of whom they are to walk worthily is at once described, as the one "who calleth you into his own kingdom and glory." Morris well remarks, "Paul rapidly turns from contemplating what men should do for God to what God does for men."[80] And there is a close connection between the two. The walk demanded of believers is so holy that if left to their own unaided powers they could never attain to it. But God is ever at work in the lives of those whom He has redeemed, aiding and directing them in the pursuit of holiness.

"Who calleth you" translates a present active participle (*tou kalountos*) and the plural pronoun (*humas*), marking the Thessalonian believers as the recipients of God's call. The present tense of the participle, standing in apposition with *God* just before it, indicates that God is continually calling them.†† The Thessalonians had of course heard and accepted God's initial call which first came to them through the preaching of the

---

††The KJV rendering, "who hath called you," translates the aorist participle which has inferior manuscript support.

gospel. But God is ever calling believers to increased efforts and higher goals. The Christian life is a matter of advancement and growth. God's call is "a continual beckoning upwards, until the privileges offered are actually attained."[81] God's call to His saints will find its consummation at the return of Christ.

Adeney proposes that the present tense here should rather be viewed as reiterative in force, that God is calling one and another here and there through the gospel.[82] But since *you* (*humas*) refers to the Thessalonian believers, the call cannot refer to the call to salvation. It is however possible that the articular participle here is timeless and is in effect the equivalent of a substantive, "your caller." Thus viewed the stress is not upon the nature of the call as continuous but rather upon the person who issues the call or invitation.

"Into his own kingdom and glory" (*eis tēn heautou basileian kai doxan*) marks the goal of the divine calling. The two nouns, "kingdom and glory" are closely connected, as shown by the one article and preposition. "The idea is chiefly eschatological. It is the kingdom and glory which will be manifested in all their fullness when Christ comes again."[83]

"His own" is emphatic by position. It implies that God's calling to believers looks forward to their intimate participation in the divine kingdom and glory, which they will fully experience at the return of Christ. This eschatological concept of the kingdom is perfectly consistent with the biblical teaching that believers are already in the kingdom (Ro 14:17; 1 Co 4:20; Col 1:13). Believers are now members of the spiritual kingdom of God and as such are already experiencing foretastes of the coming kingdom when they will share with the Messiah the glory and splendor of His rule.

The kingdom of God centers in the person of the King; it is essentially God's rule in action. It is established by the presence and power of God and is not brought about by human effort. It is now a reality in the hearts and lives of those who accept His rule, but it will have a future visible manifestation in glory when the King returns to establish His rule over the nations (Lk 1:32-33; Mt 25:31; Rev 2:26-27; 20:4).

It is the kingdom in its future aspect of glory that is the hope of the believer. Although his present lot is suffering on behalf of Christ and His kingdom (Ac 14:22; 2 Th 1:5), the saint yet rejoices amid suffering in hope of the glory of God (Ro 5:3-5). This reference to *glory* leads the thought to the final consummation of the Messianic kingdom. And thus the paragraph closes with an eschatological outlook. But this eschatological note was ethically motivated. The continuing summons of God to the future kingdom and glory is an ever-renewed inducement to holy living.

2. Renewed Thanksgiving for the Converts

2:13-16 And for this cause we also thank God without ceasing, that, when ye received from us the message, *even the word* of God, ye accepted *it* not *as* the word of men, but, as it is in truth, the word of God, which also worketh in you that believe. (14) For ye, brethren, became imitators of the churches of God which are in Judaea in Christ Jesus: for ye also suffered the same things of your own countrymen, even as they did of the Jews; (15) who both killed the Lord Jesus and the prophets, and drove out us, and please not God, and are contrary to all men; (16) forbidding us to speak to the Gentiles that they may be saved; to fill up their sins always: but the wrath is come upon them to the uttermost.

The opening *And* closely connects this paragraph with the preceding. After recounting how the gospel was delivered at Thessalonica Paul recalls how it was received. The review of their missionary labors evoked renewed thanksgiving for their converts. Thankfully he recalls how the Thessalonians received the Word of God (v. 13) and thinks of the resultant suffering for them (v. 14). The thought of their suffering for the Word of God causes a passionate denunciation of the Jewish persecutors to burst from his lips (vv. 15-16).

a) RECEPTION OF THE WORD OF GOD (v. 13). Paul begins with a statement of thanksgiving that their converts received the Word of God and then describes the nature of that reception.

(1) *Thanksgiving for the reception* (v. 13a). "For this cause," which is literally, "because of this thing" (*dia touto*), may point either to the reason for the thanksgiving or the subject matter of it. It may look backward or forward. Views differ. Those who hold that it looks backward are not agreed as to just what it connects with in the preceding paragraph. Some, like Alford, think that it refers back to the concluding words of verse 12, that God is calling them unto His own kingdom and glory.[84] Findlay holds that it "gathers its meaning from the previous paragraph: all the toil and sacrifice of the missionaries contributed to their satisfaction over the result accomplished."[85] But Frame insists that it does not relate to the contents of the entire paragraph but only "to the salient principle enounced in vv. 1-4, namely, that the gospel is not human, as the Jews alleged, but divine."[86] Of these the second suggestion seems the most natural.

Others, like Lenski, view *dia touto* as looking forward and hold that the following *that* is explanatory, elaborating the subject matter of the thanksgiving.[87] Jowett regarded *dia touto* as looking both ways: that which at first was thought of as the ground of thanksgiving, his success in preaching, became the subject matter of thankfulness.[88]

The expression of thanksgiving here stated renews the feeling of gratitude with which the epistle began (1:2), but now the subject matter of the thanksgiving is different. In chapter 1 the thanksgiving was evoked by the favorable developments at the time of writing; here the thanksgiving looks back to the time of their ministry at Thessalonica. The present tense of the verb *thank* denotes that their feeling of gratitude for the Thessalonians' reception of their message is still very real. They continue to be thankful for that response.

In contemplating the Thessalonians' response to the gospel "we also thank God without ceasing." *We* again indicates that this is the united reaction of the writers.‡‡ *Also* seems best taken to indicate "a reciprocal relation between writers and readers."[89] The writers are thankful for the readers' acceptance of the gospel, and certainly the Thessalonians are also feeling grateful that they have to come to know the saving gospel. Less probable is the view of Lünemann who holds that the *also* points rather to "every true Christian who hears of the conduct of the Thessalonians."[90]

J. Rendel Harris saw evidence in this *also* for his hypothesis that the Thessalonians had sent a letter to Paul to which he now responds. He thought it indicated that the Thessalonians had expressed their thanks, that they had welcomed the gospel and that the missionaries now reciprocated that thanksgiving.[91] The hypothesis in itself is not unlikely, but the evidence adduced for it comes short of proof. The evidence to which Harris appealed is entirely explicable on the assumption that Paul's letter is based on the carefully formulated oral report which Timothy presented upon his return (3:6).

The missionaries' thanksgiving is directed to *God*, for they recognize that the response of the hearers to their message was due to the gracious working of the Spirit of God in their hearts. They can only think of what was accomplished with sincere gratitude, expressed to God "without ceasing" (cf. 1:2). "They gave thanks without leaving gaps."[92]

(2) *Nature of the reception* (v. 13b). The matter of their thanksgiving is now explicitly stated. "That, when ye received from us the word of the message, even the word of God, ye accepted it not as the word of men, but, as it is in truth, the word of God." In reviewing their response to the gospel Paul thinks not only of their outward reception but also of their inner reaction to the divine message. The contrast is indicated in Paul's use of two different verbal forms here translated *received* (*paralambanō*) and *accepted* (*dechomai*). (Unlike the KJV, the modern versions agree in making a distinction in their renderings of these two verbs here.) The former quite literally means "to receive alongside, to take to oneself," and denotes an objective, outward receiving. The latter

‡‡Regarding it as an editorial "we" the versions of Conybeare, Montgomery, and Way again render "I."

means "to take or receive," to accept with approval, to welcome, and denotes a subjective reception. The former looks to the content of that which is received, while the latter implies a favorable evaluation of that which is accepted. The Thessalonians not only heard and intellectually understood the message but also appropriated and welcomed it into their hearts.

"When ye received" renders an ingressive aorist circumstantial participle (*paralabontes*) and looks back to the time when the Thessalonians heard the message being preached to them. It records their active response to the message, "when you took hold of the divine message" (Berkeley).

That which they took hold of was "the word of the message," literally, "a word of hearing" (*logon akoēs*). The noun *akoē*, coming from the verb *akouō* (to hear), in an active sense denotes the act of hearing and in the passive sense, that which is heard, the thing spoken, the report or preaching. Here it has the usual passive meaning and indicates that the *word* received was a spoken message. Thus Lattey puts it, "When your ears received God's message." This reference to the oral nature of the message received by the Thessalonians reminds us that at that time the spread of Christianity was largely brought about through the spoken word. "The expression marks the high place which preaching holds as a means of grace."[93]

Although Paul made skillful use of the Old Testament Scriptures in his synagogue ministry at Thessalonica (Ac 17:2-3), the distinctively Christian message was orally given. The New Testament writings had not yet been produced. Stevens remarks, "During thirty years or more after Christ's ascension the teaching 'of all nations' was done by the living preacher, not by the circulation of apostolic books among the heathen."[94]

Paul reminds his readers that they heard and received the message "from us" the missionaries who first brought it to Thessalonica. But to guard against any possible misunderstanding of the nature of the message which they received, Paul at once adds "*even the word* of God." As the italicized words indicate, the original is simply "of God" (*tou theou*). This addition stands in close connection with what has gone before to round out the concept that the message which the missionaries brought was in reality God's message. Although Moffatt feels that *of God* "comes in so awkwardly" that he is "tempted to regard it as a scribal gloss,"[95] the unexpected addition at the end of the statement emphasizes the counterbalancing truth that the gospel preached by human lips is of God. It is God's message; the missionaries were the medium. Lightfoot comments, "The Apostle betrays a nervous apprehension that he may be unconsciously making claims for himself; the awkwardness of the position of the words *tou theou* is the measure of the emphasis of his disclaimer."[96]

The converts accepted as a definite act the divine message brought by the missionaries. They "embraced it" (Weymouth) and "welcomed it" (Goodspeed, Lattey, Rotherham, and Williams) into their minds and hearts.

The nature of the message is stressed by means of a negative and positive statement. It was received "not as the word of men, but as it is in truth, the word of God." There is no word for *as* in the negative statement. Bicknell says, "Its insertion seriously alters the drift of the sentence" since Paul's thanksgiving is not due to "the attitude of the Thessalonians to the Gospel, or their appreciation of its divine origin, but the fact that the word that they accepted is divine and therefore charged with divine power."[97] Assuredly the Thessalonians recognized the Word for what it was, but Paul's words apparently are not intended to record their subjective evaluation of the gospel. Rather, he is stressing its objective character.

The negative fact is that it is "not a word of men." It is not a humanly originated message, like the teachings of the religious quacks and charlatans who were everywhere exploiting the gullible people with their pretensions. *But* (*alla*), the stronger of the two Greek adversatives, introduces the positive fact, "as it is in truth, the word of God." Whatever men may say or think about it, this is its true nature. The "word of God" here is not the written word but the oral preaching of the gospel under the power of the Spirit. It points to the nature of dynamic gospel preaching. God's messenger must "rely on the Bible; but every loyal preacher or teacher of Christ's truth is a channel of 'the word of God.' "[98]

Neil thinks that this strong emphasis upon the divine nature of the message was apparently "in reply to Jewish insinuations that Paul's was a man-made gospel."[99] Paul did not doubt that what he was proclaiming was God's message and his converts cannot think otherwise. They have the verification of it in their own experience, for it is the word "which also worketh in you that believe."§§ *Also* indicates that this message is not only divine but has the further characteristic of being active and dynamic. It *worketh*, is operative and productive, continually producing an effect in the lives of those who receive it. The thought of the activating power of God's Word is common in the Scriptures (Is 55:11; Heb 4:12; Ja 1:21; 1 Pe 1:23). Paul is fond of it. Eighteen of the twenty-one occurrences

§§Since in the Greek both "word" and "God" are masculine nouns, the masculine pronoun "which" (*hos*) might grammatically be taken with either noun. But that it should be taken with "word" is evident from the fact that "word" rather than "God" is the subject of the sentence as well as the voice (middle or passive) here used. When used of God directly the verb "worketh" is used with the active voice.

of the verb rendered "worketh" (*energeō*) in the New Testament are in Paul's letters. He alone employs the corresponding nouns *energeia*, (working) and *energēma* (activity).

In saying that this Word worketh "in you" Paul is reminding his readers that they personally know the operative power of it. The effect that it had wrought in their lives was widely known; it turned them to God from idols, committed them to the service of the living God, and gave them the hope of the return of the risen Christ as their Saviour from the coming wrath (1:9-10). Such a transforming experience convinces every believer that what he has accepted is truly the Word of God. No humanly contrived message can produce such results.

The added appositional articular participle rendered "that believe" (*tois pisteuousin*) not only defines *you* more closely but serves to indicate the condition under which the divine Word can operate in human hearts. Faith conditions its efficacy. There must not only be a hearing of the Word but also a continuing faith. The present tense marks their believing as an abiding characteristic. A genuine faith is a continuing faith. That the participle is used absolutely, with no indication of what is believed, points to the fact that from the earliest times faith was recognized as central to Christianity. "The believers" is a synonym for Christians.

b) SUFFERING BECAUSE OF THE WORD OF GOD (v. 14). The opening *For* introduces the proof that the Word was operative in their lives. The display of that fact was their suffering for the Word. Paul first speaks of the sufferers they have come to imitate and then indicates the nature of the suffering they are enduring.

(1) *Sufferers imitated* (v. 14*a*). "Ye, brethren, became imitators of the churches of God which are in Judaea." The latter part of the verse makes it clear that this imitation was in the sphere of suffering. *Ye* (*humeis*) is emphatic by position; "you on your part." The insertion of the direct address, *brethren*, voices the consciousness of the writers that they know a oneness with the afflicted readers in the brotherhood of suffering.

In 1:6 Paul mentioned that the Thessalonians had become imitators of the missionaries and of the Lord in the matter of Christian living. Here he mentions their becoming imitators in the matter of suffering for their faith. They have proved their willingness to suffer because of the gospel. Thus they "began to follow the example" (So rendered in 20th Cent, Montgomery, Goodspeed, Williams, and Way. Moffatt has "you have started to copy the churches.") of the Judean churches and had entered into the fellowship of Christian suffering for the faith. It is striking proof of the energizing power of the gospel in their lives. It demonstrated that they were not superficial, stony-soil hearers. Persecution for Christ's sake causes such to fall away (Mt 13:20-21; Lk 8:13).

It has been asked why Paul cited the example of the Judean churches to his Gentile converts. Calvin replied that thus Paul counteracted a serious temptation which might assail the Thessalonians. The Jews at Thessalonica were insinuating that the new faith which Paul's converts had accepted must be a false religion since the Jews, the only people who worshiped the true God, were constrained to oppose it. To remove any doubts they might have had, Paul reminded his readers that the first churches, started in Judea, had been made to suffer by the Jews who thus showed themselves "the determined enemies of God and of all sound doctrine."[100]

Calvin's surmise may be correct, but as Lünemann remarks, "such a design of the apostle is indicated by nothing, and its supposition is entirely superfluous."[101] He thinks that Paul selected the Judean churches because their courageous sufferings made them pertinent examples of steadfastness to the younger Christian communities.

More natural is the explanation that Paul points out the suffering of these early Judean churches to the Thessalonians to show them that from the beginning, Christians have been suffering for their faith, so they were not alone in being persecuted. Those who receive the Word of God and are united with the true people of God will always be hated by unbelieving men and be made to suffer for their belief.

This passing reference indicates that the Thessalonian believers knew about the sufferings of the Judean churches. There is no evidence that they had direct contacts with them, but it is certain that Paul, who himself did much to add to those sufferings during his pre-Christian days, would inform his converts of the story of the heroic sufferings of those early churches. And Silas, as a leading member of the Jerusalem church (Ac 15:22), would be able to supply firsthand information.

Three elements in Paul's identification of these model sufferers may be noted. They were "the churches of God" ("the assemblies of God," Darby, Young, and Rotherham). They were not merely human organizations; they belonged to God. This expression, used only by Paul in the New Testament, denotes local companies of believers.

Geographically they were the churches "which are in Judaea." Judea may be considered in its restricted sense here as denoting the province of Judea, but probably it is used in the wider sense to mean all of Palestine. The original is an appositional participle construction, "the ones being in Judaea," and points to the existence of these churches at the time of writing. Hogg and Vine think the suggestion is "that as persecution had not brought the work of God to an end in the place of its origin and the home of its fiercest enemies, it would avail as little at Thessalonica."[102]

The third element in the identification is that they were "in Christ Jesus." It adds the spiritual elements which distinguishes these assemblies from the Jewish synagogues. The difference between the Jewish synagogues and the Christian assemblies hinges on the acceptance of Jesus as Messiah. The Jews professed to believe God's Word and claimed to be God's assemblies, but when they rejected the Lord Jesus as their Messiah, who came in fulfillment of the promises in God's Word, they showed that they did not believe God's Word. It is the acceptance of Jesus as Messiah that constitutes the vital bond uniting all true Christians. The converts' faith had brought them into vital union with Him; in Him their spiritual life had its source and center.

(2) *Suffering experienced* (v. 14b). With *For*, or "because" (*hoti*), Paul states the evidence that the Thessalonian believers have begun to imitate the Judean churches. "Ye also suffered the same things of your own countrymen, even as they did of the Jews." The similarity between their experiences is stressed by "the same things," which is placed emphatically forward. The persecution is the same in character, whether inflicted upon Jewish or Gentile believers. It is a manifestation of the age-old conflict waged by the devil against God and His people. The Thessalonian believers had also come to experience this hostility. This is brought out by Paul's emphatic "ye also."

The verb rendered *suffered* is in the aorist tense and may indicate a single event in the remoter or nearer past or a series of persecutions considered collectively. If the reference is to some single event the reference might be to the flare-up in Acts 17, but more probably the reference may be to some persecution endured by the Thessalonian church since the departure of the missionaries. Timothy doubtless brought the report of it. But it seems more probable that all the sufferings they had endured as Christians are gathered up in the tense.

The similarity between their suffering and that of the Judean churches lies in the fact that both were made to suffer by their own *countrymen* (*sumphuletōn*), their "fellow-tribesmen" or "fellow-countrymen." "Your own countrymen" denotes that the persecutors are Gentiles, as indicated by the sharp contrast with "the Jews" as well as by "your own." But many commentators think that the term *countrymen* here probably has a local rather than a racial connotation and so need not exclude all reference to the Jews. Lightfoot points out that the expression then would "include such Jews as were free citizens of Thessalonica."[103] The strong invective against the Jews which immediately follows shows that Paul thought of them as being involved, although his words may, strictly taken, exclude them. The opposition to the gospel was fomented by the Thessalonian Jews, who solicited the cooperation of the Gentiles in launching their attack. Obviously, once stirred up, the Greeks of their own accord continued the hostility against the believers.

"Even as they did of the Jews" completes the statement of the parallel suffering of the two groups. *They* individualizes the sufferers indicated under the more abstract designation "the churches of God which are in Judaea." The instigators of their sufferings were "the Jews." Findlay points out that "this is the earliest example, and the only instance in St. Paul, of the designation 'the Jews' applied in the sense made familiar afterwards by the Gospel of St. John, as opposed to *Christians*."[104] The fires of persecution against the church were ignited by the unbelieving Jews in Judea; the story of Acts makes it clear that the unbelieving Jews of the dispersion kept those fires burning in the Gentile world. The remark of Tertullian fit the experience of the early churches, "The synagogues of the Jews, founts of persecution."

c) JEWS' OPPOSITION TO GOD'S WORD (vv. 15-16). At the mention of "the Jews" Paul launches into a strong denunciation of their activities. The intensity of this outburst is without parallel in his writings. Neil calls it "a polemic which is so vitriolic, and so unlike his general attitude to his countrymen, that some commentators have regarded it as an interpolation."[105] Those who favor the hypothesis of an interpolation variously include all of verses 14-16 (Holtzmann), verses 15-16 (Schmiedel), or only the closing sentence of verse 16 (Bailey).[106] Manuscript evidence gives no support to such conjectures. Instead of arbitrarily resorting to interpolation, it is better to seek to understand why Paul wrote as he did. In this passage "Paul's mind goes off at a tangent,"[107] but a study of Paul's letters reveals that there is always a reason for such so-called digressions. It is true that the portrayal of the Jewish persecutors in verses 15-16 might be removed without noticeable interruption of Paul's train of thought in the chapter, but we would lose a valuable key to the interpretation of the situation when Paul wrote.

In writing these verses Paul has been charged with giving vent to "pardonable apostolic exasperation."[108] Moffatt says, "This curt and sharp verdict on the Jews sprang from Paul's irritation at the moment. The apostle was in no mood to be conciliatory."[109] But surely Paul's words are not merely an understandable, although unjustified, outburst of momentary exasperation. Paul spoke from long and bitter experience. In his missionary labors he had been hounded from place to place by the unrelenting hostility and cunning opposition of the Jews. Perhaps at no other time during his missionary career did he suffer more from the hostility of the Jews than during the period when this letter was written.

Paul's sharp denunciation of the vicious activities of the Jewish persecutors is a justified condemnation of their crimes against the work of God. They are guilty of fierce resistance to the gospel and persistent, cruel persecution of the churches of God. The fact that these activities were persisted in far beyond the land of Judea indicates that it was a policy to which his unbelieving countrymen as a whole had deliberately committed themselves. Paul's words express the whole guilt of the Jews and his fervid, merited condemnation of them. Concerning this denunciation Denney concludes,

> What we have here is not a burst of temper, though there is undoubtedly strong feeling in it; it is the vehement condemnation, by a man in thorough sympathy with the mind and spirit of God, of the principles on which the Jews as a nation had acted at every period of their history.[110]

Paul's charges against the persecuting Jews are set forth by means of five participles standing in close apposition to "the Jews" at the end of verse 14. The first two are aorists and picture the past violent manifestations of their opposition (v. 15*a*); the remaining three participles are in the present tense and provide a sad evaluation of their opposition (vv. 15*b*-16*a*). The concluding sentence states the fateful outcome of the opposition (v. 16*b*).

(1) *Its violent manifestations* (v. 15*a*). Their violent opposition to the gracious movements of God has expressed itself in the murder of Jesus and the prophets as well as in the persecution of Christians. By saying "who both killed the Lord Jesus and the prophets," Paul combines their slaying of the Old Testament prophets and Jesus, but names Jesus first because His death was their greatest crime. The Greek separates "the Lord" from *Jesus* by placing the verb *killed* between them. This separation of the double name "brings into striking relief the Divine glory and the human character of the Slain."[111] It was none less than the exalted Lord whom the Jews killed, the one who was manifested to Israel as the historical Jesus, the Saviour. His death at their hands was no common murder. Their violent rejection of Him is the key to an understanding of all their violent deeds.

It is interesting to note that in this epistle, written about twenty years after the crucifixion of Jesus, Paul places the guilt for His death squarely upon the Jews. He was well aware that the execution was carried out by the Romans, that Pontius Pilate and Herod Antipas shared responsibility for that monumental miscarriage of justice (1 Co 2:8), but he saw clearly that the Jews were chiefly responsible, using Pilate as their tool to bring about the death of the one they hated. He well understood how the Jews in Thessalonica in a similar manner used the Gentile rabble to secure the expulsion of the missionaries from their city.

From Jesus, Paul reaches back to their violent dealings with the Old Testament prophets.|| || Christ Himself accused the Jews of killing their prophets (Mt 23:31, 37; Lk 11:47-48), and in the parable of the wicked husbandmen He pictured His own murder as the culmination of the murderous activities of the Jews (Mt 21:33-41). This charge was repeated by Stephen before the Sanhedrin in the hearing of Saul of Tarsus (Ac 7:52).

It is sometimes suggested that the words "the prophets" should rather be connected with the participle that follows to make them coordinate with *us*. This is grammatically possible and is adopted by some commentators and versions. Thus Goodspeed renders, "who killed the Lord Jesus and persecuted the prophets and us." In support of this connection it is held that to mention the killing of the prophets after the Lord Jesus makes an anticlimax; also not all of the prophets were killed. This connection implies that the prophets are not Hebrew but Christian prophets, which is less probable. The argument that not all the Old Testament prophets were killed is of little weight; the argument is nearly as strong if connected with the following participle. Thus to disconnect the prophets from the Lord Jesus blunts the force of Paul's deliberate arrangement; in slaying the Lord Jesus the Jews could not plead ignorance. His death was but the logical culmination of their violent treatment of their prophets. The connection of "the prophets" with "the Lord Jesus" under the government of the first participle is preferable.

From the manifestations of the Jews' violence before the death of Jesus, Paul turns to the manifestation of the same spirit since His death. "And drove out us" indicates that they continued to display the same hostility toward the Christian missionaries. *Us* is primarily Paul and his co-workers but they are representative of Christian missionaries as a class. The word rendered "drove out" (*ekdiōkō*) may mean either "to persecute severely" or "to drive out, expel, banish." It is composed of the simple verb *diōkō*, generally given as "to persecute," and the preposition *ek*, "out." The compound form is used only here in the New Testament. If the meaning of persecution is retained the preposition gives it an intensive force; Moffatt puts it "harassed," while Way translates "they have hounded us." It seems more probable that the *ek* here carries a semilocal significance, "persecuted out" (of a place). Hence Darby translates, "and have driven us out by persecution."

|| ||Following the *Textus Receptus*, the KJV reads "their own prophets," making it clear that they are Hebrew and not Christian prophets. While "their own" provides a correct interpretation, modern editors and most commentators agree that they are not a part of the original text.

The aorist tense of the participle may denote a specific event where Paul was driven out or a series of events viewed collectively. If the former, it records Paul's vivid remembrance of the scene told in Acts 17; if the latter, it points to Paul's repeated experiences of being forced out of a place by the Jews. The latter interpretation is reflected in the version of Conybeare, "who have driven me forth [from city to city]." In reading this letter the Thessalonians would naturally recall what had happened in their own city.

(2) *Its sad evaluation* (vv. 15b-16a). "And please not God" records the only logical conclusion that can be drawn from what has just been said. Paul does not deny that the Jews are zealously trying to please God (Ro 10:2). But their conduct is such that they "only succeeded in making themselves obnoxious to Him."[112] Paul's expression "please not God" is a deliberate understatement. The negative statement carries a strong positive connotation; they are highly displeasing to God. The present tense marks the result of their regular and continuing course of action. To persist in a course of conduct that can only evoke divine displeasure is a serious thing indeed.

"And are contrary to all men" expresses the apostolic evaluation of their attitude and conduct manward. This statement does not mean that Paul accuses the Jews of being naturally hostile to all men. The explanation for the charge lies in the statement which immediately follows, "forbidding us to speak to the Gentiles that they may be saved." The absence of the article with the participle in the original indicates that the phrase stands in close explanatory relation with the preceding clause.

The Roman historian Tacitus charged the Jews with "hostile odium" toward all men, and Gentiles generally regarded Jews as an unsociable and unfriendly race. This misreading of their true nature arose out of a misunderstanding of their religious exclusiveness which made them separate themselves from all other people. While beginning as a nation divinely called to be a separated people, the Jews had become a sinfully exclusive and bigoted nation. And when God overruled their perveted nationalism they reacted in bitter hostility. But Paul well understood that their hostility to non-Jews was grounded "not in their natural make-up, but their rejection of the Gospel, and their determination to thwart its progress."[113]

"Forbidding us to speak to the Gentiles that they may be saved" describes the manner in which the persistent hostility of the Jews showed itself toward the Gentiles. The verb rendered "forbidding" does not convey the thought of oral prohibitions but rather the thought of active, persistent efforts to hinder or prevent the preaching of the missionaries to "the Gentiles," emphatic by position. By their obstructionist tactics the Jews were actually interfering with the work of the missionaries among the Gentiles but they did not succeed in silencing them.

The Jews did not object to the missionaries having social contacts with Gentiles but they strongly opposed contacts that were specifically evangelistic in aim, "that they may be saved."## The aorist passive verb translated "be saved" is a reminder that the salvation which the missionaries offer the Gentiles is the work of God for man, man being saved by the operation of divine power toward him. Salvation is by grace, not human effort.

The Jews' opposition to the work of the missionaries among the Gentiles was not due to the fact that they were seeking to win Gentiles. The Jews themselves were vigorously engaged in this period of their history in actively proselyting Gentiles. Their fierce oppostion was due to the fact that Christian missionaries offered salvation to Gentiles without demanding that they first become Jews. Everywhere the Jews showed themselves wildly jealous at Paul's success in winning Gentiles to the Christian faith directly. By their persistent opposition the Jews deliberately sought to rob Gentiles of the salvation in Christ which they resolutely rejected for themselves. As Lenski well remarks, "The worst feature of unbelief is not its own damnation, but its effort to frustrate the salvation of others."[114] It was precisely because Paul clearly saw the seriousness of the hindering work of the Jews, that it was fraught with eternal consequences for the Gentiles they were able to turn away from the gospel, that he denounced the Jews so passionately.

The concluding phrase, "to fill up their sins always," is best regarded as modifying the entire statement concerning the violent activities of the Jews (vv. 15-16a). Their killing of Jesus and the prophets, their persistent hindering of Paul's work, their opposition to the Gentiles to keep them from being saved, are all related to their filling up the measure of their sins. The expression in the original may denote either result or purpose. Scholars are divided as to its intended significance here.

Lenski, Blackwelder, and others accept the thought of result.[115] Then the meaning is that all the activities of the Jews have produced the result that the measure of their sins has been filled up. Most scholars think that the phrase rather indicates purpose. But whose purpose? Ellicott holds that grammatically this purpose must be applied to the Jews.[116] Since we can hardly understand Paul to mean that this was the conscious and deliberate purpose of the Jews, it must be taken to mean that in their blindness and ignorance the Jews are actually pursuing this purpose. But

---

##"To speak . . . that they may be saved" is "capable of two interpretations, (1) 'to speak to them, to the end that they may be saved' or (2) 'to tell them to be saved' " (Lightfoot, p. 34). The former meaning is required by the context, although Marvin R. Vincent (*Word Studies in the New Testament,* 4:29), holds to the latter.

if purpose is meant we would naturally think of the divine purpose behind it. Ellicott recognizes that theologically considered "it mainly refers to the eternal purpose of God which unfolds itself in this wilful, and at last, judicial blindness on the part of His chosen people."[117]

It is difficult to decide whether the phrase denotes purpose or result. The two ideas are not far apart. "Purpose may be viewed as contemplated result and result as achieved purpose."[118] Plummer holds that Paul's words combine "the notions of consequence and intention. This was the result of their previous misconduct, and it was God's will that it should be so."[119]

"To fill up" conveys the common Hebrew image of a measure or cup that is being filled up. It implies that the cup is still partially empty but that it is rapidly being filled to the brim. The aorist tense looks to the time when the full measure is attained. "Each fresh act of hostility to the Gospel was an additional drop in their cup of guilt, which had been steadily filling during the ages."[120] The task at which their fathers had been diligently working, the Jews by their opposition to the Gospel were still aggressively carrying on. *Always*, placed emphatically at the end, points to the uninterrupted succession of evil acts which is filling up the measure of "their sins." The plural lays stress not on specific acts but on their aggregate sin.

Paul's words imply that there is a certain measure of wickedness which God will allow a nation, a group, or an individual to complete before His judgment falls on them. Calvin says that "this is why the punishment of the ungodly is often postponed—it is because their acts of ungodliness are so to speak not yet ripe."[121] But when the climax has been reached judgment falls. Tasker remarks "that God delays the display of His wrath till offenders have reached a kind of saturation point, beyond which they may not pass. . . . That time, Paul implies in I Thessalonians ii. 16, is now imminent."[122]

(3) *Its fatal outcome* (v. 16*b*). Such conduct could not escape divine condemnation. "But the wrath is come upon them to the uttermost." *But* (*de*) may be adversative, opposing the sin to the punishment. However, it may simply serve to introduce the additional fact that divine wrath has fallen. Although *wrath* is left undefined, its clearly denotes God's wrath. With the definite article, "the wrath," it signifies the well known and merited wrath of God which must fall upon all iniquity.

The verb translated "is come" is in the aorist tense and denotes a past point action, "came, or arrived." God's wrath has actually come upon them and still remains (cf. Jn 3:36). But the significance of the aorist is differently understood.

Lenski insists that it is simply an historical aorist; the Jews were ever filling up their cup of sin and thus the divine wrath came upon them. He holds that the wrath had already "arrived long centuries before Paul wrote," manifesting itself in the various judgments of God upon Israel.[123] But clearly Paul is not thinking here of a series of judgments in the past.

All that the aorist really says is that the wrath has come. It states the historical fact without any further specification. Vincent says that Paul's meaning is "that the divine wrath has reached the point where it passed into judgment."[124] Morris thinks that the aorist tense simply refers to the certainty of the coming judgment, while Swete holds that the aorist is a "prophetic past, looking upon the future as already settled and completed in the counsels of God."[125]

The wrath of God has already fallen and all that remains is the coming of inevitable judgment. That the judgment has already fallen is not said. The actual woes are still to come. But the Jews with their persistent opposition to the gospel, following their rejection of the Messiah, have filled their cup. God's patience with them has been exhausted. His wrath has come upon them "to the uttermost" (*eis telos*), literally, "to an end." It may have an intensive meaning, "completely, entirely, to the uttermost," or a temporal meaning, "finally, at last." Under either view the meaning is essentially the same. God's wrath has now reached its extreme limits. Judgment cannot be averted.

Various suggestions have been advanced as to the nature of the fate which Paul foresaw for the Jews. Some have thought of a great famine, the banishment of the Jews from Rome, or some definite sign of impending judgment that had just occurred. Frame holds that the picture is eschatological and means that Paul thought of the day of judgment as near at hand.[126] F. C. Baur claimed that the reference was to the destruction of Jerusalem in AD 70 and used this as an argument against the authenticity of the epistle. But there is no justification for regarding Paul's words as a reference to that event as something that has already taken place. But it is quite possible that Paul by prophetic presentiment had "foreseen the *impending* catastrophe of the Jewish people, and by means of this foresight had expressed the concluding words of this verse."[127] Paul must have been acquainted with Christ's predictions of the destruction of Jerusalem (Mt 24:1-2; Lk 19:43-44) and from the course of events realized that the fulfillment could not be long delayed.

Paul's picture here of the outlook for the Jews is dark indeed. Their fate was sealed, they were irrevocably doomed. But God has promised that He "will not make a full end of" His people (Jer 30:4-11; 31:35-37; 33:20-22). Although a dark future still awaits them, final Messianic deliverance is assured them. Paul's statement here deals with the inevitable fate of the Christ-rejecting Jews who reveal their determined opposition to the gospel by their efforts to hinder its preaching to the Gentiles. But it must be remembered that this passage does not give Paul's complete teaching concerning the future of Israel. His statement here is quite consistent with his fuller teaching in Romans 9-11. There he shows that the masses of the Jews in every period of their history have been unbelieving and therefore under the judgment of God, but always there has been an elect remnant to whom God has manifested His saving grace. Since the masses of the Jews by their persistent opposition to his work reveal that it is their settled policy to reject the gospel of Christ, Paul knows that inevitable judgment awaits them. Because of their unbelief a hardening has befallen the nation which will last "until the fulness of the Gentiles be come in" (Ro 11:25).

7

PERSONAL: SEPARATION

C. RELATIONS SINCE SEPARATED FROM THEM,
2:17—3:13

HAVING REVIEWED the missionaries' relations to the Thessalonians while with them, Paul now continues to consider their relations since being forcibly separated from them. The new topic continues through the end of chapter 3. The unity of this section would have been more evident if the new chapter had been made to begin at 2:17 instead. (The present chapter division was apparently due to the desire to have each chapter close with a direct reference to the second coming.)

This section divides into three parts, standing in a progressive relationship. In 2:17-20 Paul explains his continued absence from his beloved converts; in 3:1-5 he recalls the sending of Timothy to them to reestablish direct contact with them and to encourage them; the remainder of the section records the reaction to the return of Timothy with his report (3:6-13).

1. Desire to Revisit Them Hindered

2:17-20   But we, brethren, being bereaved of you for a short season, in presence not in heart, endeavored the more exceedingly to see your face with great desire: (18) because we would fain have come unto you, I Paul once and again; and Satan hindered us. (19) For what is our hope, or joy, or crown of glorying? Are not even ye, before our Lord Jesus at his coming? (20) For ye are our glory and our joy.

The question of apostolic relations with the Thessalonians since being separated from them is introduced with the words "But we, brethren." "But we" (*Hēmeis de*), "now to speak about ourselves," marks the return to the writers' own experiences. The *de* may be adversative, but it is better to take it as continuative, serving to add another matter, and render "now." The emphatic *we* sets the missionaries in contrast to the Jewish persecutors whom Paul has just denounced (vv. 15-16). Paul's *we* includes his co-workers, Silas and Timothy (again changed into "I" by Conybeare, Montgomery, and Way). He again takes his readers to his heart by addressing them as *brethren.* It assures his converts that they are solicitously being remembered. They are all related in Christ and it is in the interest of those spiritual family ties that this section is written.

Clearly in this paragraph Paul is continuing his defense. If the section in 2:1-12 may be called Paul's *apologia pro vita sua,* this may be called his *apologia pro absentia sua.* Paul, however, is not seeking to justify his absence as though it were a voluntary matter but is vehemently insisting that, contrary to his strong desires, he has been prevented from returning to see his converts.

Paul is countering the slanderous insinuations of his enemies at Thessalonica that he did not wish to return, that he was running away from his followers in their danger. His opponents charged that Paul loudly professed his unbounded affection for his converts while he was with them, but when danger arose because of his activities he promptly deserted them and fled. They implied that he was afraid to come back; had he not failed to show his face when his followers were taken into court because of his treasonous teachings (Ac 17:5-10)? Now that things were no longer safe for him at Thessalonica he had left the scene without wasting any further thought on his followers there. He doubtless had gone off to ensnare some new crowd of dupes who would be taken in by his blandishments, bolster up his vanity, and enable him to live in ease on their hard-earned money.

Paul answers these slanders by insisting that far from not wishing to return he twice had deliberately tried to return but his efforts had been frustrated (vv. 17-18). Although he is denied the joy of a personal reunion with them, he assures them of his deep affection for them (vv. 19-20).

a) FRUSTRATED EFFORTS TO RETURN TO THEM (vv. 17-18). The separation from their converts is not to their liking. Paul describes the feelings experienced upon the separation (v. 17*a*), recounts his efforts to return to them (vv. 17*b*-18*a*), and explains that Satan has hindered the return (v. 18*b*).

(1) *Nature of the separation* (v. 17*a*). Their forced separation from their converts Paul characterizes as "being bereaved of you." The aorist passive participle indicates that the separation was an event which was forced upon them. It was not their own deliberate act. The participle *aporphanisthentes* is a compound form, used only here in the New Testament. The verb literally means "to be orphaned," be bereft of parents; it was also used in a more general sense to denote the loss of any friend or relative, even including the bereavement of a parent. The preposition

apo, "from, away from," intensifies the meaning, "orphaned off," or "torn away from." The thought of separation is further indicated by the repetition of the preposition with the pronoun *you* (*aph' humōn*). Doubtless Paul here intended to convey the original force of the verb. It vividly portrays the desolation of soul which he felt upon being torn from his beloved converts. Chrysostom aptly commented,

> He says not, parted from you, or torn from you, or distant, or absent, but *orphaned* of you. He sought for a word that might fitly indicate his mental anguish. Though standing in the relation of a father to them all, he yet utters the language of orphan children that have prematurely lost their parents.[1]

Upon being forced out of Thessalonica the writers felt empty and bereaved like orphan children.

Paul's words reveal the strong personal ties that had been forged between the writers and the readers. Plummer remarks, "It is illuminating to remember that eight or nine months before these deeply affectionate words (which are of transparent sincerity) were written, not one of the three missionaries, so far as we know, had any acquaintance with any one in Thessalonica."[2] It was a demonstration of the ties of love and brotherhood being forged and fixed by the gospel which the missionaries were preaching. Paul did not hesitate to show them how deeply he felt even the external rupturing of those ties.

The phrase "for a short season" may be taken to imply that he had expected the separation to be only of short duration. Then both he and the Thessalonian believers had anticipated that he would be able to return as soon as the trouble died down. But it did not turn out that way. Already several months had elapsed since then.

It is more probable that the participle rendered "being bereaved" has a temporal force, "*when* we had been bereaved of you for a short season." Then the meaning is that this feeling of bereavement swept over them after they had been separated from them only "for a short season," literally, "for a season of an hour." It is a unique combination of two time designations, "for a season" (*pros kairon*) and "for an hour" (*pros hōran*), and is apparently stronger than either alone. When they had been separated from them for but a brief period, the feeling of bereavement overcame them. The length of the separation intensified the pain. That the missionaries were unable to be away from them for a single hour without a deep sense of loss proved the strength of their affection for their converts.

By adding "in presence not in heart" Paul at once interprets the separation as being only bodily. Their physical separation implied no alienation of heart. It was not a matter of "out of sight, out of mind." "Love is not bound in the fetters of place or time."[3] This refutes the charge that the missionaries did not care for their converts now that it was expedient to be gone from them.

(2) *Endeavor to return* (vv. 17b-18a). Deeply pained by the separation, the missionaries diligently endeavored "to see your face." Auberlen called this "a select phrase of love, instead of the more prosaic *to come unto you* of v. 18."[4] To bear them affectionately in their hearts was not enough; love could only be satisfied with seeing their faces and enjoying intimate face-to-face relationships. Absence sharpened the desire to behold their faces again.

The verb rendered "endeavored" means "to hasten, to give diligence." Morris remarks that it "manages to combine the two ideas of haste and earnestness."[5] The efforts to return were not dilatory or half-hearted. They had been speedily and energetically made.

The strong verb *endeavored* receives two parallel modifiers. It is enforced with a comparative adverb, "the more exceedingly." Since in the New Testament the comparative form often takes over the function of the superlative, some scholars think that it has the elative sense here, "very earnestly" (Conybeare), "extremely eager" (Goodspeed). But others would retain the strictly comparative force here. Lightfoot insists the adverb "here, as always in St. Paul, is strictly comparative."[6] Frame questions this and points to its use in 2 Corinthians 7:13 where it is doubtful that the strictly comparative force will hold.[7] The comparative force denotes that they endeavored more abundantly to see them than they would have under ordinary conditions. Then the context must indicate just what is thought of as the other member of the unexpressed comparison. Some have suggested that it was a knowledge of the perils facing the Thessalonian believers in their absence. Others find the comparison in the previously stated forced separation which only served to make them more anxious to return. Still others look to what follows and think that the obstacles thrown in their way made them more ardent in their efforts to go back. It is simpler not to press the comparative force of the adverb.

The verb *endeavored* is further modified by the prepositional phrase "with great desire," literally, "in much longing." It indicates that the missionaries were in the grip of an intense desire to return. Way renders it "with passionate yearning." The noun *desire* generally has the evil connotation of sinful desire or lust; its use here is one of the few instances in the New Testament where it has a good sense (Lk 22:15; Phil 1:23).

The diligent endeavors to return to Thessalonica were accompanied by a strong emotional desire to do so. "Because we would fain have come unto you." *Because* looks back to the great yearning they felt; in proof of this he now asserts "we would fain have come." The statement parallels the assertion concerning the missionaries' diligent endeavors to see their faces. The repetition underlines his denial of the insinuations of his enemies.

The former statement pointed to the endeavors that were put forth; this points rather to the emotional desire which they felt. The verb rendered "we would fain have" (*ēthelēsamen*) seems best taken to express a wish springing out of an emotional desire. There has been much discussion concerning the force of the verb *thelō,* which Paul uses here in distinction to the verb *boulomai.* Paul's usage makes it difficult to distinguish between them. Arndt and Gingrich say that there is no longer any difference in their meaning.[8] An attempt to distinguish shades of meaning is generally made. In discussing the difference between *boulomai* and *thelō* Thayer concluded, "the former seems to designate the will which follows deliberation, the latter the will which proceeds from inclination."[9] Others would just reverse the distinction. Thus the force of Paul's statement here is differently conceived. Milligan holds that Paul means " 'we had resolved'—with the idea of active decision or purpose,"[10] while Hendriksen renders, "we did wish."[11] Morris accepts the view that the verb *thelō* "connects with the feelings rather than the will."[12] This seems consistent with the strong emotional stress of the passage. Paul is apparently speaking of a desire arising from the emotions rather than the reason. Frame holds that the "the actual resolve" finding expression in their earnest endeavor is first expressly stated in 3:1 when Paul says "we thought it good."[13]

The parenthetical remark, "I Paul once and again," makes it unmistakably clear that Paul personally felt the strong emotional desire just asserted. The personal pronoun "I" with his own name (*egō men Paulos*) calls special attention to himself. It does not imply a lesser desire on the part of his companions but emphasizes his own. Paul rarely introduces his own name in the body of a letter and when he does it is with special emphasis. Paul felt constrained to make this personal assertion since he has been the chief object of attack in the insinuations that the missionaries did not wish to come back. Further, it was necessary to distinguish himself from his associates as Timothy, and possibly also Silas, had actually returned since the beginning of the work at Thessalonica.

This careful restriction upon the plural subject of the verb "we would fain have come" confirms the view that throughout the epistle the use of the plural "we" naturally is intended to include Silvanus and Timothy. If "we" throughout the letter is editorial and means only Paul himself there would have been no need to make the distinction here.

This strong desire to return Paul felt "once and again," literally, "both

once and twice." Scholars differ as to whether Paul means on two specific occasions or repeatedly. Those who think of two definite occasions
offer varied conjectures as to place and time. Swete thought that both
times were "probably whilst he was yet in the neighbourhood of Beraea."
Zahn suggested that the first occasion was at Berea and the second at
Athens while waiting for the coming of Silas and Timothy, while Garrod
conjectured that it was during Paul's loneliness at Athens before the arrival of Silas and Timothy and again after Timothy had been sent back to
Thessalonica. From his study of the usage of the phrase, Morris concludes that it means "more than once." Neil accepts this as more suitable
and notes that it does not involve conjecturing definite occasions for his
desire to return.[14]

(3) *Hindrance by Satan* (v. 18b). That the earnest endeavor and
strong desire were frustrated has the factual explanation, "and Satan
hindered us." *And* (*kai*) is not adversative, but coordinating; it adds
another factual statement.

Swete comments that it is remarkable "that in an epistle addressed
almost entirely to Gentile converts, and in which not a single direct quotation from the Old Testament finds place," Paul should thus refer to the
Hebrew "Satan" without any further word of explanation.[15] That the
readers were expected to understand its significance proves that Paul had
given oral instructions to them concerning the names, nature, and work
of the great spiritual adversary of Christians.

The verb rendered "hindered" literally means "to cut into." It was used
as a military term in later Greek to picture an enemy force cutting up (or
destroying) a road so as to make it impassable. It was also used to denote any hindrance in general and conveys the thought of obstacles pre-
venting the accomplishment of an intended movement.

The exact nature of the hindrances offered by Satan is not indicated.
It has been variously conjectured that the hindrances were either in the
events of Paul's own life or in conditions at Thessalonica. Some have
thought of an illness of Paul; but this would not fit Silvanus and Timothy.
Ramsay suggested that Satan had influenced the politarchs at Thessalonica to compel Jason and his friends to give bonds to assure the continued absence of Paul from Thessalonica.[16] But under this explanation it
is difficult to see how the Thessalonians could have expected Paul to
return and it takes the force out of the insinuations of the opponents that
Paul did not want to return. Still others have suggested that Paul could
not return because Satan caused the unbelieving Jews to be vigilant to
forestall any return on his part. We cannot determine just what Paul had
in mind, but it is clear that he expected the Thessalonians to understand
the reference.

That Satan did use some human instrument is entirely possible. Calvin remarked, "Whenever the ungodly cause us trouble, they are fighting under the banner of Satan, and are his instruments for harassing us."[17] Whatever the means employed, Paul was sure of Satan's activity behind it. For Paul, Satan was "undoubtedly a personality, not a personification." Ellicott aptly insists "that the language of the N.T., if words mean anything, does ascribe a personality to the Tempter so distinct and unmistakable, that a denial of it can be only compatible with a practical denial of Scripture inspiration."[18]

Paul's statement makes it clear that Satan does have the power to hinder and frustrate the work of Christ's servants. He is the great adversary who constantly opposes the work of God and disrupts God's people and their service. But Satan is not omnipotent; he is able to work only within the limits allotted to him by God (Job 1:12; 2:6). Satan may "cut in on us" and prevent us from doing what we feel is best, but the omniscient God allows it for a higher purpose.

Paul did not indiscriminately attribute all hindrances to his plans to the work of the devil. When he was prevented from preaching in Asia and Bithynia (Ac 16:6-7) he recognized the closed doors as God's negative leading. Behind the various details of his life Paul perceived the reality of the conflict between the forces of good and evil. At times he clearly recognized the hand of God in keeping him from certain courses of action. Here he knew that the hindrance was so manifestly satanic in origin as to leave the source undoubted. The indwelling Spirit enabled Paul to recognize the distinction between the two. Hogg and Vine remark that this ability to distinguish divine and satanic hindrances "is a spiritual attainment, the way to which lies through obedience to the word of God."[19] He knew how to test the spirits (1 Jn 4:1, NASB).

b) DEEP AFFECTION FOR THEM (vv. 19-20). *For* explains that behind the eager desire of Paul to return was his deep love for them, which Satan would never be able to hinder. Paul and his companions held a very high esteem for the readers. They are thoroughly "proud" of such converts. The warmth of Paul's feelings toward them is expressed in a decidedly rhetorical manner, "one of the few rhetorical passages in the Epistle."[20] But the eloquence employed is the eloquence of a loving heart. Only the Philippian church is addressed with equal emotional fervor.

Paul first asks who might be the objects of such esteem (v. 19a), asks a second question which implies the answer (v. 19b), and then makes his categorical assertion (v. 20).

(1) *Question asked* (v. 19a). "What is our hope, or joy, or crown of glorying?" The interrogative pronoun (*tis*) may be rendered either "what"

or "who." Because the three nouns are nonpersonal it is generally rendered "what," but since persons constitute the hope, joy, and crown it would be better to render "who" (Moffatt, Phillips, Berkeley, NASB).

The remainder of the verse makes it clear that the point of view in the question is eschatological. Rhetorically he asks, "Who is it that is 'our hope, or joy, or crown of glorying' in that glorious day when both writers and readers will stand before the Lord?" "Our *hope*," standing first among the three suggestions, implies that his converts will not fail him and will in that day fulfill his missionary hopes for them.

"Our *joy*" looks forward to the joy and gladness Paul anticipates in that future day. They will be true objects of the missionaries' joy when their hopes for them are realized and the beloved converts are glorified with them in that day.

"Our *crown of glorying*" looks forward to the victor's crown with which the missionaries will be rewarded for their labors in that day. The word for *crown* was used of the laurel wreath or garland with which the victors in the Greek games were crowned. Thus Paul pictures himself standing before the judgment seat of Christ and in the presence of his converts receiving his crown. It is the soul-winner's crown. But the sight of his beloved converts with him in glory will make them truly his crown "of glorying." The word for *glorying* is generally rendered "boasting" or "rejoicing." Their presence will represent success and triumph and stimulate true exultation in the heart of the missionaries. It denotes the inward feeling of joy as well as its outward expression.

(2) *Answer suggested* (v. 19*b*). Having asked who it might be that formed any one or all three of these to him, Paul now rephrases his question to strongly suggest the answer. "Are not even ye, before our Lord Jesus at his coming?" The negative introducing the question (*ouchi*, a strengthened form of *ou*) implies a strong affirmative answer. "Who could it be if it is not you?" This second question makes explicit what was implicit in the first.

Many scholars adopt an alternative punctuation for Paul's double question. They take the words "Are not even ye" as a parenthetical question thrown in before the first question is completed. Thus the Greek text of Nestle places a dash before and after them.* Milligan in accepting this view remarks that the parenthesis is "interjected into the main sentence to draw special attention to the position of the Thessalonians."[21] Moffatt phrases the verse, "For who is our hope, our joy, our crown of pride (who but you?) in the presence of our Lord Jesus on his arrival?" Lattey apparently feels the awkwardness of the parenthesis and prefers to place it

---

*The dashes are also used by Westcott and Hort and the Bible Societies' Greek text. Souter punctuates v. 19 as two consecutive questions.

as the end: "For what shall be our hope or joy or crown of glorying before our Lord Jesus at his coming? Shall it not be you?"

Lenski objects to this reduction of Paul's second question to a brief parenthesis and insists that this makes a weak and awkward break and would not occur to the ordinary reader.[22] It disregards the proper disjunctive force of the particle *ē* (or) which introduces the second question. This particle, generally omitted in the translations, serves to add a rhetorical question, "or," to state it in another way. It carries forward the preceding question to its logical eschatological conclusion. We accept the view that Paul's words consist of two correlated questions.

"Before our Lord Jesus at his coming" looks forward to that happy day when all that the writers hope and feel concerning their Thessalonian converts will be realized. Paul and his co-workers did all of their work in the light of that future day. This of course makes it unthinkable that what the missionaries are now asserting concerning their deep affection for the readers should be a false claim.

Paul's use of the title "our Lord Jesus" is a ringing testimony that he has accepted as his own Master the heavenly *Lord* who is one and the same with the historical *Jesus*. This title, "the Lord Jesus" occurs nine times in the Thessalonian epistles but is comparatively rare in the other Pauline epistles.† It is appropriate in these letters where the theme of the return of the glorified Lord Jesus is prominent. So Paul adds "at his coming."

The word rendered "coming" (*parousia*) is Paul's first use, chronologically, of this important New Testament term for the return of Christ. It is composed of *para,* "alongside of," and the substantival form of the verb *eimi,* "to be." It literally means "a being alongside of one," hence, "presence." In Philippians 2:12 Paul uses it of his personal presence in that city. In the secular language of the day it was the usual word for a royal visit to a certain city or district. In the New Testament it is one of the most frequently used words for the return of Christ. It is sometimes used in the sense of "coming, arrival" as pointing to the act by which the "presence" is brought about; but this marks only the first stage of the *parousia* which centers the attention rather on the stay which follows the arrival. Hendriksen well remarks that the term denotes "his 'coming' in order to bless his people with his presence." Walvoord points out that the contribution which this term makes to the doctrine of the second advent "is to emphasize the bodily presence of Christ—His coming as a Bridegroom for the bride." Hogg and Vine further note that the basic meaning

†The word "Christ" does not appear here in the best texts. The fuller expression "the Lord Jesus Christ" occurs 14 times in the Thessalonian epistles.

of *parousia* as "presence" involves the thought of a definite period, "a period with a beginning, a course, and a conclusion."[23]

(3) *Answer asserted* (v. 20). Following his question and his suggested answer Paul records the emphatic assertion, "For ye are our glory and our joy." *For* serves to confirm and assert what he has already implied. The *ye* is emphatic; "indeed it is really you who are our glory and our joy." It contrasts the reality with the false insinuations of the enemies of Paul. Ye *are* now, and will be in the future, "our glory and our joy." The personal pronoun *our* intensifies the *glory* or esteem in which the Thessalonian believers are held, while *joy* points to the inner feeling of delight which the missionaries have in them.

2. Sending of Timothy to Them

3:1-5   Wherefore when we could no longer forbear, we thought it good to be left behind at Athens alone; (2) and sent Timothy, our brother and God's minister in the gospel of Christ, to establish you, and to comfort *you* concerning your faith; (3) that no man be moved by these afflictions; for yourselves know that hereunto we are appointed. (4) For verily, when we were with you, we told you beforehand that we are to suffer affliction; even as it came to pass, and ye know. (5) For this cause I also, when I could no longer forbear, sent that I might know your faith, lest by any means the tempter had tempted you, and our labor should be in vain.

These verses follow as a direct consequence of what has just been affirmed (2:16-20). Since Paul's efforts to return to Thessalonica had been frustrated, the next best thing was to send Timothy to them. Paul recounts the circumstances which prompted the sending (v. 1), names and characterizes the person sent (v. 2*a*), and states the purpose in the sending in relation to the Thessalonians (vv. 2*b*-4) and to himself (v. 5).

a) CIRCUMSTANCES BEHIND THE SENDING (v. 1). *Wherefore* reaches back to all that was said in the preceding paragraph and uses it to explain the action now delineated. This paragraph contains nothing essentially new to the readers but it serves an apologetic purpose in revealing the inner feelings and motives of the writer. Paul again assures his readers that he was far from being indifferent toward them; Timothy was sent to them because he was personally unable to gratify his fervid desire to revisit them.

"When we could no longer forbear" renders a negative circumstantial participle (*mēketi stegontes*), "being no longer able to forbear." If the negative is held to retain its classical subjective tinge it points to the subjective feelings of the writers in taking the action. But this need not be insisted on since in the New Testament *mē* rather than *ou* is the regular negative with participles.

The plural participle connects with the plural subject of the following verb and again raises the question of the force of Paul's "we" in this paragraph. Morris maintains that "we" here can only refer to Paul himself; he remarks that "this seems clear from the plural form of the adjective 'alone,' which yet can only refer to Paul."[24] This is the view of numerous commentators and some of the translators.‡ But others, like Lenski, insist that the plural should be given its natural meaning as including all three of the writers, that all three agreed upon the plan adopted. Plummer comments that the plural "includes Silvanus as joining in the sending, and Timothy as consenting to the arrangement."[25] The plural of the adjective *alone* is then to be understood as stressing that the loneliness to which Paul was consigned by the plan was jointly accepted as part of the decision.

The everyday correspondence of Paul's time makes it evident that the editorial "we" was at times used, but not all the instances cited in support of it are by any means positive examples of it. Its use by Paul is possible, and if there are passages in his epistles where the "we" is best understood of Paul alone, an editorial "we" may be adopted. But Paul's consistent use of the first person plural in the Thessalonian epistles makes it probable that the plural here also carries its full weight and is intended to include his two companions.[26] That the "we" here is intended to have its full weight seems supported by the fact that in verse 5 Paul carefully employs the singular to distinguish himself from his companions.

The verbal form translated *forbear* (*stegō*) literally means "to cover." It may be used as meaning to cover that which is placed under it, "to keep in" in the sense of contain, or conceal; it may also be used as meaning to support that which is placed upon it, "to hold out against" the pressure of circumstances. Either meaning is possible here and has its adherents. Thus Rotherham renders, "no longer concealing our anxiety," while Darby has, "being no longer able to refrain ourselves." Swete refers to the figure of a watertight vessel and comments, "The floodgates of the Apostle's full heart were at length forced to open by the pressure of his love; he could no longer refrain from an expression of his inward feelings."[27] But it is difficult to see why Paul should speak about attempting to conceal his feelings when in this portion of the letter he takes pains to stress his unconcealed affections for the readers. Lünemann insists that this interpretation is "contrary to the context."[28] The meaning of endurance is preferable here, "we could endure it no longer" (Weymouth), or "stand it any longer" (Berkeley). This is in harmony with the context as well as Paul's use of the verb elsewhere (1 Co 9:12, and apparently 1 Co

‡Conybeare, Montgomery, and Way show no distinction between the "we" in vv. 1-4 and the "I" in v. 5 but have "I" throughout; Moffatt, Goodspeed, and Williams use the singular in vv. 1-3 but keep "we" in v. 4 as relating to Christians generally.

13:7). Lightfoot feels that "the usage of the word in later Greek seems decidedly in favour of" this sense.[29]

The present tense, denoting linear action, indicates that they were unable to continue enduring the suspense that they felt because of the lack of personal communication with the Thessalonians. The continued separation from their beloved converts and the lack of information about their reaction under the pressure of persecution produced a strain of suspense that was unbearable. And there was ground for feeling anxious about their converts. If the unbelieving Jews were so relentless in their antagonism to the gospel as to hound the missionaries all the way to Berea, what might they be doing to their followers at home? The load of suspense was so heavy that they felt that they had to take some action.

When the strain of suspense grew intolerable, the missionaries adopted a definite plan of action. "We thought it good" indicates that a definite decision was made. The original verb here is the same as that rendered "we were well pleased" in 2:8 and signifies that the plan of action decided upon was accepted with hearty goodwill. It was the free and deliberate choice on the part of all three.

Silvanus and Timothy concurred in the plan which meant that Paul was "to be left behind at Athens alone." This assumes the presence of Silvanus and Timothy with Paul in Athens at the time. It raises the problem of the movements of Silvanus and Timothy. From Acts 17:15 we learn that some of the Bereans conducted Paul to Athens and returned with a commandment from Paul to Silas and Timothy to join him at Athens with all speed. But Luke says nothing about Silas and Timothy joining Paul at Athens as requested; he does record that later both rejoined Paul after he had gone on to Corinth (Ac 18:5). Thus there is an apparent divergence between Acts and this epistle. This leads Plummer to remark, "The divergence in the accounts is evidence that this Epistle is not a forgery constructed out of Acts, as Baur and others have supposed."[30]

Two different ways of reconciling the Acts account with this statement have been suggested. Some propose that Timothy was dispatched to Thessalonica from Berea rather than Athens. This implies that Paul's orders for them to come to Athens were never carried out. Then apparently Silas remained at Berea while Timothy made the trip to Thessalonica, and together they rejoined Paul at Corinth.

This reconstruction presents some difficulties. It raises the question of how Timothy learned that he was to go to Thessalonica when Paul sent orders that he was to come to Athens. Lenski holds that Luke's aorist in Acts 17:15 implies that Silas and Timothy did actually come to Athens as ordered.[31] Under this view it is necessary to assume that "we" means Paul alone. Paul's words "and sent Timothy" naturally implies his presence with Paul; but under this view Paul, to be accurate, should have written "we instructed that Timothy should go" or "ordered Timothy to go." Further, this view is inconsistent with the precise meaning of the infinitive "to be left behind" (*kataleiphthēnai*) which means that Paul was "left behind" because of the departure of others. As Lightfoot points out, if Timothy was sent to Thessalonica without seeing Paul at Athens "the proper word would have been *menein* [to remain] or at most *leiphthēnai* [to be left]."[32] The view that Timothy went to Thessalonica directly from Berea is improbable.

The better reconciliation is to accept that Silas and Timothy did come to Athens as requested. They probably brought fresh news of the viciousness of the Thessalonian Jews. Upon their arrival at Athens all three felt such deep concern for the Thessalonian believers that it was decided that Timothy should hurry back to Thessalonica. The adjective *alone*, standing forcibly last, indicates that Timothy was missed by Silvanus and Paul. Apparently Silas was also soon dispatched on a mission to Macedonia, leaving Paul all alone in his work at Athens as Acts says he was. From Acts 18:5 it is clear that Silas and Timothy had both been in Macedonia before rejoining Paul at Corinth. Perhaps Paul was concerned as to what the Thessalonian Jews might do to his converts at Philippi and sent Silas back to that city. This reconstruction assumes that Luke is silent about this trip to Athens on the part of Silas and Timothy, a supposition fully consistent with the known nature of Luke's narrative. It also permits Paul's words to be taken at their full significance.

For Paul thus to be left all alone at Athens was no easy matter for him. The verb "to be left behind" may quite literally be translated "to be forsaken or abandoned" (cf. Heb 11:27; 2 Pe 2:15) and implies the feeling of loneliness and desolation which swept over him when left all alone in Athens. Paul made it a practice of having with him some co-worker whenever he began a work in a new place and apparently he was at his best when he had the assistance of another in the work. Paul's statement that he was willing thus to be left behind alone indicates that it was a sacrifice for him, "but he would not gratify himself at the expense of the Thessalonians."[33] It is another incidental proof of his genuine love for his Thessalonian converts.

The very atmosphere of the city of Athens helped to intensify Paul's feeling of loneliness. Its prevailing spirit and viewpoint were uncongenial to his ardent temperament. He saw that its inhabitants were very religious but recognized that they were hopelessly estranged from God. But most trying to him was the intellectual curiosity coupled with the moral indifference which he encountered there. Denney remarks, "Never had he been left alone in a place so unsympathetic; never had he felt so great a gulf fixed between others' minds and his own."[34]

b) Designation of the one sent (v. 2*a*). The person sent to Thessalonica is first named and then described. "And sent Timothy" states the historical fact. The verb is the general word for sending and means that Timothy was sent to do something.

It has been asked why Timothy should be able to return to Thessalonica when Paul could not. Paul does not stop to explain. It has been suggested that Timothy had not aroused the ire of the Thessalonian Jews like Paul had as the leader of the missionary party. If Timothy was at Thessalonica during the founding of the church there, as a young man he had not taken a prominent part in the work and so had not been marked out for personal attack. Lenski, however, maintains that Timothy could be sent because he, unlike Paul and Silvanus, had not been driven out of Thessalonica.[35] He assumes that Timothy did not have a part in the original mission at Thessalonica, hence could be sent without encountering the hostility of the Jews.§

Timothy is characterized as "our brother and God's minister in the gospel of Christ." Paul and Silvanus esteem the younger man as "our brother," a fellow-member in the family of God. It marks the brotherly relation maintained by servants of Christ among themselves. But perhaps *our* is not to be restricted to Paul and Silvanus; it may be used inclusively to denote that Timothy is also a brother to the Thessalonian believers. Thus Swete remarks, "As the younger brother of their father in the faith, the Christians of Thessalonica would learn to regard him very highly."[36]

"And God's minister in the gospel of Christ" describes Timothy in his relation to the Lord. *Minister* is not an official title and does not connote an ordained minister in the modern sense of the term. The word rather designates one who renders a service of some kind to another. It speaks of the servant in relation to his work, stressing his activity of serving. Our English word *deacon* is derived from the Greek term. The possessive rendered "God's" stresses that Paul acknowledges his young friend as a diligent, hard-working servant in the employment of God. The Thessalonian believers were to receive the benefit of his services.

"In the gospel of Christ" describes more precisely the sphere of Timothy's service. He renders service in connection with and in the interest of the gospel of Christ. His efforts are aimed at furthering "the gospel [the good news or glad tidings] of Christ." The genitive "of Christ" may be interpreted as either a subjective or objective genitive. Under the former it denotes the gospel which is Christ's, which He has ordained to

§See Introduction, p. 14.

be preached; under the latter it points to the gospel which tells of Christ, the good news about Him as Saviour. The latter seems to be the meaning here. The expression "the gospel of God" (2:2, 8, 9) most naturally means the gospel which is God's, which He has sent; this expression points to the gospel which tells about Christ.

There is, however, considerable confusion in the manuscripts as to the true reading for this second element in the description of Timothy. The Greek manuscripts and ancient versions have a considerable variety of readings. The textual problems are whether the true reading is "minister" or "fellow-worker" and whether to include or omit "of God." The textual critics do not agree in their conclusions. Westcott and Hort, as well as Souter, decide for "minister of God," while Nestle and the Bible Societies' text adopt "fellow-worker of God." The omission of the genitive "of God" makes a smooth reading and nicely attaches itself to the "our" before "brother." But if this was the original reading, it is difficult to account for it in the other readings. It is more probable that it represents a scribal omission than an addition. The reading "and minister of God in the gospel of Christ" has somewhat stronger manuscript support. Findlay remarks that the adjunct "in the gospel of Christ" hardly suits the reading "fellow-worker of God" "since *God's* part has been emphatically contrasted with that of His servants 'in the good news of the Christ.' "[37] Advocates of the reading "fellow-worker of God" insist that it is more probable that a scribe would alter this bold and striking expression to the more familiar "minister of God" than the reverse. But such a scribal substitution is questionable in view of 1 Corinthians 3:9. Although the expression "minister of God" occurs three times outside this passage (Ro 13:4 twice; 2 Co 6:4), this is the only place where Paul uses it of Timothy personally. Admittedly the original reading will remain a matter of debate, but it seems best to accept the better attested reading followed in our version, "God's minister in the gospel of Christ."

Different reasons have been assigned for this eulogy which Paul pronounces upon Timothy. Lünemann insisted that the epithets applied to Timothy were nothing more than Paul's spontaneous outpouring of his personal esteem for his faithful and zealous young co-worker. He objected to finding in it any apologetic significance and saw in it simply another instance of Paul's constant practice of honoring his faithful associates.[38]

Others, however, do see an apologetic significance in the characterization. Calvin held that Paul thus wished to indicate to the Thessalonians what an important emissary he had sent them and what a great sacrifice he had put himself to for the sake of the readers. Lenski insists that Paul thus speaks of Timothy "not (as Chrysostom states it) to honor Timothy, but rather to honor the Thessalonian congregation to which he was sent." Plummer thinks that it can be safely inferred "that some Thessalonians were not sufficiently aware of the value of Timothy as a teacher."[39]

That the epithets applied to Timothy were entirely without any apologetic significance seems questionable in view of the clear apologetic character of this portion of the epistle. But that it was a sincere expression of Paul's appreciation of Timothy is unquestioned. It seems best to hold that Paul thus seeks to underline the importance of Timothy's visit to Thessalonica. He had sent to them no unworthy substitute but a man fully capable of carrying out the mission assigned to him. It was another indication that Paul was concerned about the spiritual welfare of the readers.

c) PURPOSE IN THE SENDING (vv. 2*b*-5). The purpose in sending Timothy is first stated in relation to the readers (vv. 2*b*-4) and then from the side of Paul himself (v. 5).

(1) *In relation to the Thessalonians* (vv. 2*b*-4). The statement of purpose in relation to the Thessalonians falls into two parts. Paul first indicates the task assigned to Timothy (vv. 2*b*-3*a*) and then supports this with a reminder of the teaching which had been given them (vv. 3*b*-4).

(*a*) *Designated task* (vv. 2*b*-3*a*). The primary task assigned to Timothy was "to establish you, and to comfort you concerning your faith." In the original the two infinitives are united under the government of one article to form one idea; they are the two parts of a whole. The latter will be the means of achieving the former. The statement indicates the contemplated result Timothy was to achieve at Thessalonica.

In the unavoidable absence of Paul, Timothy was to *establish* and *comfort* them. The first verb means "to strengthen, to fix, make firm or solid." It contains the thought of making firm or solid by providing a support or buttress. Timothy is to establish the Thessalonian converts by providing them with the needed mental and spiritual support. Mason suggested that this "establishing" consisted in the perfecting of "their organisation," which would befit the thinking of an organizationally-minded ecclesiastic.[40] The second verb has a variety of meanings according to its context. In view of verse 3 the rendering "comfort" here seems somewhat misleading. The thought is not that the Thessalonians are to be consoled but rather that they are to be encouraged and exhorted. Timothy's task was not to soothe them in their sorrow but to fit them for the battle "concerning your faith." Milligan thinks that the preposition rendered *concerning* (*huper*) here retains "something of its original force 'for the advantage or benefit of.'"[41] Timothy's work was for the good of their faith, that they might preserve and strengthen it.

Faith here refers primarily to the personal trust which the Thessalonian believers had placed in the Saviour who had been preached to them. Although faith here does not mean "your creed," the term should not be stripped of all objective connotation; a valid Christian faith must have a definite objective content. This unexpanded expression, "your faith," indicates how central and all-comprising this concept of faith is to the Christian life. *Your* denotes that the readers had made this faith their own through their personal trust in the gospel message.

This twofold task assigned to Timothy shows that Paul was well aware that a spectacular conversion was not enough; the converts also needed to be established and grounded in the faith. No small part of Paul's missionary labors were devoted to the establishing and strengthening of his converts (cf. Ac 15:32, 41; 16:5; 18:23; Ro 1:11; 16:25). Paul felt that their premature separation from the Thessalonian converts had not given the missionaries sufficient time to establish and train them in their faith. That this important task was assigned to his young assistant demonstrates his confidence in Timothy's abilities. Ellicott remarks that this does "not seem in accord with the timid character which Alford ascribes to the apostle's faithful fellow-worker."[42]

In the first part of verse 3 we have the statement of a secondary purpose for Timothy's ministry, "that no man be moved by these afflictions." The realization of this negative purpose is dependent upon the realization of the preceding positive purpose. This articular infinitive construction stands in apposition with the preceding infinitives of purpose. They will be kept from the danger indicated if they are effectively established and grounded in the faith. The present passive infinitive with the negative indicates that this is something they must not allow to happen to them.

The precise force of the verb rendered "be moved" (*sainesthai*), occurring only here in the New Testament, is not certain. It basically means "to shake, to sway back and forth," and was properly used of a dog wagging his tail. From this it came to mean "to fawn upon, to flatter," hence conveying the thought of being deceived. Then the verb came generally to denote any act of shaking, as synonymous with *saleuō*, "to shake, to cause to move to and fro."

The Greek interpreters and ancient versions generally understood Paul's word here in the latter sense. They rendered "to be moved, disturbed, or agitated." Then the meaning is that the Thessalonians are warned against being disquieted, or wavering in their faith. This meaning is also accepted by many modern scholars. The Berkeley version translates, "so that none may be disturbed by these distresses," while Conybeare has, "that none of you should waver in these afflictions."

Milligan feels that this interpretation of the term "is to lose sight un-

necessarily of the original meaning of the word."[43] Proceeding from the
picture of a dog wagging his tail, Milligan and others hold that the word
here has a metaphorical connotation, "to fawn upon, to flatter, or beguile."
Then the meaning is that Paul feared that the Thessalonians might be
allured and drawn away from their faith amid their afflictions by the
friendly words of non-Christians who sought to induce them to give up
their new faith in order to escape persecution. Thus Williams renders,
"that none of you might be deceived amid these difficulties," and Goodspeed has, "not to be led astray, any of you, in all these troubles." Frame
holds that this latter interpretation "is on the whole preferable."[44]

Under this interpretation it is not certain whether these subtle opponents of the faith, employing professedly friendly appeals to get the
believers to renounce their Christianity, were Jews or Gentiles. Frame
thinks that it admirably fits "the cajoling insinuations of the Jews who
would coax the converts away from the new faith on the pretence that persecution is evidence that the gospel which they welcomed is a delusion."[45]
Lenski conceives of them as "pagan friends of the Thessalonians who are
sorry to see them cling to their faith and to suffer the consequent persecutions."[46] In either case the appeal would be a subtle and dangerous
form of temptation to abandon their faith. If they were the appeals of
well-meaning Gentile friends they would be especially hard to resist. Men
who could not be moved by threats have been swayed by the sincere but
misguided entreaties of well-meaning friends. "The Devil is often more
to be feared when he fawns, than when he roars."[47]

"By these afflictions" is literally "in or amid these afflictions." The
afflictions are not the instrument of temptation but the circumstances
which gave these appeals their attractiveness. "These afflictions" points
to the ill will and persecution which the Thessalonians were enduring
because of their new faith, but probably the reference includes any and
all afflictions which Christians must endure because of their faith.

(*b*) *Supporting reminder* (vv. 3*b*-4). *For* introduces a supporting
reason for the preceding negative purpose. This effort to put them on
guard against the temptation to give up their faith amid affliction was in
harmony with the teaching Paul had given them.

"For yourselves know that hereunto we are appointed." *Yourselves*
is emphatic, "as for yourselves, you well know" from previous instruction
and personal experience "that hereunto we are appointed." *Hereunto* is
literally "into this thing;" the comprehensive singular, "this," is now used
to summarize the previous plural, "these afflictions." The *we* includes
the writers as well as the readers; it is a general statement that is true
for all Christians. This is the first time in this epistle that the "we" is
thus generalized.

The verb rendered "are appointed" basically means "to lie in place," hence "to be set, appointed, destined." Believers are set or stationed at their post in life to suffer for God. The world being what it is, such sufferings cannot be avoided. They are part of God's plan for the believer in this life, and they have a necessary function to perform in the achievement of His purpose for us. Calvin remarks that afflictions "are the terms on which we are Christians."[48] To his suffering converts won on the first missionary journey Paul expressed it as a moral necessity that "through many tribulations we must enter into the kingdom of God" (Ac 14:22). Thus the suffering Thessalonians may take courage from the fact that their suffering as believers is no untoward accident which has unexpectedly befallen them; it is part of God's appointment for them. And as such they may be assured not only of its necessity but also of its beneficial purpose (Mt 5:10-12; Jn 16:33; 8:17-18; 2 Ti 2:10-13; 1 Pe 4:12-14).

Verse 4 adds the further supporting reminder that they were forewarned that affliction would befall them as believers. "For verily" (*gar kai*), "for also" (Darby), serves to stress this additional elucidation. "When we were with you" looks back to the time when the missionaries were still in a mutual face-to-face relationship with (*pros*) their readers. Then "we told you beforehand that we are to suffer affliction." The imperfect tense of the verb *told* means that this warning was repeatedly given, "we *kept* telling you in advance" (NASB). He had plainly told them *beforehand*, in advance of its actual arrival, that suffering would be the inevitable result of accepting the gospel. In this Paul wisely followed the example of Christ who graciously warned His disciples that trouble awaited them (Jn 13:19; 14:29).

To leave converts unwarned of the possible adverse personal consequences of their acceptance of the gospel is to do them a serious injustice. Of this Paul had not been guilty. Paul apparently made it a constant practice to warn his new converts that tribulation was likely to come upon them (Ac 14:22).

He repeated his prediction at Thessalonica, "we are to suffer affliction." The *we* again is general and denotes Christians as such. Montgomery renders, "that I was to suffer affliction." But thus to restrict the prediction to Paul personally is entirely unwarranted. The missionaries as well as their converts were subject to the certainty of coming affliction. The verb rendered "we are" (*mellomen*) means "to be about to, to be on the point of" doing or experiencing something. It implies that that which is to come is inevitable, destined according to the counsel of God. Thus, Way has it, "to be afflicted is our destiny."

The infinitive given as "to suffer affliction" is from the verb *thlibō*, "to press together," hence, to oppress, distress, trouble, afflict by the application of pressure from without. The present tense indicates that the pressure will be continuous or repeatedly applied while the passive voice suggests that the pressure upon believers will be exerted by an outside agent. Thus, Williams brings out the force quite well, "that we were going to be pressed with difficulties."

"Even as it came to pass" is an appeal to the facts of the case. Their experience of affliction came in fulfillment of his predictions. This verification of his words should encourage them and strengthen their faith. It is an assurance that the missionaries knew what they were talking about. "And ye know" is an appeal to their own experience. They could personally testify that his predictions had been no empty saying.

(2) *In relation to Paul* (v. 5). Having spoken of the sending of Timothy in relation to the Thessalonians, Paul now speaks of his own concern in that sending. "For this cause" looks back to verse 4, because the foretold tribulation has actually befallen the readers. His knowledge of that fact increased his personal concern for them. "I also" makes emphatic that he personally as the leader of the missionary group could not resist feeling a deep concern for his afflicted converts. The sending of Timothy as the joint action of the writers has already been mentioned; now he reverts to the singular, not as implying that the others did not share this feeling of concern, but to enable him to speak more explicitly of his own personal feeling and motive. He informs them what the sending of Timothy meant for him personally.

Paul acted to relieve the intolerable burden of suspense that he personally felt because of the lack of information as to how the Thessalonians reacted under the storm of persecution. He explains that he "sent that I might know your faith." In view of what has been said just above (vv. 1-2), Paul does not feel it necessary to repeat that Timothy was sent. The suggestion of some that Paul in his impatience sent another messenger, after the departure of Timothy, with the enquiry here stated is without foundation. The deliberate resumption of the previous wording as well as verse 6 make it unmistakable that Timothy was the only emissary sent to Thessalonica.

His own purpose in sending was "that I might know your faith." The aorist infinitive translated "know" is ingressive and means "to get to know, to ascertain." He desired to learn the condition of their faith, to gain experiential confirmation on the matter of how their faith was holding up under persecution. Mason remarks that "the form courteously implies that the faith was certainly *there*, and St. Paul only sent to 'make assurance doubly sure.' "[49]

Paul now reveals the haunting fear that assailed him, "lest by any means the tempter had tempted you, and our labor should be in vain." He sent in order that he might get the assurance that this haunting possibility had not been achieved by "the tempter." The reference is to Satan who to Paul was a very real and terrible opponent of the gospel. But Paul does not now identify the foe by his name but by his characteristic activity. The present participle pictures him as persistently engaged in the effort to destroy the faith of the Thessalonians through temptation. He never gives up his sinister efforts. This participial designation, "the tempter," is found elsewhere in Scripture only in Matthew 4:3. He who was the tempter of our Lord is also the tempter of His people. That the participial subject and the verb both are from the same stem gives emphasis to Satan's tempting activity. The verb means, first, "to try, attempt" to do something; then "to make trial of, to put to the test," and so to search out, to discover what kind of person someone is. It may be used of God or Christ in a good sense as putting men to the test in order that they may stand approved; but used of the devil it always has a bad connotation, to test in order to disapprove. It is always the devil's aim to entice men to sin and bring them to a fall.

The verb translated "had tempted" is aorist indicative and describes a past fact. Paul takes for granted that the temptation has actually taken place. He knew that the tempter had been busy at Thessalonica. But at the time of sending he did not know the outcome of that tempting activity. This uncertainty is indicated by his use of the aorist subjunctive in the expression "and our labor should be in vain." It was his apprehension of this dread possibility that caused Paul such anxiety about the Thessalonians. There was the possible outcome that "our labor," the wearisome toil which the missionaries had expended at Thessalonica, might turn out to have been "in vain" ("should come to nothing"—Darby). The possibility was that it should prove to be an empty thing, like a nut without a kernel. Paul was fully aware that the final outcome of his labors was dependent upon the steadfastness of his converts.

The return of Timothy with his report brought the glad news that Paul's fears had not been realized. But that does not mean that they were unwarranted. Knowing the fierceness of the enemy attack and the fickleness of human nature, Paul's fears were altogether reasonable. Hendriksen points out that Paul's anxiety was fully consistent with his expressed conviction that the Thessalonians were God's elect (1:4) if we observe the true time sequence.[50] Paul well remembered the enthusiastic response that the Thessalonians had given to the preaching of the gospel. But he felt that the missionaries had been driven out before it could be established whether it was a mere emotional reaction or genuine faith. With the persecution sweeping over them would they prove to be mere enthusiastic "stony-soil" hearers who would be offended and forsake the gospel when made to suffer for it? It was this uncertainty that created the burden of suspense for the missionaries and propelled the sending of Timothy. The glad report of Timothy that the Thessalonians had not failed under testing and were standing firm in their faith convinced Paul that their conversion was truly genuine and that they were verily God's elect. His statement concerning their election was made after the confirmatory evidence was received; the experience of anxiety concerning them dated to the time prior to the reception of Timothy's report.

3. Effect of Timothy's Report About Them

3:6-13 But when Timothy came even now unto us from you, and brought us glad tidings of your faith and love, and that ye have good remembrance of us always, longing to see us, even as we also *to see* you; (7) for this cause, brethren, we were comforted over you in all our distress and affliction through your faith: (8) for now we live, if ye stand fast in the Lord. (9) For what thanksgiving can we render again unto God for you, for all the joy wherewith we joy for your sakes before our God; (10) night and day praying exceedingly that we may see your face, and may perfect that which is lacking in your faith?

(11) Now may our God and Father himself, and our Lord Jesus, direct our way unto you: (12) and the Lord make you to increase and abound in love one toward another, and toward all men, even as we also *do* toward you; (13) to the end he may establish your hearts unblamable in holiness before our God and Father, at the coming of our Lord Jesus with all his saints.

A time-break of unspecified duration comes in between this and the preceding paragraph. Having just spoken of the sending of Timothy to Thessalonica, Paul again takes up the writing at the time of his co-worker's return. How long Timothy had been absent is not indicated, but clearly he had remained long enough at Thessalonica to carry out his assignment and to gain an accurate insight into the conditions and needs of the young church.

Since the beginning of chapter 2 Paul has been reviewing the past. He has made an apologetic review of his relations to the Thessalonians while with them (2:1-16) and since being torn away from them (2:17-3:5). With this paragraph he passes from the past to the present. But even here the selection of material is influenced by the criticisms launched against him by his enemies at Thessalonica. The very nature of his reaction to the report of Timothy was proof of his affectionate concern for them. The report of their spiritual stability was vitally significant to him.

The return of Timothy with his report formed the immediate occasion for the writing of this letter. Since dispatching Timothy from Athens, Paul had moved on to Corinth where he busied himself with working at his trade and preaching in the synagogue (Ac 18:1-5). Paul's subdued missionary activities at Corinth before the return of Silas and Timothy (Ac 18:5) seems to indicate that Paul was deeply depressed because of the heavy burden of suspense and uncertainty concerning the outcome of his mission at Thessalonica. The anxiously awaited return of Timothy with his good news ended the night of suspense and brought the glad morning of joy and enthusiasm. The deep emotional notes of this paragraph afford a revealing insight into his character. It shows that Paul was "a man of high-strung and ardent nature, sensitive in his affections to an extreme degree. His whole soul was bound up with the Churches he had founded. . . . He lived for nothing else."[51]

In this paragraph Paul records the fact of Timothy's return with his good news about the Thessalonians (v. 6), gives an exuberant account of the reaction to the report (vv. 7-10), and concludes with another outburst of prayer because of the report (vv. 11-13).

a) Report brought by Timothy (v. 6). *But* sets in contrast the situation at the sending of Timothy and the joyous reaction to his message upon his return. Paul first speaks of the return of Timothy from the Thessalonians and then outlines the contents of his report.

(1) *His coming from them* (v. 6*a*). The historical fact of Timothy's return is stated in the words "when Timothy came even now unto us from you." Timothy's coming is doubtless the one mentioned in Acts 18:5. *When* represents the force of the genitive absolute construction of the aorist participle with the name of Timothy, "Timothy having come." It describes the occasion for the remainder of the sentence.

The adverb rendered "even now" (just now, immediately), stands emphatically at the beginning of the sentence. Grammatically it may be connected either with the participle "having come" or with the verb *"comforted"* in verse 7. Under the latter connection, advocated by Lünemann, the meaning is that Timothy's arrival brought immediate comfort and stimulus to Paul.[52] But this proposed connection is awkward and unnatural because of all that comes between the adverb and the verb. Against it is the fact that the verb already has its own adjunct, "for this cause," which refers back to the whole preceding sentence.

It is more natural to connect the adverb "even now" with the participle standing in close proximity. Then the meaning is that the return has just taken place and that under its stimulus Paul at once began the writing of this letter. Moffatt, accepting this connection, renders "when Timotheus reached me a moment ago." Neil calls this "a pardonable exaggeration, it may have been a day or two."[53] That enough time had passed for Timothy to give a comprehensive report is obvious, but the point is that Paul sat down to write while he was aglow with the good news brought by Timothy. If Paul had not written when his heart was overflowing with the inspiration of the occasion, his letter doubtless would have lacked some of its spontaneous glow of affection and joy. Denney draws the moral that we too should guard against "procrastination as a sin" when our hearts prompt us to write that letter of congratulation or condolence.[54]

In characterizing the coming of Timothy as being "unto us from you" Paul underlines the personal element involved. The wording of the New English Bible, "has just arrived from Thessalonica," is less intimate and cordial than the original. Paul's interest was not in the fact that Timothy has come from the city of Thessalonica but that his return directly from there had brought eagerly awaited personal information of their beloved converts there. In this paragraph this "us-you" emphasis is prominent. "Unto us" may imply that Silas had returned to Corinth a little before Timothy, but this cannot be pressed since he and Timothy may have arrived together. But the *us* indicates that Silas likewise joined in the joy which Timothy's report brought.

(2) *His report concerning them* (v. 6b). Paul summarizes Timothy's report in two parts. The first relates to the spiritual condition of the Thessalonians, the second to their personal attitude toward the missionaries.

"And brought us glad tidings of your faith and love" summarizes the good news of their spiritual condition. The very wording reveals his gratifying evaluation of the report. "Brought us glad tidings" translates an aorist participle of the verb *euanggelizomai*, from which we derive our English word "evangelize."|| It means "to bring or announce good news." He might instead of it have used "reported" but he prefers this expressive term to convey the cheerful effect the report had on its recipients. Elsewhere Paul always uses this verb to mean the preaching of the good news of the gospel. The news which Timothy brought was so good that it was a veritable gospel to him. Of course that report was not a part of the gospel message but did announce the outworking of the gospel in the lives of the Thessalonian converts. It was good news concerning the good news they had preached at Thessalonica. Calvin points out that Paul's enraptured response to the report was another argument "to show how remarkable was the affection which he bore towards" the readers.[55]

If the Thessalonians sent a letter along with Timothy, as some scholars advocate, surely this would have been the place to mention it. But Paul speaks only of his reaction to the report given by Timothy. Any failure on his part to indicate his joy on receiving their letter would have been a discourtesy.

|| It is in the genitive absolute as continuing the account of Timothy's further activity.

Timothy's good news told "of your faith and love." Both nouns have the definite article, "the faith and the love of you," making them specific and distinct. *Faith* is mentioned first as central and basic to their Christian life. Timothy had been sent because of the missionaries' deep concern about the continuity of their faith (3:2, 5). Timothy's report on this point was crucially important to Paul.

Faith speaks of their characteristic attitude Godward, while *love* is their characteristic attitude manward. Their faith had its most significant exhibition in love toward others, especially their Christian brethren. If their faith separated them from the world, their love united them more closely to each other. The two terms summarize their religious and ethical excellence. The two must always go together. Calvin remarks, "In these two words he states concisely the sum total of godliness."[56]

Paul here does not mention hope as the third member of the triad of Christian virtures, as he did in 1:3. Since so much of the remainder of the epistle will be devoted to a discussion of the Christian hope, Paul stresses the other two virtues here. In view of 4:13-18, the absence of hope here may imply that because of their problems concerning the future Paul did not feel a comparable joy concerning their hope.

The second part of the report relates to the Thessalonians' personal attitude to the missionaries. "And that ye have good remembrance of us always, longing to see us." The present tense of the verb, together with the adverb *always,* indicates that this has been and continues to be their attitude.# "Good remembrance of us" does not mean that they have a clear and vivid recollection of the missionaries but that their memories and thoughts of them are kindly and affectionate, as the following clause shows. Paul had wondered whether the slanderous propaganda of the enemies would be able to alienate his converts. He was therefore deeply grateful that "you cherish a constant and affectionate recollection of us" (Weymouth). It was evidence of a true Christian attitude on their part. Swete comments, "Loving remembrance of former teachers is a Christian duty, and, in connection with faith and love, a fair evidence of Christian character."[57]

Their affectionate attitude toward the missionaries was revealed in their constant "longing to see us." The compound participle translated *longing (epipothountes)* "denotes a tender yearning towards an absent beloved."[58] The present tense marks the continuity of the feeling, while the preposition *epi* indicates the direction of the feeling. It is a favorite word with Paul; he uses it seven out of the nine times it occurs in the New Testament.

#The adverb may be joined with the preceding verb or the following participle. As in 1:2, it is best joined to the verb to indicate the unceasing nature of the remembrance.

This yearning for reunion was mutual, "even as we also to see you." The missionaries gladly reciprocated the feeling of their converts. "Even as" marks the longing as equal on both sides. This is the third time that this "we-you" relationship is mentioned in this verse. The preservation of this affectionate relationship was important for Paul. He well knew that for the development of a strong and effective church at Thessalonica such a mutual respect and appreciation between founders and followers must be maintained.

b) REACTION TO TIMOTHY'S REPORT (vv. 7-10). "For this cause" recapitulates the different parts of the preceding statement. The singular *this* gathers up into one the different facets of Timothy's report and points to the total impact made. Again Paul affectionately addresses them as *brethren*, underlining the deep fraternal feelings which the report has strengthened.

Paul first speaks of the reviving comfort or encouragement that the report brought (vv. 7-8) and then informs the readers of the thanksgiving and prayer on their behalf that it evoked (vv. 9-10).

(1) *Experience of encouragement* (vv. 7-8). The historical fact was that because of the report "we were comforted over you in all our distress and affliction through your faith." The *we* unites Silvanus with Paul in this experience of comfort, and certainly Timothy himself, in bringing the report, shared that feeling. The aorist passive verb "were comforted" records that such was the reaction wrought in them by the report. As used here the verb may mean either "comforted" or "encouraged." Those who advocate "comforted" (Lenski) think of the feeling of anxiety which the missionaries had felt but which had entirely disappeared with the reception of the report. Others prefer to translate "encouraged" (Goodspeed) or "cheered" (Moffatt) and think of the strength and courage which the report brought to the missionaries in their difficult surroundings. While both thoughts may be present, the context supports the latter emphasis.

"Over you" (*eph' humin*) indicates that the encouragement experienced was directly based on the Thessalonians. They were the personal ground for the encouragement which the missionaries received "in all our distress and affliction." The two nouns *distress* and *affliction* are linked together under one article, thus forming two aspects of the whole difficult situation in which they find themselves. The former denotes a necessity or compulsion that forces itself upon one, while the latter indicates the crushing pressure to which one is being subjected. Both terms refer to the difficult external circumstances confronting the missionaries. It is precarious to seek to identify their precise cause or character. Findlay points out that the former "signifies *outward constraint*, whether of circumstances or duty" while the latter points to "*trouble from men.*"[59] But the word rendered "in" is again the preposition *epi*, "over," and implies that the distress and afflictions continued but the missionaries were able to surmount them and no longer feel them as evil. This helped to make the report so welcome. This reference to their own distress and affliction is a tactful reminder to the readers that Paul was also facing difficulties while away from them.

"Through your faith" states the means through which this encouragement was conveyed to the missionaries. Their steadfast faith wrought the stimulus. This is the fourth time that Paul mentions their faith in this chapter. This was the central point in his concern about them (3:2, 5) and formed the leading point in the encouraging report concerning them (v. 6). The other facets of the report would have been impossible if their faith had not proved steadfast and unshaken.

Verse 8 introduces the confirmation that the steadfastness of their faith is of vital significance to the missionaries. *For* translates the causal particle *hoti*, "because," indicating the reason. "Now we live, if ye stand fast in the Lord." Before there had been a dead weight of apprehension; they felt lifeless and had no enthusiasm. But *now*, in consequence of the news which Timothy brought, "we live," feel like we truly live, not just exist. The present tense indicates that this is not just a momentary reaction but an abiding inspiration.

Paul's words are a vivid rhetorical description of the contrast between the former state of apprehension, when they were ignorant concerning the reaction of the Thessalonians under persecution, and the ease of mind and encouragement produced by the news which Timothy brought. They felt that they had been given a new lease on life, could again go on living with a sense of fullness of power and satisfaction. Had the Thessalonians apostatized it would have been a veritable deathblow to Paul. "The success of the cause of Christ, *i.e.*, the winning of souls to Him, and the continuance of such souls in Him, was St. Paul's very life."[60] The fact that their faith had proved itself steadfast was a demonstration that their work of proclaiming the gospel at Thessalonica had been successful and this made life worthwhile for them.

"If ye stand fast in the Lord" expresses his assurance that they are standing firm but also contains a reminder that they must continue to stand firm in the future. *Ye* is emphatic, for in a very real way the triumph of the gospel depended upon them, not only at Thessalonica but also in the surrounding areas (cf. 1:8). The *if* does not imply doubt but with the indicative mode expresses the strong confidence of the writers. The fact is taken for granted. Thus Goodspeed can render, "since you are standing firm." But the conditional form of the statement serves to remind them that they have a continued responsibility to "stand fast." The verb (*stēkete*) is a late formation, formed from the perfect tense of the verb *histēmi*, "to stand," and carries the idea of firmness and stability. The present tense stresses that for the future they must go on standing firm, like soldiers repelling an enemy attack. "In the Lord" points out the sphere of their steadfastness. Their faith has brought them into a close vital union with "the Lord," Jesus Christ, and they must adhere steadfastly to Him.

(2) *Thanksgiving and prayer* (vv. 9-10). *For* connects with the preceding declaration and confirms the vigor of the new life which the missionaries are experiencing. This new life shows itself in the abundance of their thanksgiving for their converts (v. 9) as well as the earnestness of their prayer for them (v. 10).

(a) *Thanksgiving because of them* (v. 9). "What thanksgiving can we render again unto God for you, for all the joy wherewith we joy for your sakes before our God?" This rhetorical question (which grammatically extends through verse 10) is expressive of deep emotion. Its main thrust is that the writers feel themselves continually unable to return adequate thanks to God for all the joy which He has given them because of their converts. Fully aware that his words are but a poor and inadequate formulation of his thanksgiving, Paul yet attempts to give expression to the deep gratitude which he feels.

"To render again" translates the aorist active infinitive *antapodounai*, "to repay, recompense, requite," and that as a definite act. The simple verb, meaning "to give," is compounded with two prepositions, *anti*, marking the idea of a return or exchange for something received, and *apo*, referring to something which is due "from" us as a debt; the thought is that of a full and complete return for the boon that has been received. No thanksgiving in their power is equivalent to the debt of gratitude they owe God because of the joy He has given them. This third outburst of thanksgiving for the readers is called forth by the news of their steadfastness under persecution.

Their thanksgiving is due "unto God." That the Thessalonians stood steadfast is due not to the missionaries, or even to the converts, but to God Himself who has upheld them under the storm of persecution. Paul viewed all spiritual blessings as coming ultimately from God. What by human standards would have been regarded as a triumph for the missionaries, Paul humbly acknowledges to be the work of God. Let Christian workers beware of taking credit for results which only God can produce.

The thanksgiving which they owe God is for *you*, "concerning you," or "on your behalf" (Weymouth). The plural *you* indicates the Thessalonian converts as a group; together they form the center around which the thanksgiving of the missionaries turns. Paul does not thank them but thanks God for them. This is high encouragement for them but no occasion for personal pride.

They owe God their inexpressible thanks "for all the joy wherewith we joy." *For* translates the preposition *epi*, "upon, or over," and marks the ground and reason for the giving of thanks. Because of "all the joy," their joy in its sum totality, they owe God a greater debt of thanks than they can express. It is a continuing joy, as the present tense of the verb indicates.

The phrase "before our God" goes with the verb "*joy*," or "rejoice," but between them Paul inserts the phrase "for your sake" to emphasize that their rejoicing is intimately connected with the readers. "For your sake" is quite literally "because of you," and again stresses that their Thessalonian converts are the reason for their joy. Findlay points out that in verses 6-10 Paul uses the pronoun *you* "with an emphasis of affection" no less than ten different times.[61] Paul's heart delights to think of them. Having experienced deep anxiety on account of them, he now knows deep rejoicing because of them. "It is the experience of sorrow that enlarges the capacity of the heart for joy."[62]

"Before our God" further defines the nature of their joy. It is a joy "which is not so much personal as religious, and which therefore finds its constant outlet" before God.[63] That they are expressing it before "our God," the God with whom they stand in intimate personal relationship, indicates its purity. It is a joy which is given free rein in the presence of God without embarrassment, for it is uncontaminated by personal selfishness or worldly motives. We have here another instance of Paul's practice of lifting everything which came into his life, whether sad or glad, into the presence of God. Thus he lived in the sense of God's presence with him.

(*b*) *Prayer in regard to them* (v. 10). In the thinking and practice of Paul thanksgiving and prayer were closely related. He freely mingled his petitions for the Thessalonians with his heartfelt thanksgiving for them. The two were simultaneous and interwoven.

The praying of the writers is described by two adjuncts, both standing emphatically before the participle. It is first of all described as being offered "night and day." The terms are in the genitive to indicate that they are praying by night and by day, not all night and all day long. Again and again during the long hours of the night as well as during the busy hours of the day they lift their prayers to God for them. Garrod well remarks, "It is evident from St. Paul's Epistles that a very large part of his private life was occupied in prayer and thanksgiving to God."[64]

Their praying is further described as being *exceedingly*. This unusual adverb, occurring in the New Testament only at 5:13 and Ephesians 3:20, is a double compound form. It is made up of *perissou*, "abundantly," *ek*, "out of," and *huper*, "above, over, beyond," and thus means "abundantly beyond all measure, exceedingly overflowing all bounds, *superabundantly*." Findlay calls this strongly emphatic adverb "an almost extravagant intensive."[65] There was nothing perfunctory or halfhearted about their praying; it was exuberant and "with intense earnestness" (Weymouth), the spontaneous overflow of their hearts.

This twofold characterization of their praying is in harmony with the meaning of the participle rendered *praying* (*deomenoi*). The verb means "to ask, to beg" and implies that it is an asking that is motivated by a sense of personal need; it is asking for a personal favor. They felt that they had a vital personal interest in the petitions made. It would be better to translate "beseeching." This word is stronger than the common word rendered "praying" which indicates devotion towards the object of worship. The use of the present tense indicates that their "beseeching" is not an isolated act but their repeated practice.

The use of the participial construction to mention this praying indicates that their petitions are subsidiary to their efforts to adequately thank God for the blessing they have received. While they felt inadequate to thank God sufficiently for the Thessalonians, they did not, however, hesitate to express further petitions. Paul knew that praying which looked toward the spiritual welfare of others was always appropriate.

The content of their petitions is twofold, "that we may see your face, and may perfect that which is lacking in your faith." The two prayer requests are united under one article and thus form a unit. The request to be able to return to them would provide the opportunity to supply that which was lacking in the faith of the converts.

The first petition, "that we may see your face," is a request on behalf of the missionaries themselves. They ask for the joy of being able to have fellowship again with their beloved converts face-to-face. This matter of his return has been the point of his defense ever since 2:17. He has informed them that his efforts to return were hindered (2:18); he has assured them of his longing to see them again (3:6); now he indicates that it is a definite point in his prayers. Thus Paul takes every means to assure them that his absence is not a matter of his own choice. This petition to return was not granted until several years later.

Their second petition is that upon returning they "may perfect that which is lacking in your faith." The petition to be allowed to return is not merely for their personal gratification; it would enable them to further the spiritual welfare of their converts. They desire to assist their faith in achieving its stability and full development.

The verb translated "perfect" has the basic idea of fitting together, to order and arrange properly. It may be used of setting right what has previously gone wrong, to repair and restore to its former condition, whether mending broken nets or setting broken bones (Mt 4:21; Mk 1:19; Gal 6:1). It was also used to signify "to complete, make good that which is still needed" (Lk 6:40; He 13:21). It is clearly in the latter sense that it is used here. The meaning is not that something has gone wrong with the faith of the Thessalonians and that rectification is needed. Rather, Paul clearly recognized that the faith of their converts needed to be brought to its full development. This is indicated by the addition "that which is lacking in your faith." Not that the faith which they had was defective, but it still needed completing and rounding out. The substantive translated "that which is lacking" is plural and is quite literally "the short-comings, deficiencies." The plural indicates that more than one thing needed completing so that their faith might be brought to the place where it would fully discharge its intended function. Paul recognized that the work begun at Thessalonica was incomplete. Because they had been prematurely torn away from the work there they had not been able to do all that was needed. The missionaries yearned to return and, like skilled artisans, complete the task and put things in top working condition.

Although Paul was overflowing with thanksgiving for his converts, he had no illusions about their actual condition. He was not blind to their deficiencies and needs. He deeply appreciated what had already been attained, but he frankly acknowledged that they had not yet arrived. Calvin comments, "We learn from this that those who far outdistance others are still a long way from their goal."[66] Conversion is only the beginning. They still needed pastoral instruction and guidance.

Their faith had shown itself strong and steadfast under persecution; their defects of faith were not on the side of zeal and loyalty but of knowledge and insight. As novices in the faith they lacked a clear and reassuring view of Christian truth and insight regarding its practical application in daily life. Their faith needed to be perfected by giving them needed enlightenment, exhortations, and warnings. Instruction and admonition were necessary, but Paul was "wise enough to convey any correction or remonstrance on the back of hearty commendation."[67]

Paul yearned and prayed to be able to return to Thessalonica to deal with the deficiencies of his converts. Had he been able to return he would have dealt with them directly and orally. Paul doubtless shared the common feeling that "personal intercourse goes farther than letters in establishing the weak and wavering."[68] But since he was not able to return he dealt with their deficiencies in the second part of his letter. If he had been able to return we would not have the benefit of this invaluable epistle. Thus the success of Satan in blocking his return was divinely overruled for the instruction and enrichment of Christ's church down through the centuries.

c) PRAYER IN VIEW OF THE REPORT (vv. 11-13). These verses amplify the prayers mentioned in verse 10. They restate the petitions already indicated but emphasize the request which will remedy the deficiencies of the readers. First, there is the petition that God will open up the way for the writers to see the readers (v. 11), and second, a more elaborate petition for the readers' stabilization (vv. 12-13).

Recognition should be given to the fact that in actual statement these verses do not form a prayer addressed directly to God. They are rather a devout prayer-wish. The God to whom prayer is addressed is spoken of in the third person and the verbs are in the optative mode, used to express a wish. Yet the solemn tone of this fervent prayer-wish approaches the language of prayer and is virtually a prayer.

(1) *Petition concerning the writers* (v. 11). "Now may our God and Father himself and our Lord Jesus, direct our way unto you." The conjunction rendered "Now" (*de*) here is not adversative but serves to add an expansion of the petitions already indicated in verse 10. Paul gives an emphatic designation of the God to whom their prayer is addressed and states the petition being made for themselves.

The pronoun translated "himself" (*autos*) stands emphatically at the beginning of the sentence; it may be either reflexive or intensive. Our versions take it as reflexive, implying that God Himself, rather than they, must open the way to see the readers. But it seems better to take it as intensive, "Now may *He*," the God before whom they rejoice and to whom they are praying (vv. 9-10), grant this request.

The two titles *God* and *Father* are united under one article to refer to one person mentioned under two aspects. He who in His eternal existence is God is also our Father. The expression brings out the characteristic Christian truth that God has revealed Himself to us as a Father in the person of His Son. *Our* is confessional; it is best taken in an inclusive sense here. He is not only the God and Father of the missionaries but also of the readers, and of all Christians.

"And our Lord Jesus" names Him as the corecipient of the petition. The original is literally, "the Lord of us, Jesus;" the name *Jesus* stands in apposition with "the Lord" as identifying the Lord with the human Jesus (cf. 2:15). The *our* again is confessional, pointing to the distinctive teaching that Christians accept this person as their own Lord.

Thus to address the Lord Jesus as the object of their prayer, equally with the Father, is to ascribe full deity to Him. To make Christ one with the Father in the prerogative of hearing and answering prayer is to bracket Him with the Father as equal in power and glory. For a strong monotheist like Paul this would have been unthinkable if he had regarded Christ Jesus as a mere man, however exalted.

His view of Christ is further underlined by the fact that the verb *direct* is singular in number although the subject is plural. One can hardly conceive of a stronger way for Paul to indicate his unquestioned acceptance of the Lordship of Jesus and His oneness with the Father. And the fact that this occurs in his prayer and not in a doctrinal discussion indicates that it was part of the accepted faith of the Thessalonians as well as Paul. Denney remarks, "It is an involuntary assent of the Apostle to the word of the Lord, 'I and My Father are one'."[69] It was an essential part of the faith of the Christian church from the very beginning. Here we see implicit in Paul's earliest letter the Lordship of Jesus Christ which is made explicit in the epistle to the Colossians. Ellicott points out the theological significance of Paul's addition of the name of Jesus, "The Eternal Son is here distinguished from the Father in respect of His Personality, but mystically united with Him in respect of his Godhead, and, as God, rightly and duly addressed in the language of direct prayer."[70]

The petition which the missionaries make for themselves is that God may "direct our way unto you." The translation "direct our way" does not clearly convey the metaphor in Paul's mind when he used the verb. It means "to make straight, to lead directly toward" a goal. Clearly Paul's request is that God will open up a way directly back to his beloved converts by removing the obstacles which Satan has thrown into the way (2:18). The verb occurs only two other times in the New Testament (Lk 1:79; 2 Th 3:5), and in each place it has the sense of divine providence controlling human action. The missionaries are making their request but they recognize that God is the supreme disposer of events. They acknowledge their dependence upon Him and know that it is His prerogative to determine the time and manner in which their prayer will be answered.

(2) *Petition concerning the readers* (vv. 12-13). The prayer for their readers is given with considerable fullness. The petition is formulated in verse 12 and its aim stated in verse 13.

(*a*) *Petition formulated* (v. 12). "And the Lord make you to increase and abound in love." The conjunction rendered "and" (*de*) is here better translated as adversative, "but," in harmony with the emphatic *you* which stands at the beginning of the sentence, "but you." "Whatever may be God's answer concerning our own request, but as for you," may "the

Lord make you to increase and abound." The missionaries are well aware that the spiritual growth and development of the readers is not dependent upon their ability to return but is in the Lord's hands.

The *Lord*, to whom alone this second petition is directed, may be either the Father or Christ. Since the designation here, as in verse 8 above, stands alone it may mean God according to the frequent usage of the Old Testament. But Paul's usage of the title by itself for Christ as well as the application of the term to Jesus in the preceding clause makes it more probable that He is meant here also. (The addition of the name "Jesus" in a few manuscripts makes this meaning explicit.) Paul's use of this term, which was familiar to readers of the Old Testament as a name of God, to denote Christ is consistent with his encounter with the glorified Jesus on the road to Damascus. Neil remarks, "It was only when he came to know Jesus that the word *Kurios*—the ordinary word for the Lord in the Old Testament—came to have a real vital content."[71]

Basil suggested that "the Lord" here meant "the Lord the Spirit," thus reading the Trinity into this passage. Swete is favorable to the suggestion and points out that it is the Spirit's office to produce love.[72] But there is no evidence in the New Testament that the Spirit is the giver of love in distinction from joy, peace, and other spiritual gifts, which are ascribed both to Christ and the Spirit as their source. It is equally appropriate to think of Christ as the indwelling power enriching their hearts unto love. That the reference is to the Spirit has nothing to recommend it except the desire to find the Trinity in this passage.

The specific petition for the readers is that the Lord will cause them "to increase and abound in love." The two verbs are both aorist optatives of wish. They are virtually synonymous in import and the use of both strengthens the expression of the prayer-wish. The former means "to become more, to increase, to be in abundance," while the latter means "to be present in abundance, to overflow." They may be rendered "to increase and to overflow" (Weymouth, Williams). The former may be viewed as "pointing to the process of growth" and the latter "to superlative attainment."[73] Then they may be thought of as standing in a relationship of cause and effect. The petition is not merely that their converts will "increase" but will be filled to overflowing "in love." It is assumed that love is already present in their lives; the request is that it may increase to overflowing fullness. Its overflowing presence is the tangible evidence of a robust faith. Genuine Christian love, whose characteristics are set forth in 1 Corinthians 13, is the one thing in the Christian life which cannot be carried to excess.

This abounding love will first of all express itself in their relations "one toward another," the fellow-believers at Thessalonica. The reciprocal pronoun indicates that this love is to be shown mutually. But it must also reach out "toward all men," not merely Christians in other places, but all men generally. For the persecuted Thessalonians this meant also loving their *enemies*, as Christ commanded (Mt 5:44). To show love to their persecutors was the true safeguard against the natural tendency to retaliate when mistreated by outsiders. Such a love is not natural to man; it can be known and practiced only as it is received as a gift from the Lord and made to increase and abound by Him.

This petition for their converts is enforced by a reference to the practice of the writers, "even as we also do toward you." The love that the missionaries have toward their converts is presented as a model and measure for them. The love of the writers "was not stationary, but living and growing."[74] The Thessalonians had seen that love in their lives when they labored among them and this letter is further evidence of their selfless concern. Following the period of anxious concern for them, the good report of Timothy had certainly stimulated anew the love of the missionaries for their beloved converts at Thessalonica.

(*b*) *Aim indicated* (v. 13). The petition for the readers is concluded with a statement of its aim, or "contemplated result" as Lenski prefers to call it.[75] The prayer for their increase in love is "to the end he may establish your hearts unblamable in holiness."

"To the end" translates the preposition *eis*, "into," and the articular aorist infinitive *to stērixai*, "to establish," is a common construction to denote purpose. While the Greek construction does not express a personal subject as does our English translation, the *he* is clearly "the Lord," not "love" as some have suggested. The Lord works through their increasing love to *establish* them, make them firm and solid (cf. 3:2), in Christian character. Only as Christ develops in them the needed inner spiritual stability will they be able to stand firm and unmoved through whatever the future holds. Timothy had been sent to Thessalonica to help establish them (3:2); this prayer is a reminder that however helpful the ministries of the Lord's servants may be, it is the Lord Himself who must work that inner stability in them.

The prayer is that "your hearts" may be established. In Scripture the "heart" is a comprehensive term standing for the whole inner life, including thought, feeling, and will (cf. 2:4). Christian stability is not achieved through outward conformity to rules and regulations, needful as that is, but through the development of conscious inner strength and stability. Such a petition for the strengthening of the inner life of the believer is timely today when much attention is given to head and hand but the inner spiritual life is often neglected.

The goal of their growth in love is inner stability "in holiness," the sphere in which their spiritual career will unfold. The word for *holiness* (*hagiōsunē*) is used only by Paul in the New Testament (Ro 1:4; 2 Co 7:1; 1 Th 3:13). It denotes not the process of becoming "holy" but rather the quality of being "holy."[76] It has an ethical quality which reveals itself in purity of life. The demand for holiness is rooted in the fact that by virtue of his acceptance of the atoning work of Christ the believer has been separated from the world and set apart as belonging unto God. That which is devoted to God must be separated from sin. Genuine holiness is motivated by the obligations which love imposes. "Since selfishness is the essence of sinfulness, love, which turns the self away from itself and towards God, is the condition of holiness, which is the antithesis of sinfulness.[77] An unloving man cannot be a holy man.

The remainder of the verse describes the holiness Paul has in view. Their hearts are to be established *unblamable* in holiness. The adjective *unblamable* means "to find no fault with, to be without blame, free from censure." It signifies that whatever charges might be made, no charge could be maintained. It points to the high standard which God sets for His children (cf. 1 Jn 2:1). It must ever be their aspiration and aim to so live that no fault may be found in them, that nothing in their conduct can be censured as evil.

"Before our God and Father" removes this holiness from the realm of fallible human evaluation and lifts it into the presence of *God* who is also "our Father." "God judges not as a brutal critic but as a loving Father."[78] The Christian must always be concerned about the evaluation that God our Father will make of our character. Our holiness of character and conduct are derived from Him and will be tested by Him.

But the whole concept of their being "unblamable in holiness" is seen to have an eschatological character by the addition "at the coming of our Lord Jesus with all his saints." Blamelessness as regards holiness is the ideal toward which believers strive in this life, but it will have its full realization at the return of "our Lord Jesus." Only those who have accepted the historical *Jesus* as their own Saviour and *Lord* and whose love inspires in them purposes that are blameless in the sphere of holiness will find His return to be a time of salvation (5:9) and not of wrath (1:10; 2:16). By virtue of their union with the Lord Jesus they will by Him be presented before God the Father as sons free from all fault and imperfection (Eph 5:27).

The return of Christ is described as being "with all his saints," or more literally, "with all his holy ones."** This at once opens up the debate as to whether Paul means the holy angels, the saints, or both. Those who

---

**"With all his holy ones"—Moffatt, Weymouth, Way, 20th Cent, and Berkeley. Williams has "with all His consecrated ones."

think Paul means angels point to the fact that in the Old Testament and in later Jewish literature, including the Dead Sea Scrolls, they are frequently so designated. Also our Lord speaks of a retinue of angels who will accompany His return in glory (Mt 25:31; Mk 8:38). In 2 Thessalonians 1:7 Paul speaks of angels in connection with the revelation of Christ.

That the expression "all his holy ones" must include the saints seems clear from the fact that this is the standard New Testament term for the redeemed. Only in Jude 14 does "holy ones" refer to angels, but Jude's expression is not identical with that here. It is Paul's consistent practice to use this expression of the saints, and advocates for this meaning see no reason to make an exception here. From his teaching in chapter 4, it seems clear that Paul means the saints.

But did Paul mean to include both men and angels, as some think? If he meant to include both it seems strange that he did not mention the angels here as he does in 2 Thessalonians 1:7. Nor need the inclusive adjective *all* be extended to include both. "All the holy ones" is a common expression with Paul to denote all believers. In view of Paul's teaching in 4:14-17 we conclude that he means only the redeemed here. The *saints* here appear to be those who have died in Christ and are brought with Him at His coming to catch away His church.

With this sublime prayer-wish the historical and personal portion of the epistle comes to a close. If Timothy's report had contained no account of "that which is lacking in your faith" (v. 10) the letter might suitably have closed here. But the mention of the deficiencies in the faith of the readers prepares the way for the second half of the letter which deals with the needed instructions and exhortations.

Some ancient manuscripts mark the close of the first part of the letter by adding an "amen" here. It is quite well attested and there is a question whether it is part of the original or a liturgical addition. Its absence may be explained as being due to omission by scribes with the feeling that it was unsuitable in the middle of a letter. On the other hand, its insertion may equally well be accounted for through the influence of liturgical usage to close the prayer. It might also be inserted by a scribe to mark the fact that the first part of the letter ended here. On the whole its insertion (Moffatt, Berkeley), rather than its omission, seems more probable. Most of our versions omit it.

8

PRACTICAL: EXHORTATIONS

CHAPTERS FOUR AND FIVE form the second major division of the epistle. This is clear from the opening formula *Finally* as well as the contents of these last two chapters. The first part was given to expressions of thanksgiving and personal narrative; this part is devoted to instructions and exhortations. Paul now passes from self-defense to a tactful treatment of the deficiencies of the readers. He now deals with his converts as a wise father with his beloved children (2:11), instructing, admonishing, and exhorting them as the need requires.

There is no need to assume that from here on Paul answers points that have been raised by the Thessalonians in a letter to him (cf. Introduction p. 21). The various topics touched upon may equally well be explained as those brought out in the discussions about their needs since Timothy's return. These exhortations and instructions are not added haphazardly but are carefully advanced to meet their actual needs as reported by Timothy.

This second portion of the epistle divides into five parts. We have first a series of exhortations concerning Christian living (4:1-12), followed by instructions concerning the dead in Christ (4:13-17), and exhortations to watchfulness in view of the Lord's return (5:1-11). Two further practical sections follow, instructions concerning church discipline (5:12-15) and directives for holy living (5:16-24).

It is instructive to notice that the teaching concerning the second advent is preceded and followed by sections dealing with daily life and conduct. Although the teaching concerning the Lord's return was clearly an exciting subject for the Thessalonians, Paul endeavored to set it into a context of practical daily living. The Christian's hope for the future must have a sanctifying influence upon the present.

A. EXHORTATIONS CONCERNING CHRISTIAN LIVING

4:1-12 Finally then, brethren, we beseech and exhort you in the Lord Jesus, that, as ye received of us how ye ought to walk and to please God, even as ye do walk,—that ye abound more and more. (2) For ye know what charge we gave you through the Lord Jesus. (3) For this is the will of God, *even* your sanctification, that ye abstain from fornication; (4) that each one of you know how to possess himself of his own vessel in sanctification and honor, (5) not in the passion of lust, even as the Gentiles who know not God; (6) that no man transgress, and wrong his brother in the matter: because the Lord is an avenger in all these things, as also we forewarned you and testified. (7) For God called us not for uncleanness, but in sanctification. (8) Therefore he that rejecteth, rejecteth not man, but God, who giveth his Holy Spirit unto you.

(9) But concerning love of the brethren ye have no need that one write unto you: for ye yourselves are taught of God to love one another; (10) for indeed ye do it toward all the brethren that are in all Macedonia. But we exhort you, brethren, that ye abound more and more; (11) and that ye study to be quiet, and to do your own business, and to work with your hands, even as we charged you; (12) that ye may walk becomingly toward them that are without, and may have need of nothing.

Paul passes to the second division of the letter with the words "Finally then." *Finally* need not be taken to imply that Paul here intended to bring the epistle to a conclusion but was carried away by the flood of further matters which he could not resist saying. So regarded, this *finally* "seems a trifle reminiscent of some sermons."[1]

The word rendered "finally" (*loipon*) is an adverbial accusative, "as for the rest," and serves to mark a transition rather than a conclusion. We have a similar use of it in the middle of the epistle to the Philippians (Phil 3:1). It implies that much has already been said and contemplates all that yet remains to be dealt with, which need not be brief. Our word *finally* is not an altogether satisfactory rendering since it commonly implies that the conclusion is at hand. A better translation would be "for the rest,"* or "further."†

Then is more literally "therefore" and serves to connect these instructions and exhortations with what has gone before. Stevens holds that it has a continuative or collective force and serves to introduce matters which are in accord with the thought of the entire letter thus far.[2] It is more probable that it looks back specifically to the prayer of 3:13. Having prayed for their establishment in holiness, Paul now exhorts them to that end. The prayer that they may be blameless in holiness at the Lord's return cannot be realized without the cooperation of those for whom the prayer is made. Paul therefore urges his beloved converts to increase in their striving after a holy walk.

This paragraph of exhortations to moral living falls into three parts. The opening exhortation is general, urging them to advance in God-

*Rotherham, Darby, Lattey; Young: "As to the rest;" Berkeley: "To go on;" Way: "I have yet to add this."

†Weymouth and 20th Cent. The wording of Phillips, "To sum up," misses the point; it denotes not a summary but a transition.

pleasing conduct (vv. 1-2). This general exhortation is elaborated in two specific areas, in regard to sanctification (vv. 3-8) and brotherly love and industry (vv. 9-12).

1. Exhortation to Advance in God-pleasing Conduct (vv. 1-2)

In this general exhortation there is an indication of the attitude of the writers in making their appeal (v. 1a), a statement of the contents of the exhortation (v. 1b), and a supporting reminder of similar previous directives given them (v. 2).

a) ATTITUDE IN MAKING THE EXHORTATION (v. 1a). The readers are again affectionately addressed as *brethren*. These appeals are being made in the interest of that spiritual brotherhood in Christ into which they have been brought. It is a loving reminder of their common interests and concerns as Christians.

The counsel is introduced with two fraternal verbs, "we beseech and exhort you." The use of two verbs instead of one stresses Paul's sense of the vital importance of maintaining becoming Christian conduct. The two verbs enforce each other and add emphasis to the request being made.

The verb translated "beseech" (*erōtaō*) in classical Greek was used only of questions, but in later Greek it came to be used also in making requests. Findlay holds that the verb here has an interrogatory force, "Will you do so and so?" and challenges the readers to give an affirmative answer. Bailey questions this interrogative quality of the verb here since in nearly half of its occurrences in the New Testament it carries the apparently simple idea of request or petition. In this latter usage it can hardly be distinguished from *aiteō*, "to ask, ask for," although "by laying greater stress on the *person* asked than on the *thing* asked for, it is more appropriate in exhortation."[3] It conveys the thought of a friend entreating a friend.

The second verb, *exhort* (cf. 2:11), here has the force of "exhort, urge, appeal" and carries an arousing note. The present tense of both verbs indicates continuing action, "we continue to request and urge" *you*, the recipients of this letter as a group. In the original the pronoun *you* stands between the two verbs, "we beseech you and exhort."

It is uncertain whether the phrase "in the Lord Jesus" should be construed with both verbs or with the latter only. Some insist that it should be taken with both; but others, like Findlay, would limit it to the last, since the apostolic exhortation rests on the divine authority of Jesus.[4] On the latter view each verb has its own modifier, "we request you" as our friends in a personal appeal, "and urge in the Lord Jesus," by virtue of our union with Him. Whether taken with both verbs or with the latter only, "in the Lord Jesus" indicates that the activity being engaged in is carried on in virtue of their union with the Lord Jesus, not "*by* the Lord Jesus" (KJV and Phillips). It is not a form of adjuration. (Williams renders, "in the face of our union with the Lord Jesus.") They are united in Him as their common Lord. Paul's appeal carries authority for them because it operates in the sphere of the regenerate life. He does not presume to advise them on the basis of personal status or special ecclesiastical prerogatives but because writers and readers are members of one family, the body of Christ. "He exhorts them not as a philosopher or teacher of general ethical truths, but as one whose place in the mystical Body is to teach and exhort his fellow members."[5]

b) Content of the exhortation (v. 1*b*). "That, as ye received of us how we ought to walk and to please God, even as ye do walk,—that ye abound more and more." The grammatical construction of the statement is broken and irregular. With *that* Paul starts to state the contents of the exhortation but before he gets to the actual statement he reminds the readers that what he has to say conforms with what they have already received from him. When he comes to the actual statement of the exhortation he graciously adds that they are already doing what he asks. He concludes by repeating *that*, to gather up what has been said, and requests that they abound the more.

"As ye received of us" tactfully reminds the readers that what he is asking is nothing new. The request is strictly conformable to what they, as their converts, had already "received" from them (cf. 2:13). These instructions had already been delivered to them while the missionaries were still at Thessalonica. Paul is thus confirming their former teachings. The Thessalonians had received them "of us" (*par' hēmōn*), "from alongside of us," as the missionaries had personally transmitted them to their converts. Their previous reception then of these exhortations implies that the writers have a right to expect that they will accept them now and act upon them.

"How ye ought to walk and to please God" states the essence of the exhortation. In the original the use of a definite article before the whole expression binds all together as a single object of the verb *received*. This is a general exhortation, covering the whole Christian life. It contains the substance of the specific instructions which follow.

The word for "ought" (*dei*) is usually translated "must" and denotes the compulsion of duty; it stresses the moral obligation resting upon them because of their personal relations to the Lord. Christian living is not a desirable option but a compelling obligation. That binding obligation is "how ye must needs walk and please God" (Rotherham). The matter of *how* they must live as Christians is central for all followers of the Lord Jesus. Paul is seeking to help them to know how they can fulfill this obligation.

"To walk and to please God" are not two separate and distinct activities; rather, the first is to result in the second. The *and* is epexegetical, explaining the logical sequence of the walk. The expression is parallel to "that you should walk worthily of God" in 2:12. They must continue so "to walk," a common figure for moral conduct (cf. 2:12), that by their walk they will please God.

To please God is the true aim and end of the Christian's walk. "The Christian does not 'walk' with a view to obtaining the maximum amount of satisfaction for himself, but in order to please his Lord."[6] Just as the writers make it their chief concern to please not men but God (2:4), so their converts must live to please God. Such an aim for the Christian's endeavor is the logical outcome of his love for his Lord. It marks the service of freedom and gladness which characterizes the believer who has been released from the bondage of the law and has entered into the perfect law of Christian liberty. Such a walk will assure the fulfillment of the prayer for blamelessness in holiness at Christ's return (3:13).

"Even as ye do walk" is a characteristic Pauline comment. It is another instance of his eagerness to give recognition to the good work that had already begun in the Thessalonian church (cf. 1:3; 7-8; 2:13-14; 4:9-10; 5:1, 4-5). He loves to give praise wherever praise is due. He fully appreciates what has already been attained by them and he would not grieve them by any apparent suggestion that they had failed to heed his former instructions. In giving them these exhortations he is not complaining or finding fault with them.

The phrase is missing in the *Textus Receptus*‡ but it has good manuscript support and may be retained with confidence. To omit it is to lose a typical Pauline touch. It is implied by the concluding remark, "that ye abound more and more." This appeal "presupposes the earlier mention of a prior commencement, and such a commencement would not be implied in the preceding text without 'even as ye do walk.' "[7]

Having gladly acknowledged that they are walking as he instructed them, his admonition can only be "that ye abound more and more." They must never be satisfied with what they have already achieved. There can be no finality in practical holiness in this life for the believer. He knows that they are abounding already but they must not give up the endeavor for still higher attainments. He who was himself constantly "pressing toward the mark" urges his followers "to keep on doing still better" (Ber-

‡Hence its absence in the KJV and those versions based upon the *Textus Receptus*.

keley), literally, "that ye may be abounding the more." Contrary to the usual way in which this verb is employed, Paul here does not name any quality in which they are to abound. This is fully in keeping with the general character of this opening exhortation. It is his desire for every area of their lives.

Lenski remarks that this opening exhortation is "psychologically perfect. It acknowledges all that the Thessalonians have hitherto achieved, and makes this the ground for achieving still more. It in no manner discourages the Thessalonians, it encourages them in the strongest manner."[8] Paul felt no need to administer a direct rebuke, for his readers are not rebellious but willing to follow his guidance. He stimulates their willingness in a masterful way.

c) REMINDER OF THE PAST CHARGES (v. 2). *For* introduces this reminder as confirmatory evidence of what has just been said. "Ye know" calls upon them to confirm that the missionaries had given them instructions in this matter while yet with them. Paul is anxious to secure their full agreement that the moral demands being set forth are no new requirement now imposed upon them in his absence. They had faithfully set before them the Christian demand for holy living while with them.

In the preceding verse the emphasis was on what the Thessalonians had *received* or accepted from their teachers; here the emphasis is upon what the missionaries *gave* or imparted to their converts. The teachings they had given them Paul describes as "what charge," literally, "what charges" or "what orders." *What* calls attention to their nature as elaborated in the remainder of this paragraph. The word rendered "charge" is a semi-military term and carries a tone of authority. It was used to designate "a word of command" received from a superior officer to be passed down to others. The plural indicates that instructions or orders had been given in specific moral areas. They had not left their readers in ignorance of what kind of a life was expected of Christians and had given "their converts something like a systematic moral teaching."[9] The term adds another touch to the ministry of the missionaries at Thessalonica as described in 2:11-12.

The missionaries had given their orders "through the Lord Jesus." The phrase points to the character of the teachings imparted, that they were stamped by the authority of Jesus the exalted Lord. But the precise wording of Paul's statement is remarkable. He does not say that the Lord Jesus gave the orders "through us" but rather that we gave them through *Him*. The meaning of course is not that the missionaries issued the orders out of their own prerogative and that they were transmitted through the Lord Jesus as their agent. Rather, the meaning is that while the missionaries were the human messengers who delivered the orders to the Thessalonians, they did so through the sanction of the Lord Jesus who had commissioned and sent them. They were given "by the authority of the Lord Jesus."§ In verse 1 Paul remarked that their exhortations were *in* the Lord Jesus, given in the sphere of His rule; here he states that the orders were given *through* Him as their source and authority.

2. Exhortation to Sanctification (vv. 3-8)

The general appeal for God-pleasing conduct is now given specific application in the demand for sanctification as applied to sexual behavior. This exhortation to sanctification is shown to have its basis in the will of God (v. 3*a*), is given specific application in the realm of moral conduct (vv. 3*b*-6*a*), and is supported by three reasons for heeding the exhortation (vv. 6*b*-8).

a) BASIS FOR THE EXHORTATION (v. 3*a*). "For this is the will of God, even your sanctification." The *For* is explanatory, showing what is involved in living God-pleasing lives in harmony with the orders which had been given them. The demonstrative pronoun *this* is the subject of the sentence and points to what follows at greater length. All that is comprehended in *this* is designated as "the will of God." The word *will*, more literally, "a thing willed," is without the article in the original and implies that their sanctification is not the whole purpose of God for them; there are other aspects of His plan not here specified (cf. 5:18). Such a setting forth of the will of God should be of vital interest to believers; it should provide the direction and inspiration of their lives. Christian conduct must have its source in the divine plan. The obligation being pressed upon them roots in God's revelation of His will for them.

The aspect of God's will here stressed is "your sanctification." Like the kindred term *holiness* (3:13), *sanctification* (*hagiasmos*) has the basic idea of being set apart for or dedicated to God upon the basis of the atoning work of Christ. It does not denote the state of holiness but rather the process of being made holy, becoming more and more in character and conduct that which God desires us to be. Since God is holy and separated from sin, this "sanctifying" must express itself in purity of life. The possessive genitive *your* means that this sanctifying process is God's will for the readers personally.

b) APPLICATION OF SANCTIFICATION (vv. 3*b*-6*a*). All that follows through verse 6 forms a grammatical unit and stands in apposition with *sanctification*, and beyond it, "the will of God." It is composed of a series of in-

§Conybeare, Weymouth, Moffatt, Goodspeed, Lattey, Williams, Berkeley, and NASB; 20th Cent has "on the authority of."

finitive clauses which unfold and apply the demand for sanctification to the moral life of the readers. There is some uncertainty as to the precise coordination of the clauses as well as the intended meaning of some of their terms. We accept the view that three coordinated points are advanced. The application of God's will concerning their sanctification finds expression in three demands: to abstain from fornication (v. 3*b*), to know how to possess one's own vessel (vv. 4-5), and to avoid wronging a brother (v. 6).

(1) *To abstain from fornication* (v. 3*b*). "That ye abstain from fornication" states the negative aspect of sanctification in its application to sexual conduct. The second personal pronoun *ye* marks this as a demand upon the readers directly. The infinitive rendered "abstain" in the middle voice means "to hold one's self off from, to keep away from, to abstain," while the durative present denotes that they must constantly keep aloof from fornication. The thought of separation in the verbal form is further strengthened by the preposition *from*.

Fornication is used here in its comprehensive meaning to denote every kind of unlawful sexual intercourse. A few manuscripts even insert the word *all* to stress the inclusiveness of the prohibition. The readers must realize that fornication was once one of the greatest enemies of Christian sanctification. Alexander remarks, "St. Paul insists, with great solemnity, upon a truth which at various times, even in the Church, has been, if not denied, yet half forgotten, that *moral* evils are always *spiritual* evils of the first magnitude."[10]

We need not infer that Timothy had brought back a report that actual cases of immorality existed in the Thessalonian church. The absence of any direct censure for immorality (such as that given to the church at Corinth), as well as the commendatory tone of the epistle, seems to indicate that this advice is intended to be preventive. Writing from Corinth, a notoriously licentious seaport, Paul well knew the penetrating moral taint to which his converts in the seaport of Thessalonica were constantly exposed. Further, the warning was timely since many of the readers, until a few months before, had lived by the low moral standards prevailing in the pagan world around them. Paul well knew that he could not assume that their conversion would automatically undo the moral habits of a lifetime. He was aware that strong temptations to licentiousness constantly assailed them. Constant admonitions and urgent warnings were always needed, and the New Testament epistles repeatedly touch upon the subject. It may well be that Timothy had reported that some of the members were finding it difficult to maintain the moral standard which the missionaries had taught.

Fornication was one of the conspicuous forms of immorality in all areas of the pagan world. It was regarded as a matter of indifference and even defended as a necessity of nature, like eating and drinking. The well-known proneness of the pagan gods to sensuality had a degrading influence on public morals. Fornication received ritual sanction in some of the religious cults of the day. Adultery was a common subject of poetry and all the arts were employed to make it a pleasing and seductive practice. The disclosures from Pompeii and Herculaneum bear painful testimony to the moral degradation that pervaded even the most civilized portion of the heathen world.

The strong position of the New Testament against impurity in all forms shows that Christianity did not adapt its moral standards to the practices of contemporary society. Its moral demands stand in stark contrast to the immoral practices of that day. The Christian church insisted that abstinence is an essential and ever present need for the development of personal holiness and God-pleasing conduct. Unlike the pagan cults, it refused to tolerate, much less foster, immoral practices among its members. Its demands for chastity root in the fact that the body of the Christian belongs to God and is the temple of the Holy Spirit (1 Co 6:13-20). In these days of neopaganism the Christian church must again aggressively reemphasize and promote the New Testament moral standards for the Christian life. "The new morality is only the old immorality brought up to date."[11]

(2) *To know how to possess himself of his own vessel* (vv. 4-5). These two verses form a second infinitive clause parallel to the preceding negative clause and emphasize the same basic truth in a fuller way, restating it positively (v. 4) and negatively (v. 5).

"That each one of you may know how" indicates that the demand being made applies to each individual member of the church. The same moral standards hold for all. It also asserts that it is God's will that each one should know how he must act in the matter of sex. To *know* is not here used as a euphemism for sexual relations. It rather means "to understand" how one must act in this matter. It implies that chastity is a matter that requires instruction and self-discipline. The word *know* carries the force of the present tense and indicates that "purity is not a momentary impulse, but a lesson, a habit."[12]

(a) *Positive duty* (v. 4). Each believer has the duty to know "how to possess himself of his own vessel in sanctification and honor." The statement presents difficulties of interpretation; uncertainty exists concerning the intended meaning for the words *possess* and *vessel*. Two distinct meanings are advocated for each. Does the verb mean "to possess" or "to acquire," and does "his own vessel" mean "his own body" or "his own wife?"

167

4:4 _The Thessalonian Epistles_

In classical Greek the verb rendered *possess* (*ktaomai*) in the present tense meant "to procure for oneself, to acquire," and only in the perfect tense did it have the meaning "to possess." But the verb used here is present. Both ancient and modern commentators have felt this fact to be a major difficulty in accepting the meaning of "body" for the word *vessel*. Since it would be quite pointless to ask the readers to "acquire" their own bodies, it is held that Paul must be referring to acquiring or procuring a wife, getting married. But the use of the verb in the papyri indicates that in the popular language of the day the meaning "to possess" was not confined to the perfect tense; the present tense also took this meaning. This relieves the major difficulty to the view that the body is meant. In view of its papyrus usage Moulton and Milligan suggest that in our passage the verb probably has the meaning "gradually obtain the complete mastery of the body."[13] This is in harmony with the fact that attainment to the Christian moral standard involves a struggle which must be won by persistent effort.

Advocates of the view that by vessel Paul means "a wife" insist upon the usual meaning of the verb. They point out that it is used in Ruth 4:10 (LXX) to signify "getting a wife by purchase," and that there is evidence in the rabbinical literature that "vessel" was used to mean wife. It is also said that in favor of this meaning is 1 Peter 3:7 where the wife is spoken of as "the weaker vessel." But 1 Peter 3:7 cannot be used to support this view since Peter is thinking of both the husband and the wife as vessels. It is maintained that the Greek pronoun rendered "his own" (*heatou*), standing in an emphatic position, cannot refer to the body because "a reference to the *body* of an individual cannot be emphatic."[14] But this claim is contradicted by 1 Corinthians 6:18, "He that committeth fornication sinneth against his own body" (cf. also 1 Co 7:4). There is no reason why one's own body should not be emphatically referred to; nothing material is more a man's own than his body.

Against the view that *vessel* means "a wife" it is pointed out that this "would imply a low estimate of the woman's position quite foreign to St. Paul."[15] If *vessel* means wife then Paul in this verse would be forbidding celibacy altogether. The continuous action in the verb *know* does not favor this meaning; it has the force of the present tense, thus it does not denote any one act (the taking of a wife) but a continuing knowledge or state (the continued control over the body with its cravings and passions).

The view that Paul means the body is consistent with a recognized New Testament usage of the term *vessel*. Thus in 2 Corinthians 4:7 Paul speaks about having "this treasure in earthen vessels," and in 2 Timothy 2:21 he refers to the man who purges himself from impurity as being "a vessel unto honor." The use of the word vessel as a reference to the body would be familiar to Old Testament readers from 1 Samuel 21:5, "The vessels of the young men were holy." Paul's Greek readers would be quite familiar with the thought of the body as the vessel or instrument of the soul. If the reference is to the body, verses 4 and 5 enjoin a fundamental duty which applies to every believer, whether man or woman, married or unmarried. We accept Paul's expression as a reference to one's own body.

Our modern English translations deal with this problem verse in different ways. Some, like the American Standard Version, retain Paul's figurative term *vessel* (Also Darby, Rotherham, Young, Lattey, NASB). Others boldly set forth their understanding of Paul's intended meaning, whether "wife" (Moffatt, Goodspeed, Weymouth, Montgomery, Williams, 20th Cent) or "body" (Conybeare, Way, Phillips). The Revised Standard Version may be quoted as representative of the former, "that each one of you know how to take a wife for himself," while the New English Bible may represent the latter, "each one of you must learn to gain mastery over his body."

Each believer must know how to bring his body under full control, to gain continuous mastery over it. This is to be done "in sanctification and honor." The two concepts are linked together under one preposition. *Sanctification* indicates that this mastery over the body is to be achieved in the sphere of personal consecration, in the realization that the body must be set apart for the service of God. Such a sanctifying use of the body excludes impurity; impurity dishonors the body. To use the body as a sacred instrument devoted to the service of the Lord is to give it true *honor*. Plummer comments, "Honour for the human body as something sacred is to a large extent a Christian idea. Heathen philosophers often regarded it with contempt."[16]

If Paul's exhortation means "to know how to take a wife," then "in sanctification and honor" means that entry into marriage must be in purity and honor, or "out of pure and honorable motives" (Williams). Certainly Christians should know how to conduct themselves in getting married so as to avoid impurity and scandal.

A few scholars, like Frame, place quite a different interpretation upon verse 4. They propose to place a comma after the word *vessel*, interpreted as "wife," and divide the verse into two parts. They take *know* to mean "know the value of, treat with respect" (cf. 5:12), and *possess* is taken to mean "acquire, get."[17] Then the verse reads somewhat as follows: "that each one of you [who is already married] respect his own wife; that each of you [who are not yet married] get his own wife in the spirit of consecration and honor." Although grammatically possible, such an interpretation seems improbable. If this was Paul's meaning, it is doubtful that he would have expressed it in this harsh and ambiguous way.

(*b*) *Negative description* (v. 5). Added without a connecting particle, "not in the passion of lust" gives a negative description of the Christian's use of his body. It stands in direct antithesis to "in sanctification and honor." The body must not be used for immoral purposes under the influence of "the passion of lust." *Passion* denotes not so much the violence of the feeling as its ungovernable nature. The term is related to the verb "to suffer" and expresses the lustful feeling which the individual suffers. *Lust* denotes active desires, cravings, longings, whether good (as in 2:17) or bad, as here. Trench compares *passion* to the diseased condition of the soul and *lust* to the active disease which springs out of that condition.[18] The combination of the two terms indicates the surrender of an individual to his passions so that he is overwhelmed and carried away by them. "When men allow themselves to whet their desires, there are no bounds to their lustful emotions."[19] Christians must not allow their desires to dominate them and make them the slaves of passion.

The conduct here forbidden for the believer is typical of that prevailing among the Gentiles. "Even as the Gentiles" points to the exact correspondence between the conduct prohibited and the vicious practices of the pagan world. The term *Gentiles* generally denotes the non-Jewish nations, but sometimes, as here, it means non-Christians, those who are outside the Christian church. Writing to the Thessalonian believers who were predominantly of Gentile origin, Paul divides the world into Christians and Gentiles, a division based upon the fact of Gentile ignorance of God. The Gentiles are characterized as those "who know not God." In the original this negative expression has the article prefixed to it and stands in apposition to "the Gentiles." It points to "the Gentiles' ignorance of the one true God as their peculiar property and the cause of their sinfulness."[20]

The Gentiles knew gods who were the personification of their own ambitions and lusts but they did not know the true God, the God who is Himself holy and wills the sanctification of His followers. In Romans 1 Paul traces the origin and development of the world's wickedness to its suppression of the knowledge of God which even the heathen had from their observation of God's works in creation. This suppression led to idolatry, and idolatry led to immorality.

This reference to Gentile ignorance of God is a pointed reminder to the readers. They have just been brought out of the ignorance of paganism and have come to know the true God (1:9) and His orders for the Christian life (4:2). With their new knowledge, to fall back into the immoral practices of paganism would be especially reprehensible.

If by *vessel* Paul means "wife," this negative description in verse 5 is "a further elucidation" of "the contrast between Pauline and pagan ideals of marriage."[21] Pagan marriage was only too commonly marked and governed by passionate lust. This obviously is the wrong motive and the wrong way for a Christian to enter the marriage relationship.

(3) *To avoid wronging the brother* (v. 6a). "That no man transgress, and wrong his brother in the matter" translates an articular infinitive construction standing in apposition with *sanctification*, of which it is another specific exemplification. The verb translated "transgress" literally means "to go beyond" and carries the thought of passing over the line that divides right from wrong. The present tense with the negative (*mē*) has the force "that there be no going beyond." It is not certain whether it is used here intransitively or transitively. If it is used absolutely, to be marked off by a comma, as in our version, it means "to go beyond what is proper, to exceed the proper limits," hence to *transgress*. Then the nature of the transgression is only to be discerned from what follows. It may, however, be taken transitively, the accusative "his brother" being construed with both verbs. Then it has the sense "to get the better of," and so wrong the brother. Darby translates, "not overstepping the rights of and wronging the brother."

The verb translated "wrong" has the root meaning "to have more," and so it is used to mean "to take advantage of, to defraud, to cheat." The verb does not indicate the nature of the wrong being done but the idea of selfish and self-seeking fraud is involved in the term. The present tense prohibits the continuation of such a practice.

The object of this reprehensible practice is "his brother." Views differ as to whether *brother* here means a fellow Christian or a fellow creature. Hogg and Vine acknowledge that "there is no other instance in Paul's epistles of the use of this word of mankind in general," yet they feel it difficult to suppose that Paul "here limited its meaning to the Christian relationship." Lightfoot supports this larger view with the remark that "this is a duty which extends to the universal brotherhood of mankind, and has no reference to the special privileges of the close brotherhood of the Gospel." Others, like Stevens, hold that " 'his brother' denotes, as below in ver. 10, a fellow-believer." Then Paul is simply thinking of the immediate circle in which Christians stood without thereby intending to exclude the wider circle. "He uses the name of brother as an argument against unbrotherly overreaching."[22] To accept the term *brother* here in its usual restricted sense does not imply that Paul is accepting a double standard, as though it were allowable to wrong a non-Christian. The standard demanded in the Christian circle would also apply to the wider circle. Lenski comments, "Christian ethics treat a Christian brother as a clear example of how to treat other people, and thus differ from all worldly ethics (Mohammedan, Masonic, and other mere humanly arranged brotherhoods)."[23]

The sphere of the conduct prohibited is "in the matter." The definite article makes it specific, pointing to the matter under discussion, and therefore should not be translated generally, "in *any* matter" (KJV). But what is meant by "the matter?" The expression is apparently intentionally obscure to avoid a too precise statement of a distasteful subject. Two distinct interpretations are advocated, sexual impurity and dishonesty in business.

Advocates of the latter view, holding that Paul means "in your business dealings with your brethren," thus find two sins condemned in this passage, sexual impurity and dishonesty in business. It is held that this is to be expected since "the two outstanding vices of paganism were sexual and commercial vileness and greed."[24] Paul's readers, living in the bustling commercial city of Thessalonica, would need to be warned against both evils.

The following arguments are advanced for consideration of this view.

1. The articular infinitive at the beginning of verse 6 indicates that a new topic is introduced, namely, the sin of dishonesty in business. Opponents reply that the articular infinitive does not prove that a new topic is being introduced; the articular construction simply shows that this is another appositional expansion of *sanctification*. The construction in itself does not decide the interpretation.
2. "All these things" shows that more than one subject is being treated. But strictly taken even two topics do not fully account for the scope of the expression. Advocates of the other view insist that the expression is more adequately accounted for as referring to the various forms of sexual impurity being condemned.
3. The meaning of the verb rendered "wrong" points to a covetous, grasping spirit which expresses itself in dishonest business practices. This interpretation is strengthened by the fact that the noun is generally translated "covetousness." In reply it may be acknowledged that the verb is agreeable to this interpretation but it may also be used of sexual vice viewed as depriving a brother of his rights because of selfishness.
4. Fornication and covetousness are found in similar juxtaposition in other New Testament passages (Eph 5:3, 5; Col 3:5; Heb 13:4-5). That the two sins may be dealt with together is clear, but that does not prove that Paul does so here.
5. The word rendered "matter" (*pragma*) is a regular commercial term,

meaning "business, a matter of business," therefore it should be taken to have that meaning here. In the plural the term does have this meaning but it is singular here. Milligan points out that "no other adequate example of *pragma* in this sense in the singular has been produced."[25] Should evidence be forthcoming that in the linguistic usage of that day the singular was used to mean "business" a major difficulty to acceptance of this view would be removed. The term occurs elsewhere in the New Testament ten times, four times in the plural, but it nowhere has the undisputed interpretation of business dealings.

Advocates of the view that sexual impurity is still under consideration insist that it is more reasonable to regard the entire paragraph (vv. 3-8) as a unity, dealing wholly with the matter of sanctification in relation to sexual purity. They maintain that the definite article "the matter" cannot be taken to introduce some new topic but points to the specific matter which has been under consideration. Milligan asserts that "the words are too closely connected with what precedes and what follows (v. 7 'uncleanness') to admit of any such transition to a wholly new subject."[26] Moffatt concludes that "Paul is still dealing with the immoralities of men, but now as a form of social dishonesty and fraud. The metaphors are drawn from trade, perhaps as appropriate to a trading community."[27] The view that sexual promiscuity, regarded as a matter of defrauding another of his rights, is meant is in keeping with the fact that the verb rendered "wrong," like the noun form, is frequently associated with words relating to sins of the flesh. We agree that it is best to interpret "the matter" as a euphemistic generalization for all sorts of sexual uncleanness.

It is generally held that Paul here narrows his remark to the sin of adultery, which obviously is a violation of the rights of another. But it is not necessary to restrict the evil to adultery. Morris remarks, "Promiscuity before marriage represents the robbing of the other of that virginity which ought to be brought to a marriage. The future partner of such a one has been defrauded."[28] Any illegitimate sexual relationship has in it the potential for social complications which cannot be calculated in advance.

c) REASONS FOR THE EXHORTATION (vv. 6*b*-8). With *because* Paul passes from the contents of the exhortation to the motives for obeying it and gives three reasons for doing so. Sexual purity must be maintained because its violation brings God's vengeance (v. 6*b*), it is in harmony with God's call (v. 7), and to reject it is to reject not man but God (v. 8).

(1) *Its violation will bring God's vengeance* (v. 6*b*). "The Lord is an avenger in all these things." The first motive for obedience is prospective, what the Lord will do to those who violate His demand for sexual purity.

As usual in this epistle, "the Lord" refers to the Lord Jesus Christ through whom God will judge the world (Jn 5:22; 2 Th 1:7-9). He is characterized as "an avenger," one who avenges or punishes, who extracts legal justice from a culprit. He satisfies justice by inflicting the due punishment upon the wrongdoer. In the Old Testament to take vengeance is a prerogative which Jehovah retains for Himself (Deu 32:35; Ps 94:1; Ro 12:19), but as Plummer points out, "Paul constantly takes expressions which in the O.T. are used of Jehovah and uses them of Christ, as if the transition was natural and obvious."[29] Christ will be the sure and just judge "in all these things," all the different forms of carnal impurity.

This first reason appeals to the fear of the consequences of disobedience. Paul might have appealed to the bitter physical, psychological, and social consequences of immorality. His emphasis rather is eschatological, the coming judgment day. A just God and a coming day of judgment are factors which cannot be left out of consideration when dealing with moral practices.

The added words, "as also we forewarned you and testified," again remind the readers that this eschatological motive was nothing new to them. The aorist tense of the verb *forewarned* speaks of the warning as a past event, given while Paul was with them. It was part of the basic moral instruction which the missionaries gave their converts. The preposition *pro* (before) prefixed to the verb is often taken to mean "before the day of vengeance," but it seems better to take it to mean "said before, told you beforehand." Lattey translates "told you plainly," but there is no clear instance of this meaning of the verb in the New Testament.

The added verb *testified* adds solemnity to what was told them. The form used here is stronger than that used in 2:11. The prefixed preposition (*dia*) adds force to the verb so that it means "to solemnly testify, to solemnly affirm." It was a warning intended to penetrate their conscience. "Men's dullness," says Calvin, "is such that unless they are struck forcefully they have no sense of the divine judgment."[30]

(2) *Its harmony with the divine call* (v. 7). The second reason is retrospective, looking back to what God has done. "For God called us not for uncleanness, but in sanctification." *For* indicates that the warning that Christ will judge is justified in view of what He has already done. Immorality must be avoided as being inconsistent with God's gracious call. The aorist tense of the verb looks at the divine call as a past historical event, the time of their conversion. The first personal pronoun *us* denotes that the writers as well as the readers are the recipients of the call. In the original, *God*, the subject, stands after both the verb and its object, thus placing the emphasis upon the fact that *God* issued the call. The active voice, rather than the passive "ye were called," brings out the fact

that He took the initiative in bringing us into union with Christ. That call, mediated through the preaching of the gospel at Thessalonica, took the readers out of paganism and placed them into God's blessed kingdom. That call carries moral implications, both negative and positive.

God's purpose in calling us was "not for uncleanness." *Not* (*ou*), used in the denial of an objective fact, occupies an emphatic position to stress that it was not "for uncleanness" that God called us. *For* is the translated Greek preposition *epi* ("upon") and indicates that the call was not issued on the basis of or with the understanding that we should continue to live in *uncleanness*, that which is morally impure (cf. 2:3). It was not included in His call. This negative note, marking the moral demands made on Christ's followers, is not superfluous; it stands in contrast to certain pagan cults which involved their votaries in immoral ceremonies.

"But in sanctification" states the positive aspect of the divine call. *But* marks the strong contrast between the two aspects. Instead of allowing them to continue in uncleanness, the ones who are called must follow through their call *in* the sphere of *sanctification*, the sphere of progressive holiness. God called us into union with Christ as the moral atmosphere in which we are to work out a life of sanctification.

(3) *Its rejection is a rejection of God* (v. 8). The inferential conjunction rendered "therefore" (*toigaroun*) occurs in the New Testament only here and in Hebrews 12:1. Composed of three participles, *toi*, *gar*, and *oun*, it means "for this reason, for on this account therefore" and serves to introduce an emphatic logical conclusion from the preceding. This appeal unites the former two in that it recalls both the severity and the goodness of God.

"He that rejecteth" translates a present active articular participle and pictures an individual who has the character of an active, deliberate rejecter. The verb means "to set aside, to nullify, to make void or cancel." He takes God's demand for sexual purity so lightly that he makes it void by refusing to obey it.

No object of that which he rejects is named but the reference seems to be to the call for holiness mentioned above and indirectly to Paul as the channel through whom the call was given. He who rejects the divine call to holiness and maintains that he can go on living in uncleanness rejects "not man, but God." The literal order is "not man he rejects but God." There is an unqualified contrast between *man* and *God*. His rejection is not the flouting of any man but God Himself. Behind the command of the missionaries was the authority of God. It is another reminder to the readers that the message given them was not of human origin but rooted in the revelation of God (cf. 1:5; 2:4, 13).

The God who demands moral purity of believers is further described as "who giveth his Holy Spirit unto you." The original is an articular present participle standing in apposition with *God*, "the One giving to you."‖ Some manuscripts read an aorist participle, "the One who gave," but the weight of the manuscript evidence is in favor of the present.# It is accepted without question by the critical texts. The present may be interpreted to mean that God "is ever renewing this witness against uncleanness in fresh accessions of the Holy Spirit."[31] It is better to regard the present participle as substantival, "the Giver of the Holy Spirit." The aorist participle would point to the giving of the Spirit to the readers at their conversion. Then God is characterized as the great Giver who by the gift of His Spirit is actively empowering the saints' struggle for holiness.

God's supreme gift to His people is his Holy Spirit. In keeping with the emphasis of the section, the emphatic word in the expression is *Holy*. The original is quite literally, "His Spirit, the Holy." The nature of the imparted Spirit is holy. Holiness is always the mark of His work.

The readers are reminded that God gave His Spirit "unto you." Some manuscripts have "unto us" and this is the reading of the *Textus Receptus*, followed in the KJV. But the preponderance of manuscript evidence is strongly for "you." It is accepted by all modern critical editors. The use of "us" would have made the statement general, but the use of the second person makes it personal to the Thessalonians. And the construction used (*eis*, "into," and the accusative, rather than the simple dative) "brings out more pointedly the entrance of the Spirit into the heart and life."[32] Therefore they are responsible to Him whose Spirit is resident in them. The obligation to live holy lives arises out of their reception of the Holy Spirit, who sanctifies and makes holy. For them to go on living in impurity is a direct insult to the divine Giver and a sin against the Holy Spirit who is the power unto holiness. He supplies not only the desire but also the ability to live a life of purity. His indwelling puts "an end to the pagan plea that man has no power to resist impure desires."[33] For believers to go on living in immorality is to repudiate the gracious provision of God for holiness and invites His sure judgment as the avenger of sin. "The way to escape the Avenger is to fly to the Giver and accept and cherish His gift."[34]

‖A number of manuscripts have the conjunction *kai*, "also," just before the participle. The critical texts are not agreed on its authenticity. Westcott and Hort, also Souter, omit it, while Nestle admits it. The Bible Societies' text retains it but encloses it in brackets to indicate it is of dubious textual validity. The reading has good support. Its retention adds the significant thought that God not only calls but also gives the Spirit as the blessed means of realizing the call.

#If the original reading were "unto us" rather than "unto you," the present participle might be viewed as having iterative force, denoting the giving of the Spirit to each successive convert.

3. Exhortation to Brotherly Love and Industry (vv. 9-12)

But marks the transition to a new topic. This paragraph offers a further elaboration of what is involved in a God-pleasing life (vv. 1-2). It may, however, be regarded as "another illustration of sanctification."[35] The paragraph consists of a commendation of the readers for their love of the brethren (vv. 9-10*a*) and a twofold exhortation to those who are already practicing this love (vv. 10*b*-12).

a) COMMENDATION OF THEIR LOVE (vv. 9-10*a*). Their love of the brethren is commended by the assertion that it is a subject about which they need not be written to (v. 9*a*); this assertion is supported by two points of confirmatory evidence (vv. 9*b*-10*a*).

(1) *Commendatory statement* (v. 9*a*). "Concerning love of the brethren ye have no need that one write unto you." These words imply a contrast with the subject of the preceding paragraph; there was a need for the warning concerning sexual purity. This commendation of their love of the brethren is to be taken as a simple statement of fact. It was an honest and courteous recognition of an attractive feature of the Thessalonian church. Paul's own love for them made him eager to acknowledge it.

In classical Greek *love of the brethren* (*philadelphia*) was used for affection or love for a brother or sister by birth, but in the New Testament it always denotes love for fellow believers, those who are members of the family of God in virtue of the new birth. Christian love does not undervalue or disregard natural family ties; it gives them their due importance and condemns those who are without natural affection (Ro 1:31; 2 Ti 3:3). But Christian love transcends these limited natural ties and finds its wider sphere of affection in the redeemed family of God's children (Lk 8:21). This love which Christians cherish for each other as brethren is not just a passive disposition of fondness; it manifests itself in overt acts of kindness toward the brethren.

The practice of this "brother-love" was one of the outstanding features of the early Christian Church. Jesus had exhibited it in His own person and ministry and it was present in the Christian community from the first (Ac 4:32). And wherever the gospel took root in remote Greek cities this family feeling also sprang up among the converts. It was this feature of its corporate life that made the church so distinctive and drew many yearning hearts into its fold. Tertullian (c. 192) quotes the heathen as remarking in amazement, "Behold how these Christians love one another."

The missionaries gladly acknowledged that on this subject the readers had "no need that one write unto" them.** Explicit instructions on the matter were unnecessary. "Love was engraved on their hearts, so that there was no need of letters written on paper."[36]

(2) *Confirmatory evidence* (vv. 9b-10a). *For* at once introduces the evidence for the preceding statement of fact. "For ye yourselves are taught of God to love one another." The emphatic "ye yourselves" contrasts the readers with "we," the writers, understood in the preceding statement. The fact is that the readers themselves are "taught of God" (*theodidaktoi*). This compound verbal, made up of *theos* (God) and the passive verbal *didaktos* (taught), occurs only here in the New Testament. It does not refer to any past historical teaching, as God's word in the Old Testament or Jesus' commandment of love (Jn 13:34), nor to the teaching of New Testament writers; it signifies the teaching in their hearts by God Himself through the indwelling Spirit. It is God rather than a human being who is the Teacher, and the teaching "refers not only to a partial and fragmentary lesson, but to a permanent relation established between the human mind and the Divine Teacher. We are pupils all our life through in the school of God."[37]

"To love one another" conveys not only the content of the teaching but also the purpose or aim of the divine teaching. The form of the original (*eis to agapan*) signifies, "ye are God's pupils for this purpose—that ye may be loving one another." He has many lessons to teach them but this is the supreme reason why He is teaching them. The present tense indicates that this love is to be no occasional, sporadic matter, but a continual, habitual practice. The reciprocal pronoun indicates that this love is mutual. Christians are to lavish upon each other that same self-sacrificing love which was shed abroad in their hearts by the Holy Spirit (Ro 5:5).

Being 'taught of God" is an inner, spiritual experience which is not subject to outward observation. That individuals are the recipients of this inner, subjective teaching must be demonstrated by their objective practice of this love toward other Christians. "For indeed" at once introduces this objective, historical evidence to confirm the assertion that the Thessalonians are truly taught of God. *For* serves to confirm the fact that they are being taught of God to love, while *indeed* looks forward to the fact that they are actually practicing it, "for indeed ye do it toward all the brethren that are in all Macedonia." They need not be urged to acquire this virtue, for they are already practicing it. Only those who are

** The original expresses no subject for the infinitive "write" but "we" or the indefinite "any one" is rightly supplied from the context. The original construction is a little lax, literally, "not a need ye have to write to you." Regularly the infinitive "to write" would be in the passive, as in 5:1. The use of the active for the passive is amply vouched for in similar combinations and need occasion no difficulty. A few scribes smoothed out the construction by writing "we have."

taught of God keep on loving one another. The present tense indicates that it is their continuing practice.

Timothy doubtless had seen the evidence that they were showing love "toward all the brethren." The preposition rendered "toward" (*eis*) points not only to the direction but also the destination of this love, it is a love that reaches out unto "all the brethren." They are not allowing their personal predilections to make their love selective. True to the inner promptings of love, they are expressing their love not only to their own members but also toward all fellow Christians "in all Macedonia," the Roman province of which Thessalonica was the capital. Their expression of love toward other believers was as wide as their opportunities. The geographical location and political status of Thessalonica brought them frequent opportunity to show this love toward believers coming to their city. In what practical way their love manifested itself is not stated, perhaps in hospitably opening their homes and hearts to them. That persecutions causing dispersion gave them further opportunities to show this grace is not improbable. At any rate the expression implies knowledge of neighboring Christian churches and lively communication with them.

We know of established sister churches in Macedonia only at Philippi and Berea, but it is highly probable there were groups of believers in other cities or surrounding villages of which we have no information. That the gospel had spread with great rapidity from these known centers seems clear, yet the expression need not be pressed to mean that there were numerous believers all over Macedonia. But the claim is quite groundless that it proved that the Thessalonian church had already existed for a considerable time, hence this epistle could not have been written by Paul.

b) EXHORTATIONS TO THOSE LOVING (vv. 10*b*-12). *But* is mildly adversative, setting the following exhortations in contrast to the commendation that has just been given. The very fact that they are already loving the brethren justifies the following exhortations. They are exhorted to abound yet more in love (v. 10*b*) and to be industrious (vv. 11-12).

(1) *Exhortation to abound in love* (v. 10*b*). "We exhort you, brethren, that ye abound more and more." The verb rendered *exhort* (cf. comments on 2:3) conveys a feeling of tender personal concern yet leaves no doubt as to the urgency of the exhortation. The present tense denotes that it is an appeal which the missionaries desire continually to press upon their converts. The affectionate address, *brethren*, marks the exhortation as grounded in the spiritual brotherhood into which the readers have been brought. In 3:12 the writers recorded their prayer for the growing love

179

of the readers; now they are actively urging them to a greater personal realization of that love.

"That ye abound more and more" expresses the solicitude of the missionaries that their love may be active and increasing to an overflowing measure. There is always room for increase and growth in love. Like a living plant, it must continue to grow and bear still more fruit. In their practice of love, believers can never sit back satisfied and feel that they have done enough. In this life we never reach the goal of ethical perfection. Love must always be stretching out after a closer approximation to the divine standard of love in Christ.

This is the third occurrence of the verb *abound* in this letter. The term is characteristic of Paul's understanding of the Christian life. Paul's ever active qualities of mind and heart found in the gospel an endless source of divine energy for abundant living. And he yearned to have his converts avail themselves of the varied and abundant resources of the gospel for an overflowing life. Knowing the exuberant qualities of the Christian life, Paul could never be complacent when believers lived barren and mediocre lives. He always aspired to lead them into the abundant life which Christ came to bring.

(2) *Exhortation to be industrious* (vv. 11-12). *And* carries a conjunctive force and places this exhortation in a construction parallel to the preceding. Ellicott remarks that it stands in "close grammatical, though somewhat more lax logical, connection with what immediately precede."[38] Lünemann insists that we must "consider vv. 11, 12 as a new exhortation, internally distinct from that in vv. 9, 10, and which only happens to be united with it, as both refer to the moral furtherance of the Christian life."[39] In keeping with this view some commentators treat these two verses as a separate and distinct topic. But others, in keeping with the grammatical structure of the verses, hold that this exhortation is closely connected with the preceding. Thus Neil insists, "Brotherly Love is the subject of the whole passage, issuing firstly in hospitality, secondly, in every man recognizing his Christian duty to contribute his share of honest work to the community as a whole."[40] Riggenbach well remarks that "the new exhortation is added with a view to saving brotherly love from being damaged."[41] Our faithful performance of the everyday duties of life is intimately related to our love for our associates.

The exhortation "that ye study to be quiet" indicates that there was a spirit of restlessness in the young Thessalonian church. It was due, apparently, not to political influences but rather to the new religious experiences and hopes which had gripped their minds. Although there is nothing to prove that this restlessness was caused by their excited anticipation of the impending return of Christ, such a connection, nevertheless, seems probable. The inspiring expectation of Christ's return, whereby earthly interests were reduced in importance in their eyes, had become the center of their excited interest. This connection seems justi-fied from the fact that Paul immediately follows this exhortation with his treatment of the second advent, thereupon to return to further practical exhortations concerning daily living. Paul urges that this "eschatological restlessness" be turned into the proper channel. Instead of allowing their excited expectation to lead them to neglect their daily duties, let them use this enthusiasm faithfully to fulfill those duties.

These two verses contain the statement of the exhortation (v. 11a), make a passing reference to past similar charges (v. 11b), and set forth the motivating purpose of the exhortation (v. 12).

(a) *Contents of the exhortation* (v. 11a). The exhortation is threefold: "that ye study to be quiet, and to do your own business, and to work with your hands." The three phrases apparently relate to three phases of the trouble in the Thessalonian church—mental excitement, meddlesomeness, and idleness. Timothy had noted the beginnings of these tendencies in the church, but we need not conclude that the problem was serious. There is the probability that these exhortations were intended primarily to be preventive. The reference to past similar charges indicates that these matters had formed part of the teaching the missionaries had imparted while with them. But it is clear from the second epistle (3:6-15) that these brief words did not arrest these undesirable tendencies and the problem became more acute later on.

They are first of all urged to be calm, "that ye study to be quiet." The infinitive translated "study" quite literally meant "to be fond of honor, to be actuated by love of honor," hence, "to be ambitious for, to aspire to," from a love of honor to strive eagerly to bring something to pass. In later Greek it came to denote restless eagerness in any pursuit, hence, "to strive eagerly, to be zealous." Findlay holds that even in the latter sense "there clings to it the connotation of some *desire to shine* or *pursuit of eminence.*"[42] It is not certain just which sense Paul intended the term to have here. If he meant "and to be ambitious to be quiet" (Rother-ham),†† he urges that the restless energy and activity associated with ambition for eminence be channeled into the task of living a quiet and calm life. More probably, in harmony with later usage, it has the mean-ing "to seek earnestly to be quiet" (Darby),‡‡ urging them to be zealous-

††Similarly Conybeare, Weymouth, Williams; 20th Cent, Berkeley, NEB, and NASB. Phillips has, "and to make it your ambition to have no ambition!" but that is not quite the point. Way paraphrases, "to make it a point of honour to avoid religious excitement."
‡‡Similarly Moffatt, Montgomery, Goodspeed, Lattey.

ly active in endeavoring to live quiet lives. In either case the advice is paradoxical.

The infinitive "to be quiet" basically means "to be at rest" and was used of silence after speech, rest after labor, peace after war, and the like; it was also used of tranquility or peace of mind; here it is used to urge the living of a calm, restful life. The present tense in both verbal forms stresses that they must constantly strive to lead such a life. They must eagerly endeavor to be eminent in the effort "to be quiet," live tranquilly and restfully. Instead of allowing them to succumb to fanatical excitement, Paul desires to recall them to restfulness of mind and a balanced outlook upon life. If they will develop a quiet, restful attitude, the outward manifestations of restlessness will cease.

Calvin proposed to separate these two infinitives, taking *study* by itself and referring it back to the command to brotherly love. He held that Paul, having commanded them to increase in love, now "commends to them a holy rivalry, so that they may vie with one another to mutual affection."[43] Then the following infinitive, "to be quiet," begins a new construction, standing parallel with the next two infinitives. But if this was Paul's meaning we would expect a connective "and" between them. It is much better to take the two infinitives together, as in our versions. This avoids the harshness of construction which results from Calvin's proposal and gives the most natural interpretation.

The following two duties explain how they are to go about living quiet lives. They must direct their attention to their own proper duties, "to do your own business." The infinitive translated "to do" means "to busy oneself with, to be occupied with, to practice," hence, to mind or give attention to "your own business," more literally, "your own things," your own personal affairs. The present tense points to this as their continual duty. They are to serve God by a faithful performance of their own individual tasks. It is a warning against meddlesomeness in the affairs of others. While having a proper concern for the needs of the brethren, they must avoid the neglect of their personal affairs. Let them have the habit of attending to their own interests and responsibilities.

They are further exhorted "to work with your hands." The verb specifically means "to work, to labor," and the added "with your hands" makes it unmistakable that manual labor is meant. The present tense marks this as their standing duty. Their excitement about the future must not keep them from their daily work. Paul knew that pious idlers can be a serious danger to the peace of the brotherhood.

The expression indicates that the majority of the Thessalonian church members practiced some handicraft. It is not probable that the term should be interpreted to exclude skilled labor. It clearly was a working-man's church. There would be dock workers, and others doing heavy manual labor, as well as craftsmen working by hand at their trades, many of them requiring training and dexterity. That there were a few wealthy members in the church is probable (Ac 17:4), but Plummer points out that the Thessalonian epistles contain "no exhortations to the wealthy, and no warnings as to the deceitfulness of riches, although there was much wealth in Thessalonica."[44]

Paul's teaching and personal example at Thessalonica had underlined the dignity of manual labor. In this he sided strongly with the Jews against the Greeks. Among the Greeks manual labor was regarded as degrading; it was an indispensable but contemptible necessity fittingly performed by slaves. The Jews, on the other hand, upheld the dignity of all forms of labor. Work was regarded as obligatory, and every Jewish boy, however wealthy his family, was taught a trade. The Jewish rabbis worked at a trade to earn their livelihood.

Christianity finds nothing inconsistent between honest toil and personal holiness. It holds that all things which believers do should be done as service to Christ (Col 3:17). Denney remarks, "If we cannot be holy at our work, it is not worth taking any trouble to be holy at other times."[45]

Lenski finds in these last two exhortations two distinct groups, businessmen and common laborers.[46] This view serves to add another touch to the figure of the businessman whom he finds in verse 6 above. But it is improbable that any such a rigid distinction can be drawn. These admonitions are directed to the church in general, although obviously they would apply to some more directly than to others.

(b) *Reminder of past charges* (v. 11b). "Even as we charged you" again reminds the readers that these demands are nothing new to them. The aorist tense of the verb *charged* (cf. 4:2) points to a definite action in the past. The historical fact was that the missionaries had given them explicit instructions on these issues while still with them. "Even as" insists upon the exact correspondence between those orders and the present demands. Those who were succumbing to these undesirable practices had no excuse for their misconduct.

It is not certain whether this phrase is meant to be taken with all three of the preceding infinitives or only with the last. Ellicott takes it with all three. This would mean that mental excitement, meddlesomeness, and idleness had already begun to manifest themselves while the missionaries were still in the city. He concludes, "The very first publication of Christianity in Thessalonica seems to have been attended with some manifestations of restlessness and feverish expectation."[47] But others, like Frame, hold that this reminder relates directly only to the last.[48] This restricted reference is in full harmony with the contents of the following verse. By teaching and personal example the missionaries had inculcated the dignity as well as the duty of manual labor.

(c) *Purpose in the exhortation* (v. 12). There was a twofold purpose for the demand that the readers should be diligently engaged in daily labor. "That ye may walk becomingly toward them that are without" points to the effect their behavior had on non-Christians. Paul is anxious that his converts walk (conduct themselves) becomingly (with gravity and seemly deportment.) The adverb *becomingly* (*enschēmonōs*), composed of *eu* (well) and *schēma* (form, fashion), means "in good form, decorously, in an honorable manner, so as to cause no offense." Believers can never be indifferent to the impact produced by their example. For them to spend their time in idleness would bring discredit upon the cause of their Lord.

Paul is anxious that his converts set a good example "toward them that are without." *Toward* translates the preposition *pros* and points to the social relations in which they stood. The way they behaved would influence "them that are without," unbelievers, whether Jews or Gentiles, those who are outside the family of God. These nonbelievers might not understand the blessings of the gospel but they were fully able to appreciate the difference between order and confusion, between idleness and diligence in the lives of professed followers of the gospel. Paul was ever concerned that believers should not offend the moral sense of unbelievers. Paul's deep, God-given concern for "them that are without" is evident from his varied references to them in his letters (1 Co 5:12-13; Col 4:5; 1 Ti 3:7).

"And may have need of nothing" further challenges them to work in order that they may maintain a dignified independence. Self-support, where possible, is a moral duty.

The word rendered "nothing" (*mēdenos*) may be either masculine, "no one," or neuter, "nothing." Either makes good sense. If it is masculine the meaning is that they must be working to earn their own livelihood so that they will not be dependent upon others for alms. "Christianity has no place for drones."[49] For members of the church to be parasites and continue to live off other members of the brotherhood is morally degrading. Lünemann objects to the view that *mēdenos* is masculine with the remark, "To stand in need of *no man*, is for man an impossibility."[50] It may be replied that it is equally impossible for a man to be in need of *nothing*. As absolutes, both are impossible.

Since the expression "to have need of" is generally used with the genitive of the *thing* needed, the neuter seems more probable. Adeney supports this view with the remark, "We do not want to feel that we have need of nobody. The notion is churlish."[51] While men obviously need fellowship, the neuter stresses that they must make proper provision for themselves and their families by their personal labors. Their own industry must foster a healthy spirit of financial independence. This is essential if their love of the brethren is to continue and to abound. Those who deliberately impose upon the generosity of others are not living in love.

9

PRACTICAL: INSTRUCTIONS

B. INSTRUCTIONS CONCERNING THE DEAD IN CHRIST

4:13-18 But we would not have you ignorant, brethren, concerning them that fall asleep; that ye sorrow not, even as the rest, who have no hope. (14) For if we believe that Jesus died and rose again, even so them also that are fallen asleep in Jesus will God bring with him. (15) For this we say unto you by the word of the Lord, that we that are alive, that are left unto the coming of the Lord, shall in no wise precede them that are fallen asleep. (16) For the Lord himself shall descend from heaven, with a shout, with the voice of the archangel, and with the trump of God: and the dead in Christ shall rise first; (17) then we that are alive, that are left, shall together with them be caught up in the clouds, to meet the Lord in the air: and so shall we ever be with the Lord. (18) Wherefore comfort one another with these words.

ALTHOUGH THE ESCHATOLOGICAL NOTE has already been heard on several occasions (1:10; 2:12, 19; 3:13), two whole paragraphs are now devoted to matters associated with Christ's return. They reveal that the deficiencies of the faith of the Thessalonians were on the doctrinal as well as the practical side. The two paragraphs are both eschatological in outlook yet are sufficiently distinct to be treated separately. In both paragraphs the teaching of Christ's return is not presented by way of indoctrination but as a matter already familiar to the readers. But the readers were in need of further explanation and admonition. The first paragraph offers needed instruction concerning the relation of their dead to the return of Christ; the second deals with the point of the time of His return and the resultant need for watchfulness. The distinctness of the two paragraphs is evident from the fact that Paul ends each with a practical exhortation (4:18; 5:11). The present paragraph is the classic New Testament passage on the rapture of the church.

There is no asserted connection between this new topic and what has preceded. The opening *But* (*de*) is transitional and indicates that a new subject is being introduced which may be more or less closely connected with the preceding. It would be appropriate here to render it "Now." Our modern versions do not agree on the rendering of this particle here.*

Lenski questions the existence of any close connection between this paragraph and what has gone before, but Bicknell insists that "when we look below the surface there is a real continuity of thought."[1] This thread of continuity he finds to be the practical effect that the hope of the return of Christ had made upon the minds of the readers. It has caused some of them to lose their mental balance, resulting in restlessness and idleness. So, Paul turns to deal with the source of their agitation. Alexander, however, thinks the link of connection is the theme of brotherly love with which the preceding paragraph closed. He remarks, "Christian 'brotherly love' includes love for, and thought of, those who sleep in Jesus. This is indicated by the very order and sequence of this Epistle."[2]

It may be granted that there was a mental association for Paul between the preceding and the present section, but it is not necessary to seek to identify any close and logical connection.

We need not suppose that the Thessalonians had sent Paul a letter inquiring about the fate of those believers who had died. It is enough to suppose that Timothy had told him about their anxiety and sorrow. Timothy certainly would have done what he could to clear up their questions, but now Paul sends written instructions to settle their misgivings and fears concerning the dead in Christ.

These words of instruction and comfort concerning the dead in Christ may be divided into three parts. The authoritative character of the instructions is indicated in verse 13; the contents of the instructions are recorded in verses 14-17; verse 18 assures the comfort to be derived from the instructions.

1. Character of the Instructions (v. 13)

"We would not have you ignorant, brethren" characterizes the attitude of the writers in imparting the needed instruction.† The words are a not infrequent formula of transition in Paul's epistles used to introduce some new subject which he is anxious that the readers should understand.‡ The negative formula is positive in meaning, "we wish you to know" (cf. 1 Co 11:3; Col 2:1). The positive form is very common in the papyri. The expression does not carry an implied rebuke like "Know ye not?" nor does it make an appeal to previous knowledge and instruction. It

---

*"Now" is the rendering of Lattey, Weymouth, Phillips; "but" is used by Conybeare, Darby, Rotherham, Montgomery, Berkeley, RSV, and NASB; Williams has "also" while Young and Way use "and." The particle is omitted entirely by Moffatt, Goodspeed, 20th Cent, and NEB.

†The *Textus Receptus* here has the singular pronoun, "I," but the plural is strongly authenticated. The singular is correct in Ro 1:13; 11:25; 1 Co 10:1; 12:1.

‡It occurs six times: Ro 1:13; 11:25; 1 Co 10:1; 12:1; 2 Co 1:8; 1 Th 4:13.

seems always to relate back to something that has happened and to which attention is called to correct a misunderstanding or to relieve anxiety. The precise point of this paragraph concerns a matter upon which the missionaries had not dwelt in their teachings while yet in Thessalonica. But the writers are anxious that their readers should not remain uninformed on this eschatological matter. Clearly Paul did not feel that eschatological subjects should be avoided. He knew that "ignorance concerning spiritual realities is always bad for the believer."[3]

Each time that Paul uses the formula "we would not have you ignorant" he adds the affectionate address, *brethren,* as if the information given is due to his concern for the readers. It softens an expression "which otherwise might seem to be dictatorial or imply reprehensible ignorance in those to whom he writes."[4]

"Concerning them that fall asleep" states the precise subject of the paragraph. "Them that fall asleep" translates an articular present participle; the action may be interpreted either as continuous, "those sleeping" or "lying asleep," or as repeated, "those falling asleep from time to time." The *Textus Receptus* has the perfect tense, "those who have fallen asleep," but the present tense has strong manuscript support and also lends "itself more readily to the thought of a future awakening than the perfect would have done."[5]

This well-known euphemism for death did not originate with Christianity. It was a common metaphor among the Jews and was current even among pagans. The figure was apparently suggested by the stillness of the body and its apparent restfulness upon death; it was used even where there was no hope of resurrection. Having been used by the Master Himself (Mk 5:39; Jn 11:11), Christians readily accepted the term as a witness to their faith concerning death. The figure is not distinctively Christian, yet, as Morris well remarks, it is "much more at home in a Christian context than elsewhere."[6] It indicates the restful effect of death for the child of God and points to its temporary nature. The risen Lord robbed death of its sting and horror for the believer and has transformed it into sleep for those in Christ. And so the early Christians called their burial-places *koimētēria,* (cemeteries or dormitories.)

But the figure of death as sleep cannot be pressed to establish the teaching that in the intermediate state the soul is in unconscious repose (soul sleep). The state of the soul after death is not in Paul's mind in this metaphor; the body only is thought of as being asleep, no longer in communication with its earthly environment. As sleep has its awakening, so the body of the believer will have its awakening. The theory of soul sleep is inconsistent with Paul's assertion in 5:10 that God's purpose for us is that whether we live or die we should live together with Christ.

At death the believer's "earthly house of our tabernacle" is dissolved (2 Co 5:1) and returns to the dust, but the spiritual part of man, the soul, his self-conscious personality, departs "to be at home with the Lord" (2 Co 5:8). Since to depart from this world in death to "be with Christ" is described by Paul as "very far better" (Phil 1:23) than the present state of blessed communion with the Lord and happy activity in His service, it is evident that "sleep" as applied to believers cannot be intended to teach that the soul is unconscious.

"That ye sorrow not, even as the rest," indicates the practical aim of the writers in imparting these instructions. The negative (*mē*) with the present tense indicates that their aim is to stop the sorrowing of the readers. They are not to go on sorrowing like others. They hope to cure their sorrow by removing their ignorance. The verb means "to pain, to grieve," and in the passive, as here, "to be sad, to be distressed, to grieve."

The reason for their grief is not explicitly stated but a general inference can safely be drawn from the context. Clearly some of the Thessalonian believers had died since the missionaries left and those who had lost loved ones were assailed with grief because of their death. There is nothing in this paragraph to suggest that they thought that "these dead were lost" as Lenski thinks.[7] Verse 15 rather indicates that they feared that those who failed to live until the coming of Christ would be at an irreparable disadvantage at His return. They thought that there was a peculiar advantage attached to survival until the end time (cf. Dan 12:12). They fancied that those who had departed would miss the blissful reunion, or at least come behind those who lived until the *parousia*. Thus their grief was not just a natural sorrow for their own loss but grief for the supposed loss of their loved ones sustained by their death before the return of the Lord.

This is an argument for the early date of this epistle. Such an anxiety could only be entertained in the first period of their existence as a church, and would naturally arise with the first deaths in their midst. It points to a time when their apprehension of Christian doctrine concerning death was still quite imperfect.

They are not to go on sorrowing "even as the rest," the non-Christians. The force of the original is to prohibit all sorrow for their dead. We need not assume that Paul intended to prohibit that natural sorrow and sense of loss we feel at the death of loved ones, but he is prohibiting all sorrow which mourns the supposed loss sustained by loved ones because of their death. Such sorrow is not for Christians. For them to give way to their grief would be to act like the pagan world.

"The rest" is an expression synonymous with "them that are without" in verse 12 above. Findlay notes the difference between the two terms in remarking that the earlier expression "implies *exclusion,* this implies *deprivation.*"[8] The non-Christians are deprived of the hope and comfort that the Christian faith, rightly understood, provides. "Even as" does not introduce any comparison between the sorrow which Christians might rightly feel and the wild abandonment to grief manifested by the unsaved. It rather states the contrast between Christians and "the rest, who have no hope."

"Who have no hope" translates an articular participle standing in apposition with "the rest." It characterizes them as a class having no hope. *Hope* is not further defined and it is not certain whether hope of life in Christ or hope of resurrection is intended. Apparently the latter should be construed, in view of the context. The expression points to the hopelessness which characterized the pagan world.

It has been remarked that the nonchristian world was not completely without hope. It is true that the Pharisees believed in a resurrection, although the Sadducees denied it. Had Paul been writing to a Jewish audience he doubtless would not have expressed it so strongly. But even in the heathen world there were occasional utterances of hope for the future. The best and truest of the ancient philosophers held, with more or less distinctness, to the immortality of the soul. Plato taught immortality§ and Ovid could write concerning death:

> Souls have no share in death: when their earlier haunt is abandoned,
> They dwell in their new abodes, and live on in the home that receives
>   them (*Met.* xv. 158-59).

But as speculation increased and confidence in their traditions grew dim, faith in a future life wavered. The Stoics expressed serious doubts concerning man's future state, and at best could offer only conditional immortality. The Epicureans, whose teachings were frankly materialistic, naturally disbelieved in immortality.

But Greek and Roman philosophy agreed in holding out no hope for the future of the body. Any future bliss for the souls of men was thought of in terms of escape from the body, regarded as the "prison-house" of the soul. There was a common hopelessness in the fact of death. Four typical assertions are: "Of a man once dead there is no resurrection" (Aeschylus); "Hopes are among the living, the dead are without hope"

§Plato puts these words into the mouth of Socrates: "Death is one of two things; either such that the dead is nothing and has no perception; or else it may be a removal and change of the soul's residence from this place to another. . . . If, then, death be such as this [an unconscious sleep] I call it gain: for in that case all time seems to the dead no longer than a single night. But, on the other hand, if it be a departure from hence to another region, and the saying be true that in that other world are all the dead; what could be a greater blessing than this? . . . They that are there are every way happier than those who are here; and above all, for the time to come they are immortal, if what is said holds true" (*Apology of Socrates* 40c).

(Theocritus); "Suns may set and rise again but we, when once our brief light goes down, must sleep an endless night" (Catullus); "No one awakes and arises who has once been overtaken by the chilling end of life" (Lucretius). The mystery religions did offer their devotees some form of victory over death, but their weird views of resurrection offered little ground for hope and confidence. It may well be remarked that the speculations and surmises of pagan philosophy and religion did not offer any certain basis for hope since they lacked any revelation on the subject.

Among the common masses of the pagan world hopelessness and despair prevailed in the face of death. This hopelessness was well known to the Thessalonian Christians. Conybeare and Howson refer to a heathen sepulchral inscription at Thessalonica which proclaimed that "after death there is no revival, after the grave no meeting of those who have loved each other on earth."[9] Lightfoot remarks that nowhere is the gloomy despair of the Roman world more forcibly brought out than by their monumental inscriptions; he calls attention to the amazing contrast seen between the dreary wail of despair in the tombs above ground on the Appian Way and the exultant notes of hope in the ill-written, ill-spelled inscriptions of the catacombs.[10] It is Christ alone who has abolished death, and brought life and immortality to light through the gospel (2 Ti 1:10).

2. Contents of the Instructions (vv. 14-17)

The sorrowing of the Thessalonians for their dead is inexcusable in view of the hope that Christians have. Christian hope is grounded in the revelation which we have in Christ Jesus. It is the pagans' ignorance of that revelation that explains their hopelessness.

The nature of the Christian hope is now logically unfolded. The readers are given a basic assurance concerning their dead (v. 14); this is supported by the revelation of the two groups at Christ's return (v. 15); and this in turn is confirmed by a portrayal of the manner and events at Christ's coming (vv. 16-17).

a) ASSURANCE CONCERNING THEIR DEAD (v. 14). *For* introduces the reason why the readers are not to sorrow for their dead. The historical facts of the death and resurrection of Jesus are the guarantee concerning the future of the believing dead. Christian faith and hope are anchored in history: "For if we believe that Jesus died and rose again." *If* does not imply doubt and uncertainty concerning Christ's death and resurrection but instead assumes it as a recognized truth. It is a condition of reality and might well be translated "since."‖ *We*, both writers and readers,

‖Moffatt and RSV use "since" and Lattey and 20th Cent use "as." The NEB makes it a simple declarative statement.

"we as Christians," accept the fact of Christ's death and resurrection as the great major premise of the Christian faith. They are the sure foundation of Christian hope. The two facts must be kept together. "St. Paul bases his Gospel not on the Cross taken in isolation, but on the Cross as followed by and interpreted by the Resurrection."[11]

"Jesus died" asserts the past historical event. *Jesus* is the name of a human being and calls attention to His experience here on earth. His experience of death as our Redeemer has significance for our own experience. Death was not final in His case, neither will it be in ours. It is not said that Jesus "fell asleep" but rather that He *died*. He experienced death, the result of sin, in all its grim horror. But His death brought the death of death; in dying as our sin-bearer He transformed death for believers into sleep with a future awakening.

Jesus not only died, but also rose again. Both are definite historical events. His resurrection was the climactic event which demonstrated His victory over sin and death. If Jesus did not actually arise from the grave our Christian hope has no justification. It may be noted that both verbs, *died* and *rose*, are in the active voice; to have used passives would have meant that He was acted upon by others. The active voice depicts Him as voluntarily laying down His life and taking it up again (Jn 10:17-18). Christian faith embraces as its Saviour this Jesus, who voluntarily died and rose again. His victory assures our victory.

> No longer must the mourners weep
>   And call departed Christians dead;
> For death is hallowed into sleep,
>   And every grave becomes a bed.
>
> Now once more, Eden's door
>   Open stands to mortal eyes!
> Now at last, old things past,
>   Christ is risen! We too shall rise![12]

From his premise of Christian faith Paul draws the conclusion, "even so them also that are fallen asleep in Jesus will God bring with him." Rolston remarks, "The connection between the two parts of this statement [verse 14] is not obvious. It is one thing to believe that Jesus died and rose again; it is quite another to believe that God will bring with Jesus at his coming those who have fallen asleep."[13] But the connection which Rolston misses is implied in "even so," pointing to the complete accord between Christ and His saints. In the words of Gloag, "The apostle's argument proceeds on the supposition that Christ and believers are one body, of which Christ is the Head and believers are the members; and that consequently what happens to the Head must happen to the members."[14] The resurrection of Christ is at once the assurance and type of the resurrection of His people.

The statement of this conclusion is slightly irregular. Having said, "If we believe, as we do, that Jesus died and rose again," we would expect, "even so we also believe that . . . ." Instead, the conclusion is given as a direct assertion, not as a matter of faith. Paul thus instinctively avoids any impression of uncertainty concerning the truth declared in the conclusion.

The order in the original makes *God* emphatic, stressing that He is the Actor in what is to take place. Young reproduces the order of the original in the following (somewhat awkward) rendering, "so also God those asleep through Jesus he will bring with him." The God who raised up Jesus will also associate Christ's people with Him in resurrection.

"Them that are fallen asleep" translates an articular aorist passive participle; it looks back to the definite event of their death, again described under the consolatory term *sleep.* The participle in itself is timeless; with the future verb it denotes all those who will have died prior to the return of Christ. It is probable that the passive participle here is passive in meaning as well as form; if so, it would be more accurate to render, "them that were put to sleep." Then the very act of dying is "compared to putting to sleep, as with a child whom his mother hushes to slumber."[15]

The chief difficulty of the verse is the significance of the phrase translated "in Jesus," quite literally, "through Jesus" (*dia tou Iēsou*). It is not certain whether it should be taken with the participle just before it, "those fallen asleep," or with the verb "will bring" immediately after. Were the original reading "in" rather than "through" the former would be the unquestioned connection. This uncertainty is reflected in our versions. Darby may be quoted as representative of those holding to the former connection, "so also God will bring with him those who have fallen asleep through Jesus,"# while Weymouth may represent the other connection, "in the same way also through Jesus God will bring with Him those who have fallen asleep."**

If "through Jesus" is connected with the verb, it means that while God effects the resurrection, Jesus is His agent in both the bringing and the resurrection. The primary reason for holding to this connection seems to be the difficulty of the expression "fallen asleep through Jesus." But this proposed connection with the verb creates its own difficulties. It destroys the natural parallelism of the sentence: "Jesus died . . . those

---

#The NASB has "in Jesus" connected with "asleep." Rotherham, Young, Way, Lattey, and Berkeley rightly have "through Jesus" and connect with "asleep."
**Williams, 20th Cent, and RSV translate "through Jesus" and connect with "will bring." The NEB paraphrases, "and so it will be for those who died as Christians; God will bring them to life with Jesus."

fallen asleep through Jesus;" but connected with the participle, the two subjects stand in clear and illustrative antithesis. To connect "through Jesus" with "will bring with him" makes a redundant conclusion, "through Jesus . . . with him." If "them that are fallen asleep" has no modifier those "asleep" would include all the dead; but that goes beyond the scope of this passage. It is desirable to have a modifier with the participle to define the character of those asleep.

The grammatical construction leaves it an open question as to which connection Paul intended. We accept the connection with "them that are fallen asleep" as the more probable. But what is the meaning of the unusual expression "fallen asleep through Jesus?" Two interpretations are advanced.

Some hold the meaning to be that they have "fallen asleep through Jesus" as martyrs for the faith. But in that case we would expect the accusative with the preposition rather than the genitive (*dia ton Iēsoun*), "on account of" or "for the sake of" Jesus. Moreover, Lünemann asserts that "the indications in both Epistles do not afford the slightest justification of the idea of persecutions, which ended in *bloody death*."[16] To restrict the reference to martyrs would inappropriately limit this message of comfort to a very small portion of believers. Clearly the problem agitating the Thessalonians was wider than death by martyrdom; it is natural to assume that since the missionaries had left, some of the members had died a natural death.

The more probable meaning is that through the atoning work of Jesus what was stark death for men without hope of the resurrection has become simply sleep. Through His death and resurrection Jesus has disarmed death and removed its sting for believers. "Through the Jesus" points to an effect wrought by "the Jesus" mentioned in the first part of the verse; His death and resurrection have changed the nature of death. "Death is to the Christian no longer a penalty, but a falling asleep; and this belongs to the Christian's death in whatever form it may come, and with whatever accompaniments."[17]

That those who have fallen asleep "God will bring with him" is the fundamental declaration in Paul's reply to the unenlightened sorrowing of the Thessalonians. They have no cause to sorrow for their departed loved ones because when God acts to bring back the risen Christ at the *parousia* they will return with Him. The verb rendered *bring* is frequently translated "lead" and serves to picture the departed saints as following the lead of their Lord in His triumphal train in His return from heaven. This verb stresses the "blessed association of departed Christians with their Lord at His *parousia*, in which the Thessalonians feared their sleeping brethren would have no part."[18]

Since Paul has just spoken of the resurrection of Jesus we might have expected him to say that God will also "raise up" the departed believers. Instead he speaks of their association with Jesus at His coming. It indicates that the worry of the Thessalonians was not whether those who had died would rise, but whether they would have a share in the glories at Christ's return.

b) REVELATION CONCERNING THE TWO GROUPS (v. 15). *For* introduces the authority for the statement just made. It was based upon a revelation from the Lord. The verse indicates the character of the revelation (v. 15*a*) and states the corrective for their sorrow (v. 15*b*).

(1) *Character of the revelation* (v. 15*a*). "For this we say unto you by the word of the Lord" characterizes the authority upon which the preceding declaration was based. *This* refers not to what precedes but is an emphatic introduction to all that follows the first *that* of this verse. "Unto you" has an emphatic position and stresses that the revealed truth now being spoken is given in the special interest of the readers. It is a message from "the Lord," Jesus Christ, given by Him for their special instruction and comfort.

"By the word of the Lord" indicates the source of the revelation. *By* is literally "in"; the revelation was made in connection with a communication from the mouth of the Lord. The expression has been understood in three different ways.

Some propose to find this *word* in some recorded utterance of Jesus while He was here on earth. But there is nothing in the recorded prophetic utterances of Jesus in the gospels which covers the present statement.

Others suggest that Paul is quoting some unrecorded saying of Jesus known to him through tradition, like the memorable utterance in Acts 20:35. Morris regards this explanation as "the simple one" which makes the others unnecessary. But Milligan feels that the "very want of similarity with any 'recorded' saying should make us the more chary of postulating an 'unrecorded one'."[19] If Paul was actually referring to some unrecorded saying of Jesus it is probable that he would have given the utterance more directly, as in Acts 20:35.

More probable is the view that the reference is to a revelation made to the writers directly, to Paul personally, or possibly to Silas (cf. Ac 15:32), to meet the special circumstances that had arisen. The opening formula "we say unto you" is agreeable to this view; it has a parallel use in the Old Testament. In 1 Corinthians 15:51-54 Paul speaks of "a mystery" in setting forth the transformation of the living at the rapture of the church. This "mystery," undoubtedly a direct revelation to Paul, may well be a further unfolding of the revelation given him to meet the perplexity of the Thessalonians. This view is in full accord with the scriptural records that Paul did receive direct communications from the risen Lord from the very beginning of his ministry (cf. Ac 9:5-6; 22:17-21; Gal 1:12; 2:2; 1 Co 11:23). The version of Moffatt reflects this view, "For we tell you, as the Lord has told us." The rendering of Weymouth, "And this we declare to you on the Lord's own word," would suit either of the other two views.

(2) *Corrective in the revelation* (v. 15b). "That we that are alive, that are left unto the coming of the Lord, shall in no wise precede them that are fallen asleep" provides the corrective for their sorrowing. The revelation that the living will not have any advantage over the dead at the return of Christ makes any further feeling of sorrow for their dead wholly unjustified. The two classes of believers at the Lord's return, those that are still alive and those that have died, will unitedly share the same destiny.

The one class at the Lord's return is designated as "we that are alive, that are left." This group designation is introduced with an emphatic first person pronoun, "we," marking the sharp distinction from them that are fallen asleep. This "we" is modified by two articular participles, "the living, the ones surviving." The present tenses are characteristic, describing all those who will be alive at the return of Christ. Paul writes "we" because both the writers and the readers are among that class of believers who are still living here on earth. In opposing the two classes he naturally includes himself with the living. He could not have said "they who are alive" without denying his own hope of seeing the return and robbing his own generation of that hope. The present participles characterizing this group are in themselves timeless; they reflect the time of the future verb they are used with. This revelation deals with the two classes of believers at the Lord's return, not who will be in each class.

Calvin ingeniously explains that although Paul knew by "a special revelation that Christ would come at a somewhat later date," he yet here speaks as though he would be among the living "to arouse the Thessalonians to wait for it, and to keep all the godly in suspense."[20] But Paul's indication that he was looking for the Lord's return was no pious pretense perpetrated for the good of the church. He sincerely lived and labored in the anticipation of the day, but he did not know when it would come. The *time* of the return remains unrevealed (cf. Ac 1:7; Mt 24:36). "The last day is hidden, that every day may be regarded" (Augustine).

It cannot be demonstrated from his letters that later on Paul gave up this hope and expected death instead. As he grew older he well realized that the chances of his survival were diminishing, but that did not eliminate the hope. In 2 Corinthians, written some five years later, Paul deals with his personal attitude to the alternatives of death and the coming of the Lord (2 Co 5:1-10). In it he again uses "we." In verses 2-4 he expresses his yearning for that which cannot take place until the Lord's return; in verse 6 he asserts that he is of good courage in the face of death, and in verse 8 he reasserts that he is willing "to be absent from the body, and to be at home with the Lord." Clearly he still yearns for the *parousia*, which is certain to come, but is unafraid of death which may come first.

In the epistle to the Philippians, written perhaps some five years later still, he describes his own attitude toward death in language akin to that in 2 Corinthians and indicates that death for him is no remote possibility (Phil 1:21-24). Yet he uses "we" and "our" in 3:20 to describe the characteristic attitude of believers toward the coming of Christ.

Even in the pastoral epistles, written last of all, Paul uses "we" in connection with the hope of the second advent. In Titus 2:11-13 Paul speaks of the grace of God instructing us that "we should live . . . looking for that blessed hope." Even in 2 Timothy, where he uses language that can only mean that he was anticipating a speedy execution, he still speaks of the reward awaiting those who love His appearing (2 Ti 4:8). Clearly Paul shared that attitude of expectancy which should characterize each generation of believers. He did not know that he would be alive until the *parousia*, neither could he affirm that he would not be.

Plummer remarks that Paul's use of *we* offers "incidental evidence of the authenticity of the letter. A forger writing after the Apostle's death would not have attributed such words as 'we who are alive' to him."[21]

The second designation, "that are left unto the coming of the Lord," defines more specifically whom Paul means by the living. They are the ones who will "remain over," or "survive" unto the *parousia* (cf. 2:19). There will be a whole generation of Christians who will be alive at that time and will never experience physical death.

The revelation concerning these survivors is that they "shall in no wise precede them that are fallen asleep." "Shall in no wise" translates a strong double negative,†† "by no means, not at all." It offers the sorrowing Thessalonians unquestionable assurance that the living will not "precede them that are fallen asleep." The living will not *precede*, "come before, get a head start" on those who have died. (This was the meaning of "prevent" when the KJV was published in 1611). The living will have no advantage over those fallen asleep; they will not meet the returning Christ ahead of the dead, nor will they have any precedence in the

††*Ou mē* with the aorist subjunctive is comparable in force to *ou mē* with the future indicative (cf. Jn 6:35).

blessedness at His coming. The loss which they felt their loved ones had sustained through death is an imaginary one.

c) PORTRAYAL OF CHRIST'S RETURN (vv. 16-17). *For*, better translated "because" (*hoti*), again justifies the preceding statement by a fuller description of the Lord's return. It pictures the manner of His return (v. 16*a*), the events at His return (vv. 16*b*-17*a*), and the abiding consequence of His return for believers (v. 17*b*).

(1) *Manner of His return* (v. 16*a*). It will be emphatically personal, "the Lord himself." The words point to Christ's "own august personal presence."[22] He will not merely send His angelic deputies to call the saints; He will return personally for them in His glorified body. "The Lord" Jesus, under whose lordship believers stand in life or death (Ro 14:7-9), will Himself "descend from heaven," where He now sits enthroned at the right hand of God (Ro 8:34; Eph 1:20; Col 3:1). He will leave the throne to "descend" (go down) "from heaven" (*ap' ouranou*). The preposition *apo* (off, away from) views the descent from the standpoint of heaven. (In 1:10 "from heaven" is *ek ouranōn* and contemplates the expected coming from the standpoint of earth where the waiting saints are.)

Three prepositional phrases, standing before the verb in the original, describe the accompanying circumstances at the Lord's descent, "with a shout, with the voice of the archangel, and with the trump of God." *With* in each phrase represents the preposition *en*, "in, in connection with," denoting the attendant circumstance.

"A shout" will accompany Christ's descent and last throughout it. "The momentariness of the descent itself is thus set forth. One shout, and all will be done: the descent will have been accomplished."[23] The noun rendered *shout* means "a shout of command" and implies authority and urgency. It was variously used of a general shouting orders to his troops, a driver shouting to excite his horses to greater speed, a hunter encouraging his hounds to the pursuit of the prey, or a captain of rowers exciting them to more vigorous rowing.

The shout is left undefined, no definitive genitive being added. Nothing is said as to who gives the shout, or to whom it is directed. It may well be the shout of Christ Himself, the mighty conqueror over death, awakening the bodies of the dead in Christ to immortal life (cf. Jn 5:28-29; 11:43-44). Others would attribute it to the archangel as His agent.

It may indeed be that the references to the three sounds are to be understood as descriptive of one great signal from heaven. The fact that the second and third clauses are joined by *and* suggests that they stand in an epexegetical relationship to *shout*, serving more fully to describe the shout. Thus as Findlay suggests, "The three phrases may express a single idea, that of 'the voice of the Son of God' by which the dead will be called forth, His 'command' being expressed by an 'archangel's voice,' and that again constituting the 'trumpet of God'."[24] Hogg and Vine paraphrase, "with a shout in the archangel's voice, even with the voice of the trump of God."[25]

Others would distinguish two distinct sounds. Thus Hendriksen takes the shout as uttered by Christ, "proceeding from *his* lips," while the next two phrases, united by the conjunction, are taken "together, so that the archangel is represented as sounding God's trumpet."[26]

Still others insist upon three distinct sounds, following each other in rapid succession. Riggenbach identifies them as follows: "the Commander's call of the King Himself; the voice of the archangel summoning the other angels; the trumpet, which awakes the dead, and collects the believers."[27]

Whatever the procedure in detail may be, it is clear that the signal from heaven will have great significance for the saints. They will hear and instantly respond to the summons when it goes forth. Clearly the rapture does not seem to be a silent affair. It seems that a tremendous reverberating sound will actually encircle the earth. Some seem to think that the world will be unaware of the rapture of the church, that the saints will silently slip away and the world will hardly note their absence. Others think that the rapture, described as a truly "noisy affair," will be known to all, that the voice of the archangel and the sound of the trumpet will be heard by all. An intermediate position seems to be nearer the truth. The unsaved world will realize that something extraordinary and supernatural has taken place, but it does not necessarily follow that they will understand the significance of the sound and will realize exactly what has taken place. Stanton well remarks, "The world shall hear the shout of His coming, much as those who traveled with Saul on the road to Damascus, who heard the sound of a voice, but evidently did not hear articulate words, and who saw no man (Acts 9:7; 22:9)."[28] When the voice spoke to Jesus from heaven during Passion Week all those present heard a sound but it was differently interpreted by various groups (Jn 12:28-30).

"The voice of the archangel" may denote a vocal utterance by the archangel or a sound or tone produced by him, namely, with the trumpet. The latter is the meaning if the two phrases are taken together. The original has no definite article with either *voice* or *archangel*. Both are qualitative. It may be rendered, "a voice [or tone] such as an archangel uses."

The word *archangel* occurs elsewhere in the New Testament only in Jude 9 where it is directly associated with Michael. Whether or not there is more than one archangel cannot be categorically answered from Scripture. It is possible that Michael is the only archangel, but the reference in Daniel 10:13 to Michael as "one of the chief princes" makes it possible that there are others beside him. The only other angel named in the Bible is Gabriel, an august being, who described himself to Zacharias as "that stand in the presence of God" (Lk 1:19).

"The trump of God" again is qualitative, neither noun having an article. It denotes a trumpet belonging to God, such as is used in His service. The mention of this eschatological trumpet has raised the question of its relationship to other end-time trumpets mentioned in Scripture. It is clearly parallel to "the last trump" in 1 Corinthians 15:52 since both passages relate to the rapture of the church. That this trumpet should be equated with "the seventh trumpet" in Revelation 11:15 is highly improbable.[29] The subjects are different: here it is the church; there a wicked world. The results are different: here it is the glorious catching up of the church to be with the Lord; there it is further judgment upon a godless world. Here "the last trump" signals the close of the life of the church on earth; there the "seventh" trumpet marks a climax in a progressive series of apocalyptic judgments upon the living on earth.

Others would equate this trumpet in 1 Thessalonians 4:16 with that in Matthew 24:31; but this too is improbable.[30] There is a similarity between the two since in both the blowing of the trumpet is associated with a gathering of the Lord's people; but there are marked differences. The subjects are different: here the reference is to the church; there the Olivet discourse portrays Jewish believers during the great tribulation. The circumstances are different: here the trumpet is connected with the raising of the believing dead; there no mention is made of a resurrection but it is connected with a regathering of the elect who have been scattered over the earth. The result is different: here the blowing of the trumpet results in the uniting of the raised dead with the living as one body to be caught up to meet the Lord in the air; there the elect are the living believers who are regathered from all parts of the earth at the command of their Lord who has returned to earth in open glory.

(2) *Events at His return* (vv. 16b-17a). By means of *and* two events are next directly connected with the Lord's descent from heaven. They relate to the two distinct groups of believers seen in verse 15.

"The dead in Christ shall rise first." "The dead in Christ" is an alternative description of "them that are fallen asleep" (v. 14). It limits the scope of the dead to those who experienced physical death while in spiritual union with Christ. Although physically dead they are still "in Christ;" death did not sever them from Him. "Membership in the body of Christ is in no way impaired by death."[31] Those now in heaven in a disembodied state, will Christ bring with Him (v. 14) to receive their resurrection bodies. The raising of their bodies will take place *first*, the first act in the drama to take place at the *parousia*. *First* is not used here to distinguish the resurrection of the saved from the later resurrection of the lost; the unsaved are not in view here. This picture is not to be equated with Revelation 20:1-10. *First* means that the dead believers will be resurrected before the living are caught up. The survivors will have to wait a moment as it were. Thus the saints who have died will not be at any disadvantage when the Lord returns.

The second act in the drama follows at once, "then we that are alive, that are left, shall together with them be caught up in the clouds." *Then* marks an order of events but does not necessarily indicate any long interval. "In a moment" in 1 Corinthians 15:51-52 makes it clear that no appreciable interval between the raising of the dead in Christ and the transformation of the living saints is implied. The qualifying phrases for *we* are again repeated for emphasis. Paul here does not stop to speak of the transformation necessary for the living before they can be caught up, but 1 Corinthians 15:53-54 makes it clear that they will receive glorified bodies without passing through death; for them "what is mortal shall be swallowed up of life" (2 Co 5:4).

The raising of the Christian dead *first* does not, however, give them any advantage over the living saints. Those that are alive "shall together with them," the resurrected, "be caught up in the clouds." "Together with them" denotes that the two groups will unitedly and as one company arise to meet the Lord. It implies the full association and equality of the two groups. For the living it will mean not only recognition of but reunion with their departed loved ones.

The verb *caught up* denotes a sudden and forcible seizure, an irresistible act of catching away, due to divine activity. It might also be rendered "snatch up, sweep up, carry off by force." The Latin for the Greek verb is *rapturo*, from which we derive our English word "rapture." Here is the revelation of the bodily snatching up of the church to meet her returning Lord. With this catching up "for the first time the church of all times and all lands will be with one another. . . . Till then there exist only churches (in the plural, Rev 22:16), and the church of a *generation* living at any one time on earth."[32] This picture of the rapture of the church is a distinctly Christian revelation. "There is no parallel to this rapture in Jewish literature of similar date."[33]

The catching away is described as being "in the clouds," literally, "in" or "amid clouds." The *clouds* form the element with which those caught up are surrounded. That literal clouds are meant seems clear from Acts 1:9 where they are associated with Christ's ascension, as here with the ascension of His saints. Lightfoot compares the clouds to a chariot on which the saints will be borne aloft.[34] Findlay remarks, "There is something wonderful and mystical about the clouds,—half of heaven and half of earth; their ethereal drapery supplies the curtain and canopy for this glorious meeting."[35]

The immediate purpose of the catching up is "to meet the Lord," literally, "into a meeting with the Lord." In Hellenistic Greek the expression had become a kind of technical term denoting "a ceremonial meeting with a person of position."[36] In papyrus usage it was used of an official delegation going forth to meet a newly appointed magistrate, or other dignitary, upon his arrival in their district.[37] Hogg and Vine remark, "Almost invariably the word suggests that those who go out to meet him intend to return to their starting place with the person met."[38] Paul here breaks off his account of events and does not say whether those caught up to meet the Lord return to heaven with Him or come back to earth with Him. From John 14:2-3 it is clear that Christ's coming to take His own unto Himself is for the express purpose of taking them to the heavenly mansions now being prepared for them. But that does not mean that they will not come with Him when He returns to earth to establish His kingdom. On the other hand, it is precarious to assert that those who have been caught up will *immediately* return to earth with Him. A posttribulational rapture cannot be demonstrated on the basis of this expression.[39]

The meeting with the Lord takes place "in the air," between heaven and earth. In five of its seven occurrences in the New Testament the word *air* (*aera*) means the atmosphere.‡‡ Nor does it seem necessary to depart from that meaning here or in Ephesians 2:2. Yet the term need not be pressed to mean that the meeting will take place in the immediate vicinity of the earth, that is, "below the mountain tops," as Wuest asserts.[40] Rather, with Hogg and Vine we may say that "the word 'air' attracts the attention upward without particularly defining the place of the meeting."[41] But there well may be a deep significance in this place of meeting. In Ephesians 2:2 Satan is described as "the prince of the powers of the air." In what was Satan's domain this meeting now takes place. Morris remarks, "That the Lord chooses to meet His saints there, on the demons' home ground so to speak, shows something of His complete mastery over them."[42]

(3) *Consequence of His return* (v. 17*b*). "And so shall we ever be with the Lord" records the glorious climax for the believer of these apocalyptic events. Rotherham aptly preserves the order and emphasis of the original in rendering, "And thus evermore with the Lord shall we be!" The

‡‡Ac 22:23; 1 Co 9:26; 14:9; Rev 9:2; 16:17.

emphatic adverb *so* (in this manner, thus), points to what has preceded in order to indicate that this glorious consummation is in consequence of the catching up to meet the Lord in the air. As Frame points out, Paul does not say "'and there,' as if the air were the permanent dwelling-place."[43] The important thing is not the place but the fact of the permanent union with the Lord. Wherever the Lord is, there His glorified church will be.

The *we* is comprehensive, covering all believers. Both the living and the dead will share the same glorious destiny of being *ever*, (always, at all times), "with the Lord." This will not be a matter of mere companionship but one of intimate union. Ellicott points out that the preposition rendered *with* (*sun*) indicates "not merely an accompanying, but a *coherence* with" the Lord.[44] "The entire content and worth of heaven, the entire blessedness of life eternal, is for Paul embraced in the one thought of being united with Jesus, his Saviour and Lord."[45] This will be the acme of heaven's bliss.

3. Comfort in the Instructions (v. 18)

This verse points out the practical value for the readers of the revelation just stated. "Wherefore," in consequence of what has just been told them, "comfort one another with these words." The verb *comfort* points to any kind of animating and cheering speech. Its exact shade of meaning is determined by the context. Views differ as to whether it should here be translated "comfort"§§ or "encourage."|| || The rendering "comfort" places the emphasis upon the consoling impact that it imparts to those who are sorrowing the loss of loved ones; "encourage" suggests that there is solid ground for encouragement and confident hope in the face of the fact that loved ones have passed away.

Paul does not himself seek to comfort or encourage his readers but rather bids them actively to comfort or encourage "one another." The present imperative places upon them the continuing duty to do so, both in private conversation and in the public services. Those who have lost loved ones will find personal comfort in what Paul has said and will pass that comfort on to others; those who may not have experienced the personal loss of loved ones will use the message to mutual encouragement.

They are to comfort each other "with these words," literally, "in these words." The comfort to be experienced lies in the very words which the writers have given them. These very words contain not only the antidote to their sorrow but proclaim a message of encouragement and hope. There is solid comfort in these words for believers when they stand

§§Conybeare, Lattey, Montgomery, Young, Way, 20th Cent, RSV, NASB. Rotherham and NEB use "console."
|| ||Darby, Goodspeed, Moffatt, Phillips, Weymouth, Williams, and Berkeley.

beside the grave of loved ones. Their rich comfort stands in striking contrast to the insufficiency of the comfort which the pagan world had to offer in such an hour. The helplessness of the pagan world in the face of death is well illustrated by a second-century papyrus which Deissmann quotes: "Irene to Taonnophris and Philo, good comfort. I was as sorry and wept over the departed one as I wept over Didymas. And all things, whatsoever were fitting, I did, and all mine, Epaphroditus and Thermuthion and Philion and Apollonius and Plantas. But, nevertheless, against such things one can do nothing. Therefore comfort ye one another. Fare ye well."[46]

The blessed prospect of the rapture as described in 1 Thessalonians 4:13-18 may rightly be called the polestar of the Christian church. It constitutes a precious revelation that has brought comfort and cheer to believers in all ages. But the very preciousness of this hope has naturally turned attention to the problem of its precise time relationship to the great tribulation. This is a question that has evoked wide discussion and there is no agreement today concerning the answer. Three different positions are advocated, each held by godly and diligent students of the Scriptures. It is not our purpose to enter into any extended discussion of this thorny problem. We propose simply to state briefly the three views, indicate our preference, and point out the relationship of the problem to these epistles.

The pretribulational rapture view holds that the church in its entirety will be resurrected and translated, removed from the earthly scene in the rapture, before any part of the great tribulation runs its course. This view insists on a clear distinction between the rapture of the church and the revelation of the Lord, His return to earth in open glory. It holds that the rapture, the next great prophetic event, is imminent and that believers should be expectantly prepared for it.[47]

The midtribulational rapture view holds that the church will be raptured at the midpoint of the great tribulation, at the end of the first three and a half years of the seventieth week of Daniel (Dan 9:24-27). It holds that the rapture is an event distinct from the revelation but does not accept that the rapture is imminent, holding that some prophetic events must first occur before the rapture can take place.[48] This view is a compromise between the pretribulational position and the posttribulational view.

The posttribulational rapture view holds that the church will remain on earth throughout the great tribulation and will be caught up to meet the Lord in the air at the end of the tribulation as He comes from heaven and will immediately return with Him to earth in open glory. While accepting that the rapture and the revelation are essentially different events, this view sees no appreciable time interval between them and in effect fuses them into one eschatological occurrence.[49]

These epistles do not explicitly state the chronological relationship of the rapture to the great tribulation. The problem arises out of the natural effort to set forth a harmonious sequence of end-time events. Walvoord, an advocate of a pretribulational rapture, says, "The fact is that neither posttribulationism or pretribulationism is an explicit teaching of Scripture. The Bible does not in so many words state either."[50] And Ladd, an advocate of a posttribulational rapture, remarks, "With the exception of one passage, the author will grant that the Scripture nowhere explicitly states that the Church will go through the Great Tribulation. . . . Nor does the Word explicitly place the Rapture at the end of the Tribulation."[51] (Ladd's "one passage" is Rev 20).

The view one accepts will be determined largely by doctrinal and exegetical presuppositions. This writer accepts the view of a pretribulational rapture. It is in harmony with his understanding of prophecy in general, his views concerning biblical interpretation, and the implications of these epistles as they relate to the discussion.

In 1 Thessalonians 1:10 the Thessalonian believers are pictured as waiting for the return of Christ. The clear implication is that they had a hope of His imminent return. If they had been taught that the great tribulation, in whole or in part, must first run its course, it is difficult to see how they could be described as expectantly awaiting Christ's return. Then they should rather have been described as bracing themselves for the great tribulation and the painful events connected with it.

In 1 Thessalonians 4:13-18 Paul assured his converts that those believers who had died would share equally with the living in the rapture. This was his answer to their grief at the supposed loss of those who had died. But if they had been taught that the church must go through the great tribulation the logical reaction for them would have been to rejoice that these loved ones had escaped that great period of suffering which they felt was about to occur.

Posttribulationists assert that Revelation 20:4-6 shows that the resurrection (hence also the rapture) takes place after the great tribulation. Pretribulationists reply that there will be a resurrection at the beginning as well as at the end of the great tribulation. Wood points out that Revelation 20:4 has in view two distinct groups. "The first group is pictured as already living and thus able to occupy thrones; but the individuals of the second group 'lived and reigned with Christ a thousand years.' Thus, the resurrection of the latter group takes place at this posttribulational time. But the former group must have been raised at a previous time in order to be able to occupy their thrones."[52] Pretribulational rapturists have not been in agreement as to whether the resurrection at the end of the great tribulation involves only the tribulation martyrs or includes all the Old Testament saints.[53]

First Thessalonians 5:1-11 appeals for appropriate conduct on the part of the readers in view of the coming "day of the Lord." If it is recognized that this term denotes a prophetic period which begins with the rapture and includes the return in glory, the passage clearly offers no proof that the church must pass through the great tribulation, in whole or in part. The exhortation is made in view of the prophetic prospects as a whole. The entire paragraph appeals to the readers to live a godly life, not because they must be prepared to face the prospect of enduring the great tribulation but because God's purpose for them is not wrath but salvation.

In 2 Thessalonians 1:3-10 the readers are commended for their growing faith and love and are assured that because of their praiseworthy attitude amid present persecution they will be given "rest" while their persecutors will certainly be recompensed with severe punishment. But if the church must pass through the great tribulation, then Paul should have warned them that still more intense suffering lay ahead.

Second Thessalonians 2:1-12 has been appealed to by opponents of a pretribulational rapture as proving that the rapture cannot be imminent, since certain events are mentioned which must first take place. In reply it is pointed out that the Thessalonians had received the erroneous idea that the day of the Lord had already begun but that they were urged, in the interest of their hope of the rapture, not to be shaken by this teaching. Paul assured them that the prophetic day of the Lord could not yet be running its course since two specific events had to be fulfilled. Paul's description of events during that prophetic period demonstrated that the predicted day of the Lord was still future. The view that they were already in that day was inconsistent with the hope of their "gathering together unto him" at the rapture (v. 1), the hope so clearly set before them in 1 Thessalonians 4:13-18.

Equally devout and sincere students of Scripture will doubtless continue to hold different views on the question of the time of the rapture. Advocates of their respective views must avoid attributing unworthy motives or insincerity in exegesis to each other because they do not agree. It is appropriate and proper that diligent efforts should be given to the study of the evidence for a chronology of end-time events. But these efforts must not be allowed to lead to a preoccupation with uncertain details so that the sanctifying power of this blessed hope for daily living is lost sight of. "Every one that hath this hope set on him purifieth himself, even as he is pure" (1 Jn 3:3).

10

PRACTICAL: WATCHFULNESS

C. EXHORTATION TO PERSONAL WATCHFULNESS

5:1-11 But concerning the times and the seasons, brethren, ye have no need that aught be written unto you. (2) For yourselves know perfectly that the day of the Lord so cometh as a thief in the night. (3) When they are saying, Peace and safety, then sudden destruction cometh upon them, as travail upon a woman with child; and they shall in no wise escape. (4) But ye, brethren, are not in darkness, that that day should overtake you as a thief: (5) for ye are all sons of light, and sons of the day: we are not of the night, nor of darkness; (6) so then let us not sleep, as do the rest, but let us watch and be sober. (7) For they that sleep sleep in the night; and they that are drunken are drunken in the night. (8) But let us, since we are of the day, be sober, putting on the breastplate of faith and love; and for a helmet, the hope of salvation. (9) For God appointed us not unto wrath, but unto the obtaining of salvation through our Lord Jesus Christ, (10) who died for us, that, whether we wake or sleep, we should live together with him. (11) Wherefore exhort one another, and build each other up, even as also ye do.

THIS PARAGRAPH is an appropriate companion piece to the preceding. It is the second half of the distinctively eschatological block of material in the epistle. The former offered needed instruction concerning the dead in Christ; this gives a word of needed exhortation to the living.

In the preceding paragraph (4:13-18) the main cause for restlessness among the Thessalonian believers in relation to the anticipated coming of Christ was allayed. They had thought that only those who were alive at the time of the *parousia* would witness and share in its glories. As long as they held this view they would feel impatient at any prospect of postponement in His return since it cast a shadow upon their own hope of personal survival to share in that glory. All grounds for this feeling were removed with the assuring revelation that there will be no essential difference in the lot of those who have died and those who are alive when Christ returns for His own.

But a further word needed to be directed to the readers. The solemn truth is that the returning Lord will be the Judge of all. It is their duty

207

to so live that they will be prepared to meet the Lord whenever He comes. In view of the uncertainty as to the time of His coming, it is imperative that they give diligence to be morally and spiritually ready. The pastoral heart of the writers leads them thus to exhort their beloved brethren.

In the preceding paragraph the writers addressed themselves to the ignorance of their readers; in the present paragraph they address themselves to their knowledge. In saying "ye have no need that aught be written unto you" they indicate that they are now dealing with what was already known to them. The purpose is not to give them new information but to urge them to profit by what they already know. They do not need further instruction but encouragement to live in accord with what they have already been taught.

They are reminded of the uncertainty as to the time of Christ's coming (vv. 1-2). The result of this uncertainty for the unprepared is graphically declared in verse 3, while their own need to live as sons of the day is set forth at length in verses 4-11.

1. Uncertainty of the Time of Christ's Coming (vv. 1-2)

The connective particle translated "But" (*de*) is again transitional; it indicates that a new subject is being introduced. The majority of our modern versions render it "but,"* thus suggesting that a contrasting thought is being introduced. Then the contrast seems to be between the certainty of Christ's coming as set forth in the preceding section and the uncertainty as to its time. While some interpreters hold that this paragraph is simply a continuation of the discussion in 4:13-18, it seems clear that a new aspect of the *parousia* is now to be considered. Thus the particle (*de*) is best taken not as adversative but transitional and may well be rendered "now."†

a) Their information concerning the times and the seasons (v. 1). The new aspect of the eschatological teaching is "concerning the times and the seasons." The expression "times and seasons" repeats the words of our Lord in Acts 1:7 and indicates that the writers were familiar with the teaching given there by Christ. The expression here implies that the Thessalonians already were acquainted with it. Apparently Paul is using traditional language concerning the time of the *parousia* (cf. Dan 2:21).

While the words *times* (*chronoi*) and *seasons* (*kairoi*) are synonymous and are on occasion used interchangeably, they are not equivalent terms. Both relate to time. The ancient writer Ammonius remarked that the

---

*Conybeare, Darby, Goodspeed, Lattey, Phillips, Way, Weymouth, Williams; RSV, 20th Cent. Young uses "and," Moffatt has "as regards," while Berkeley and NEB omit it entirely.
†So rendered by Montgomery and NASB.

first denotes quantity and the second quality. The first designates time in its duration, whether a longer or shorter period; the second draws attention to the characteristics of the period. The first deals with the measurement of time, the second with the suitable or critical nature of the time.

Both terms are in the plural. "The times" point to the chronological ages which may intervene before the *parousia* takes place; "the seasons" indicate the times in their critical character, the occurrences which will distinguish these times. Riggenbach remarks that the plurals point "to the possibility of a repeated alternation of periods of development and crises of decision, and so to a possibly longer duration."[1] We may use the rendering "the eras and the crises." The New American Standard Bible renders "the times and the epochs," while Weymouth, Goodspeed, and Williams have "times and dates."‡

The fact that "ye have no need that aught be written unto you" indicates that the readers already knew about these times and seasons. Not that instruction on this point was not useful, but they already possessed it. By contrast the clear implication is that there was need for the instruction given in the previous section (cf. 4:13).

The mention of "writing" seems to suggest a contrast to oral teaching. The implication is that the Thessalonians had already received oral teaching on the point. Teaching concerning the second advent formed an important part of the instruction given by the missionaries while at Thessalonica, and this matter about "the times and the seasons" had not been neglected. It had been made plain to them that the coming of the Lord was not an event which they could mark as a fixed date on the calendar. They had been told that "times and seasons" are a matter of divine determination (Ac 1:7), and not a proper subject for Christian speculation. Biblical interpretation transcends its legitimate function whenever it presumes to establish fixed dates for coming prophetic events. The Scriptures do not sanction the senseless practice of setting dates for the return of Christ. The failure of such attempts only serves to bring the prophetic hope into disrepute.

b) THEIR KNOWLEDGE CONCERNING THE DAY OF THE LORD (v. 2). The connective *for* introduces the reason why it is not necessary to write to them about the times and seasons. "Yourselves know" is another appeal to the personal knowledge of the readers. It made further teaching on the subject unnecessary. They already knew "perfectly that the day of the Lord so cometh as a thief in the night."

Nothing is stated as to the source of their knowledge but as new converts they had obviously received it from the missionaries. And the apos-

‡The NEB reverses the order; Berkeley has "periods and dates," and 20th Century, "the times and the moments;" Moffatt, "the course and periods of time."

tolic teaching seems clearly grounded in the teaching of Christ on the
point (Mt 24:43-44; Lk 12:39-40). This became a regular part of the
apostolic teaching (2 Pe 3:10; Rev 3:3; 16:15). The suggestion of some
that the Thessalonians had derived their knowledge from their study of
the gospel of Luke, or that of Matthew, which had already come into their
hands is very unlikely.[2] There is no evidence that either gospel had already been written this early.

The adverb "perfectly" characterizes the knowledge of the readers on the
subject. They knew "perfectly well" (Rotherham) or "accurately" about
the subject. Their information did not need correction or supplementa-
tion. It implies an exactness of knowledge as the result of careful teaching. "There was no haziness about the missionaries' instructions on this
point."[3] In dealing with prophetic subjects the missionaries had been
accurate teachers. It is an essential characteristic for all biblical teaching.
The writers' statement involves a paradox, "You know accurately that
nothing accurate as to the precise date for the day of the Lord can be
known."

While nothing definite can be known as to the actual date, they definitely know that "the day of the Lord so cometh as a thief in the night." The
coming of that day is certain. The use of the present tense, rather than
the future, "lends vividness and certainty to the whole idea."[4] The present
tense is regularly used in doctrinal statements and indicates the abiding
reality of the truth asserted. Findlay comments, "The event is certain
and in preparation; *when* it will arrive none can tell."[5]

Paul uses the expression "the day of the Lord" without any definite
article. The absence of the definite article lays stress upon the character
of the *day*, it is a day belonging to the *Lord*. It is His day, when He will
display His character and work in judging the wicked and vindicating
His justice in the establishment of His righteous rule. As the expression
is used in the Old Testament "the Lord" denotes Jehovah, but for Paul it
means Christ. Plummer remarks, "We have here another instance of the
easy way in which what in the O.T. is said of Jehovah is transferred in
the N.T. to Christ."[6]

"The day of the Lord" is a familiar Old Testament expression. It
denotes the day when God intervenes in history to judge His enemies,
deliver His people, and establish His kingdom.[7] As a day of judgment,
it is associated with darkness and sorrow for the wicked but deliverance
and joy for the godly. It is a day especially connected with the open
activity of God in human affairs. Barclay feels that as used in the Old
Testament the day of the Lord has three characteristics: "(i) It could
come suddenly and unexpectedly. (ii) It would involve a cosmic up-

heaval in which the universe was shaken to its very foundations. (iii) It would be a time of judgment."[8]

Clearly Paul uses the term "the day of the Lord" with its Old Testament connotation of the Lord coming in judgment to establish His kingdom. It is thus to be distinguished from His coming for His saints, the rapture as described in the preceding paragraph. As a prophetic period the day of the Lord is inaugurated with the rapture of the church as described in 4:13-18, covers the time of the great tribulation, and involves His return to earth and the establishment of His messianic reign. In this passage Paul is dealing only with the judgment aspect of that day.

The day of the Lord "so cometh as a thief in the night." Robert Young's translation brings out the literal order of the original in rendering, "the day of the Lord as a thief in the night doth so come." The "as-so" construction (*hōs-houtōs*) strongly stresses the similarity between the coming of the day of the Lord and the coming of the thief. The comparison lies in the suddenness and unexpectedness of both events. The thief comes suddenly and at a time that cannot be predetermined; so the day of the Lord will come suddenly when people are not expecting it. But this analogy of the coming of the thief must not be pressed beyond the intention of the context. To assume that the coming Lord is Himself being represented as a thief, "one who takes property by stealth," is to misuse the analogy.

The thief comes slyly "in the night," when men are asleep rather than awake and watching. The phrase "in the night" serves to strengthen the thought of the manner rather than the time of his coming. It speaks of the unhappy surprise that his coming brings to those who are not watching and are therefore caught unprepared. Although the phrase is added only here, the thought is present in the teaching of our Lord (Mt 24:43; Lk 12:39).

The original makes it perfectly clear that it is the thief who comes in the night, not that the Lord will come in the night. Yet the tradition early arose in the church that the Lord would come again at night. It was apparently stimulated by Paul's phrase "in the night" as well as the reference in Christ's teaching about a coming at night. (That it will be night for some on this globe when He returns is self-evident.) Later tradition fixed this coming as on Easter Eve. This expectation gave rise to the observance of night vigils as an expression of the hope to be overtaken in a waking condition by the returning Christ. But it is obvious that Paul's words do not justify such a view. The coming of the thief *at night* simply serves to emphasize his secretive and unannounced coming. Swete draws a spiritual parallel when he remarks, "Night is the time

211

when robbers are abroad: and so 'the times of this ignorance' and sin usher in and will last until the Coming of the Lord."[9]

2. Result of the Uncertainty for the Unprepared (v. 3)

The fatal result of being unprepared for the coming of the day of the Lord is vividly portrayed. "When they are saying, Peace and safety, then sudden destruction cometh upon them." The absence of any connecting particle in the best manuscripts places this verse in close connection with the preceding.

The subject, *they,* is left undefined, but the contrast expressed in verse 4 makes it clear that the reference is to the unbelieving world, not the church. The reference is to "all unregenerate men in so far as they give any thought to future events."[10] The vast masses of mankind will be preoccupied with the things of this world and will show no interest in preparing for the Lord's coming. This fact is clearly illustrated by our Lord in His comparison of the days before His return to the days of Noah (Mt 24:37-39; Lk 17:26-27) and of Lot (Lk 17:28-30).

Instead of anticipating and preparing for the coming day of judgment, they will be wrapped in a fatal, self-deceiving sense of security. They will be saying, "Peace and safety." Thus they will be assuring themselves that there is peace everywhere and everything is safe and secure. The two terms are used together only here in the New Testament. *Peace* here points to circumstances that do not evoke a feeling of alarm; *safety* has the thought of being unshaken, secure from enemies and danger. Ellicott distinguishes the two terms thus: "the first betokens an inward repose and security; the latter a sureness and safety that is not interfered with or compromised by outward obstacles."[11] They feel that everything is safe and secure and see no outward evidence to dispute the feeling.

In view of the devastating judgments that the prophetic Scriptures portray as sweeping over the world in the end-time, we may ask, from what do they feel themselves secure? If they are thinking of national or international conditions, it seems surprising indeed that such a claim should even be advanced. But it may be that Revelation 13:4 points to a time when such a claim might have a show of justification. With the rule of the beast so strong that none would dare to attack him, they might well feel that at last peace and security had been attained.

Hogg and Vine hold that their assertion of peace and security does not have reference to international conditions but rather denotes "the sense of security from Divine interposition that will possess the hearts of men up to the very moment at which God breaks the long silence and once again intervenes directly in human affairs."[12] Having blunted their consciences against the repeated warnings of coming judgment and having deliberately rejected the love of the truth, they will readily accept the devil's lie and feel secure from divine intervention (cf. 2 Th 2:10-12).

But their feeling of security is a fatal delusion. At the very time that they are uttering their confident claims to security "then sudden destruction cometh upon them." The word order in the original is arresting, "then sudden upon them cometh destruction." The adjective *sudden* stands emphatically at the beginning of the clause but we must wait until the recipients are indicated and the verb has been written before we read that terrible word *destruction*.

"Sudden" indicates that the doom which overtakes them is unexpected and unforeseen, catching them totally unprepared. The noun rendered "destruction" (*olethros*), used only by Paul in the New Testament, does not imply annihilation but "carries with it the thought of utter and hopeless ruin, the loss of all that gives worth to existence."[13] It does not denote loss of being but rather loss of *well*-being, the ruination of the very purpose of their being. From 2 Thessalonians 1:9 it is clear that by destruction Paul does not mean physical annihilation but rather the eternal separation from Christ of the lost. Destruction is the opposite of the salvation awaiting believers (vv. 7-10).

The inescapable and fatal nature of this destruction is well illustrated by the catastrophe that befell unbelievers in the days of Noah and of Lot. Barnes notes that Paul's assertion here is wholly inconsistent with the teaching of universal salvation.[14]

The verb here rendered *cometh* (*epistatai*) means "to stand upon or over, to stand by." It is frequently employed of a coming that takes one by surprise. It indicates that they will be oblivious to the coming of the judgment but will suddenly become aware of it "as it presses close upon the doomed transgressors and is on the point of overwhelming them."[15] *Them* marks the ones upon whom the destruction falls, the unbelievers, those who have spurned all warnings of coming judgment and rejected the offers of grace.

Paul adds a further figure to characterize this destruction, "as travail upon a woman with child." The expression, which literally rendered is, "even as the travail to her in womb having," is a common Greek idiom for a pregnant woman. Here it is used in its literal sense, but the word *travail* or "birth pangs" is a common figure for intense pain and sorrow. Paul's figure may be reminiscent of our Lord's teaching (Mt 24:8; Mk 13:8), but more probably it comes from the Old Testament where the figure is common (Is 13:8-9; Jer 4:31; Ho 13:13; Mic 4:9).

Some, like Milligan, hold that the point of the illustration is the suddenness with which the destruction comes. Lenski insists that this thought of suddenness and consequent helplessness "is the sole point here." But from the very nature of the illustration the thought that it is inevitable cannot be excluded. Hogg and Vine remark, "Just as the figure of the thief suggests the unexpected character of the catastrophe, so this suggests its inevitableness." Findlay finds three thoughts implied in the comparison, "inevitable certainty, suddenness, and intense pain." Swete quotes Gill as adding "another point of similarity: the cause of their anguish will be *in themselves*." But the figure must not be pressed to imply that Paul felt he knew the approximate time of the advent. Thus (regrettably), Lünemann suggests that as the woman knows the near approach though not the very hour of her travail, so the apostle thought the unknown hour of the second advent would be within his own times.[16]

The solemn and inescapable nature of the coming judgment for the unprepared is now literally stated, "and they shall in no wise escape." *They*, the subjects of this inevitable doom, goes back to the first part of the verse, to those who were assuring themselves that everything was safe and secure. They stand in sharp contrast to the believers, addressed in verses 4-11, who will escape.

When the unexpected judgment falls "they shall in no wise escape." Every effort to get out and flee will be futile. This inability to escape is stressed by the use of the emphatic double negative (*ou mē*).§ Way's rendering well brings out the decisiveness of the event, "There shall be no escape for them—none!" Williams renders, "but they shall not escape, no, not at all." Inescapable will be the doom falling upon the unbelieving world in the eschatological day of the Lord. The reference is to those who are living on this earth at the time of the Lord's coming in judgment; no reference in this passage is made to the judgment of the dead, although that will certainly follow in due season. Kelly stamps as "unspiritual ignorance, not to say folly" the attempts of some to say this refers to the destruction of Jerusalem in A.D. 70.[17] Neither can it be interpreted to mean the day of each man's death.

3. Life of Believers as Sons of the Day (vv. 4-11)

"But ye brethren" sets the Thessalonian believers in sharp contrast with those mentioned in verse 3, the unthinking and unbelieving world caught unprepared by the day of judgment. The personal pronoun *ye* (*humeis*) is emphatic, sharpening the contrast. The renewed direct address, *brethren*, further underlines the contrast. Findlay remarks that by their repetition of *brethren* "the Apostles instinctively drew their friends near to themselves under the shadow of the solemn future."[18]

In contrast to the presumptuous skeptics, the life of believers as sons of the day is now set forth at considerable length. Believers are charac-

§See comments under 4:15.

terized negatively and positively (vv. 4-5); this provides a basis for exhortations to preparedness (vv. 6-8); and this call to preparedness is consistent with the salvation that God has appointed for believers (vv. 9-10). The paragraph concludes with an exhortation to mutual edification (v. 11).

a) CHARACTERIZATION OF BELIEVERS (vv. 4-5). The Thessalonian believers are first described negatively, "ye are not in darkness." It indicates their contrast to the unbelieving world as to the sphere of their life. Unbelievers have their existence in the realm of "darkness," a common religious metaphor for sin and evil. Darkness is emblematic of the condition of the moral and spiritual estrangement and ignorance of the unredeemed. It has penetrated their hearts and minds, blinding them to spiritual realities and making them oblivious to impending judgment. Spiritual darkness is the habitual sphere in which the man of the world lives and moves.

The missionaries record the happy fact that their readers as believers "are not in darkness."|| They have been spiritually enlightened, have passed out of the darkness of ignorance and unbelief. They have been delivered out of the power of darkness and transplanted into the kingdom of the Son of God's love (Col 1:13).

In consequence of their enlightenment they have been delivered from the conceived result "that that day should overtake you as a thief." The construction *hina . . . katalabē* is best taken to denote contemplated result rather than purpose. If purpose is insisted on in accordance with classical usage it must denote "the purpose contemplated by God in His merciful dispensation."[19] But later usage definitely favors the meaning of result, "so that." Unbelievers, immersed in the realm of darkness, will be overtaken, but not they.

"That day," literally, "the day," is the day of the Lord mentioned in verse 2. It is the day par excellence. They are assured that that day, here personified, will not *overtake* them, will not come upon them by surprise and lay hostile hands on them. The day of the Lord as a time of destruction will fall upon those living in the darkness of sin and in estrangement from God. But believers do not live in that realm. They have nothing to fear from that day. They will already have been taken up in the rapture (4:13-18), the event which inaugurates the day of the Lord as the day of judgment upon the world.

The coming of that day will not catch believers "as a thief." It will not come upon them like an intruding thief who seizes the owner of the house in order to plunder his goods (cf. Mt 12:29).

|| The sentence is unquestionably indicative, not imperative. To make it a command is inconsistent with Paul's teaching concerning the nature and position of the believer (Eph 5:8; Col 1:12-14; 2 Cor 6:14).

Some scholars here accept a variant reading, "thieves," which gives a somewhat different meaning.# Milligan, although acknowledging that the reading is quite uncertain, accepts the plural and explains it thus, "The figure of the 'thief' is now transferred from the *cause* of the surprise (v. 2) to its *object*, the idea being that as the 'day' unpleasantly surprises the thief who has failed in carrying through his operations, so 'the day' will 'overtake' those who are not prepared for it."[20] In favor of this unusual reading it is argued that no copyist would deliberately change "as a thief" to "as thieves," but the reverse would be natural. It is also pointed out that such a swift change of metaphors is consistent with Paul's style.[21] But it seems improbable that "as thieves" is the original reading. The variant may well be due, not to deliberate scribal change, but to mechanical corruption; the plural (*kleptas*) may have been accidentally written because of the ending of the word "you" (*humas*) before it. The meaning of the plural does not seem to fit the context. The illustration stresses "*a thief-like surprise* that 'the day' brings with it; not such a suprise *as falls upon thieves* at their night's work."[22] Morris further points out that "in this context the sons of darkness who are surprised are not awake and watchful, like thieves, but asleep or drunken."[23] Accepting the singular, the picture is the same as that in verse 2.

The opening *for* of verse 5 confirms the preceding negative characterization with a more specific positive declaration. It explains why they will not be surprised by that day as by a coming thief. "For ye are all sons of light, and sons of the day." The pronoun *ye* is again an emphatic form and *all* is also emphatic by its position at the beginning of the sentence. This assertion concerning their nature holds true for all the Thessalonian believers, including the weak and faint-hearted. The missionaries were well aware that some of the Thessalonian believers had weaknesses and faults which needed to be rebuked, yet they knew of no exception among them to the assertion that they were "sons of light and sons of the day." The transformation in them that the missionaries had observed under the preaching of the gospel assured them of this fact (cf. 1:3-10).

The expression "sons of light" is a Hebraic formula describing their nature as belonging to the light. The figure, moreover, expresses an intimate relationship, that they were as closely related to the light as children to their parents. The Hebrews described a person as "the son of" anything which completely dominated and controlled him. Thus the expression means that spiritual light is the pervading element of their character. "Believers are called 'sons of light,' not merely because they have received a revelation from God, but because in the New Birth, they

---

#The plural, *kleptas,* is accepted by Westcott and Hort on the basis of A, B, and the Bohairic version. Souter, Nestle, and the Bible Societies' text retain the singular, *kleptēs,* which is strongly supported by manuscript evidence.

have received the spiritual capacity for it."[24] They "are now light in the Lord" (Eph 5:8). They passed from a life in the sphere of darkness into the realm of light at the time they were brought to the knowledge of Christ as their Saviour. Believers now live in the light and move forward to the day when they will become "partakers of the inheritance of the saints in light" (Col 1:12).

They are further asserted to be "sons of the day." The doubling of the idiom produces emphasis. The significance of "the day" has been differently understood. Neil takes it as a reference to "the Day of the Lord, i.e. they will be partakers in its glory."[25] They already belong to that eschatological day, are already sharing in essence the light and life that will be brought to full manifestation when the Lord comes to redeem His own. But most interpreters hold that there is no direct reference to the day of the Lord. There is no definite article with *day* in the original and the expression is qualitative. They are "sons of day" (Rotherham), belonging to spiritual "day" rather than "night."

Lightfoot remarks that "sons of day" is an advance upon "sons of light." "Not only have ye an illumination of your own, but you are also living and moving in an enlightened sphere."[26] Day is the realm in which they are now living as light-possessed men.

This positive characterization is followed by another negative statement. "We are not of the night, nor of darkness." "The negative throws the affirmative into the boldest relief by being placed before and after it."[27]

By the change to the first person plural the writers tactfully identify themselves with their readers. The assertion concerning the nature of believers is now to be made the basis for exhortation to live as sons of day; but before stating their exhortations the writers thus indicate that they themselves are eager to assume the responsibilities entailed by Christian privileges. By thus uniting themselves with their readers the missionaries show that the responsibilities to be pressed upon them are common to all believers. The use of the "we" extends through verse 10.

This negative statement parallels the preceding positive assertion, but with a difference. The restatement drops the Hebraic figure and states the plain denial. The repeated negative with the genitive, "not of the night, nor of darkness," indicates the domain to which they do not belong. To be "of night" is stronger than to be "in night." Neither noun has the article in the original, "not of night, not of darkness." The assertion is qualitative. *Night* and *darkness* are again figurative; *night* being the state of man's alienation from God who is light, and *darkness* the realm of sin and iniquity. *Night* corresponds to *day,* and *darkness* to *light,* but the previous order has been reversed so that the first word corresponds with the fourth and the second with the third:

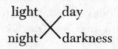

The result is the rhetorical figure called chiasma, from the Greek word meaning to place cross-wise, like the letter X, pronounced *chi*. Such an arrangement occurs in various parts of the Scriptures and is quite frequent in Paul's writings (Ro 10:9-10; 1 Co 4:10; 2 Co 6:8).

In these statements concerning the position and nature of believers, both negative and positive, there is a decided note of assurance and victory. Lenski aptly remarks, "These writers know of no twilight zone or condition."[28]

b) EXHORTATION TO PREPAREDNESS (vv. 6-8). "So then" (*ara oun*) introduces a logical and necessary conclusion from what has just been said. This combination of the two particles is peculiar to Paul. According to the Nestle text he uses it eleven times. The former introduces a conclusive statement as a logical inference of thought, while the latter draws out the practical consequence. What he urges now is supported by both reason and duty.

A twofold exhortation follows. They are exhorted to watchfulness (vv. 6-7) and to being spiritually armored (v. 8). The possession of spiritual privilege must lead to conformable personal conduct.

(1) *Exhortation to watchfulness* (vv. 6-7). The exhortation is stated in verse 6 and is confirmed by the observation in verse 7.

(*a*) *Statement of the exhortation* (v. 6). The statement is both negative and positive. Negatively, "let us not sleep, as do the rest." The word *sleep* is here used metaphorically to denote indifference to spiritual realities on the part of believers. It is a different word than that in 4:13-15 for the sleep of death. It covers all sorts of moral and spiritual laxity or insensibility. Believers who would succumb to sleep thereby become idle and morally inert and expose themselves to the dangers resulting from sin. The present tense of the verb stresses that as sons of day they must constantly keep themselves from falling into such a condition.

In saying "let us" the writers unite themselves with the readers in warning against yielding to this danger. They too stood in need of the warning. Even superior spiritual attainments do not provide immunity against lethargy. Hogg and Vine point out that while the apostles frequently join themselves with their readers in such exhortations, the Lord Jesus "never thus identified Himself with those whom he addressed, whether the multitude or His disciples."[29] This observation provides another glimpse of His uniqueness.

Because they have become "sons of light" believers must not conduct themselves "as do the rest," the unbelievers. *Sleep,* the figure of spiritual insensitivity, is the characteristic attitude of the unsaved. The non-Christian may be wide awake and shrewd in dealing with the things of this world, but when it comes to the welfare of his immortal soul he shows himself overcome with stupor or is fast asleep.

But (alla), the stronger of the two Greek adversatives, introduces the positive statement of the exhortation, "let us watch and be sober." Over against the single negative stands the twofold positive.

"Let us watch" is the opposite of *sleep.* It conveys the demand for morally and spiritually wakeful activity, being on the alert against the assaults of sin and unrighteousness. Stevens calls this "a broad maxim of Christian duty, summing up in itself the temper and attitude appropriate to the life of faith."[30]

The exhortation reflects the eschatological teaching of our Lord (Mt 24:43-44; Mk 13:33-36; Lk 12:37). The believer must not only be alert to the dangers around him but must be looking for the return of his Lord. The Scriptures make this waiting for the return of the Lord one of the chief objects of Christian watchfulness (1 Co 1:7. Titus 2:13; Heb 9:28; 2 Pe 3:12).

"And be sober" expands on the duty of watching. It is not enough just to watch; the watcher must also be *sober,* rational and self-possessed, in perfect control of all his senses. Without this sobriety true vigilance is impossible. He must keep free from the stupefying effects of sin and self-indulgence. This is the opposite of being drunk (v. 7), but Paul is not here using the term in its literal meaning of abstinence from intoxication. It is rather the moral attitude and temper of those who are "sons of day." Such a calm and self-possessed posture enables the believer effectively to deal with whatever threatens. It will also assure his readiness to meet the Lord when He comes.

(b) Confirmation of the exhortation (v. 7). For is again confirmatory. The preceding exhortation is fitting for believers because the opposite practices characterize those who are of the night. "For they that sleep sleep in the night; and they that are drunken are drunken in the night." Here are two characteristic activities that belong to those who are of the night. While sleep may here have something of its previous moral connotation, it seems that Paul is using it in its literal sense. There are some things that are appropriate to the night, and sleep is one of them. "They that sleep sleep in the night" is the statement of a recognized fact. The argument is that as sleep is natural in the night, so indifference to God is

the natural characteristic of the unregenerate man who is spiritually in the night. But the believer no longer belongs to the realm of night, hence cannot properly indulge in moral sleep. He must be awake and watching.

But there was another way in which unbelievers spent the night, "and they that are drunken are drunken in the night." The practice of spending the night in drunken revelry was common in pagan society. But it was an activity that was associated with the night. To be drunken in broad daylight was a monstrous thing, the evidence of deep debauchery (Ac 2:15; 2 Pe 2:13). But such self-indulgent activities are wholly inappropriate to believers as those who belong to light and to day.

The two occurrences of "are drunken" represent two different words in the original. The first, *methuskō,* in the active voice means "to make drunk, and in the passive, as here, "to get drunk, become intoxicated." The second, *methuō,* means "to be drunk." There is no essential difference in meaning between the two words here, except that the former denotes the act of getting drunk, while the latter indicates the state of being drunk. The distinction is observed in rendering, "and those who get drunk, are drunk at night" (Weymouth).**

(2) *Exhortation to be armored* (v. 8). *But* again introduces a contrast between those who engage in activities characteristic of the night (v. 7) and believers who belong to the day. This contrast is sharpened by the use of the emphatic personal pronoun *we* (*hēmeis*), marking the difference between believers and "the rest" (v. 6). This difference justifies the renewed exhortation, "But let us, since we are of the day, be sober, putting on the breastplate of faith and love; and for a helmet, the hope of salvation."

"But let us, since we are of the day, be sober" is literally "But we, being of the day, let us be sober" (Rotherham). The plural participle *being* is slightly causal in force, hence the rendering in our version, "since we are of the day." Since we as believers have our sphere of life in that realm characterized as "day," we are obligated to be *sober.* The present tense of the hortatory verb again calls for a continuing condition of being sober. Sobriety must be the habit of believers.

The verb *sober* resumes the exhortation of verse 6, yet here receives added force from verse 7 and the two participial clauses which modify it. As the one independent verb of verse 8, this exhortation draws renewed attention to the vital need for sobriety. Such inward alertness and self-possession is consistent with the fact that we belong to "the day." And this demands that we be appropriately armored, "putting on the breastplate of faith and love; and for a helmet, the hope of salvation." The verb

**Likewise Williams and the RSV. It is also possible to take the first term as in the middle voice and render with Young, "and those making themselves drunk, by night are drunk."

"putting on" conveys the thought of "clothing oneself with" and introduces Paul's favorite metaphor of the Christian armor. This military metaphor was prepared for and suggested by the sober vigilance just advocated, the proper characteristic of the sentry. The believer is not only a watchman but also a warrior. He must not only be alert and self-possessed but also equipped to resist the onslaught of the enemy. While awaiting the return of his Lord, the believer must be on his guard, for he waits in a hostile world.

"Putting on" translates an aorist middle participle which is attached to the present tense verb "let us be sober." The difference in the tenses is suggestive. Believers must continue in a state of sobriety, but the matter of putting on their armor is not a continuous or repeated action. The present tense would have suggested that there were times when they might put off their armor, later to put it on again; but this the Christian may never do. The aorist tense indicates that the armor must be put on as a definite act, hence to be kept on. Thus having on the armor is a characteristic aspect of their vigilance. The middle voice indicates that this putting on of the armor is a matter that involves their own interests.

The putting on of the armor is for the purpose of resisting present spiritual enemies. There is of course no thought of being defensively prepared against the coming of the Lord as a thief. In Ephesians 6:13-17 this picture of the Christian's armor is drawn out in greater completeness; here only two parts of the whole armor are mentioned, both defensive weapons, since the picture is that of the soldier guarding himself against surprise attack.

The first piece of the armor, "the breastplate of faith and love," is indispensable. The *breastplate* was a piece of armor which covered the soldier's body from neck to waist and protected his heart, the very center of his life and the spring of his vital forces. The term is here used figuratively, as in Ephesians 6:14; the believer's spiritual breastplate consists "of faith and love." These two appositional genitives are Christian virtues, both indispensable for the believer's security against spiritual assault.

The breastplate is pictured as being double or having two sides. *Faith* denotes the proper inner attitude of the believer toward Christ as his Redeemer and Lord, while *love* is the proper outward expression of the Christian life toward the saints. John Trapp remarked, "Faith is the forepart of this breastplate, whereby we embrace Christ, and love the hinder part thereof, whereby we embosom the saints."[31] While the breastplate is thus pictured as being double, it is in reality a unity; Christian faith and love cannot be separated, for "where the one goes the other follows."[32] No objects of the faith and love are mentioned; they are themselves well-known realities of the Christian life and need no further definition.

The second piece of the armor named is the helmet, "and as a helmet, the hope of salvation." The *helmet*, meaning literally, "around the head," gave protection to the head of the soldier. It was "the crown of the soldier's armour, its brightest and most conspicuous piece."[33] It invited the special attack of the enemy.

The believer's helmet, giving protection to his head, is "the hope of salvation." The nature of this *hope* is at once defined as being the hope "of salvation." This objective genitive denotes that the hope is directed toward salvation, the future eschatological deliverance of believers at the *parousia*. It is the antithesis of the wrath mentioned in the next verse. It is this hope of the future consummation of our salvation that "lifts up the head toward heaven, and wards off all the power of the blows inflicted by Satan and this world."[34]

While we believers already know the blessed experience of salvation from the bondage of sin, we are eagerly awaiting the coming consummation of our salvation with the return of the Saviour who will climax our salvation with the glorification of our bodies (Phil 3:21; Ro 8:23). This blessed hope must inspire present purification of life (1 Jn 3:2-3). It also encourages the believer to resist the enervating influences of the present evil age. It makes the dangers and trials of this earthly life seem light and endurable (Ro 8:18).

c) SALVATION APPOINTED FOR BELIEVERS (vv. 9-10). The causal conjunction *For* (*hoti*) introduces a further reason why as believers we must put on our armor, especially the helmet, the hope of salvation. Our hope is reasonable because it is in harmony with the act and intention of God regarding us. The salvation which He intends for us is described as to its nature (v. 9*a*), its agent (vv. 9*b*-10*a*), and its goal (v. 10*b*).

(1) *Nature of salvation* (v. 9*a*). "God appointed us not unto wrath, but unto the obtaining of salvation." Our salvation proceeds from God's appointment. It is connected with the past act and deliberate purpose of God. The verb rendered "appointed" (*etheto*) means "to set, put, place" in connection with material things, and in connnection with persons, "to place, to appoint" to a position or service or "to destine" them *unto* (*eis*) the realization of a definite goal. The middle voice indicates that God thus acted in His own interest, while the aorist tense denotes the action as an event of the past. Acting according to His own will and good pleasure, God has "destined"†† us unto salvation as His gracious intention for us. The divine intention concerning us is stated both negatively and positively.

††"Destined" is the rendering used by Lattey, Weymouth, Moffatt, Goodspeed, 20th Cent, Berkeley, RSV, NEB, and NASB. Darby renders, "God has not set us for wrath."

Negatively, God's intended goal for us believers is "not unto wrath." The *not* is emphatic by position.‡‡ As in 1:10 *wrath* here is used in its eschatological sense, the wrath of God upon the sinner in the coming day of judgment. God wills not our destruction but our salvation. He has no intention that we should become the subjects of His wrath, fall under its punitive action, when the day of "sudden destruction" (5:3) falls upon the unsaved. He cherishes no angry purposes toward His redeemed children; the divine wrath against sin was diverted from us when by faith we were united with "the Son of his love" (Col 1:13). Wrath is the destiny of Christ-rejecting souls.

This negative assertion seems clearly to assure that believers will not have part in the coming great tribulation, when God's wrath falls upon a Christ-rejecting world (Rev 6:15-17; 14:10; 19:15). They are looking forward not to the coming of that day when God will display His wrath in divine judgment but to the coming of the Lord Himself who will deliver them from the very presence of sin.

But (*alla*), the stronger of the two Greek adversatives, introduces the positive aspect of the divine intention for us, "unto the obtaining of salvation." In what follows the essence of this salvation is described as being eternal fellowship with Christ (v. 10; cf. 4:17*b*).

"The obtaining" translates an anarthrous noun (*peripoiēsin*) which in its active sense means an act of acquiring something; the genitive, "of salvation," indicates that which is acquired, namely, salvation in its completeness. But some interpreters shy away from this meaning of the term since it might imply that salvation is obtained through our own efforts. They prefer to take the word in its passive meaning, something acquired for us, a possession given us. Thus Lightfoot puts it "for the adoption of salvation" and asserts that this acquiring is "the act of God."[35]

The active suits the context better. To be sure, those who obtain this salvation do so according to the appointment and calling of God, but they must make a willing response to the call and exert personal effort toward its realization. The divine calling necessitates a human response. While salvation is of God, the actual gaining of our salvation as a personal possession demands on our part "a wakeful, soldierlike activity, such as will be crowned by the 'winning of salvation,' the glorious end for which 'God destined' them when He first 'called them to His own kingdom and glory' (ii. 12)."[36] Each believer must give diligence to make his calling and election sure (2 Pe 1:10). It seems clear from the hortatory nature of the context that the emphasis here is upon the human activity needed actually to obtain the salvation. Our versions accordingly use such terms as

‡‡The original order, which makes very awkward English, is, "for not appointed us God unto wrath."

acquiring, winning, and *to gain salvation.*§§ Those who now by faith accept God's salvation and actively endeavor to make it their personal possession will enter into "the full attainment of salvation" (NEB) when the Lord comes.

(2) *Agent of salvation* (vv. 9b-10a). While diligent effort on the part of believers is needed, the added phrase "through our Lord Jesus Christ" leaves no uncertainty as to the real source of all salvation. Salvation can only be obtained through Him. He is the Mediator of salvation, and through Him whom we have accepted as "our Lord" our hope of salvation will assuredly be realized.

He who is the medium of our salvation is further appositionally identified as the one "who died for us." His function as our Redeemer from "the wrath" is linked directly with the fact of His atoning death. The aorist indicative verb *died* looks back to Calvary as a historical fact. It asserts that He "experienced death" (Berkeley) in all the grim reality of the term. The active voice of the verb points to the voluntary nature of His death; He was not "killed" but was willing to die of His own accord.

But the significance of His death lies in the fact that it was "for us" (*peri hēmōn*). Plummer notes that the preposition *peri* indicates that it "was 'about us' that He was thinking when He willed to die. He died a death in which he had a special interest."[37] This is the only instance in the Thessalonian epistles where our interest in the death of Christ is asserted. But the precise connection between His death and our salvation is not drawn out. Pointing to the preposition used, Denney remarks, "It is the most vague expression that could have been used to signify that Christ's death had something to do with our salvation."[38] Yet the very vagueness and brevity of the remark indicates that the writers assumed that their readers would understand its significance. It assumes that the Thessalonian believers had received adequate instruction concerning the meaning and value of Christ's death.

That the significance of Christ's death is not discussed in the Thessalonian epistles simply shows that this doctrine, contrary to the situation in the Galatian churches, was not being brought into question at Thessalonica. Any assumption that the preaching of the cross of Christ had received little attention in the apostolic proclamation at Thessalonica is unwarranted. From 1 Corinthians 15:1-3 it is clear that this was at the very heart of the apostolic preaching from the very first. Paul was busy preaching a fully developed theology of the cross at Corinth at the very time that this epistle to the Thessalonians was written (1 Co 2:1-2; 1:17-18). In this passing reference to Christ's death 'for us" we must therefore

§§Rotherham and Young; Montgomery, Lattey, Way, 20th Cent; Goodspeed, Moffatt, Williams.

recognize a latent reference to the whole theology of the cross as Paul had preached it at Thessalonica.

There is some uncertainty as to whether the original reading translated "for us" is *peri hēmōn,* (concerning us), or *huper hēmōn,* (in our behalf).|| || The former reading is more indefinite and does not directly assert that Christ died as our substitute. The latter is the regular preposition for the thought of substitution in the Koine Greek.[39] There are other passages where the manuscripts show this variation in the preposition used. Both are used in different places concerning the death of Christ.## The latter preposition (*huper*) asserts the thought of His substitionary death, while the former (*peri*) assumes it. The truth of the vicarious death of Christ cannot be eliminated from this passage. The death of Christ "for us" is the meritorious cause for our deliverance from the wrath of God against sin (2 Co 5:21).

Hogg and Vine point out that this appositional phrase, "who died for us," might be omitted without impairing the general sense of the passage.[40] Clearly it was added to underline the fact that our salvation in its inception as well as its consummation is wholly due to the atoning work of our Lord. Without His redemptive work on the cross there could be no salvation for sinful men.

(3) *Goal of salvation* (v. 10*b*). The salvation which God has appointed for believers through our Lord has as its ultimate goal "that, whether we wake or sleep, we should live together with him." This glorious purpose will be fully realized at Christ's return "whether we wake or sleep." This parenthetical clause summarizes the comfort given the Thessalonians in the revelation concerning the two classes of believers at the Lord's return for His own (4:13-18).

There is not complete agreement among the interpreters as to the meaning of the verbs *wake* and *sleep.* To interpret them as natural wakefulness or physical sleep, as though the goal of the salvation will be realized whether the advent occurs in the daytime or at night, is a view which Lünemann well stamps as "feeble and trifling."[41] Others would interpret it in an ethical sense, "whether watchful and alert or lax and drowsy in our spiritual condition, as true believers we will surely participate in the rapture." But it seems inconceivable that after the writers have been urging the duty of watchfulness they should now present it as a matter of little difference whether believers are spiritually vigilant or negligent. While participation in the rapture will not be determined by

---

|| ||*Peri* is the reading adopted by Westcott and Hort and by Nestle; *huper* is the reading of the *Textus Receptus* and is retained by Souter and the Bible Societies' text.

##Four different prepositions are used in the New Testament to describe the relation of Christ's death to men—*anti, dia, peri, huper.*

any advanced spiritual attainments of believers but solely because of their union with Christ, that is not the point here.

The words *wake* and *sleep* seem clearly to have a figurative meaning here to denote "live or die." (Cf. Ro 14:8-9). Through the atoning death of our Lord we have been brought into a living relationship with Christ, the consummation of which is not dependent upon our being physically alive when He comes. The outcome for us will not be determined whether we are "waking in life or sleeping in death" (Moffatt).

When our Lord returns, both the living and the dead believers will receive their glorified bodies (1 Co 15:51-54; 1 Th 4:16-17) and the grand purpose of God for us will be realized, "that . . . we should live together with him." Then both groups will enter into life in all its fullness. Forever to "live in fellowship with Him" (Williams) is the highest description of our apocalyptic salvation in the Scriptures. This will be the very essence of eternal life.

The aorist tense of the verb "should live" states our future living with Christ as a simple fact without reference to its progress or completeness. It is the realization of that goal that is stressed.

The previous mention of the death of Christ was not associated with His resurrection, as is generally the case (4:14; Ro 4:25; 1 Co 15:4). But the fact of His resurrection is here assumed. "His risen Life, His Enthronement with God, are not here explicitly affirmed; but all else that is affirmed depends absolutely and solely on these things being facts, being true."[42] If Jesus Christ did not arise from the grave this hope of our future life of fellowship with Him is groundless.

But the strengthened form "together with him" (*hama sun autō*) indicates that not only will believers live with their Lord but also that both the living and the dead *together* will be living with Him (cf. 4:17). Both groups, the living and the dead, will be living together, united with Him. Ellicott points out that "to live with Christ" forms "the principal idea, while the *hama* [together] subjoins the further notion of aggregation."[43]

d) EXHORTATION TO MUTUAL EDIFICATION (v. 11). This concluding exhortation of the eschatological section of the epistle is introduced by the strong inferential conjunction *wherefore* (*dio*). Meaning "on account of which thing," it grounds the exhortation in the explanation concerning the Christian hope just given.

The exhortation is given a double statement. They are first of all urged to "exhort one another." The present imperative sets this forth as their continuing duty. The verb rendered "exhort" (*parakeleō*) occurs more than fifty times in the letters of Paul and has a variety of meanings ac-

cording to the context.*** The commentators and translators are not
agreed as to its exact force here. From the analogy of its use in 4:18,
some advocate the rendering "comfort."††† Conybeare agrees with the
American Standard Version in using "exhort," thus stressing the hortatory
nature of the mutual appeal. Many commentators and most of our modern
versions‡‡‡ hold that the better rendering is "encourage," since the
section being concluded is definitely calculated to cheer the hearts of the
readers and to encourage them to diligence and perseverance in their
Christian life. But comfort as well as encouragement may well be implied in the verb, depending upon the individual need.

The reciprocal pronoun rendered "one another" denotes that this is to
be a mutual activity. As each seeks to comfort or encourage the other
there will be a mutual benefit. Our honest efforts to aid the spiritual life
of others bring a blessing to our own life.

The second exhortation given them is "and build each other up." Here
we have another of Paul's favorite metaphors, an architectural figure used
to convey a spiritual concept. The familiar sight of a building being constructed is employed to stress the thought of the assured spiritual growth
of the believer as the result of patient labor. Each individual believer is
viewed as a building, a holy temple, in process of construction. This
building up of the believer is a continual activity, lasting throughout his
earthly life.

Here again the activity is to be mutual. They must continually build
up "each other" (*heis ton hena*).§§§ Howson points out that with Paul
this verb (*oikodomeō*) "is always a social word, having regard to the
mutual improvement of members of the Church, and the growth of the
whole body in faith and love."[44] "Each other" is literally "one the one"
and indicates that no individual is sufficient unto himself in this matter
of his spiritual development. Each needs the mutual assistance of other
believers for the attainment of full spiritual maturity. Each believer has
something to contribute to the others in the building up of the church
"unto a fullgrown man, unto the measure of the stature of the fulness of
Christ" (Eph 4:13). This process of mutual up-building takes place
through all of the constructive experiences that the believer encounters
from his fellowship in the church. Neil comments that these words indi-

***See comments under 2:3. The verb occurs at 2:11; 3:2, 7; 4:1, 10, 18; 5:11, 14.
The noun appears in 2:3.
†††Lattey, Montgomery, Young, Way.
‡‡‡Darby, Goodspeed, Moffatt, Weymouth, Williams; Berkeley, 20th Cent, RSV,
and NASB. Rotherham uses "console," Phillips, "go on cheering;" the NEB has
"hearten."
§§§The suggestion that we read *eis ton hena*, "into the One," that is, Christ or the
church as one body, is unsuitable here.

cate that "the Church member's role is not one of passive absorption, but of active evangelism."[45]

"Even as also ye do" is praise and encouragement for the readers based upon their actual practice. Moffatt calls it "another instance of Paul's fine courtesy and tact. He is careful to recognize the Thessalonians' attainments, even while stirring them up to further efforts."[46]

It is clear that in the primitive churches the care of souls was not delegated to an individual officer, or even the more gifted brethren among them; it was a work in which each believer might have a share. Adeney sees here an indication of a free order in the Thessalonian church "which allowed free scope to the members of a church to address the brotherhood."[47] That this activity of mutual edification was carried forward in their assemblies is obvious. But it seems implied that the believers also took advantage of their occasions of private conversation to talk about these subjects for mutual strengthening. Wherever believers encourage and strengthen each other in private conversation as well as in their assemblies by considering the eschatological truths that have been presented in these two paragraphs, there will be a healthy and flourishing church.

11

PRACTICAL: ASSEMBLING

D. INSTRUCTIONS CONCERNING ASSEMBLY
RELATIONS

5:12-15 But we beseech you, brethren, to know them that labor among you, and are over you in the Lord, and admonish you; (13) and to esteem them exceedingly highly in love for their work's sake. Be at peace among yourselves. (14) And we exhort you, brethren, admonish the disorderly, encourage the fainthearted, support the weak, be longsuffering toward all. (15) See that none render unto any one evil for evil; but always follow after that which is good, one toward another, and toward all.

THE CONNECTIVE PARTICLE rendered "But" (*de*) is transitional, indicating that a new subject is being introduced. The connection between this new paragraph and the preceding eschatological section is not obvious. Bicknell thinks that "the connexion of thought with the previous passage is the duty of mutual edification."[1] Then what follows may be viewed as practical guidance in how they are to build up each other. The immediate reference to their leaders would remind them that such mutual edification is not inconsistent with high respect for their leaders.

More probably the connection is to be found in the exhortation to watchfulness in the preceding section. The readers have been urged to live in preparedness for the glorious future that awaits them in connection with the return of their Lord. Paul has been pointing them to the future, *but* there are present duties to which they must turn their attention. Their watchfulness and soberness must be evident in their daily relations to each other. With that in mind, practical guidelines are now set forth.

Whatever may have been the precise point of transition in the mind of Paul, it is clear that he is now resuming the line of exhortations begun in 4:1-12 and is seeking to deal with further deficiencies in the Thessalonian church (cf. 3:10). This return may best be indicated by rendering the particle "now."[*]

[*]"Now" is used by Lattey, Rotherham, Way, and Weymouth, and "but" by Darby; NASB, and RSV. It is omitted entirely by Conybeare, Goodspeed, Moffatt, Montgomery, Phillips, Williams; 20th Century, Berkeley, and the NEB.

The attitude of the writers as they focus on these matters is indicated in the words "we beseech you, brethren." The verb "we beseech" (see comments under 4:1) does not carry the note of an authoritative command but rather that of a friend making an urgent appeal to a friend. The term suggests that those making the request stand in a position of familiarity with those being entreated. We may render, "Now we are requesting" or "begging you."† In keeping with this is the insertion of the affectionate address, *brethren.*

The solicitous tone indicates that the writers were aware that difficulties did exist in the Thessalonian church regarding the subject now being dealt with. It must be borne in mind that Timothy had just returned from Thessalonica and had given a detailed report of the situation in the church. Sound principles of guidance for their assembly relations are therefore now set forth. Instructions are given concerning their relations to their leaders (vv. 12-13) as well as their duties as a congregation toward faulty members (vv. 14-15).

1. Instructions Concerning Their Leaders (vv. 12-13)

It is obvious that these instructions, directed to the *brethren,* are addressed to the members of the church apart from its leaders. They are urged to maintain a proper attitude toward their leaders (vv. 12-13a) and to preserve peaceful relations among themselves (v. 13b).

a) ATTITUDE TOWARD THEIR LEADERS (vv. 12-13a). A double demand is made upon them in regard to their leaders. They are to know them (v. 12) and to esteem them (v. 13a).

(1) *To know them* (v. 12). It seems obvious that some feelings of tension and misunderstanding had arisen between the members and their leaders. The members seemingly had not appreciated or rightly understood the nature and function of their leaders. Therefore they are urged "to know them." They must not remain in ignorance concerning their leaders but by reflection come to a full understanding of their true character and work. But the verb here clearly carries the further thought that they must "appreciate" these leaders as they recognize their true value. This rather unusual meaning for the verb (*oida*) can now be supported by parallels in extra-canonical literature.[2]

Ministers are often urged, and rightly so, to "know" their members, but here the members are called upon to "know" their leaders. And surely much of the tension that at times develops between the pastors and mem-

---

†Our versions here use several words to render this verb: "beseech"—Conybeare, Lattey; RSV; "entreat"—Montgomery; "ask"—Young; "request"—Rotherham; NASB; "beg"—Darby, Goodspeed, Moffatt, Way, Weymouth, Williams; Berkeley, the NEB, and 20th Cent.

bers would be dissipated if the members would learn to know and appreciate the duties and ministries of their spiritual leaders. Such a recognition and appreciation of their spiritual leaders is "a purely spiritual exercise possible only to spiritual persons. Non-spiritual persons cannot recognize, and would not acknowledge, spiritual workers or their work."[3]

The leaders are described as "them that labor among you, and are over you in the Lord, and admonish you." The Greek construction is three participles united under one article, thus indicating that they are not three distinct groups but one class of men discharging a threefold function. While no official terminology is employed further to identify them, it seems natural to assume that they were the elders or presbyters of the Thessalonian church.

Some scholars hold that the terminology indicates they are not ordained officers in the church but rather voluntary workers. Certainly the three present tense participles stress the work of these men rather than the dignity of the office, but that does not prove the Thessalonian church was still without duly appointed leaders. From Acts 14:23 it is clear that it was Paul's practice to appoint elders in his recently established churches. And even if we accept the assertion of some that the missionaries were driven out of Thessalonica before they had time to appoint elders over their converts, that does not prove that the church remained unorganized. Those who had been former attendants of the Jewish synagogue would be familiar with the basic organization of the synagogue and would thus know how to secure the needed leadership for the church. That the need for a definitely constituted leadership for the group would soon be felt is certain. That they remained without the needed organization and appointed leaders is highly improbable. If the church had not been properly organized and remained without qualified leaders, would not Timothy have attended to that need while he was there? This exhortation to the members takes it for granted that the ministerial oversight of their leaders was an essential function in the church. When this passage is combined with 2 Thessalonians 3:6-13 "it becomes plain that this was a community which had an accepted leadership and a pattern for enforcing conformity to the standards of the Christian community."[4] But it is clear that their organization was simple and thus nothing like the organized hierarchy operative in many churches today.

The plural *them* points to a plurality of elders in the church. This is in harmony with Paul's practice of establishing leaders for his churches (Ac 14:23). These men were naturally chosen from among their own numbers on the basis of their willingness and abilities. Since they apparently continued their secular employment for a livelihood, several would be chosen to work together in giving the needed oversight and leadership to the group of believers.

The work of these leaders is set forth with three present tense participles, delineating their continuing activities. The use of participles instead of nouns of office presents these leaders as exercising specific ministerial functions rather than being given official status.

They are first identified as those "that labor among you." This general designation points to their work as requiring strenuous effort resulting in weariness.‡ Those who faithfully carry out their pastoral responsibilities well know that it demands hard work. Calvin draws the pungent deduction from the term "that all idle bellies are excluded from the number of pastors."[5] Apparently Paul intended that the term should serve as a rebuke to the idlers at Thessalonica.

"Them that labor among you" is broad enough to include various types of work and might in itself include Christian workers in the church who held no office of any kind. It might be allowed to involve any service to the church by any of its members. But the following two participles, linked to the preceding by *and*, make it clear that their leaders are in view: those who "are over you in the Lord, and admonish you." Their labors are in the realm of leadership and admonition.

The participle rendered "are over" (*proistamenous*) literally means "standing before," hence "to be at the head, to direct, to rule." It may denote informal leadership or management of any kind, but papyrus usage establishes that it can be used of various kinds of officials.[6] It points to the spiritual guidance these men are giving to the church, a recognized function of the elders.

The added phrase "in the Lord" defines the nature and scope of their leadership. They are not secular leaders dealing with civic or political affairs but rather preside in connection with the spiritual concerns of the saints. Their position does not stem from personal ambition but rather from their spiritual maturity. Their position of leadership in the church is based upon the recognized fact that both they and those being led are "in the Lord." "His Lordship underlies their leadership."[7] Their authority is not that of a formal ecclesiastical hierarchy but rather is "one exercised in the warmth of Christian bonds."[8]

The third function of the leaders is to "admonish you." *Admonish* quite literally means "to put in mind" and usually carries an implication of blame attached, calling attention to faults or defects. It is the activity of reminding someone of what he has forgotten or is in danger of forgetting. It may involve a rebuke for wrongdoing as well as a warning to be on guard against wrongdoing. It directs an appeal to the conscience and

‡See comments on *labor* under 1:3.

will of the one being admonished in order to stir him to watchfulness or obedience. Morris remarks, "While its tone is brotherly, it is big-brotherly."[9]

(2) *To esteem them* (v. 13*a*). A coordinating *and* at once adds a further duty toward their leaders, "to esteem them exceeding highly in love." The word translated "esteem" generally means "to think, consider, regard," to give careful and deliberate consideration to something or someone. But its parallel construction with "to know" suggests that here it has the unusual meaning "to esteem." They are to value and respect their leaders because of their intrinsic worth. The present tense points to this as their continuing attitude.

Two further phrases amplify this demand to esteem their leaders. "Exceeding highly" renders a very strong double compound superlative adverb meaning "abundantly out of all bounds, beyond all measure."§ It calls for a degree quite beyond all imagination.

"In love" points to the affectionate nature of their esteem toward their leaders. In verse 12 they were urged to think rightly of their leaders; now they are admonished to have an affectionate feeling toward them. Whenever love does not dominate, the admonitions of the leaders, however much they may be deserved by the members, will always tend to provoke resentment against those giving the admonition. If they are to have cordial relations between leaders and members, love must prevail. When they have genuine love they will not merely tolerate the admonitions of their leaders but will graciously accept them.

The intended emphasis in the expression, "to esteem them exceeding highly in love," has been differently understood, depending on whether "to esteem" is directly connected with "in love" or with "exceeding highly." Under the former connection the central emphasis is that the esteem given their leaders is to be in love, with the adverb inserted in between to stress that this love is to be without reserve. Under the latter connection the emphasis is that they are to esteem their leaders very highly, with "in love" added as a loose adjunct to the whole phrase. The latter connection, taking the words in the order in which they stand, seems the more natural. But unquestionably both attitudes are being urged by Paul. As Lattey has it, "and to esteem them very highly and lovingly."

"For their work's sake" points to the reason that their leaders are to be held in high and affectionate esteem. The expression may mean "because of the *nature* of their work," because it is the Lord's work, or "because it is the proper response to the good work they are doing." The latter seems to be the intended meaning here. Their attitude toward their

§The form here is *huperekperissōs*; in 3:10 and Eph 3:20 it is *huperekperissou*, which some manuscripts also have here. See comments under 3:10.

leaders is not to be governed by personal partiality or prejudice but rather by an objective evaluation of the intrinsic worth of what they are doing.

That no counter-requests are added for the leaders is worthy of note. It indicates that they were performing their duties faithfully. We may assume that Timothy had reported nothing on their part that demanded correction.

b) PRESERVATION OF PEACEFUL RELATIONS (v. 13*b*). "Be at peace among yourselves." This imperative is added without any connecting particle. Some, detaching these words entirely from the preceding, regard them as "a new exhortation, entirely independent of the preceding."[10] There is admittedly no stated formal connection, and such injunctions to be at peace do not require a disciplinary context. Yet it seems that in thought this command is closely connected with what has just been urged upon the members of the church. Right relations with their leaders are essential for the maintenance of peace in their midst.

"Be at peace" is a present imperative, meaning that they are not urged to make peace but rather to maintain it. It is a compliment to them, implying that their peaceful relations had not been broken. Let them continue. The use of the imperative form, rather than "beseech" as above, stresses the importance of this point. "No Church could grow spiritually without its members being at peace among themselves."[11]

The duty is to maintain peace "among yourselves." This reflexive pronoun makes the duty equally binding on members and leaders. Both have a share in maintaining the peace in the church. To have said "be at peace with them" would have indicated that the members must submit to the leaders so that peace can be maintained and would have placed all of the responsibility on the side of the members. An alternative reading, which none of the modern critical editors accept, it "be at peace through them" and would imply that their leaders must be recognized and accepted as the true center for congregational peace and unity.

2. Instructions Concerning Faulty Members (vv. 14-15)

There is some question as to whether this series of precepts is addressed to the church as a whole or to the leaders in particular. Lightfoot notes that the Greek commentators regarded them as addressed to the presbyters, but he holds that "there is nothing in the form of the sentence to indicate this restriction."[12] The use of the address *brethren*, which would otherwise here have an unusual restriction in its scope, and the similarity of the introductory words with those in verse 12 support the view that the whole church is addressed. Dealing with faulty church members is admittedly in a special measure the responsibility of the leaders, but it is not confined to them. All believers must be ready to minister to the needy as here indicated. Hogg and Vine remark, "There is no hard and fast line drawn between the elders and the people."[13]

The opening formula, "And we exhort you, brethren," introduces a fresh series of exhortations. The thought now turns to those members in the Thessalonian church who have made necessary the previous exhortation concerning their attitudes toward their leaders. They are urged to work with various individuals who need help (v. 14) as well as to promote proper relations with others (v. 15).

a) WORK WITH VARIOUS INDIVIDUALS (v. 14). Three types of individuals needed special attention in the Thessalonian church: the disorderly, the fainthearted, the weak. Each needed different treatment. The use of the imperative form with each type makes these demands stronger than the infinitive construction used in verses 12-13. The present tense in each case marks that which is enjoined as a perpetual duty.

"Admonish the disorderly." These individuals must continually be admonished with the aim that their fault will be corrected. "The disorderly" (*tous ataktous*) are apparently those who were neglecting their daily tasks. The basic meaning of the word is "out of order, out of place," and was used as a military term to denote a soldier who did not keep the ranks, or of an army advancing in disarray. Then it was further applied to those who quit the ranks and did not perform their duty. By an easy transition the word came to mean disorderly or irregular living of any kind.[14] In the papyri the cognate verb is used with the meaning "to be idle."[15] Milligan concludes that Paul's reference is to those Thessalonian members "who, without any intention of actual wrong-doing, were neglecting their daily duties, and falling into idle and careless habits, because of their expectation of the immediate Parousia of the Lord."[16] Thus the command here is to stir up these loafers and order them to do their duty,

"Encourage the fainthearted." These individuals have a different need and must de dealt with accordingly. "The fainthearted" (*tous oligopsuchous*) means literally "the small souled," the discouraged and despondent. The word does not carry any implication of mental deficiency as the KJV "feebleminded" might suggest. They are members who have become discouraged for some reason, perhaps because of adverse circumstances or because of their deep consciousness of their own sinfulness, causing them to despair of being able to live the Christian life.

These timid, discouraged individuals needed to be encouraged, cheered up, stimulated, and helped along. They did not need to be rebuked and warned like the "disorderly" but rather needed to be encouraged through the use of helpful words to continue the battle for the Lord. Let such souls, who instinctively fear the worst, learn to take courage from the gentle Lord who would not break the bruised reed nor quench the smoking flax (Mt 12:20).

"Support the weak." "The weak" (*tōn asthenōn*, those without strength), here are not the physically weak or sick, but rather the morally or spiritually weak. They need sympathetic assistance. The verb rendered "support" (*antechesthe*) literally means "to hold one's self over against." It thus conveys the idea of supporting another by keeping one's self directly opposite the weak one so as to sustain him. Let the strong put their arms around the weak and hold them up. They need to be assured that they are not forgotten or despised because of their helplessness.

Neil well remarks that the presence of weak believers in the church is "no Thessalonian peculiarity. . . . Weak souls are the normally frail human stuff of which the Christian Church consists."[17] Truly converted people may yet be weak for various reasons. "Some believers are weak through lack of knowledge of the will of God, some through lack of courage to trust God; some, who are timorous or over-scrupulous, hesitate to use their liberty in Christ, some, through lack of stability or purpose, are easily carried away; some lack courage to face, or will to endure, persecution or criticism; some are unable to control the appetites of the body or the impulses of the mind."[18]

These three classes of individuals needing the assistance of the whole church may be identified with three groups who have already appeared in the letter. The *disorderly* may be identified with the idlers of 4:11-12; the *fainthearted* are those who are anxious about their departed loved ones (4:14-17) or are worried about their own salvation (5:9-11); the *weak* are those who are suffering from temptations to lapse into immorality (4:2-8).[19]

These instructions concerning three classes of faulty members are rounded off with the general command, "be longsuffering toward all." In dealing with these faulty members they will experience the constant need to be longsuffering, literally, "long-tempered." Longsuffering is that admirable quality which refuses readily to yield to anger and retaliation in the face of provocation or irritation. This ability to be patient, to bear with those who try us, is an ingredient of Christian love (1 Co 13:4) and is the fruit of the Spirit (Gal 5:22).

The intended scope of the words "with all" is not certain. If a close connection with the preceding injunctions is insisted upon, the meaning will naturally be "all the believers, whatever their character."[20] Others, like Plummer, hold that its scope is all-inclusive, not only the faulty members but also "Jews and heathen, whether persecutors or not."[21] Plummer points to verse 15 to support this inclusive meaning.

This inclusive interpretation would be obvious if we accept the suggestion of Frame that this last clause of verse 14 should be taken with verse 15.[22] This arrangement would give us another set of triplets. It is simply a matter of re-punctuating. Then we have a triplet of commands in verse 14 each dealing with limited groups, while verses 14d-15 would then constitute another triplet of commands which are comprehensive in scope. This suggestion is attractive and in harmony with the frequent arrangement of the material in triplets in the concluding portion of this epistle. That Paul was deliberately arranging his material in triplets here is not certain. It seems best to retain the usual connection of this last clause with the three commands in the first part of the verse. But we need not thereby limit *all* to believers only; in accepting the wider scope we have in it a natural bridge to the general injunctions which follow.

b) PROMOTION OF PROPER RELATIONS WITH OTHERS (v. 15). It is clear from the last clause of the verse that the duties now enjoined, both negative and positive, have a wider scope than just the congregation. "See that none render unto any one evil for evil." *See* is a present imperative with the force, "be careful, be on your guard." It implies that watchfulness is necessary to keep the prohibited practice from creeping in. The plural imperative, "see *ye*," is clearly addressed to the church as a whole, not just the leaders. All have a standing duty to see to it that this undesirable practice does not gain entrance. The temptation to retaliate generally comes on the personal level, hence each member must see to it that he on his part does not give in to it. The danger was real because of the persecution being experienced by the members of the church.

The verb *render* means literally "to give back," hence, to repay, to recompense. It is in the aorist tense and indicates that they must constantly be on their guard that there may not occur a single instance of any one paying back "evil for evil" (*kakon anti kakou*). The preposition *for* (*anti*) conveys the idea of exchange and thus denotes the deliberate return of evil for evil received. *Evil* here has the meaning of that which is injurious or harmful, harm caused by evil intent. It is a categorical prohibition against retaliation. Calvin remarks that the prohibition includes not only the act but also the tendency. "For if it is forbidden to *render evil for evil*, every desire to do injury is wrong."[23]

This prohibition runs counter to "one of the strongest impulses of fallen human nature, for no vice is more certainly regarded as a virtue among men than is retaliation."[24] The prohibition against retaliation is distinctly Christian. It is grounded in the teaching of our Lord (Mt 5:38-48) and was inculcated by the apostles (Ro 12:17-21; 1 Pe 3:9). Compliance with this demand constitutes one of the sternest tests of Christian character. Milligan points out that this lofty spirit found occasional expression in heathen philosophy but that "Christianity first made 'no retaliation' a practical precept for all, by providing the 'moral dynamic' through which alone it could be carried out."[25]

But introduces the counterpart to the preceding prohibition. Christianity does not merely prohibit the practice of evil but seeks to replace it with active good. "Always follow after that which is good." *Always* insists that there are to be no exceptions to this injunction. It is to be observed "on every occasion," no matter how trying the circumstances may be.

"That which is good," emphatic by position, is here the direct opposite of the evil prohibited. *Good* therefore does not refer to the ethical ideal of goodness but rather to acts that are beneficial and helpful, rather than harmful. They must make such kindly acts their constant pursuit, even in the face of open hostility. "Always keep looking for ways to show kindness" (Williams).

The present tense imperative "follow after" (*diōkete*) indicates that what is now demanded will not come naturally and without effort. It is a goal that must be continually and earnestly pursued, like a hunter persistently stalking his prey. The verb has the double meaning "to pursue" and "to persecute." The former meaning is intended here but perhaps its use was meant to remind the Thessalonians that although their enemies are persecuting them they must continue to pursue that which will be beneficial to their persecutors.

The beneficial practice is not limited but should be followed in their dealings "one toward another" as fellow believers. This does not prove that there were hostile or strained relations between different members in the church but it does remind them that such feelings toward each other would be entirely unwarranted. But such beneficial activities must also be extended "toward all," all men with whom they come into contact. "The aim of the Christian must always be to secure the greatest GOOD for ALL."[26]

12

PRACTICAL: CONDUCT

E. INSTRUCTIONS FOR HOLY LIVING

5:16-24 Rejoice always; (17) pray without ceasing; (18) in every-thing give thanks: for this is the will of God in Christ Jesus to you-ward. (19) Quench not the Spirit; (20) despise not prophesyings; (21) prove all things; hold fast that which is good; (22) abstain from every form of evil.

(23) And the God of peace himself sanctify you wholly; and may your spirit and soul and body be preserved entire, without blame at the coming of our Lord Jesus Christ. (24) Faithful is he that calleth you, who will also do it.

IN THIS CONCLUDING PARAGRAPH of the epistle the writers offer their beloved converts some general instructions for Christian living. The writers give a series of terse principles basic to holy living (vv. 16-22), and then conclude the body of the letter with a grand prayer for the entire sanctification of the readers (vv. 23-24).

1. Principles for Holy Living (vv. 16-22)

No connecting particle joins this paragraph to the preceding, and no close connection between the two need be insisted upon. Yet clearly the social duties just enjoined will not be burdensome if the principles now set forth are vitally operative in their lives. The principles inculcated naturally fall into two groups: verses 16-18, principles for the inner life; verses 19-22, directives for corporate spiritual life.

a) PRINCIPLES FOR THE INNER LIFE (vv. 16-18). The attitude that must characterize their inner life is set forth in three terse commands (vv. 16-18a), which deal with their life in relationship to God. The commands are justified by the assertion that such is God's will for them (v. 18*b*).

(1) *Triplet of commands* (vv. 16-18a). "Rejoice always; pray without ceasing; in everything give thanks." Uttered without any connecting particles, these crisp injunctions ring out with arresting terseness, delineating the attitude that must characterize their inner life. In each of these com-

mands, which Moffatt calls "diamond drops,"[1] the modifier stands emphatically before the verb: "Always rejoice ye; continually pray ye; in everything give thanks" (Young). The present tense in all of these imperatives marks them as continuing duties. Here are attitudes that must be characteristic of their lives.

The command "rejoice always" is remarkable in view of the sufferings of the readers already mentioned (1:6; 2:14; 3:2-4). But this note of rejoicing was something with which the readers were already acquainted in their own experience (1:6). A vital Christian experience unlocks the whole of man's nature; it influences his outward conduct and stimulates his affections and emotions.

But the remarkable part of this command lies in the emphatic *always*. This adverb of time (*pantote*) is a favorite with Paul[*] and occurs here for the sixth time in this epistle (1:2; 2:16; 3:6; 4:17; 5:15). It stresses the duty to rejoice "at all times," not just when circumstances are pleasant. Paul held that joy was a distinctive and abiding characteristic of the Christian. But Paul was no blind optimist. He well knew that in leading the Thessalonians to faith in Christ he had shared with them a heritage of suffering (cf. 3:2-3). But he also knew that suffering for the Lord was not incompatible with rejoicing in the Lord. He could testify to the paradoxical experience of joy amid sorrow and suffering (2 Co 6:10). His explanation for this paradox is found in Romans 8:18 and 2 Corinthians 4:16-18. He had learned the secret that sorrow and suffering voluntarily endured for Christ open a new spring of joy (2 Co 12:10; Col 1:24). Paul's later letter to the neighboring Philippian church, written from prison, may well be read as "a descant on this theme."[2]

Also for the suffering Thessalonian believers this command to rejoice came as no startling innovation. Their own experience had already taught them the reality of Christian joy amid suffering for their faith (1:6; 2:14). They well knew that this was no natural joy but rather the product of the indwelling Holy Spirit. It was the exhibition of this joy amid suffering that was one of the distinctive features of the early Christian church, amazing the heathen world, and drawing many to Christ.

The imperative statement is an appeal to their will; it reminds them that they have a part in maintaining this experience of joy. It is a call to them not to allow adverse circumstances to rob them of their joy. "God wishes his people to be happy, and does not suffer them to be indifferent to their own peace. He commands them to rejoice."[3] Christian joy is not dependent upon external circumstances; it springs out of the fact that the believer is "in Christ" and is rooted in the unfathomable blessings flowing from that union. Believers therefore have ample reason to rejoice

[*]It occurs 27 times in Paul's letters and 15 times in the rest of the New Testament.

even amid unfavorable circumstances. They know that their sinful past has been forgiven, that in Christ they are now well-pleasing to God, and that the hope of an eternity with Christ lies before them. Consequently the believer has no right to continue to be despondent and miserable. Mason concludes, "The Christian who remains in sadness and depression really breaks a commandment: in some direction or other he mistrusts God—His power, providence, forgiveness."[4]

The second guiding principle for their inner life is "pray without ceasing." *Pray* is a comprehensive term covering all forms of reverent approach to God. It suggests the reverential attitude of the one praying rather than the length of the petitions being offered. They must maintain such a reverential approach to God as a continuing practice.

Again it is the emphatic adverb "without ceasing" (*adialeiptōs*) that makes the command arresting. This call to pray "unceasingly" obviously does not demand that they engage constantly in the act of uttering prayers.[†] Clearly Paul is not laying upon the Thessalonians a demand to maintain an uninterrupted prayer vigil.[‡] Such an interpretation of the term would be inconsistent with Paul's own claim that he prayed "unceasingly" (Ro 1:9; 1 Th 1:2-3) amid his busy missionary activities.

The adverb does not mean uninterrupted praying but rather constantly recurring prayer. But the command means more than "never give up praying" (Goodspeed) in the sense that they must not give up the practice of prayer. Rather, he is asking for a life that is pervaded with the spirit of unceasing prayer. The practical demands of life make it impossible for them to give themselves to constant praying, but they are to live in a spirit of constant communion with God. In the Christian life the act of prayer is intermittent but the spirit of prayer should be incessant. "It is not in the moving of the lips, but in the elevation of the heart to God, that the essence of prayer consists."[5] But such a spirit of prayer will manifest itself in repeated utterances of prayer to God. "The spirit of prayer is only known by constant secret acts of prayer."[6] Milligan suggests that as a commentary on this command we should note "the constantly interjected prayers in this and the later epistle."[7]

He who lives in a spirit of unceasing prayer will ever be ready and fit to approach God in worshipful prayer. His praying is not limited by time or place. He is not restricted to set hours of prayer. Neither is he restricted to any specific place of prayer, "but the believer is not in a right place if he cannot continue to pray there."[8]

---

†Neither in 1:3 or 2:13 does this adverb have the connotation of an uninterrupted action.

‡"It is a characteristic petrification of Christianity when certain Religious Orders keep up worship in relays all day and all night." (R. Mackintosh, "Thessalonians and Corinthians," in *The Westminster New Testament*, pp. 63-64.)

"In everything give thanks" is likewise a startling injunction. Such a reminder to express thanks is characteristic of Pauline practice and teaching (Ro 1:8; 1 Co 1:4; Eph 1:16; 5:20; Phil 1:3; Col 1:3, 12; 3:17; Phile 4). But it is again this emphatic adverbial phrase "in everything" that lifts this admonition above the level of natural practice or possibility. It is a duty that is not dependent upon gratifying circumstances. They must practice thanksgiving "in every circumstance" (Montgomery). The preposition *in* (*en*) points to the circumstances of their thanksgiving, "in connection with everything," and *everything* makes the injunction all-inclusive. The previous two commands are continuous as to time; this one is universal in scope.

The Christian should meet adverse circumstances of life not with a spirit of stoic resignation but with a spirit of unfailing gratitude. Paul and Silas had exemplified this spirit when imprisoned at Philippi (Ac 16:25). Such an attitude is made possible only by the grace of God. It can become a vital reality only when the truth of Romans 8:28 is experienced. When we realize that God works all things out for good to those who love Him and are yielded to His will, thanksgiving under all circumstances becomes a glorious possibility. "He who can say 'Amen' to the will of God in his heart will be able to say 'Hallelujah' also."[8]

(2) *Justification for the commands* (v. 18b). *For* introduces the fact that this triplet of commands is justified because of God's will for the readers. "For this is the will of God in Christ Jesus to you-ward."

There is some uncertainty as to the intended scope of *this* (*touto*). Is it to be restricted to thanksgiving alone, or does it include all three injunctions? Ellicott feels that the peculiar stress which Paul always seems to lay on thanksgiving renders the restriction to the last command more probable.[9] Adeney further argues for this restriction from the fact that the pronoun *this* is singular, rather than "these things."[10] But it may be replied that the three commands are sufficiently homogeneous in character to allow their inclusion under the singular. Findlay remarks that "they constitute one habit and temper, the spirit of a true devotion to God, so that *touto* includes them collectively."[11] The context favors this inclusive reference. Rejoicing, prayer, and thanksgiving form a trio which are closely related and must not be separated in practice. If the dove of Christian joy is continually to mount upward it must fly on the wings of prayer and thanksgiving.

Rejoicing, prayer, and thanksgiving are expressly asserted to be God's will for them.§ As in 4:3, the word *will* is without the definite Greek

---

§"Otherwise it would soon in the declension of Christendom have been counted levity and presumption." (William Kelly, *The Epistle of Paul the Apostle to the Thessalonians*, p. 72.)

article, indicating that this triple command does not exhaust God's will for His saints. The assertion underlines the fact that the exalted spiritual life just set before them is not merely Paul's own ideal for believers but is specifically God's *will*, His gracious design and purpose for them. Whedon remarks that this fact must eliminate for the believer an attitude of pessimism in relationship to the events of life.[12]

Joy, prayer, and thanksgiving are God's will for them "in Christ Jesus." He is the pattern and source of such a life. It found supreme manifestation in His earthly life and it is only in union with Him that such a life is possible for the believer. It is the product of the new life received from Him and is made operative in them by the indwelling Holy Spirit.

The added phrase "to you-ward" assures the Thessalonians that this aspect of God's will can have specific application to their own lives. The phrase is literally "into you" (*eis humas*) and indicates that the truth stated is to reach out and become operative in them. The obligation resting upon them is practicable by them. "The argument is not, 'You *must* do it, for God so wills, but 'Knowing that it is God's will, you *can* do it.' "[13] God does not demand that which He does not give the power to perform.

b) PRINCIPLES FOR CORPORATE SPIRITUAL LIFE (vv. 19-22). This further series of commands stresses responsibility of the readers toward the workings of the Spirit in their assembly. The preceding series (vv. 16-18) stressed their personal relationship to God; this stresses their duty to react properly to the operation of the Holy Spirit in their midst.

Five terse commands are given. In each the object is placed at the beginning and the verb at the end, making both emphatic. All the verbs are in the second person plural, indicating that the duties inculcated are intended for the entire membership of the Thessalonian church. The first two commands are negative (vv. 19-20), the remaining three positive (vv. 21-22).

(1) *Negative commands* (vv. 19-20). "Quench not the Spirit; despise not prophesyings." The literal order is, "The Spirit do not quench, prophesyings do not despise" (Rotherham). In both commands the use of the negative (*mē*) with the present imperative prohibits the continuation of a course of action already in progress; it must be stopped. The first is general, the second particular.

"The Spirit" in verse 19 does not refer to their human spirit, nor to the new spirit which characterizes their new community relations, but to the Holy Spirit Himself. This unmodified designation, "the Spirit," can only denote the Spirit par excellence, the divine Spirit who indwells them and pervades the communal life of the Thessalonian believers. This is confirmed by the next clause which deals with the manifestation of the operation of the Spirit in their midst through prophesyings.

"Quench not" is a command based upon the familiar image of the Holy Spirit as a flame. On the day of Pentecost the outpoured Spirit manifested His presence to the waiting disciples in the form of tongues "like as of fire" (Ac 2:3). This figure of the Spirit as fire goes back through John the Baptist (Mt 3:11) to Isaiah 4:4. This emblem of the Spirit points to His sudden and vehement activities in human hearts. It implies "His gifts of warmth for the heart and light for the mind and His power to kindle the human spirit."[14]

The word *quench*, when used of literal fire, means "to extinguish, to put out;" metaphorically it means "to suppress, to stifle." The reference is not to the person of the Holy Spirit Himself, for He can never be extinguished, but to His activity in the human heart. Since fire is always extinguished by something outside itself, this prohibition is directed against some hindrance to the Spirit's operation in their midst. It is not indicated whether they are quenching the Spirit in themselves or in others. Both thoughts may be included in this general injunction, yet the connection with verse 20 seems to indicate that the suppression of prophetic utterances in the assembly was primarily in view.

The precise situation in the Thessalonian church calling forth this injunction is not clear. Many interpreters hold that it arose out of the operation of the charismatic gifts in the Thessalonian church. Apparently speaking with tongues had led to disorders and confusion in the assembly, as at Corinth, and consequently some of the more staid members had reacted strongly against these spiritual manifestations, endeavoring to restrain them. Under this view the situation was exactly the opposite to that at Corinth. There Paul had to restrain enthusiastic excesses in the exercise of spectacular gifts, but here he must warn against an undue checking of the moving of the Spirit. Such an interpretation of the situation is possible, but it seems to read a lot into this simple injunction.

The general character of the prohibition would certainly leave room for a wider interpretation. Anything which might be permitted in their assembly, or in their own hearts, which was contrary to the nature and work of the Spirit would quench His operations. The Spirit's fire is quenched whenever His presence is ignored and His promptings are suppressed and rejected, or the fervor which He kindles in the heart is dampened by unspiritual attitudes, criticisms, or actions. Certainly any toleration of immorality and idleness, against which they have been warned (4:1-12), would quench the Spirit's working in their midst. They must not allow the operations of the Spirit to be suppressed either through yielding to the impulses of the flesh or by imposing a mechanical order upon the services which would hamper the free movements of the Spirit.

"Despise not prophesyings" names a specific action whereby the Spirit may be quenched. The verb rendered "despise" is a strong word, meaning "to set down as of no account, to set at naught, to treat with contempt." The negative with the present tense forbids the continuation of such an attitude. Williams well conveys the force in his rendering "Stop treating the messages of prophecy with contempt."

Prophesyings refers to the utterance of various declarations of the divine counsels under the immediate inspiration of the Spirit. The plural noun without the article denotes the individual cases as the Spirit spoke through the prophets for the instruction and edification of the church.

The prophetic function held an important place in the life of the early church. In Ephesians 4:11 the prophets are named next to the apostles as Christ's gift to the church. They were the human channels through whom the Spirit made known His will and purpose for His people. The prophetic revelation might at times concern the future (Ac 11:28), but not necessarily so. The prophetic message generally was in the nature of instruction and guidance concerning the present (Ac 13:2).

The basic function of the prophet was to "speak forth" the counsel of God.|| Through this important gift the Spirit guided the development of the life and doctrine of the young church. With the completion of the divine revelation in the New Testament canon such direct communication of new spiritual revelation has ceased. Today the prophetic ministry in the church is not the disclosure of new revelation directly from the Spirit but rather the proclamation of God's message for His people as gathered from the inspired Scriptures under the illumination of the Spirit and made relevant to the contemporary situation. Believers need to be on guard against any professed revelation from the Spirit today which goes beyond or is inconsistent with the revelation embodied in the Scriptures.

This verse makes it clear that some members of the Thessalonian church had a low evaluation of prophesying. Obviously some local circumstances had brought it into disrepute. Those who view the preceding injunction in connection with the operation of charismatic gifts assume that some of the members had been carried away by their possession of the more spectacular gifts, such as speaking in tongues, and consequently tended to demean the less spectacular gift of prophecy. According to this view Paul is seeking to establish a proper balance, reminding them that to

|| The word "prophet," from *pro*, "forth," and *phēmi*, "to speak," means "one who speaks forth." "A prophet in fact is (1) A *for*-teller, *i.e.* one who speaks *for* God; (2) A *forth*-teller, *i.e.* a herald, proclaimer; (3) A *fore*-teller, *i.e.* one who predicts." (G. W. Garrod, *The First Epistle to the Thessalonians*, p. 143.)

despise the gift of prophecy is to quench the Spirit. This also seems to read a lot into the text.

Possibly some had developed a disparaging attitude toward prophecy because of its abuse in the church. Frame conjectured that the idlers in the church had abused the gift of prophecy by proclaiming as a professed utterance from the Spirit that they were to be supported from funds under the control of the church.[15] In reaction to this abuse of prophecy other members had come to doubt the validity of the Spirit's operation in prophecy. Such a reconstruction of the actual abuse eliciting this command seems improbable; we would then have expected the writers to be more explicit concerning it.

More probable is the suggestion of Morris that this despising of prophecy was due to second-advent speculations in the church.[16] From the second epistle (2:3-4) it is clear that, at least a little later, certain self-deceived individuals considered their own speculations on the subject to be the voice of the Spirit. Such abuses of prophecy would naturally cause the more calm and discerning to react against the gift.

Whatever the exact nature of the abuses that evoked the tendency to undervalue prophecy, they must guard themselves against the easy reaction of despising all prophesying. Believers need to remember that wherever the Spirit of God is at work, the devil will seek to introduce confusion. They must not disparage the true manifestations of the Spirit, but be alert to detect the false.

(2) *Positive commands* (vv. 21-22). Three positive commands are set over against the preceding negative commands. The American Standard Version uses no particle to mark the transition to the positive but has a marginal note that "many ancient authorities insert *but.*" This particle (*de*) has good manuscript support and is probably part of the original.# This adversative adds to the force of the text. It serves to counterbalance the preceding injunctions. The missionaries are not advocating credulity toward all that claims to be a message from the Spirit. They need to realize that a false supernatural report may mimic the true. "The simple fact of a preternatural inspiration is not enough to establish the claims of a spirit to be heard. There are inspirations from below as well as from above."[17]

The objects in these positive commands stand emphatically before the verbs. Young's rendering preserves the original order: "all things prove; that which is good hold fast; from all appearance of evil abstain ye."

The Thessalonians are urged to "prove all things." The verb *prove,* a

---

#The *de* does not appear in the *Textus Receptus*, nor in Souter's text; Westcott and Hort have it in brackets; but Nestle and the Bible Societies text accept it as a true part of the original.

favorite with Paul,** has the basic meaning "to test, to examine, to test with the expectation of approving" (see the discussion under 2:4). The present tense denotes that the testing demanded is not an isolated action but is rather to be the settled rule and continuing practice. Williams conveys this linear action in his rendering, "but continue to prove all things until you can approve them."††

"All things" has primary reference to the things that are being set forth as the message of the Spirit in their midst. But the command is in itself general, extending the principle to all things that affect their religious life. The duty to test prophesyings is thus brought under the universal rule that Christians must practice the testing of all things that ask their acceptance as being from God. Ignorant and untested acceptance of all that claims to be from God is not demanded in any area of the Christian life. Believers are specifically warned, "Believe not every spirit, but prove the spirits, whether they are of God" (1 Jn 4:1).

Ellicott would restrict this command to those who had the special gift of discerning the spirits (1 Co 12:10),[18] but since this command, like the others, is addressed to the church as a whole there is no need thus to limit it. Certain individuals did have the special ability to discern the spirits, yet all Christians have the responsibility to practice discernment in spiritual matters.

Findlay remarks that this command "vindicates 'private judgement' in religion."[19] At Berea the apostolic teaching was tested by the members of the Jewish synagogue and Luke commends the attitude and action of the Bereans (Ac 17:11). So also in our day, when new religious teachings are being proclaimed, believers must continually test them to determine whether or not they have their origin in God. But this command does not mean the establishment of rationalism as the criterion for the testing of spiritual realities. Mere intellectual acumen is unable to make this test. "Now the natural man receiveth not the things of the Spirit of God: for they are foolishness unto him; and he cannot know them, because they are spiritually judged" (1 Co 2:14). "It is spiritual discernment rather than intellectual sagacity that is required."[20]

The Thessalonians are not told how this testing is to be effected, but clearly it must proceed upon a spiritual standard. The Bereans tested the apostolic teaching on the basis of its agreement with the Scriptures

**Seventeen of its twenty-three occurrences in the New Testament are found in the letters of Paul.

††Many of the early Christian writers connected this command to "prove all things" with a saying frequently attributed to Jesus, "Be approved bankers" or "money-changers," that is, men who professionally evaluated various coins in commercial exchange and were keen in detecting spurious coins. If the words of our epistle were written with that saying in mind, the thought would be that the readers must become experts in discerning the true value of that which presents itself as spiritual currency. (For a listing of the patristic references see Lightfoot, p. 85.)

(Ac 17:11). The Scriptures are our sole and sufficient criterion for the testing of all teachings which claim to have divine origin and authority. It is the function of the Holy Spirit to quicken the spiritual perception of the believer so that he is enabled to detect spiritual error in the light of the Word of God (Jn 14:26; 16:13; 1 Jn 2:20-27). The acuteness of the believer's spiritual perception is dependent upon the spirituality of his daily walk (2 Pe 1:8-11).

The testing of all things must result in one of two reactions, according to the outcome of the test. "Hold fast that which is good" indicates the proper reaction toward that which has commended itself. The original order, "the good hold fast," stresses the character of that which is to be retained. "The good" (*to kalon*) denotes the intrinsic value of that which has been tested. It is to be accepted like a coin that is found to be genuine. The adjective signifies that which is excellent, fair, and pleasing in its nature. It may thus be distinguished from the word *good* (*agathon*) in verse 15 above, which carries the thought of that which is beneficial. While admittedly the two words in common usage are not always sharply distinguished, the context makes it clear that they are here employed with their distinctive significance.

The verb rendered "hold fast" (*katechete*) is used with two basic meanings, "to hold fast" or "to hold back." The former is clearly the meaning here. The preposition prefixed to the verb gives it a perfective force, "to hold down, to hold firmly." It adds energy to the action. They must not only approve that which has been found to be good but must actively lay hold on it and firmly retain it. "Cling to what is good" (20th Cent). And, as the present tense stresses, this must be their habitual course of action.

On the other hand, "abstain from every form of evil." This must be their reaction to all that is found to be spurious. "Every form of evil" stands in antithesis to "the good." *Evil* (*ponēros*) is a strong term and is properly distinguished from *kakos*. The latter term points to the base nature of a thing, its lack of those qualities and conditions which would make it worthy of the claim that it makes; the former term is active and denotes that which is destructive, injurious, and evil in its effect.[21] It is malignant evil, blasting and destroying that which it touches. It includes the doctrinal as well as the moral. Lenski asserts, "The worst forms of wickedness consist of perversions of the truth, of spiritual lies."[22]

The term *form* (*eidous*) literally means "that which is seen," the external appearance. It points to the external form in which evil presents itself. "Every form" stresses the inclusiveness of this command. They are to shun evil in whatever form or appearance it may present itself. But the rendering "all appearance of evil" (KJV) must not be interpreted to mean that they are to avoid that which *looks* wicked to those who see it, although in itself it may not be so. The term does not denote semblance as opposed to reality. Such a dictum might enable them to shun some unpleasant duty. "It is a poor heart that is much afraid of *seeming* evil in a good cause."[23] While believers should abstain from actions which will knowingly offend others, it is not always possible to abstain from everything which may appear evil to a narrow and foolish judgment.

In contemporary Greek usage the term *form* was also used to mean "sort, kind, species." This gives the best meaning here. We may then render "from every sort of evil" (Williams). Evil has many forms in which it presents itself. "The essence of evil does not change, but ever seeks new and attractive forms through which it may embody itself."[24] These must be recognized and resisted. Evil has a complexity which stands in striking contrast to the simplicity of the good.

From wickedness in all its forms they must "abstain" (*apechesthe*), quite literally, "hold yourselves off from." The present middle imperative marks this as a continuing personal obligation. In such a course lies their safety.

There is a verbal correspondence between the two commands, "hold fast" (*katechete*) and "abstain from" (*apechesthe*) which is not generally apparent in our English versions. Darby suggests it in his rendering "hold fast the right; hold aloof from every form of wickedness." In both commands the verb is "to hold" (*echō*), with a different preposition. The first verb is active and means that they must "hold fast" the *thing*, while in the second the middle voice stresses that they must "hold off" *themselves* from all wickedness.

These two commands must not be separated in Christian experience. Both are necessary for the development of true Christian character. Christian growth requires not only the assimilation of the good but also the rejection of the evil. The intensity of our adherence to the good, will be measured by the strength of our rejection of the evil.

2. Prayer for Their Entire Sanctification (vv. 23-24)

This prayer is linked to the preceding exhortations by the connective particle *And* (*de*). It is frequently translated "but" when a contrast with what has preceded is intended. Some hold to this meaning here and see an intended contrast "between the futile efforts after holiness of which they in themselves were capable, and the almighty power of sanctification exercised by God."[25] But it is not obvious that such a contrast is actually intended here. The writers certainly are not disparaging the personal efforts of their readers toward holiness. It seems better to take its force here as being continuative, "now" or "moreover," as introducing a further fact that must be added. The full picture demands clear recognition of the necessity of God's sanctifying work in them if the preceding exhortations to holiness are to be realized in experience. He alone is the source and author of true sanctification in the life of the believer. Thus the instructions concerning holy living (vv. 16-22) are appropriately concluded with a prayer for God's sanctifying work in them (vv. 23-24).

a) STATEMENT OF THE REQUEST (v. 23*a*). "And the God of peace himself sanctify you wholly." This title of God is appropriate in view of the conditions at Thessalonica but it cannot be concluded that those conditions dictated its choice here. It is characteristically Pauline and occurs at the close of several Pauline epistles.‡‡ Both nouns have the definite article in the original, "the God of the peace." It points to that God whom the Thessalonians have come to know, whose abiding character is one of peace and whose prerogative it is to bestow the well-known Christian peace upon those who have been reconciled to Him through Christ. He can work in sanctification only in those who have ceased to be in rebellion against Him.

The pronoun rendered "himself" (*autos*) stands emphatically at the beginning of the sentence. Only He can work the needed sanctification in them; all their own efforts would be utterly unavailing apart from the divine working.

The specific request of God for the Thessalonians is that He may "sanctify you wholly." The primary meaning of *sanctify* is "to set apart, to consecrate," but it also carries the thought of the resultant holiness of character in the consecrated. The note of holiness was already sounded in 3:13 and 4:3-8.

The verb here is an aorist active optative (*hagiasai*), expressing a realizable prayer-wish for their future. Some insist that the aorist here points to the crisis experience of entire sanctification,[26] but it is generally accepted that the action is best viewed as constative, a process of sanctification occurring during this present life and viewed as consummated at the return of Christ. Even those who insist upon the meaning of an initial crisis experience stress that it must be followed by a continuing process of sanctification.

The prayer of the writers for their beloved converts is that God may sanctify them "wholly." This adjective (*holoteleis*), occurring only here in the New Testament, is a compound of *holos*, "whole, entire," and *telos*, "end." Its basic connotation is "wholly attaining the end, reaching the intended goal," hence has the force of no part being left unreached. The prayer is that the divine sanctification may extend to every part of their

‡‡Ro 15:33; 16:20; 2 Co 13:11; Phil 4:9; in 2 Th 3:16 we have "the Lord of peace." Cf. 1 Co 14:33; also Heb 13:20.

being, leaving no area untouched by the pervasive power of divine holiness. It is tragically true that "many are satisfied with a partial Christianity, some parts of their life are still worldly."[27]

b) ELABORATION OF THE REQUEST (v. 23*b*). "And may your spirit and soul and body be preserved entire, without blame at the coming of our Lord Jesus Christ." The conjunction *and* indicates that what follows is a restatement of the request from another viewpoint.§§ The word order in the original is arresting. Rotherham preserves this order in his rendering, "And entire might your spirit and soul and body,—[So as to be] unblameable in the Presence of our Lord Jesus Christ,—Be preserved!" The prayer that they may be wholly sanctified is now carried forward with the petition that they may be preserved in all parts of their being until the return of Christ. Sanctification and preservation go together.

The original order brings the two adjectives rendered "wholly" and "entire" (*holoteleis* and *holokleron*) into juxtaposition. They are synonyms, both being built upon the adjective *holos*, "whole, entire." Both stress the thought of wholeness. Findlay distinguishes them as follows, "The former is collective, the latter distributive—the one implying a totality from which no part is excluded, the other an integrity in which each part has its due place and proportion."[28] The latter, compounded with *kleros*, "a lot, a portion received by lot," properly denotes "that which retains all that was allotted to it," hence, without lack or deficiency, complete and whole in all its parts. It was used of "unhewn stones, as having lost nothing in the process of shaping and polishing."[29] Here it is used in an ethical sense; the thought is that all the virtues which belong to the sanctified believer may be complete in them.

The adjective *entire* is predicate, rather than attributive,|||| and should be closely joined with the verb *preserved*, "be preserved as entire." It is to be construed as relating to the three substantives "spirit and soul and body," but it is neuter singular because governed by the first term (*to pneuma*).

"Your spirit and soul and body" enumerates the areas of the desired preservation. *Your*, going with all three nouns, indicates that the prayer is specifically for the Thessalonian believers. All three areas stand in need of the sanctifying and keeping power of God. It is a prayer that is applicable only to believers.

The three terms are arranged in the order of merit, the highest first. The enumeration begins with that which is highest and purest in man and

§§The addition in the KJV "I pray God," is unnecessary. If any addition were needed it should be "*we* pray God," since Silas and Timothy are never wholly forgotten throughout the letter.

||||The rendering "your whole spirit" in the KJV makes it an attributive adjective and restricts it to "spirit" only.

ends with the outward and material part of man. The divine sanctification begins with the inner and spiritual and reaches down to the outward and material.

The precise implication of this threefold enumeration for the essential nature of man has been much debated. Is man presented as a trichotomous (three part) or dichotomous (two part) being? Down through the ages the answers of Christian scholars have been divided on the question.## All agree that man in his essential nature is both material and nonmaterial. The *body* is the outward, material part of man, the instrument through which the inner life expresses itself. It is an essential part of man as created by God (Gen 2:7) and in the biblical view man is incomplete without a body. Our salvation will not be completed until we receive our glorified bodies at Christ's return (Heb 11:40; Phil 3:20-21).

"Spirit and soul" relate to the nonmaterial part of man.*** The Bible at times speaks of man as a bipartite being, referred to as composed of "body and spirit" (Ja 2:26; 2 Co 7:1) or of "body and soul" (Mt 10:28). But here, as in several other places (e.g. Heb 4:12), man is viewed as tripartite. This raises the thorny problem of what is meant here by "spirit" and "soul." Both terms are used with various shades of meaning in the Scriptures.[30]

The view of Jowett that Paul probably attached "no distinct thought" to each of these terms is unacceptable in view of Paul's known care in the use of his terms.[31] The common suggestion that these terms are simply a rhetorical piling up of words for emphasis is rejected by Ellicott with the remark that such a position is "plainly to set aside all sound rules of scriptural exegesis."[32] Bible students who accept the accuracy of Scripture have always believed that a distinction between the two terms was intended here. If there is no difference between them it is difficult to see how the Spirit of God can distinguish them as in Hebrews 4:12. That there is a distinction between "soul" and "spirit" is clear from Paul's use of the adjectives *psuchikos* (soulish) and *pneumatikos* (spiritual) in 1 Corinthians 2:14-15 and 15:44.

The *spirit* is the highest and most distinctive part of man. It is the life principle imparted to man by God who is Spirit, enabling him to know and communicate with God. But with the fall, man as a spiritual being was separated from God and spiritual death resulted. The impartation of

##For a convenient summary of the two views and their leading advocates see Augustus Hopkins Strong, *Systematic Theology*, pp. 483-488.

***The suggestion of Frame that "your spirit" probably "designates that portion of the divine Spirit" which permanently indwells the believer must be rejected. Paul would never thus place the divine Spirit in the same category with man's soul and body; nor is it clear how he could pray that the divine Spirit needed to be preserved entire (Frame, p. 211).

a new spiritual nature in the new birth is necessary so that man can again have direct communion with God.

The *soul* may be viewed as the self-conscious life of man, the seat of personality.††† The self-conscious personality reaches out in two directions. In its relation to the world the soul is entirely dependent upon the body for its information and responses. Through his spirit, man reaches up to the spiritual world, Godward. The fallen man has an awareness of the reality of God and the spiritual, but in his unregenerated condition he has no direct contact with God. Thus the unregenerated man can only understand a religion of the senses. With the new birth he is brought into direct relation with God through the renewed spirit, enabling him to worship God in spirit and truth.

Hebrews 4:12, however, suggests that it is very difficult to distinguish between spirit and soul. Scriptural usage indicates an overlapping of functions. Nor need we try to keep them in watertight compartments. Students of Scripture are not agreed as to whether the distinction between spirit and soul in our passage is substantial or functional. Trichotomists hold to the former, dichotomists to the latter.

The prayer for the Thessalonian believers is that they may "be preserved" in spirit and soul and body. The verb is again an aorist optative of a prayer-wish. The action is best viewed as constative; "the continuous preservation of the believer is contemplated as a single complete act, without reference to the time occupied in its accomplishment."[33] The passive voice points to God as the agent of the preservation. Although the subject of the verb is "your spirit and soul and body" the verb is singular, thus stressing the fact that complex man is in reality a unity, one being.

The quality of the desired preservation is indicated in the adverb rendered "without blame" (*amemptōs*). It denotes a condition of being unblamable, "so that there is no cause for censure."[34] It does not imply a condition utterly without defect but rather a condition where no just cause for complaint can be raised. The prayer is that they may so live that no just charge can be made against them. Milligan points out the interesting coincidence that this adverb, occurring only in this epistle in the New Testament, has been found on certain sepulchral inscriptions at Thessalonica.[35]

This prayer for their preservation is offered in connection with the hope of the Lord's return. The reality of this keeping will be made manifest "at the coming of our Lord Jesus Christ." "At the coming" is literally "in the parousia." (cf. 2:19). It is in view of that anticipated coming that

†††In the KJV *psuchē* is rendered "soul" 58 times, "life" 40 times, "mind" 3 times, and "heart" once.

the prayer for their preservation is offered. Were there no future *parousia*, this preservation would be quite pointless. The prayer for their preservation is significant in view of what that day will disclose. It will assure that then they will be found as blameless.

c) ASSURANCE CONCERNING THE ANSWER (v. 24). Assurance that this penetrating and far-reaching prayer for the readers is not a cry of despair is found in the nature and activity of God. "Faithful is he that calleth you" assumes rather than asserts a reference to God. The construction puts the emphasis upon His faithfulness as caller and doer. It is this fact that assures the consummation of their salvation.

God is *faithful*, to be trusted, reliable concerning all that He has said. The faithfulness of God is one of the central themes of Scripture.‡‡‡ He never lies in making a promise and never begins a work without carrying it through to completion. Here is indeed comforting assurance. "If you enjoy His *calling*, rejoice in His *faithfulness*, who will do it."[36]

"He that calleth" renders an articular present participle. The present may be taken to mean that God "renews his call to service every day of our lives."[37] More probably it is to be taken as a substantive, "your Caller." The construction, in context, calls attention to God's person as their caller rather than to His activity.

The accusative plural *you* reminds the Thessalonian believers that they themselves are the objects of God's effective call, the beneficiaries of His gracious call through the gospel (2:12; 2 Th 2:14). That call is the pledge of His desire for their entire sanctification.

"Who will also do it" stresses the correlation between the divine calling and fulfillment. The verb has no expressed object in the original. This absolute use of the verb "sets in bold relief the *doing* with which God accompanies His *calling*."[38] *Also* underlines the fact that the God who called can be relied upon to complete what He began in calling them. The primary reference is of course to their sanctification and preservation, but the statement is too comprehensive to be restricted to these requests. It is a basic truth that motivates all areas of the Christian life.

‡‡‡Gen 28:15; Deu 7:9; Ps 36:5; Ro 11:29; 1 Co 1:9; 10:13; 2 Th 3:3; 2 Ti 2:13; 1 Pe 4:19; 1 Jn 1:9.

13

CONCLUSION

5:25-28 Brethren, pray for us.
(26) Salute all the brethren with a holy kiss. (27) I adjure you by the Lord that this epistle be read unto all the brethren.
(28) The grace of our Lord Jesus Christ be with you.

THESE BRIEF VERSES form a postscript to the body of the letter. This conclusion appends three further exhortations and adds a final benediction. It is thus composed of four independent matters: the request for the prayers of the readers (v. 25); the affectionate greeting to all the readers (v. 26); the instruction that the letter be read to all the brethren (v. 27); and the concluding benediction of Christ's grace (v. 28).

Unlike that of the second epistle to the Thessalonians, this conclusion makes no reference to the apostolic autograph. Just how much of it was penned by Paul's own hand is not clear. Some hold that he wrote verses 26-28; others feel that he took the pen at verse 27; while still others think that he wrote only verse 28. Who the amanuensis was is not known.

A. REQUEST FOR THEIR PRAYERS (v. 25)

"Brethren, pray for us." The affectionate address, *brethren*, is emphatic by position. This is the only instance in this epistle where it is placed as the first word in the sentence. The request for their prayers is thus prefaced by the recognition of the ties of Christian brotherhood. Those ties justify and motivate the request, "pray for us." The present tense denotes that they are asking for the continued prayers of the readers, "be praying for us" (Rotherham). Let this be their practice.

In view of the next verse it seems clear that the writers desire to be remembered not only in their private prayers but also during the public worship services of the Thessalonian church. The imperative form of the request lays this upon them as a duty.

"For us" (*peri hēmōn*) centers the requested prayers around the writers, Paul and Silvanus and Timothy (1:1). The preposition rendered "for" literally means "around, about," and pictures the prayers of the readers as surrounding the writers and their work. They were keenly conscious of their need for the supporting prayers of fellow believers for success in their missionary labors.

Paul believed in the efficacy of prayer. He makes it a practice at the beginning of his letters to assure his readers that he is praying for them and at the close to urge their prayers on his behalf. This request assures the readers "that it is the privilege of the saints to pray for the most honoured servant of the Lord, and that he seeks and values their prayers!"[1] Surely the widespread prayer support which Paul was able to enlist is one of the keys to the power of his ministry. Paul "knew of no faster way to get the Gospel through the enemy lines than by recruiting Christian converts into the secret service of prayer. . . . He depended upon it as his basic weapon."[2]

Plummer makes the significant observation that Paul's requests for prayer for himself point out the great difference between Paul and Christ. "The Apostle prays for himself and for his disciples, and he charges them to pray for themselves and for others, and in particular for himself. Christ prays for Himself and for His disciples, and He charges them to pray for themselves and for others; but He never asks them to pray for Him."[3]

This request for their prayers was a reminder to the afflicted Thessalonian believers that the missionaries' life at Corinth also had its problems and frustrations. They too knew the reality of unpleasant experiences and harassing difficulties in their work for the Lord.

Some ancient manuscripts have "also" in this verse, "pray also for us."* Its claim to be part of the original is beset with serious doubts, yet its insertion is not inappropriate. If it is a part of the original, two views of the intended connection are possible. It may be taken as a call for interchange in prayer; the missionaries have just prayed for their converts (v. 23), now let them pray for the missionaries. The reference, however, may be viewed as going back to verse 17; they have been told to pray without ceasing, and such praying must not be limited to themselves but also include others, even their missionaries.

B. GREETING IN MUTUAL LOVE (v. 26)

There is some uncertainty as to the intended recipients of the order, "Salute all the brethren with a holy kiss." It is generally held that it was primarily the elders of the church who are instructed to greet the other

---

*It is lacking in the *Textus Receptus* and Souter, placed within brackets by Westcott and Hort and by Nestle, and accepted as part of the original in the Bible Societies' text, but with admitted uncertainty.

members for the writers. Others hold that this is an over-refinement and maintain that this directive, like the preceding, is addressed to the whole church. Admittedly there is no intention on the part of the writers to greet the rest of the members second-hand, yet obviously the greeting would be delivered to the church as a whole by the elders to whom the letter would be delivered.

Salute does not suggest any stiff formality. In the papyri it is regularly employed at the end of a letter to convey friendly greetings to others. Such salutations were a common feature of the epistolary communications of the day. The verb means "to greet, to bid welcome."

As a definite act the greetings of the writers are to be conveyed to "all the brethren," including, of course, the sisters in the assembly. This would naturally be done when on the Lord's Day the members assembled for their united service of worship. *All* insists that as members of the inclusive brotherhood of the saints, they are to share equally in the greeting. It tactfully includes those whom the writers have found it necessary to rebuke in this letter (4:11-12).

The greeting is to be given "with a holy kiss" (*en philēmati*), either in connection with or by means of the kiss. *Holy* underlines that it is not to be an expression of romantic love but of distinctly Christian love toward fellow believers. It is the sign of a sanctified spiritual relationship. As *holy* (*hagiōi*), the kiss must be "free from anything inconsistent with their calling as saints, *hagioi*."[4]

While defining its spirit, there is no indication that these words were intended to inaugurate a new Christian practice. The kiss upon the cheek was a common form of Oriental greeting among friends. The custom, common in nonchristian circles, was taken over by the Christian church, but purified and sanctified. It was exchanged among believers as they assembled for worship. Apparently at this time the sexes were segregated in the assembly and the men kissed the men and the women the women.[5] The kiss was exchanged on the basis of brotherly love among members of one spiritual family.

Plummer maintains that "nowhere in the N.T. is the holy kiss connected with public worship."[6] The New Testament references to the kiss do not demand any liturgical connection.† But the literature of the subapostolic age reveals that by that time the kiss had become a secure part of public worship, with liturgical significance.[7] When the kiss came to be exchanged between men and women it became the occasion for their critics to charge the Christians with impurity. The resultant embarrassments

†Ro 16:16; 1 Co 16:20; 2 Co 13:12; 1 Th 5:26; 1 Pe 5:14.

gave rise to numerous regulations concerning the practice by the early church councils.

C. LETTER TO BE READ BY ALL (v. 27)

"I adjure you by the Lord that this epistle be read unto all the brethren." The use of the singular "I" which has occurred previously only at 2:18 and 3:5, stresses that this is a wish from Paul personally. As the one most responsible for the contents of the letter, he makes this his own strong request.

The rare verb rendered "adjure" (*enorkizō*), occurring only here in the New Testament, means "to put under an oath," or, according to Lightfoot, "to bind by an oath."[8] Paul thus puts them under oath to perform that which he requests. The plural *you* seems best taken as a reference to the leaders of the Thessalonian church. The courier of the letter would naturally deliver it to one of the elders; as a group they would be held responsible to see that his request was carried out. The adjuration is made "by the Lord,"‡ that is, the Lord Jesus Christ. The use of the expression here is an indirect testimony to the true deity of Christ.

Paul's specific wish is "that this epistle be read unto all the brethren." While at times the verb may simply mean "to read," it here retains its classical meaning "to read aloud."[9] The aorist tense contemplates a definite (as a opposed to a repeated) occasion when "this letter" will be read to the assembled brethren. "This letter" is literally "the letter," since "the Epistle is regarded as already concluded, and these words occur in the postscript."[10] As a substitute for his personal presence with them, Paul clearly intends that the letter is to be received as having the same authority as his oral instructions.

Paul desired that the letter should not merely be passed from hand to hand, lest some might be omitted. Nor is it certain that all the members of the Thessalonian church would be able to read it for themselves. His suggestion is that the letter be read publicly when "all the brethren" assemble for their united worship service. Whether the reading would take place before, during, or after the service is not clear.

The request that the letter be read to *all* the brethren makes clear that Paul intended this letter to be recognized as the possession of the entire Thessalonian church.§ It guards against any thought on the part of the elders that the letter was only for them and that they might "communicate its contents to those whom they chose to take into their confidence."[11]

‡The Greek verb takes a double accusative, the person to whom the oath is administered and the divine person by whom the adjuration is made.

§There is no evidence that "all the brethren" meant the members of the other churches in Macedonia.

Paul insisted that its message was for *all* who were *brethren*.|| There were to be no inner and outer circles in their brotherhood. Christianity has no esoteric teachings which are reserved for the initiated few. The message of the gospel is an open secret.

This particular phrase is unique among the New Testament epistles. That Paul should be anxious to have this letter read to all the members at Thessalonica is not surprising, but the solemn earnestness of his statement is indeed arresting. Various reasons for this have been suggested: (1) this was his first letter to them and inaugurated a new practice in his churches; he worded it so strongly to assure that the letter would be publicly read; (2) he felt so strongly about the importance of this letter that he felt compelled to assure that it would be read to all; (3) since the letter was a substitute for his personal presence, Paul was afraid that a feeling of disappointment at his absence might cause the church to neglect the letter; (4) he thus sought to guard against garbled reports of its contents being circulated under the claim that they were his true teachings; (5) a primary intention of the letter was to comfort those who had lost loved ones and this objective would be lost if these did not themselves hear the message the letter contained; (6) Timothy had reported that certain troublemakers had indicated they would not pay heed to any such epistolary admonitions and would refuse personally to read the letter; (7) Paul was suspicious that the elders might suppress parts of what the letter contained; (8) there were two congregations in Thessalonica, a Gentile section and a Jewish section, and Paul thus sought to assure that the letter would reach both groups. This last suggestion is entirely devoid of support from the letter itself.

That something in the report of Timothy gave rise to this strong request is quite probable, but the true reason or reasons can only be surmised. Probably several considerations were operative. The adjuration implies divine punishment if they failed to do as asked, but there is no bitterness in Paul's statement. It is in keeping with the brotherly ties stressed in verse 25.

D. BENEDICTION OF CHRIST'S GRACE (v. 28)

This concluding benediction, "The grace of our Lord Jesus Christ be with you," inaugurated a typical Pauline practice. A reference to *grace* appears in each of the concluding benedictions of the Pauline epistles.

|| Some manuscripts insert the adjective "holy" before "brethren." This is the reading of the *Textus Receptus*, hence its appearance in the KJV. But it is omitted by the critical editors on the basis of manuscript evidence. The expression "holy brethren" is not found elsewhere in the New Testament. Nor is it probable that Paul would use it here in view of his insistence that sanctification is God's will for all believers. Any thought that he has in view a special class of believers whom he characterizes as "holy" as distinguished from other believers is unacceptable.

It matches the mention of grace in the opening salutation of each epistle. Thus all the contents of the epistle are encompassed with grace. It is specifically the grace of Him whom both writers and readers worship as "our Lord Jesus Christ." His grace is the alpha and omega of Paul's letters.

The concluding benedictions in all the Pauline epistles are essentially the same with some variations. The shortest is simply "Grace be with you" (Col 4:18; 1 Ti 6:20; 2 Ti 4:22), while the fullest is the trinitarian formulation in 2 Corinthians 13:14. At times he adds the pronoun "all" (2 Th 3:17; Titus 3:15), or says "with your spirit" (Phil 4:23; Phile 25). The second person pronoun *you* (*humōn*) makes the benediction personal for the readers. Only in Ephesians is this pronoun not used; there the benediction is expressed impersonally in the third person (Eph 6:24).

Like the opening greetings of his epistles, Paul's epistolary conclusions are always distinctly Christian. His benediction of grace displaces the customary epistolary "farewell" (cf. Ac 15:29).

Some manuscripts add an "Amen" but it lacks strong support. It is doubtless a later liturgical addition to the text.

The subscription, "To Thessalonians, First, was written from Athens," is not part of the original. It is a later scribal addition, dating perhaps from the second century. "Written from Athens" is a scribal blunder, based upon a misinterpretation of 3:1. The epistle was written from Corinth.

Part 2

SECOND THESSALONIANS

14

AN INTRODUCTION TO
2 THESSALONIANS

SECOND THESSALONIANS, like other New Testament "second" epistles, is a logical sequel to 1 Thessalonians. Since both epistles place strong emphasis upon the second advent they are rightly known as the eschatological epistles among the Pauline writings. All of 2 Thessalonians centers around the truth of the second coming of Christ.

THE AUTHENTICITY OF 2 THESSALONIANS

The authenticity of 2 Thessalonians seems never to have been questioned in the early church. The external attestation to its Pauline authorship is early and strong. Milligan remarks that "the external evidence on its behalf is both earlier and fuller than in the case of the First Epistle."[1]

Attacks upon the Pauline authorship of 2 Thessalonians began at the opening of the nineteenth century. The critical doubts proceed entirely upon internal grounds and in general have taken two forms.

ESCHATOLOGICAL CONTENT

The first line of attack was upon the eschatological content of this epistle. It was maintained that Paul could not have written the detailed eschatological passage about the man of sin since this figure does not appear elsewhere in Paul's writings. It is true that Paul does not elsewhere mention this important personage, but that he did not have occasion to do so twice does not prove that he could not have done so when the occasion demanded. Paul tells the Thessalonians that he did speak about these matters while he was with them (2:5). Surely it cannot be held that this picture is inconsistent with Old Testament prophecy, and Paul's inquisitive and penetrating mind would certainly seize upon the Old Testament prophecies underlying his picture.

Others have claimed that this passage must be post-Pauline since the whole idea of the man of sin is based upon the Nero Redivivus myth, that the infamous emperor had not died, but was waiting the chance to return and bring calamity upon his enemies or the whole world. But recent research has shown that the claim that this passage must therefore be dated not earlier than the last two decades of the first century is groundless. Paul's picture clearly comes not from the myth concerning Nero but from the current Antichrist teaching which reaches back to a time long before Paul. Milligan justly remarks that this teaching "was firmly rooted in Jewish soil even before the Christian era."[2] Paul's picture is in fact grounded in the Old Testament prophetic Scriptures.

It is asserted that Paul could not have written 2 Thessalonians since its eschatology is contradictory to that in 1 Thessalonians; in 1 Thessalonians the second coming is thought of as being imminent and occurring suddenly while in 2 Thessalonians it is preceded by definite signs. It is generally admitted today that this objection has no real weight. It is common in apocalyptic literature to find the elements of suddenness and signs occurring side by side. Wikenhauser points out that "even in the eschatological discourse of Jesus we find harbingers of the *parousia* mentioned (Mk 13, 6 sqq.), alongside the warning to be vigilant because the day is uncertain (Mk 13, 33 sqq.)."[3]

Even the critics today admit that the asserted difference in teaching is no proof that Paul could not have written both epistles. Some say that it simply shows "how confused a maze of eschatological conceptions could co-exist in one and the same person."[4] Others suggest that it simply shows that Paul as a wise and practical man felt free to alter his position under the stress of circumstances.[5]

But conservative scholars, maintaining a high view of inspiration, see no need to resort to such explanations. They hold that both epistles can be accepted as being accurate as they are. Scroggie holds that any supposed eschatological inconsistency between the two epistles disappears when it is recognized that the rapture and the revelation as two different phases of the second advent are dealt with.[6] Even those who do not stress the clear distinction between the different aspects of the second advent insist that there is no real inconsistency between the teaching of the two epistles. In the first epistle the *parousia* is presented as *sudden*, coming as a thief; the second asserts that the day of the Lord has not actually arrived and that signs will precede it. But from the signs it will not be possible accurately to determine the day, and when it comes people will be taken by surprise.

The arguments from the eschatological features of this epistle are now commonly recognized to have little weight. Lake remarks that recent research has served "decisively to remove the eschatological argument from the list of possible objections to the authenticity of 2 Thessalonians."[7]

LITERARY RELATIONSHIP

The second line of attack upon the authenticity of 2 Thessalonians is based upon the literary relationship of the two letters.

It is said that the two epistles are too much alike to believe that Paul should have written them both to the same church. It is held to be psychologically improbable that a man of Paul's originality and mental freshness should write two letters so alike within a short period of time to the same community. This similarity, it is claimed, suggests rather that 2 Thessalonians is the work of a clever imitator. While there are remarkable resemblances, the actual likenesses must not be overstated.* The parallelisms do not extend to more than one third of their entire contents, and the actual parallels in language are often not contained in corresponding sections but are drawn from the epistles as a whole.

It is certainly highly arbitrary to deny an author the right to borrow freely from his own previous work when he is writing to the same church under overlapping circumstances within a short period of time. Zahn suggests that these similarities may well be due to the fact that Paul read again the preliminary draft copy of the previous letter before writing 2 Thessalonians.[8] This is all the more probable if this letter was occasioned by a misunderstanding at Thessalonica of some parts of the first letter. But if 2 Thessalonians is the work of an imitator of Paul it is difficult to see why he did not make greater use of 1 Thessalonians, and why he should limit himself to 1 Thessalonians and not also draw in material from the other Pauline epistles.

On the other hand, it has been claimed that the difference in tone in the two letters points to a difference of authorship. The writer of 1 Thessalonians reveals himself as warmly sympathetic and deeply affectionate in relation to his readers, while the tone of the writer of 2 Thessalonians is rather chilly and officially formal. But this supposed lack of cordiality in 2 Thessalonians is in the use of certain phrases (cf. 1:3; 2:13) and is only superficial. Frame points out that the warmth and closeness in the first epistle is due to the vehemence of the self-defense in the first part of that epistle and remarks, "Omit the self-defence from I and the differences in tone between I and II would not be perceptible."[9] The more chilly and officially formal tone which the critics find in 2 Thessalonians is naturally explained as due to the changed circumstances at Thessalonica and the resultant change in the writer's mood. The report of unfavorable developments at Thessalonica would naturally give rise to a more restrained and sober tone when dealing with these matters.

*Compare 2 Th 1:3 with 1 Th 1:2; 2 Th 1:5 with 1 Th 2:12; 2 Th 1:7 with 1 Th 3:13; 2 Th 2:16-17 with 1 Th 3:11-13; 2 Th 3:8 with 1 Th 2:9; 2 Th 3:16 with 1 Th 5:23; 2 Th 3:18 with 1 Th 5:28.

The German critic Wrede in his *Die Echtheit des zweiten Thessalon-icherbriefs* claimed that the contents of the two epistles made it impossible to accept that both had been written by the same man to the same church. He insisted that 1 Thessalonians implied a purely Gentile community, while 2 Thessalonians showed a strong Jewish coloring and assumed a greater knowledge of the Old Testament than Gentile Christians would possess. He concluded that 1 Thessalonians was written to a Gentile church and 2 Thessalonians to a Jewish church, hence both epistles could not be letters of Paul to the Thessalonians. The genuineness of 2 Thessalonians must therefore be rejected.

Such a conclusion is not justified by the evidence. There is nothing in 2 Thessalonians which a Gentile believer could not have appreciated. Whenever people of non-Jewish background became members of a Pauline church they followed Paul's leadership in accepting the Old Testament as authoritative and soon became familiar with its contents through the Septuagint. The account of the founding of the Thessalonian church in Acts (17:1-4) shows that Paul gave prominence to the Old Testament in his preaching at Thessalonica. In view of the apocalyptic section in Mark's gospel (ch. 13), which was undoubtedly written to Gentile believers, it cannot be established that the apocalyptic content of 2 Thessalonians would be unintelligible to them either. Further, Gentile members of the Thessalonian church had been given acquaintance with such teaching through Paul's oral ministry while yet with them (2:5).

Those who deny the authenticity of 2 Thessalonians cannot give a satisfactory explanation of how this epistle came to be unhesitatingly accepted as genuine. It is difficult to believe that the Thessalonian church, having one authentic letter from Paul, would be so gullible that in later years they would receive as genuine a fictitious letter also addressed to them.

It is psychologically improbable that a later Pauline imitator would be able to produce a letter that is so characteristically Pauline. Goodspeed concludes that this letter "has too much of the characteristic Pauline trenchant vigor to be dismissed as an imitation."[10]

It is now generally conceded, even by liberal scholars, that the critical attacks have not overthrown the authenticity of 2 Thessalonians. Thus Moffatt, himself not a conservative, remarks,

> It is fair to say that almost every one of the features which seem to portray another physiognomy from that of Paul can be explained, without straining the evidence, upon the hypothesis that he wrote the epistle himself (so most recent editors).[11]

And so after a century and a half of critical discussion the consensus of scholarship once more supports the position of conservative Christianity in upholding the authenticity of 2 Thessalonians.

THE RELATIONSHIP BETWEEN THE TWO EPISTLES

Even among those who are unwilling to sacrifice the authenticity of 2 Thessalonians, the problem of the relationship between the two epistles has led to views contrary to the traditional position. Two of these divergent views call for some comment.

DIVIDED CHURCH

Harnack, impressed by the views of Wrede, sought to save the Pauline authorship of 2 Thessalonians by postulating that "alongside of the Gentile community implied by the First Epistle there was a smaller and earlier Jewish community to which the Second Epistle was directed."[12] He thought that this division of the Thessalonian church was hinted at in 1 Thessalonians 5:27, where Paul asked that the "epistle be read unto all the brethren," as though there was another group beside the one being addressed. For further support he appealed to the questionable rendering of 2 Thessalonians 2:13 as, "God chose you as firstfruits." The statement obviously could not be made of the Gentile church at Thessalonica since they were not the first converts in Macedonia, but it did point to the Jewish section since they were the first Jewish converts in the province.

But this reading of the situation is highly unlikely. Guthrie well points out that "it is inconceivable that Paul the universalist would foster such a division by separate letters to the rival sections."[13] His strong condemnation of disunity within the local church at Corinth makes it unthinkable that he would condone it at Thessalonica. The existence of such a division in the Thessalonian church is inconsistent with the fact that in 1 Thessalonians 2:14 Paul holds up the Judean churches as models for the assumed Gentile section at Thessalonica.

The identical superscription in both epistles points to the logical conclusion that both were addressed to the same group. Harnack's conjecture that the address of 2 Thessalonians originally read "to the church of the Thessalonians, those of the circumcision," and that the last four words were later dropped, only demonstrates the weakness of his case.

REVERSAL OF ORDER

The common view is that our 1 Thessalonians was written before 2 Thessalonians. This is asserted by the titles which have been affixed to them. But some scholars maintain that the order of these epistles must be reversed. Manson, while rejecting the proposal of Harnack concerning the recipients of the two letters, holds that the problem can be solved by reversing the order of the letters. He insists that this reversal removes doubts concerning the genuineness of 2 Thessalonians and rescues it from the unjust evaluation of being regarded merely as "a pale ghost of its neighbour."[14] A number of arguments are advanced in support of this reversal.

In 2 Thessalonians the church is seen as undergoing persecutions (1:4-7), whereas they are referred to as in the past in 1 Thessalonians (1:6; 2:14-15; 3:2-4). But this observation does not establish the conclusion that the sufferings were entirely past when 1 Thessalonians was written. In 1 Thessalonians 3:4 Paul warns the readers that tribulation was to be expected at any time. In 1 Thessalonians the references to persecution occur in the portion where Paul reviews the past and his statements therefore naturally relate to the past.

It is held that the reference to his signature as the sign of genuineness in 2 Thessalonians 3:17 "is pointless except in a first letter."[15] But Paul did not always refer to such an identifying sign in his first letters. His joyous response to the report brought by Timothy did not call for such a safeguard in 1 Thessalonians. But when the second letter was written there was definite need to guard them against accepting professed letters from his hand which were spurious (2:2).

It is maintained that the internal difficulties dealt with in 2 Thessalonians are "a new development of which the writers have just heard," while "in I Thess. they are referred to as completely familiar to all concerned."[16] Thus 1 Thessalonians 4:10-12 needs 2 Thessalonians 3:6-15 to be understood. But it is just as natural to hold that the gentle hint to the busybodies in 1 Thessalonians was ineffectual in producing the desired result and necessitated the stronger measures in 2 Thessalonians. If 2 Thessalonians with its instructions on how to deal with the troublers came first it is difficult to see why 1 Thessalonians makes no reference to these deliberate violators of the instructions given them.

The mention of the death of some of the Thessalonian members is asserted to be more understandable if 1 Thessalonians was written later and a longer time had elapsed since the founding of the church. But the fact that some deaths had occurred does not establish that a long time interval is necessary. Certainly only a very few deaths among the believers would raise the problem that 1 Thessalonians deals with. The acknowledged interval between the departure of the missionaries from Thessalonica and the return of Timothy with his report of affairs there provides ample time for this problem to arise.

It is claimed that Paul's remark in 1 Thessalonians 5:1, "But concerning the times and the seasons, brethren, ye have no need that aught be written unto you," is relevant if 2 Thessalonians precedes it. But the statement is equally valid in a first epistle in view of the accurate oral teaching they had received on the point.

It is felt that the organization implied in 1 Thessalonians 5:12-13 requires a longer time interval than that allowed if 1 Thessalonians was written first. The organization of the church implied in 1 Thessalonians is quite simple and really demands no lengthy period of development. Paul certainly would see to it that elders were appointed as soon as a consistent group had been formed (cf. Ac 14:23).

It is claimed that the church "in 1 Thessalonians looks more advanced than it is in 2 Thessalonians."[17] Thus in 2 Thessalonians 3:7 the readers are reminded how they ought to imitate the missionaries whereas in 1 Thessalonians 1:6-10 they had become imitators and had themselves become examples to others. But the point of the imitation in the two instances is quite different and therefore does not establish the asserted greater maturity in 1 Thessalonians. In 1 Thessalonians the reference is to their conversion while in 2 Thessalonians the demand is for a calm and orderly life as believers.

It is held that the shorter 2 Thessalonians would naturally come first and that 1 Thessalonians supplements it since it "is much fuller and introduces much new material as, for instance, chapter 5 with its many cryptic injunctions."[18] But there is no valid reason for insisting that a first epistle must be shorter than a second. Nor can 1 Thessalonians be proved to be a supplement of 2 Thessalonians. Where both epistles deal with the same points the discussion in 2 Thessalonians is usually the longer.

Manson holds that the recurrence of the formula "Now concerning" in 1 Thessalonians 4:9, 13; 5:1 points to further problems which the Thessalonians have raised in a letter to him since 2 Thessalonians did not answer all their questions.[19] But the argument is quite inconclusive. It does not prove that Paul was answering a letter from the Thessalonians, for the formula is adequately explained as referring to matters to which Timothy had drawn attention in his oral report about conditions at Thessalonica.

This effort to reverse the canonical order of the epistles raises difficulties. Thus in reconstructing the order of events Manson conjectures that Timothy was sent back to Thessalonica from Athens (1 Th 3:1-5) bearing 2 Thessalonians. Timothy was sent back for the very purpose of getting more information about conditions at Thessalonica; it is therefore difficult, under Manson's reconstruction, to see how Paul could write so definitely about conditions there before he received the report of Timothy. Furthermore, if 2 Thessalonians had already been written to them, it is difficult to see why Paul failed to refer to that letter in 1 Thessalonians as further proof of his deep concern for the Thessalonians.

Second Thessalonians contains no indication of any intention, or even longing, on Paul's part to return to Thessalonica such as is touchingly expressed in the first letter. Since 2 Thessalonians contains no hint of such a longing it cannot properly be inserted before the writing of the first epistle. Second Thessalonians naturally belongs to Paul's stay at Corinth when he knew that it was not the Lord's will for him to go back to Thessalonica (Ac 18:9-11).

In 2 Thessalonians there appear to be references to a previous letter (2:2, 15; 3:17); if 2 Thessalonians was written first we must postulate another letter now lost. First Thessalonians contains no hint of any previous correspondence therefore it is more natural to accept the traditional order.

In support of the traditional order Hendriksen points out that in 1 Thessalonians emphasis is placed on Paul's *personal* contacts with the readers which are vividly remembered as recent, whereas 2 Thessalonians mentions a *letter* to them. The first epistle records how the readers accepted the gospel by faith, while in the second epistle Paul expresses his gratitude that their faith is growing. In 1 Thessalonians Paul gives them needed teaching concerning the "rapture" (4:13-18), while in 2 Thessalonians 2:1 he indicates that they have received previous instruction on the subject.[20]

If the traditional order is retained there is logical order and development apparent in their contents. Thus Neil remarks,

> In each of the topics dealt with—persecution, Second Advent, idleness— there is an obvious intensification of the difficulties, and development of the situation, as described in the first letter, which make any alteration of the sequence impossible.[21]

We conclude that there is no justification to depart from the canonical order of these epistles. This has been accepted by the church as the natural order ever since the second century.

THE PLACE AND DATE OF 2 THESSALONIANS

PLACE

Paul, Silvanus, and Timothy were together when the epistle was written (1:1). Since 1 Thessalonians was written from Corinth during Paul's initial ministry there,† it seems clear that shortly afterward this letter was also written from that city. This is supported by the fact that the three men do not appear together again in the New Testament story following

†See Introduction to 1 Thessalonians under Place and Date.

Paul's departure from Corinth. McNeile, indeed, points out that this is an argument from silence and suggests that the three men may actually have worked together at Ephesus (Ac 19:1-20) and that this epistle might have been written from that city.[22] But the close connection between the two letters makes it highly unlikely that such a long interval occurs between them.

DATE

The date assigned to 2 Thessalonians will depend upon the time interval assumed between the two epistles. This has variously been given as being only a few days[23] to a whole year.[24] Either suggestion seems extreme. It is generally accepted that some two or three months elapsed between the writing of the two letters. Then, in harmony with our dating of the first epistle, 2 Thessalonians may be dated in the fall or early winter of either 50 or 51 AD.

THE OCCASION AND PURPOSE OF 2 THESSALONIANS

OCCASION

The immediate occasion for the writing of 2 Thessalonians was the nature of the further information received by Paul concerning his beloved Thessalonian converts. It is possible that the bearer of 1 Thessalonians had remained there long enough to note the developments and had returned with the report. The close commercial connections between Thessalonica and Corinth would afford opportunities for reports to reach Paul.

The report concerning developments at Thessalonica contained both favorable and unfavorable elements. He rejoiced at the news that the Thessalonians were growing in their faith and love (1:3) and were remaining steadfast under persecution (1:4).

But some extreme ideas concerning the day of the Lord had taken root in part of the church and these ideas were producing a nervous excitement which was apparently having a bad effect upon their daily life. Carried away in the zeal of their transforming Christian experience, some members felt that the new age, the day of the Lord, had dawned and that the Messiah would openly appear at any time (2:1-3). It was the report of these conditions that called forth this second epistle.

PURPOSE

The epistle reflects favorable as well as unfavorable features of the report from Thessalonica. Paul took the occasion to commend his converts for their remarkable growth in faith and love (1:3) and to encourage them to steadfastness under persecution with the assurance that their afflictions would be justly recompensed when the Lord returned in judgment (1:5-12).

But the real purpose in writing was to deal with the doctrinal error concerning the day of the Lord and to rebuke the disorderly conduct of certain members. In chapter 2 Paul corrects their erroneous view that "the day of the Lord is already here" (Williams) and then in chapter 3 strongly rebukes the reprehensible conduct of the disorderly. No cause and effect relationship between these two problems is asserted in these epistles. While some interpreters deny any clear relationship between them,[25] it is generally accepted that the exciting teaching about the day of the Lord naturally promoted the idleness of certain members. This connection would mean that the entire epistle has a bearing on the matter of the second advent.

15

AN OUTLINE OF 2 THESSALONIANS

I. Salutation, 1:1-2

II. Comfort Given Them in Their Affliction, 1:3-12
   A. Thanksgiving for their growth and steadfastness, 3-4
      1. Character of the thanksgiving, 3a
      2. Reasons for the thanksgiving, 3b
      3. Glorying of the writers, 4
   B. Encouragement in view of Christ's return, 5-10
      1. Indication of God's righteous judgment, 5
      2. Description of the judgment, 6-8
         a) Outcome of the judgment, 6-7a
         b) Revelation of the Judge, 7b
         c) Subjects of the judgment, 8
      3. Consequences of the judgment, 9-10
         a) Destruction of the lost, 9
         b) Lord's glorification in His saints, 10
   C. Prayer for them in their affliction, 11-12
      1. Nature of the prayer, 11a
      2. Substance of the prayer, 11b
      3. Purpose of the prayer, 12

III. Events Preceding the Day of the Lord, 2:1-12
   A. Corrective for their erroneous view, 1-5
      1. Appeal for calmness, 1-2
         a) Subject of the appeal, 1
         b) Aim of the appeal, 2a
         c) Nature of the erroneous teaching, 2b
      2. Events which must precede, 3-4
         a) Warning against deception, 3a
         b) Events indicated, 3b-4
      3. Reminder of past oral teaching, 5

    B. Restraint upon the mystery of lawlessness, 6-7
        1. Purpose of the restraint, 6
        2. Removal of the restrainer, 7
    C. Career of the lawless one, 8-12
        1. His Career terminated by Jesus, 8
        2. His power over the lost, 9-12
            a) Description of his power, 9-10*a*
            b) Subjects of his power, 10*b*
            c) Judgment upon the deluded, 11-12

IV. Renewed Thanksgiving and Prayer for Them, 2:13-17
    A. Thanksgiving for God's choice of them, 13-14
        1. Character of the thanksgiving, 13*a*
        2. Grounds for the thanksgiving, 13*b*-14
            a) Because of the divine choice, 13*b*
            b) Because of the divine call, 14
    B. Exhortation to those chosen, 15
    C. Prayer for the chosen, 16-17

V. Exhortations Concerning Practical Matters, 3:1-15
    A. Request for their prayers, 1-2
        1. Request stated, 1*a*
        2. Petitions indicated, 1*b*-2
    B. Confidence concerning their progress, 3-5
        1. Faithfulness of the Lord toward them, 3
        2. Confidence in their obedience, 4
        3. Prayer for their growth, 5
    C. Discipling of the disorderly, 6-15
        1. Command to withdraw from the disorderly, 6
        2. Facts supporting the command, 7-10
            a) Apostolic example given them, 7-9
                (1) Their knowledge of the example, 7*a*
                (2) Nature of the example, 7*b*-8*b*
                (3) Purpose behind the example, 8*c*-9
            b) Practical maxim taught them, 10
        3. Information requiring the command, 11
        4. Command to the disorderly, 12
        5. Instructions to the faithful members, 13-15
            a) Appeal for continued well-doing, 13
            b) Instructions concerning those refusing to obey, 14-15

16

SALUTATION

1:1-2 Paul, and Silvanus, and Timothy, unto the church of the Thessalonians in God our Father and the Lord Jesus Christ; (2) Grace to you and peace from God the Father and the Lord Jesus Christ.

THIS THREE-PART SALUTATION differs from that in 1 Thessalonians only in two places. (See 1 Th 1:1). The deviations consist of two additions, both of which are in harmony with Pauline usage elsewhere.

The first addition is the pronoun *our* with *Father* in the second member of the salutation. "Our Father" stresses God's relationship with His people; when used alone *Father* denotes His person, the first Person of the Trinity. *Our* includes the Thessalonians as well as the writers; it brings out this common relationship as the bond between writers and readers. In their mutual experience they know God as "our Father," the One who is their nourisher, provider, and protector.

The second difference is the addition of "from God the Father and the Lord Jesus Christ" to the familiar greeting of "Grace to you and peace." This addition, naming the source of the grace and peace, is characteristically Pauline.° *Grace* and *peace* are presented as coming *from* (*apo*), emanating from, a double source, "God the Father and the Lord Jesus Christ." Both are placed under the government of one preposition and connected by *and*, thus placing them on a basis of equality. For a strict monotheist like Paul to put the two in juxtaposition would be unthinkable if he did not accept the deity of Jesus Christ. God the Father and the Lord Jesus Christ are conjointly named as the source of grace and peace. This is mentioned as an accepted axiom of the faith.

In our materialistic age, believers need to be reminded again that all our blessings have their origin in God the Father whom we have come to know through the Lord Jesus Christ. "God the Father" (*theou patros*) points to His person as distinguished from the Son whom believers acknowledge as "the Lord Jesus Christ." Some early manuscripts here also

°In his epistles it is missing only in 1 Thessalonians. In Col 1:2 only "our Father" is named.

read "God our Father" but the "our" here apparently has been added by the scribes because of its common occurrence in the Pauline salutations.†

Findlay remarks that " 'God the Father' is the ultimate spring, 'the Lord Jesus Christ' the mediating channel of 'grace and peace.' "[1] But Paul's statement here makes no such distinction. It is not in view here.

The content of 2 Thessalonians is essentially eschatological; all of the epistle has a bearing upon that theme. But there is no general agreement as to the number of its main divisions, nor where the accepted divisions occur. Aside from the opening salutation (1:1-2) and the conclusion (3:16-18), the number of major divisions made by the interpreters varies from two to six. Furthermore, Plummer appropriately remarks, "It is not easy to find accurately appropriate headings for each portion of this Epistle."[2]

Many commentators are content to make three main divisions, corresponding to the chapter divisions. This division is attractive in that it makes each section end with a prayer for the readers (1:11-12; 2:16-17; 3:16). But this threefold division labors under the difficulty that the second division is composed of two parts which do not bear any marked unity of thought. The latter part of chapter 2 (2:13-17) seems to be an insert which is more or less independent from what precedes as well as what follows. Some, indeed, connect it with the preceding section about the man of sin, while others regard it as belonging to the third division. It seems best to regard 2:13-17 as a separate division and thus make four main divisions for the epistle.

In the first division (1:3-12) the writers encourage the persecuted Thessalonian believers by expressing their thanksgiving for them and the assurance that justice will be meted out to all at Christ's return. In the second division the readers are given corrective instruction concerning the day of the Lord and the events connected with it (2:1-12). Thanksgiving, exhortation, and prayer for the readers make up the third section (2:13-17). The concluding division of the epistle is hortatory, urging upon the readers varied practical Christian duties (3:1-15). A brief section (3:16-18) concludes the letter.

---

†The *Textus Receptus* reads "God our Father" but the pronoun is not accepted as the true reading by modern editors. Paul has "our Father" as the source of "grace and peace" in the opening salutation in Ro 1:7; 1 Co 1:3; 2 Co 1:2; Gal 1:3; Eph 1:2; Phil 1:2; Col 1:2; Phile 3. It does not appear in the greeting in the pastoral epistles.

17

COMFORT IN AFFLICTION

1:3-12 We are bound to give thanks to God always for you, brethren, even as it is meet, for that your faith groweth exceedingly, and the love of each one of you all toward one another aboundeth; (4) so that we ourselves glory in you in the churches of God for your patience and faith in all your persecutions and in the afflictions which ye endure; (5) *which is* a manifest token of the righteous judgment of God; to the end that ye may be counted worthy of the kingdom of God, for which ye also suffer: (6) if so be that it is a righteous thing with God to recompense affliction to them that afflict you, (7) and to you that are afflicted rest with us, at the revelation of the Lord Jesus from heaven with the angels of his power in flaming fire, (8) rendering vengeance to them that know not God, and to them that obey not the gospel of our Lord Jesus: (9) who shall suffer punishment, *even* eternal destruction from the face of the Lord and from the glory of his might, (10) when he shall come to be glorified in his saints, and to be marvelled at in all them that believed (because our testimony unto you was believed) in that day. (11) To which end we also pray always for you, that our God may count you worthy of your calling, and fulfil every desire of goodness and *every* work of faith, with power; (12) that the name of our Lord Jesus may be glorified in you, and ye in him, according to the grace of our God and the Lord Jesus Christ.

THIS OPENING PARAGRAPH begins with fervent thanksgiving for the readers but soon passes into direct encouragement to them and explicit prayer on their behalf. There is no formal break in the flow of words until the end of verse 10. It is another illustration of Paul's habit of "allowing his sentences to grow one out of the other, like shoots from a vine stalk."[1] The paragraph may be divided into three parts. It opens with an expression of thanksgiving for the readers because of their spiritual growth and steadfastness under persecution (vv. 3-4). Without a full grammatical break, the next part is devoted to encouragement for the readers from the truth that the returning Lord will mete out justice to all (vv. 5-10). The paragraph closes with prayer for the afflicted Thessalonian believers (vv. 11-12).

A. THANKSGIVING FOR THEIR GROWTH AND STEADFASTNESS (vv. 3-4)

These two verses indicate the nature of the writers' thanksgiving (v. 3*a*), the reasons for the thanksgiving (v. 3*b*), and their own glorying in the readers (v. 4).

1. Character of the Thanksgiving (v. 3*a*)

"We are bound to give thanks to God always for you, brethren, even as it is meet." The plural pronoun *we*, as in 1 Thessalonians, naturally denotes Paul, Silvanus, and Timothy, the designated writers (v. 1).* The thanksgiving is the united expression of the writers.

The writers present their thanksgiving for the readers as being obligatory, "we are bound to give thanks." The verb *bound* (*opheilomen*) literally means "to owe" and pictures the thanksgiving as a debt. The present tense indicates that the feeling of personal obligation is lasting. The infinitive "to give thanks" stands emphatically at the beginning of the sentence to stress the nature of the felt duty, and the present tense expresses the thought of repeated thanksgiving.

This continual thanksgiving the writers acknowledge as due "to God" (*tō Theō*), the true God whom the readers now also know and serve. The added *always* underlines the lasting and unvarying nature of this obligation Godward. This duty to thank God is not a general sense of gratitude but is specifically "for you, brethren." The thanksgiving centers around the readers, affectionately addressed as *brethren*.†

While Paul often remarks that he gives thanks for his readers, only in this letter does he say "we are bound to give thanks" (1:3; 2:13). Some critics have maintained that the remark that the thanksgiving is obligatory indicates that Paul's feelings toward the readers have changed, and the thanksgiving is now more formal, cool, and half-hearted. But such an evaluation of the expression is reading a lot into his words. If taken without bias or presuppositions, this unusual expression rather implies a high compliment. The implication is that the writers could not justly hold back their thanksgiving for the readers even though they should attempt to do so. The expression must be interpreted in the light of verse 4. Their thanksgiving for the readers is not an obligation which they are reluctant to grant; it is rather a privilege which they are eager to fulfill. Hendriksen correctly observes that "the writers reveal themselves as men who are elated rather than reluctant, exuberant rather than hesitant."[2] The mis-

---

*The plural is changed to "I" in the translations by Conybeare, Montgomery, Phillips, and Way under the assumption that the "we" is editorial. (See the discussion under 1 Th 1:2.)

†See under 1 Th 1:4 concerning this address in these epistles.

sionaries are sincerely grateful for their converts. They held a tender place in Paul's heart, for the report of their steadfastness had produced a life-giving sense of relief and encouragement in him during a time of personal discouragement (1 Th 3:7-8).

This feeling of gratitude for the readers is not merely subjective. The added words, "even as it is meet," indicate that it is objectively justified. The adjective rendered "meet" (*axion*) means "equal in value, comparable in worth," hence, "fitting and proper." Their feeling of gratitude for their converts was right on the ground of moral fitness; "it is right to do so" (Williams). "Even as" marks the true correspondence between the subjective feeling and the objective fact. Their actual spiritual condition made the feeling of the missionaries wholly befitting.

Paul was well aware of the shortcomings of the Thessalonian believers, but he did not allow their faults to blind him to their strong points. He was deeply appreciative of the transforming change that had been wrought in them. "He never forgot what they had been like in their pre-Christian days, and never forgot to thank God for what He had achieved in them."[3] He will faithfully deal with their failings but first he is eager to give praise where praise is due. Instead of criticizing, he is eager to commend. Bicknell comments, "Power of appreciation is a real test of character."[4]

2. Reasons for the Thanksgiving (v. 3*b*)

The conjunction rendered "for that" (*hoti*) here has a causal force and is best translated "because."‡ Two reasons for thanksgiving are indicated.

The first reason is that "your faith groweth exceedingly." The verb is placed emphatically forward, "because increase greatly doth your faith" (Young). "Groweth exceedingly" (*huperauxanei*) is a compound verb occurring only here in the New Testament. The simple verb "groweth" (*auxanō*) is used of the growth or increase of living things, as a plant or a tree. Here the prefixed preposition *huper*, "over, above," intensifies the thought of the growth as being abundant and unusual. "Because your faith grows beyond measure" (Weymouth). Its growth was entirely beyond natural expectation.

Paul is fond of such compounds with *huper*. He uses them ten times in his epistles. Lünemann remarks that "they are an involuntary expression of his overflowing feelings."[5] Such forms suited Paul's fervent nature and readily served to bring out the great and surpassing importance of the subjects he dealt with.

"Your faith" denotes the personal confidence and absolute trust God-

---

‡The ASV here stands alone among our versions in rendering "for that." The others, except Phillips who omits it entirely, have "because."

ward which had been evoked in the Thessalonians through the preaching of the missionaries. Their personal appropriation of the gospel is showing itself to be a vital force; it is "constantly budding and branching forth in fresh beauty and vigor."[6] The storms they have endured have not destroyed their faith but rather strengthened its roots. This was indeed a just reason for the missionaries' thanksgiving.

The second stated reason for thanksgiving is because "the love of each one of you all toward one another aboundeth." Here again the verb stands emphatically at the beginning of the statement. Young's literal rendering reproduces the original order, "and abound doth the love of each one of you all, to one another." The verb *aboundeth* means "to become more, increase, be present in abundance." In contrast to the preceding verb which suggests an inner, organic growth, this implies an outward diffusion, "as of a flood irrigating the land."[7] The present tense records that their love is continually increasing, overflowing its normal limits like a river.

This overflowing love is being revealed by "each one of you all." *Each one* particularizes this manifestation while *all* asserts that it is true of every member without exception. And that love was being mutually expressed "toward one another." "Every individual member was a radiating centre for a love that extended itself to each and all throughout the church."[8] Swete remarks that their mutual loving and being loved illustrates "the 'self-balancing nature' of Christian love."[9]

The fact that hope is not now mentioned with faith and love (cf. 1 Th 1:3) does not imply that their hope has died. Its presence is implied in the *patience* mentioned in the next verse. Yet it may well be that Paul does not now speak of their hope because an unwarranted interpretation of the Chrisitan hope was creating confusion in their midst, and for this he could not give thanks. In this thanksgiving the matters that needed correction are wisely kept in the background.

The growing faith and increasing love of the Thessalonians was a direct answer to the prayers of the missionaries. In the first epistle (3:10, 12) both were mentioned as matters that needed improvement and were receiving attention in their prayers for the readers. Now they record their thanksgiving to God that the prayers have been answered. They are thankful that the continued afflictions endured by their converts have not undermined their faith nor dried up the springs of their love.

3. Glorying of the Writers (v. 4)

The conjunction "so that" (*hōste*) indicates consequence and introduces a statement of the effect that the growing faith and increasing love of the readers have upon the writers themselves. "So that we ourselves glory in you in the churches of God." "We§ ourselves" is strongly emphatic, calling attention to the writers themselves. The order of the two pronouns (*autous hēmas*)|| stresses that, contrary to their usual modesty, they "themselves glory in you in the churches." As the founders of the church they would be slow to boast of anything to their own credit, but they are doing so now. Such boasting on their part was unusual, but the unusual qualities of their converts constrained them to this unusual action. Others are talking about the Thessalonians, and the founders, justly proud of their converts, cannot restrain themselves from doing likewise. It is indeed high praise for the readers, intended to encourage them in their affliction.

The writers *glory* in their converts, "speak proudly of" them (NASB). The present tense indicates that this is not an isolated event; it is rather their practice to speak about them with elation. The word order in the original, "So that we ourselves in you are boasting in the assemblies of God" (Rotherham), makes prominent the truth that the missionaries are glorying in their readers specifically.

They glory in their converts "in the churches of God." The only description given of these churches is that they belong to God, being "the congregations of God's people" (NEB). No geographical limitations are added. It is usually held that Paul means the churches in Corinth and its neighborhood. Swete suggests that Paul "probably itinerated through the surrounding towns and villages" and wherever groups of believers had been formed he proudly spoke of the Thessalonian believers.[10] The expression does not necessitate Paul's personal presence in these churches, nor need it be confined to oral communication. If these different churches are limited to the vicinity of Corinth a considerable time interval must be allowed between the mission at Thessalonica and the writing of this letter. But this is not necessary.

Where the churches in view were actually located we cannot say, other than Corinth. Certainly Paul does not mean all the churches in existence at the time, nor should we restrict his meaning to Corinth and vicinity. This glorying was doubtless also expressed to churches at a greater distance with whom Paul kept in contact, either by personal messengers from them or written communication to them. The widespread commercial activities centering in Corinth would naturally give Paul varied opportunities to contact these churches in different parts of the Mediterranean world. Surrounded by a sea of paganism, these scattered Christian

§Conybeare, Montgomery, and Way again shrink this "we" to "I."

|| The *Textus Receptus* and Souter have the order *hēmas autous*, but Westcott and Hort, Nestle, and the Bible Societies' text without question accept *autous hēmas* as the correct reading.

communities naturally took the deepest interest in reports concerning the welfare of fellow believers in different parts of the empire. And Paul did not hesitate to praise one church to another in order to provoke them to further good works, and he did not hesitate to tell them that he was doing so (cf. 2 Co 8:1-8; 9:1-5).

The subject matter of the boasting concerning the Thessalonians is unfolded in the addition "for your patience and faith in all your persecutions and in the afflictions which ye endure." Their boast is "for your patience and faith," or more literally, "over your endurance and faith" (Rotherham). Their glorying spreads itself "over" (*huper*) their endurance and faith, covering these two features of their spiritual life. "Patience and faith" are closely united under the government of one article. *Patience* (*hupomonē*) does not denote a meek submissiveness but rather a heroic endurance under trial (cf. comments under 1 Th 1:3). This endurance or perseverance# is closely linked to their *faith*. Without a vital faith they would not have been able to remain steadfast under their afflictions. Their endurance manifested the reality of their faith.

The suggestion of Lünemann that, because of its close connection with patience, faith here means "fidelity" is arbitrary.[11] In 1 Thessalonians 1:3 patience was connected with hope, but here it is connected with faith as the source of their steadfastness. The point of the apostolic boasting is that the Thessalonians are maintaining their unwavering trust in the Lord amid persecution for their faith.

"In all your persecutions and in the afflictions which ye endure" sets forth the circumstances under which their faith-inspired endurance manifested itself. "Persecutions" and "afflictions" both relate to the same difficulties being experienced, but the latter is more general and comprehensive than the former. *Persecutions* designates the hostile actions of the enemies of the gospel, while *afflictions* relates to the varied pressures and painful experiences they have endured because of their faith. *All* indicates that the persecutions have been numerous and varied, while the added phrase, "which ye endure," the verb being in the present tense, shows that the antagonisms which marked the beginning of the Thessalonian church (1 Th 1:6; 2:14; 3:3; Ac 17:5-9) were still continuing or had been renewed. Amid these difficult circumstances they continue to *endure* (*anechesthe*), which quite literally means "to hold oneself up." It pictures them as bravely holding themselves erect and firm under the sufferings endured because of their faith.

#"Patience and faith" is rendered "endurance and faith" by Rotherham, Young, Darby, Williams, Phillips, Way; Berkeley; "steadfastness and faith" by Conybeare, Montgomery, Goodspeed, Moffatt; RSV and NEB; and "perseverance and faith" in the NASB.

B. ENCOURAGEMENT IN VIEW OF CHRIST'S RETURN (vv. 5-10)

A distinct train of eschatological thought begins with verse 5 and runs through verse 10. This significant apocalyptic portrayal is introduced to comfort the persecuted Thessalonian believers both with reference to the present and the future. This initial apocalyptic passage of the epistle also skillfully prepares the way for the further eschatological discussion in chapter 2.

In the readers' steadfast suffering for the gospel, Paul found an indication of the righteous judgment of God (v. 5). This led him to a description of the judgment (vv. 6-8) and its consequences (vv. 9-10).

1. Indication of God's Righteous Judgment (v. 5)

The transition to the eschatological teaching is abrupt and somewhat awkward. As indicated by the italics, the expression "*which is* a manifest token of the righteous judgment of God," contains no verb in the original. Two different explanations of the connection are possible. The expression may be regarded as an elliptical nominative with the words "which is" to be understood, as is done in the above rendering.** Or more probably it may be regarded as an accusative in apposition with the whole preceding sentence.†† This view might best be represented by a dash at the end of verse 4. Under either view the sense is essentially the same.

The word rendered "a manifest token" (*endeigma*), a passive form used only here in the New Testament, quite literally means "a thing pointed out, a thing proved," hence, "evidence, plain indication."‡‡ But what does Paul regard as "a plain indication" (NASB) "of the righteous judgment of God?" He can hardly mean the fact that the readers are suffering for their faith; their suffering while seeking to do the will of God seemed to contradict the righteousness of God. The reference is rather to the whole preceding statement concerning their steadfast endurance and faith amid their sufferings for the gospel. It was evidence that the righteous judgment was still future and grace was still calling them to endure. That they were enabled to endure was evidence to themselves that a new life had been imparted to them, and God's present working in them indicates that He will not allow their unjust sufferings to go unrewarded.

"The righteous judgment of God" looks forward to the future day of

---

** In effect also the following versions, Conybeare, Young, Goodspeed, Moffatt, Weymouth, Montgomery, Williams, Phillips, Way; KJV, 20th Cent, RSV, NASB, Berkeley, NEB.

†† Rotherham, Darby, Lattey.

‡‡ The difference between the passive *endeigma* and the active *endeixis*, "proof," is negligible.

judgment at Christ's return. This future reference is evident from the definite article and the singular number as well as the following verses. God's *judgment* (*krisis*), the act of distinguishing and separating the good from the evil, is *righteous,* just and without partiality. This demands that "the Judge of all the earth" shall come to set aright the enormities that now prevail.

Paul also thought of their heroic sufferings in the light of the effect upon the sufferers. Their sufferings were being permitted "to the end that ye may be counted worthy of the kingdom of God." The expression rendered "to the end that" in classical Greek served to express purpose. Frame holds that this is also the usual meaning of the construction when Paul used it.[12] This is the meaning commonly accepted here. Way renders, "a token . . . of His purpose that you be adjudged worthy." Then Paul refers to the divine purpose in permitting their present sufferings. But because of the weakening of the telic force of the construction in later Greek, others insist that here it denotes result, conceived or actual. Then the reference is to the outcome or result at the judgment. In the day of judgment their present sufferings will be seen to have been beneficial. Findlay combines both ideas here and holds that the statement expresses "half purpose and half result."[13] Then the divine purpose in permitting their sufferings will in the day of judgment be found to have produced the result that they will be accounted worthy.

Under either view the statement is a direct encouragement to the suffering readers. They are assured that their sufferings are significant. The conviction that suffering has a moral purpose and is connected with some larger movement is always a stabilizing force amid present difficulty.

The contemplated result will be "that ye may be counted worthy of the kingdom of God." The passive infinitive rendered "be counted worthy" is a judicial term and means, not "to make worthy" (as given by Moffatt, Phillips, Berkeley, RSV) or "to be worthy," but "to reckon worthy, to be considered deserving."[14] The aorist tense looks forward to the judgment day when such a verdict will be pronounced upon them. The sufferings are not meritorious, procuring their entry into the kingdom, for their sufferings are the outcome of having already been saved by faith.

Morris aptly comments,

> By his choice of this word the apostle is excluding human merit even in a section where he is drawing attention to a noteworthy piece of endurance, and is emphasizing that attainment to the kingdom is not the result of human endeavour at all, but of the grace of God.[15]

Yet such steadfast suffering on behalf of the kingdom now will show that there is a moral fitness in then admitting them into "the kingdom of God,"

His divine rule in its future, open manifestation. "There must be apparent a fitness of character in those admitted to God's heavenly kingdom, if His judgment in their favour is to be recognized as 'righteous.' "[16]

"For which ye also suffer" brings their sufferings into intimate relations with the kingdom. The preposition rendered *for* (*huper* with the ablative) means "in behalf of, for the sake of," thus indicating the reason why they continue willingly to *suffer* (present tense), to undergo affliction and evil experiences. They are motivated by their allegiance to the King and His kingdom. It was well worth suffering for.

Also has been understood in two different ways. Some view it as marking the correspondence between present suffering and future glory. More probably the *also* was intended to remind the readers that their sufferings unite them with the experiences of the missionaries. They too are enduring suffering because of their interest in God's kingdom.

2. Description of the Judgment (vv. 6-8)

Mention of the coming righteous judgment of God leads to a vivid description of that judgment. Paul indicates the contrasted outcome of the judgment (vv. 6-7a), the majestic revelation of the Judge (v. 7b), and the subjects of God's vengeance (v. 8).

a) OUTCOME OF THE JUDGMENT (vv. 6-7a). The judgment of God is based upon the reality of a great spiritual principle, "if so be that it is a righteous thing with God to recompense." The form of the conditional sentence (first class) does not imply any doubt but assumes the reality. "If indeed" (*eiper*), an intensified form, stresses the reality as an undisputed fact, "as it certainly is."§§ The accepted principle is stated conditionally in order to use it as an unassailable argument concerning the outcome of the divine judgment. The judgment will be righteous because it is "a righteous thing with God" to judge righteously. His verdict will never be arbitrary or capricious but in strict harmony with that which is just. "With God" (*para theō*), literally, "alongside of God," indicates that such is His viewpoint in exercising judgment. This assertion concerning the character of God and His judgment was intended to afford strong consolation to the afflicted readers. "The pious sufferers of all ages have stayed their souls upon the truth of an eternally righteous God."[17]

God's righteous character in judgment assures a twofold outcome in the judgment. He will mete out strict justice to both the evil and the good. As to the former, He will, as a definite act, "recompense affliction to them that afflict you." The verdict on the afflictors will be retributive. His action will be "to recompense" them in kind, "to give back to those

§§According to the critical text, this form is used only by Paul in the N.T. Ro 8:9, 17; 1 Co 8:5; 15:15; and 1 Th 1:6. The *Textus Receptus* has it in 1 Pe 2:3 also.

troubling you—trouble" (Young). They will receive due and full compensation for what they have done. In 1 Thessalonians 3:9 the verb is used of repaying good received; here it refers to requiting evil conduct. Those characterized as *afflicting* (present tense) the Thessalonians, repeatedly subjecting them to the crushing pressure of persecution, will be dealt with in kind by the Judge.

This principle of just requital lies at the basis of our belief in a moral universe. Our sense of justice demands such a requital. Not good but evil creates a moral problem for us. In the face of present injustices our conscience tells us that there must be a future retribution. A world in which justice was not done at last would not be God's world at all.

This principle of moral justice also assures that the divine verdict on the afflicted will be remunerative, "and to you that are afflicted rest." For them it will bring a reversal of present experiences. This assurance is applied directly to the readers, "to you, to those afflicted." For them the outcome will be *rest*, welcome relief. The word carries the picture of the loosening or relaxing of a taut bowstring, hence suggests the thought of relief through the relaxing of tension or pressure. It thus suggests rest, not from toil and fatigue, but from tension and suffering. Their endurance was now continually on the stretch, but with the reversal of circumstances, welcome relaxation and refreshment would come. The ultimate abolition of tension in the Christian life awaits the second advent. Paul connects this hope not with the thought of dying but with the Lord's return. This assured rest "characterizes the glory of the kingdom of God according to its negative side as freedom from earthly affliction and trouble."[18]

This rest the readers will then experience "with us," that is, with Paul, Silvanus, and Timothy. They too knew what it meant to be under hard pressure for the sake of the kingdom of God. They too found comfort in the prospect and will share with them the enjoyment of the rest. "Both the reunion and the recognition of the Saints in glory are here implied."[19] If the Thessalonians are associated with the missionaries in present suffering (v. 5), they will also share with them the enjoyment of the coming rest. It is characteristic of Paul thus to unite himself with his readers (2 Co 1:7; 4:14; Phil 1:30; 2 Ti 4:8). On these words "with us" von Dobschütz aptly remarks, "These two little words belong to the genuine Pauline touches for the sake of which no one, with any feeling for the way in which the mind of Paul works, can give up the authenticity of this brief epistle."[20]

b) REVELATION OF THE JUDGE (v. 7*b*). The cessation of affliction for believers will be brought about by a supernatural invasion from outer space by the righteous Judge. It will occur "at the revelation of the Lord Jesus from heaven." The force of the preposition here rendered *at* (*en*) seems to be more than temporal, indicating the time of judgment; it also has instrumental implications, suggesting that the revelation is the means by which the requital is accomplished. The retribution is a part of the *revelation*, when the Judge as righteous in His judgment will be unveiled. Paul is fond of this term which has the basic meaning of "an uncovering, a removal of the veil."|| || Implying a manifestation of what is already in existence, it speaks of the future appearing of Christ in open glory. Findlay asserts that "this Biblical term implies always a supernatural disclosure."[21]

The one thus to be revealed is identified as "the Lord Jesus," the human Jesus, now enthroned in glory at the right hand of the Father, whom believers now confess as "the Lord" of their lives (see the discussion under 1 Th 1:10). Although now unseen by human eyes, believers already know and love Him and await His manifestation in glory.

Three added prepositional phrases further characterize this revelation. "It is not the action of sovereign grace which translates the saints waiting for Him to heaven, but the display of judicial righteousness by the Lord when He appears in glory."[22] His revelation will be "from heaven." The preposition *apo*, "from, away from," indicates that the revelation involves a departure from heaven, where at His ascension he sat down "on the right hand of the throne of the Majesty in the heavens" (Heb 8:1).

The coming is further described as "with the angels of his power." He will be accompanied by *angels*, supernatural messengers of God. Jesus spoke of angels attending Him at His return in glory (Mt 16:27; 25:31). These heavenly beings are characterized as "angels of his power."## *His* does not modify angels but rather power. The *power* belongs to Christ and the angels will be its agents, the executors of His commands. This mention of power is part of the consolation offered to the readers; now "power" belongs to the persecutors, but when Jesus returns this will be the attribute of the one who will punish the persecutors.

A third prepositional phrase is used, "in flaming fire," literally, "in a fire of flame." The manuscripts vary between "in a flame of fire" and "in a fire of flame," but the latter has the better support here. A question at once arises whether this phrase is to be taken with what precedes or what follows. By placing a comma after *power* the phrase may be connected with what follows to depict the fire as the instrument of vengeance. This is the view accepted in the King James Version, Darby, and Phillips, as

---

|| || In the N.T. 13 of the 18 occurrences of the noun are by Paul; the verb form occurs 26 times, 13 by Paul.

The absence of an article makes the expression qualitative, angels such as are associated with His power.

indicated by the comma and verse division. But it is doubtful that the original readers would have made the break in the thought which this view requires. It is more natural to connect this phrase with what has gone before as a further description of the returning Judge. This is the view accepted by most interpreters. Milligan remarks, "There is certainly no thought here of 'fire' as the actual instrument for the destruction of the ungodly."[23] As descriptive of the returning Lord, it pictures Him as encircled, as it were, with a fiery robe, like a flame leaping and blazing forth. The Old Testament theophanies were frequently marked by the presence of fire (Ex 3:2, 19:18, 24:17; Ps 18:12; Is 30:27-30; Dan 7:9-10), speaking of the divine majesty and indignation against sin. This Old Testament concept of the fiery manifestation of Jehovah's presence is now ascribed to the returning Lord Jesus. It is an indirect but unmistakable Pauline testimony to the true deity of Jesus Christ. His return will indeed be a terrible sight for His enemies.

c) SUBJECTS OF THE JUDGMENT (v. 8). The returning Judge will act in "rendering vengeance" on His enemies. (The gender of the participle *rendering* makes it clear that it connects with "the Lord Jesus" rather than with "fire of flame" just before it.) The precise formula (*didontos ekdikēsin*) occurs only here in the New Testament. The present participle *rendering*, "giving" or "taking," is descriptive of the action of the Judge meting out *vengeance* (that which proceeds out of justice). The term does not contain the idea of human revenge but rather denotes infliction of full justice on a criminal, giving him all, but no more, than his guilt deserves. The punishment is in full harmony with the fact that the judgment of God is righteous (v. 5) and is consistent with the principle of divine justice (v. 6). "It is of His own nature that God is a God of love; it is because of the existence of sin that He is also a God of 'vengeance'."[24] (See comments under 1 Th 1:10).

In the Old Testament the rendering of vengeance is asserted to be the prerogative of Jehovah (Deu 32:35; Ps 94:1; Ro 12:19). But here that dread prerogative is transferred to Jesus Christ. It is in harmony with the assertion of our Lord, "The Father . . . hath given all judgment unto the Son" (Jn 5:22).

The recipients of His vengeance are given a double identification, "to them that know not God, and to them that obey not the gospel of our Lord Jesus." The repeated article in the original makes it clear that two groups are intended. But it has been questioned whether two separate groups are intended or the same group is described in two different ways. The latter view is urged by those who hold that the context limits the reference to the ones persecuting the Thessalonian believers; then the double designation points to the two factions among them, the Gentiles who did not know the true God and the Jews who rejected Christ. Then the statement is "readily understood as an example of synonymous parallelism."[25] Williams brings out this view in rendering "those who do not know God, that is, those who will not listen to the good news." This makes the second designation a more explicit formulation of their heinous guilt. They are ignorant of God because they have deliberately rejected the knowledge of Him offered in the gospel.

While this explanation of the double statement is attractive, it is more natural to accept the grammatical construction as denoting two distinct classes. Then the first class, "them that know not God," are the heathen, "all Gentiles who have refused such knowledge of God as is to be had from the light of Nature, cp. Acts 10. 34, Rom. 2. 10-15."[26] In support of this identification Lünemann points out that the expression "not knowing God" is "with Paul a characteristic designation of the Gentiles (I Thess. iv. 5; Gal. iv. 8; comp. Rom. i. 28; Eph. ii. 12)."[27] While the second designation, "them that obey not the gospel," is an accurate portrayal of the Jews, it should not be limited to them. It includes both Jews and Gentiles who have heard the gospel and definitely rejected it. Under this view the picture is not to be limited to persecutors of the Thessalonians. We would agree with Riggenbach that such "excessive strictness of historical reference is not at all advisable; Paul speaks generally of the judgment of the world."[28]

The second class is more guilty than the first. The first class is guilty of ignorance of God, but it is a reprehensible ignorance, resulting from their rejection of the light that they did have (Ro 1:18-23). The second class is identified by its refusal to *obey*, to listen and submit to, the gospel. The present tense marks their disobedience as characteristic of them. It is a willful refusal. "No soul believes the supernatural mysteries revealed by God, unless by a submission of his will he brings his *intellectual* faculties into captivity to the obedience of Christ (2 Cor. x. 5)."[29] They reject "the gospel of our Lord Jesus," the good news concerning *Jesus* the Saviour and the demand that He be accepted as *Lord*. They not only reject the knowledge offered in the gospel but also refuse the obedience which the gospel demands.

3. Consequences of the Judgment (vv. 9-10)

The picture now passes to the abiding consequences of the judgment. Paul first speaks of the destruction befalling the lost (v. 9) and then sets forth the contrasted glorification of the Lord in His saints (v. 10).

a) DESTRUCTION OF THE LOST (v. 9). The fate befalling the two classes mentioned in verse 8 is set forth in the words "who shall suffer punishment." *Who* (*hoitines*) is the plural qualitative relative pronoun, "who are such as," have this character. The two groups are now united because of their common enmity against God. Their fate will be in harmony with their nature.

"Shall suffer punishment," an expression occurring only here in the New Testament, is rendered quite literally, "a penalty shall pay" (Rotherham). The word rendered "punishment" (*dikē*) is connected with the same root as the Greek word for "judge" and "righteous." Its first meaning is "right, justice;" then a judicial hearing to establish the right, "a suit at law;" and then the right exacted, "the penalty paid." The last is its meaning here. It is a "punishment determined by a lawful process."[30]

An appositional adjunct further describes the punishment, "even eternal destruction." In 1 Thessalonians 5:3 the destruction befalling the unsaved was called *sudden* as depicting its unforeseen and unexpected coming. Here the adjective *eternal* (*aiōnion*) points to its duration. This adjective is derived from the noun *aiōn*, "an age, a period of undefined duration," hence *aiōnios* denotes "age-long," whatever the length of the period. The adjective occurs seventy times in the New Testament according to the critical text, but only in three instances (Ro 16:25; 2 Ti 1:9; Titus 1:2) is it used of a period that is not endless. In the remainder of the New Testament occurrences it denotes an endless and therefore undefined period. Frame points out that the exact duration intended by the adjective depends upon the writer, but "in the N.T. the age to come is of unlimited duration; hence *aiōnios*, 'belonging to the age' means to Paul 'eternal' and 'everlasting'."[31] Thayer says the term "gives prominence to the immeasurableness of eternity."[32] This eternal destruction or "everlasting ruin" (Berkeley) is the opposite of the "eternal life" which belongs to the age to come. Swete says that this is "the most express statement in S. Paul's Epistles of the eternity of future punishment."[33] In reply to those who attempt to give *aiōnios* only a *qualitative* aspect Ellicott points out that "the early Greek expositors never appear to have lost sight of its *quantitative* aspects."[34] Findlay asserts, "There is no sufficient reason for interpreting the destruction of the reprobate as signifying their *annihilation*, or extinction of being; they will be *lost* for ever—lost to God and goodness."[35]

The punishment is further described by two parallel prepositional phrases, "from the face of the Lord and from the glory of his might." The preposition *apo*, *from*, is capable of two different interpretations; it may have a *causal* force, "proceeding from," or a *local* force, "away from." Conybeare accepts the causal force and renders, "And from the presence of the Lord, and from the brightness of His glorious majesty, they shall receive their righteous doom." The Twentieth Century New Testament gives strong expression to the local interpretation, "everlasting Ruin—

banishment 'from the presence of the Lord and from the glorious manifestation of his might'."

The idea of separation is generally accepted as the intended meaning and is in full harmony with the context. It permits us to give the ordinary meaning to the expression "the face," or presence, "of the Lord," and does not simply reduce it to mean "the Lord." It keeps this verse from being a mere repetition of the idea in verses 7-8. To hold that *from* designates separation from the Lord, thus describing the abiding nature of the destruction, gives a fuller picture than merely to view it as giving the source of the punishment.

This banishment from the presence of "the Lord," the glorified Jesus, will be the very essence of eternal punishment. The result will be a "negative vacuum"[36] for them, depriving them of the Lord's favor and all which gives meaning and blessedness to life. Bicknell remarks that the expression "from the face" "sums the Christian doctrine of hell. Heaven is primarily the presence of God. Hell is the loss of that presence."[37] It is thus the very opposite of the bliss Paul held before the Thessalonians in 1 Thessalonians 4:17. Paul does not often speak of the destiny of the lost and his description of their fate is restrained. He paints no lurid pictures of their sufferings but stresses rather their negative spiritual relationship. Although he leaves the destiny of the lost largely to awful inference rather than definite portrayal, not to be overlooked are Paul's positive assertions concerning their fate in his use of such terms as *wrath, indignation, affliction, punishment, death, destruction* (Ro 1:18; 2:5-9; 6:21; Phil 3:19; 1 Th 1:10).

The lost will be irrevocably separated from "the glory of his might," the outward and visible splendor which the saints will share with their Lord (v. 10). It is the *glory* that belongs to His *might* (*ischuos*), the inherent strength resident in Him which enables Him to produce these judicial consequences of His coming. In verse 7 the synonymous term rendered *power* (*dunamis*) denotes inherent capability, power relevant for its use. Here the use of *ischus* stresses the might which is His, enabling Him to perform. During His earthly ministry the Lord Jesus did not use this might on His own behalf, but at His return as the Judge in glory this might will be operative in open display with a terrible impact upon His enemies.

b) LORD'S GLORIFICATION IN HIS SAINTS (v. 10). The fate that will befall the lost stands in striking contrast to the destiny of the saints to be displayed when Christ returns in open glory. The temporal clause "when he shall come," more literally, "whenever he shall come," accepts the fact of His coming, viewed as a definite event, as unquestioned, but indicates that the time is left undetermined.

Paul's double statement, "when he shall come to be glorified in his saints, and to be marvelled at in all them that believed," makes the returning Lord, rather than the saints, the subject. The Lord is central to the picture; the saints are viewed in relationship to Him. The two infinitives may be taken to denote both the purpose and the result of His coming.

He will come "to be glorified in his saints." The parallelism with *believed* in the following clause makes it clear that "his saints" (*tois hagiois autou*), "his holy ones," are redeemed men, not angels. They have been set aside as belonging to Christ, *his* because of their union with Him by faith. They are the rank and file of believers who have now been made perfect. In verse 7 the angels manifested Christ's power; here the saints are related to His glorification. The verb *glorified* is an unusual compound form occurring only here and in verse 12 in the New Testament. The preposition *en* prefixed to the verb and repeated with *saints* stresses that Christ will be glorified not only "among" but *in* the saints. The passive voice indicates that He is the recipient of glory in connection with them. The meaning may be that His glory will be reflected in the saints, being as it were mirrors reflecting His glory. But more probably the meaning is that Christ will be glorified when it is openly displayed what He has wrought in His saints, now assembled with Him in glorified bodies and perfected in spirit.

The parallel clause, "and to be marvelled at in all them that believed" restates the scene. "To be marvelled at" indicates the mingled surprise and admiration evoked in the spectators. Christ will be the object of wonder and admiration. But who will do the marvelling? That the saints themselves will feel such an adoring admiration toward their Lord is unquestioned, but the preposition *in* (*en*) again indicates that they themselves are the occasion for this wondering admiration. The reference probably is to the angels of heaven who had sought to understand the salvation of the saints (1 Pe 1:12) and had beheld in the formation of the church a demonstration of the manifold wisdom of God (Eph 3:10). Swete holds that those marvelling includes "still more the unbelieving world, who had hitherto held them in contempt (I Cor. i. 28), and had seen no beauty, either in the Master or in His disciples. Such unbelievers will now 'behold, and wonder and perish' (Acts xiii. 41)."[38] But Paul does not stop to identify the spectators since the focus of his attention is upon the glorified Lord.

"All of them that believed" parallels the preceding "saints." *All* stresses "the inclusiveness of the sainthood."[39] It implies a great multitude of the saved. The aorist tense of *believed* looks back to the decisive event here on earth when by faith the saving message of the gospel was appropriated. The saints, now entering the temple of glory, had first to pass through the temple of faith. *Saints* points to God's sanctifying work in them; *believed* records their active personal response.

The picture is suddenly given a strongly subjective turn by the parenthetical clause "because our testimony unto you was believed," relating it directly to the readers. It stresses that they are assuredly among that great company that believed. "Was believed" stands emphatically at the beginning of the clause to mark the personal response that the readers gave to the apostolic preaching. (Cf. 1 Th 2:13). "Our testimony" indicates that the preachers not only proclaimed the truths of the gospel but also bore personal witness to the reality and power of those truths. Their testimony was "unto you," literally, "upon you" (*eph' humas*), the preposition apparently being "intended to emphasize the direction the testimony took.°°°[40]

Instead of the verb "was believed" (*episteuthē*) Hort conjectured that the verb should read *epistōthē*, "was confirmed."[41] This conjecture is accepted by Moffatt and Goodspeed in their versions, but it is improbable. It has no significant manuscript support and it destroys the intended assurance to the readers in the repeated "believed."

"In that day," standing emphatically at the close of the whole sentence, connects with the two preceding infinitives, "to be glorified" and "to be marvelled at." It concludes with solemn emphasis the eschatological picture following the brief parenthesis which Findlay characterizes as "an interjectional outburst of the author occurring as he dictates to his secretary."[42]

C. PRAYER FOR THEM IN THEIR AFFLICTION
(vv. 11-12)

The eschatological picture just held before the readers to encourage them in their affliction now furnishes motivation to pray for them. It is characteristic of Paul thus to turn his teaching into prayer. His teaching was given in a spirit of prayer. He felt no inconsistency between the assurance of the divine working in them (1 Th 2:13; 4:9) and fervent prayer for them (1 Th 5:23-24). He regarded such intercessions for the elect (1 Th 1:4) as necessary links in the chain of salvation stretching from eternity past to eternity future.

°°°The construction is unusual. Lightfoot holds that the phrase should be connected with "believed" in the sense "belief in our testimony directed itself to reach you" (*Notes* on the Epistle of St. Paul, p. 105).

This is the first of four formulated prayers for the readers in this brief epistle. Indicated are the nature of the prayer (v. 11*a*), its substance (v. 11*b*), and its purpose (v. 12).

1. Nature of the Prayer (v. 11*a*)

"To which end" (*eis ho*) closely links the prayer with the teaching in verses 5-10. The prayer is offered "with this in view" (Williams), that is, in view of the coming glorification of Christ in His saints and is in the interest of its realization.

The missionaries assure the readers, "we also pray always for you." *Also*, standing prominently before the verb, states this praying as an additional activity by the missionaries. Varied connections with the foregoing have been suggested. Findlay proposed a connection with *testimony* in verse 10, indicating that it was carried on with prayer.[43] But the testimony relates to their past ministry among them, while this seems to suggest an additional present activity. Others hold that the connection is with verse 3; not only do the missionaries thank God for the readers, they also pray for them. This is obvious, but we may also include the fact of their boasting about them (v. 4). It shows how thoroughly the missionaries are occupied with their converts. Personally they thank God for them; when in contact with other believers they boast about them; in their united devotions they regularly *pray* (present tense) for them. The added *always* underlines the regularity of the intercessions "for you;" they faithfully pray for their converts every day. "The duties of a preacher or evangelist do not cease with the utterance of his message."[44]

2. Substance of the Prayer (v. 11*b*)

The content of their prayer is given a double statement, "that our God may count you worthy of your calling, and fulfill every desire of goodness and every work of faith." In the original the subject and predicate are reversed, placing *you* emphatically at the beginning of the whole statement. The Thessalonian believers are explicitly the objects of their prayers. The prayers are addressed to "our God," the God whom both writers and readers now know and serve. After the prominent *you* we might have expected "your God" but Paul prefers to write *our* to intimate the close connection between writers and readers.

The first petition is that God "may count you worthy of your calling." It looks back to verse 5. There the thought was of being reckoned worthy to enter the eschatological kingdom; here the prayer is that God may deem them worthy of their *calling*, "the calling" which they have received from God. The divine call is a prominent theme in Paul's writings. Usually it refers to the initial gospel call which results in the conversion

of those called (Ro 8:30; Eph 4:1; 1 Th 4:7). That seems to be the meaning of the calling here. But in view of the future they must now "walk
worthily of the calling wherewith [they] were called" (Eph 4:1). Utterly
unworthy in themselves when called, they cannot make themselves worthy
by their own efforts, but they must diligently seek to so live that God
may count them worthy of His calling. The call to salvation looked forward to its consummation in the coming kingdom (1 Th 2:12). That
prospect must have a sanctifying effect on their lives now. But God
must work the necessary holiness in them. "Only God can fit and equip
His people by His grace to fill the role for which He has chosen them,
namely, to glorify Him in the Kingdom of His Son at His Parousia and
for ever."[45] As saved people they are heirs of the coming kingdom, but
they must undergo a period of moral ripening to be fitted for that glorious
destiny.

And connects this with the further petition that God may "fulfill every
desire of goodness and every work of faith, with power." This indicates
the means whereby God will work in them that fitness which will enable
Him to count them worthy to enter the final kingdom. The prayer is
that God may *fulfil*, bring to completion, to full expression, their "every
desire of goodness and every work of faith." The double statement covers
both their inner desire and outward activity. Both must be wrought by
God (Phil 2:13). God counts men worthy as they consent to and endeavor
to do that which He works in them.

Some would refer "desire of goodness" (*eudokian agathōsunēs*) to God
(cf. "his" in KJV). Thus Phillips renders, "that he will effect in you all
that his goodness desires to do." In Ephesians 1:9 *eudokia* does denote
God's "good pleasure" but the context here indicates that it must be
related to the Thessalonians. The parallel "work of faith" requires that
both be related to the readers. And Paul's use of *goodness* elsewhere
(Ro 15:14; Gal 5:22; Eph 5:9) always denotes a human quality.

Desire is literally "good pleasure," that which seems good, and points
to a favorable reaction to a good object in view. It conveys the thought
of a resolve which is willingly made. It is the good resolve of the regenerate man (Ro 10:1; Phil 1:15). *Every* points to the diversity and inclusiveness of these desires. The added genitive, "of goodness," is open to
two different interpretations. If the genitive is objective it means "every
desire for goodness" (Weymouth), the desire to be and do good, their
aspirations after goodness. If it is subjective it means "every desire
prompted by goodness," springing out of personal goodness. This implies
a goodness which God has wrought in the readers. The subjective meaning is favored by the fact that the genitive in the next expression is certainly subjective. This inner moral quality of *goodness*, the virtue which

desires to be beneficial, was already present in the readers (v. 3). The prayer is that God may bring to completion every aspiration that springs out of their regenerate nature.

"And every†††† work of faith" is the necessary complement to "desire of goodness." The reality of the inner desire must prove itself in outward activity. "Work of faith" (cf. 1 Th 1:3) denotes that work or activity which faith prompts. Such work proves the vitality of faith. A living faith is a working faith (Ja 2:17).

"With power," standing emphatically at the end of the sentence, connects with the verb *fulfil* and marks the manner of the desired working of God in them. Their own efforts would be ineffectual apart from God's *power* (*dunamis*), the characteristic power inherent in His nature, and only His power can produce these results. It is characteristic of the ardor of Paul that nothing less than the mighty operation of divine power in them will satisfy him.

3. Purpose of the Prayer (v. 12)

The ultimate purpose of the prayer for the readers is "that [*hopōs*] the name of our Lord Jesus may be glorified in you, and ye in him." Since the gospel call to the readers had this in view (v. 10), God's design in fulfilling the prayer on behalf of the readers is that the name of our Lord Jesus may be glorified in them.

In biblical terminology "the name" stood for the revealed character and attributes of the individual whom it represented. It is through His revelation of Himself that we are able to apprehend God (Is 52:6). In the Old Testament "the name of the Lord" is a designation for Jehovah (Gen 4:26; Ex 33:19; Deu 5:11; Is 42:8; 56:6). By a natural transition Paul applies this terminology to Christ. At His return in glory His name shall be glorified not simply as "Jesus" but as "our Lord Jesus." (The addition of "Christ" here lacks adequate manuscript authority.) Then will be manifested the fullness of His attributes as our Saviour and Lord. And this shining forth of His glory will be "in you," the Thessalonian believers now afflicted for that name.

But the glorification will be reciprocal, "and ye in him."‡‡‡ This mutual glorification implies the essential unity between the Lord and His own, brought to its consummation at the second advent. The manifestation of the saints in glory awaits Christ's return in glory (Col 3:4). "The servants come in for a share of the honour of the master whose livery they wear."[46]

---

††††Although "every" (*pasan*) is not repeated before "work" in the original, its position indicates that it is to be taken with both expressions.

‡‡‡"In him" (*en autō*) may mean "in it" (the name) or "in him" (the Lord Jesus). The latter connection, accepting the nearer antecedent, is the probable meaning.

The norm as well as the source of this mutual glorification is set forth in the words "according to the grace of our God and the Lord Jesus Christ." Only *grace*, the unmerited favor of God, will be able to account for this glorification; all human merit is ruled out. Our salvation is due to His bounteous grace from beginning to end. And indeed "that Christ should find His glory in men, and share His glory with them, is the greatest conceivable favour."[47]

It is not certain whether the genitive construction "of our God and the Lord Jesus Christ" refers to one or two persons. The use of only one article with the two nouns makes possible the rendering "of our God and Lord, Jesus Christ." This restricts the grace to Christ who is then designated as both God and Lord. Against this interpretation is the fact that "Lord" is often used as a proper name and does not here need the definite article to bring out the double reference. Lenski, who holds to the single reference, calls this grammatical argument weak. He insists that the single reference is in keeping with the fact that "Paul loves to bring his thoughts to a unified conclusion, not concluding at random or with a duality."[48] This weighty designation of Jesus Christ as both God and Lord is in keeping with the profound eschatological picture just given. It is further in keeping with the known practice of the Christians from the latter part of the first century onward to call Jesus "our Great God and Saviour" in reaction to the familiar contemporary practice of applying titles of deity to rulers, often the worst of men.

Although the interpretation which finds only a reference to Jesus Christ in the construction is quite possible and even probable, it is not generally accepted. It is held that the double designation is in harmony with Paul's usual practice of discriminating between the Father as "God" and Christ as "Lord." At any rate, the construction used marks the unity and equality of the Father and the Son, if the double designation is adopted. For Paul there was no great distinction between them.

18

DAY OF THE LORD

2:1-12 Now we beseech you, brethren, touching the coming of our Lord Jesus Christ, and our gathering together unto him; (2) to the end that ye be not quickly shaken from your mind, nor yet be troubled, either by spirit, or by word, or by epistle as from us, as that the day of the Lord is just at hand; (3) let no man beguile you in any wise: for *it will not be*, except the falling away come first, and the man of sin be revealed, the son of perdition, (4) he that opposeth and exalteth himself against all that is called God or that is worshipped; so that he sitteth in the temple of God, setting himself forth as God. (5) Remember ye not, that, when I was yet with you, I told you these things? (6) And now ye know that which restraineth, to the end that he may be revealed in his own season. (7) For the mystery of lawlessness doth already work: only *there is* one that restraineth now, until he be taken out of the way. (8) And then shall be revealed the lawless one, whom the Lord Jesus shall slay with the breath of his mouth, and bring to nought by the manifestation of his coming; (9) *even he*, whose coming is according to the working of Satan with all power and signs and lying wonders, (10) and with all deceit of unrighteousness for them that perish; because they received not the love of the truth, that they might be saved. (11) And for this cause God sendeth them a working of error, that they should believe a lie: (12) that they all might be judged who believed not the truth, but had pleasure in unrighteousness.

THIS PARAGRAPH constitutes the very heart of the epistle. It is crucial because of its momentous eschatological import. No other portion of the prophetic Scriptures covers precisely the same points of revelation here given. This weighty and difficult passage has been the occasion for much critical discussion and has been rejected as non-Pauline by not a few radical critics who have felt that Paul could not have written such a fantastic prophecy. Even those scholars who accept it as Pauline find it difficult because of its "fantastic apocalyptic signs." Thus Neil writes, "This section, dealing with the indications which may be expected to herald the end of the world, provides us with the weirdest piece of writing in all the epistles and one that has never yet been satisfactorily explained."[1] Morris points out that our difficulty of interpretation arises from "the fact that it is a supplement to his oral preaching. . . . He could take it as known, and simply add what was necessary to clear up the misunderstanding that had arisen."[2]

Paul here deals with an eschatological error that was harassing the young Thessalonian church. The excitment produced by this doctrinal error stimulated the practical problem that Paul found it necessary to deal with in the third chapter. The paragraph may be divided into three parts. Paul sets forth the corrective for their erroneous view that the day of the Lord was already present (vv. 1-5), indicates the fact of a present restraint upon the mystery of lawlessness (vv. 6-7), and pictures the brief career of the lawless one (vv. 8-12).

A. CORRECTIVE FOR THEIR ERRONEOUS VIEW
(vv. 1-5)

The opening *Now* (*de*) is a transitional particle marking the passing to a new subject. The particle may be used without any adversative force, but here it seems to have a mild adversative implication as marking the contrast between his prayer for them (1:11-12) and his task of correcting their erroneous view. He makes an affectionate appeal for calmness (vv. 1-2), indicates the events preceding the day of the Lord (vv. 3-4), and reminds them of his former teaching on the matter (v. 5).

1. Appeal for Calmness (vv. 1-2)

The opening words, "We beseech you, brethren," indicate the attitude in which the matter is being approached. The attitude of the writers is not impersonal, cold, and didactic, but personal, warm, and affectionate. *Beseech* (see discussion under 1 Th 4:1) implies a familiar relationship of equality and the direct address, *brethren*, suggests that the appeal is prompted by common Christian concerns. "The Apostle, who has a right to *charge*, rather *implores* as a brother."[3] He indicates the subject matter of the appeal (v. 1), its aim (v. 2a), and the nature of their disturbing error (v. 2b).

a) SUBJECT OF THE APPEAL (v. 1). "Touching the coming of our Lord Jesus Christ, and our gathering together unto him" states the subject matter of the appeal. The preposition rendered "touching" (*huper*) has the root meaning of "over," hence, "on behalf of, in the interest of." The appeal is being made "in the interest of" the truth concerning the Lord's coming. The writers are anxious that it should cease being a source of alarm and confusion to their converts due to an erroneous conclusion. The appeal is intended to be corrective, to remove their misunderstanding concerning "the coming of our Lord Jesus Christ." (On *coming* see comments under 1 Th 2:19). The full title, "our Lord Jesus Christ," adds solemnity to the appeal.

The aspect of the coming in view here is made clear by the added expression "and our gathering together unto him." The government of the two nouns under one article makes it clear that one event, viewed under two complementary aspects, is thought of. It is a summary statement of the teaching given them in 1 Thessalonians 4:13-18. The pronoun *our* in both parts emphasizes the deep personal interest that writers and readers (and all true believers) have in the one who is coming and the resultant "gathering together" (*episunagōgē*). The term denotes the act of gathering together, then the congregation thus assembled. It includes both the dead and the living saints in "our final muster before Him" (Williams) at His coming for His own. The noun occurs again in the New Testament only in Hebrews 10:25 where it is used of the ordinary assembling of the saints for worship. These assemblies are a precious foretaste and anticipation of that future assembling of the saints "unto him" when our Lord will be present, not as now by His Spirit only, but in the visible glory of His person. The preposition rendered "unto" (*epi*) marks "the point to which the gathering together was directed."[4] Christ Himself is the convening center for His saints both now and in that coming day. His coming will mean *our* gathering *unto* him; the pronoun *our* contrasts our movement toward Him with His coming for us. This is the calming hope they must hold fast. "The blessed hope of being caught up to the Lord at His coming or presence is a most intelligible preservative against the false and disquieting rumour that the day of His judgment of the earth had come."[5]

b) AIM OF THE APPEAL (v. 2*a*). "To the end that ye be not quickly shaken from your mind, nor yet be troubled" states the content and aim of the appeal. "To the end that" (cf. 1:5) may denote either content or aim, but here we clearly have a mingling of the two ideas since the very statement of the content indicates the aim of the appeal. The appeal is stated in the form of a double negative purpose. The writers are anxious to calm the excitement that has been aroused in the Thessalonian church. They need to have their mental equilibrium restored.

"That ye be not quickly shaken from your mind" warns against the mental agitation that has assailed them. The adverb *quickly* does not mean "after so short a time," so soon after they had received the truth from the missionaries. The reference is rather to the quality of their action. They are reacting "hastily" or "rashly," responding to the exciting teaching without due consideration.

The verb *shaken* denotes a rocking motion, a shaking up and down, like a building shaken by an earthquake (Ac 16:26), or a ship tossed on a stormy sea. The passive voice points to an outside force; they were being shaken by the false eschatological teaching being promulgated there by some false teacher (v. 3). The verb was sometimes used of a ship that had been insecurely anchored and was being blown from its moorings.

Way renders, "Not to drift storm-tossed from your mental moorings." The aorist tense points to the initial shock of excitment that has shaken them "from your mind," disturbing their mental poise and throwing them off balance. They are not permitting their mind to perform its proper function but are swayed by emotional reactions. It is a reminder to them that "believers are not to be controlled by the emotions, whether of dread or of desire, but by the mind, enlightened by the revelation of the mind of God."[6]

"Nor yet be troubled" adds a second feature to the prohibition. The verb *troubled,* coming from a noun meaning "clamor, tumult," meant "to be frightened, to cry aloud," and thus conveys the thought of a feeling of fright and alarm. The present tense points to a state of alarm, of nervous excitement. The aorist tense of the preceding verb pointed to the initial shock produced by the false teaching, but the present tense here denotes the resultant excited, fluttery state. It implies that the symptoms of disquietude and alarm have already appeared among them. "Nor yet" (*mēde*) suggests that although they may have experienced the initial shock, they should not yield to such an unstable condition.

The means producing the shock and alarm are indicated by three phrases, "either by spirit, or by word, or by epistle as from us." The triple use of *by* (*dia*) enumerates three distinct means or instruments that may have started the disturbing reports. "By spirit" denotes some prophetic utterance professedly given under the operation of the Spirit. The second means, "or by word," points to some vocal utterance as distinguished from the following "by epistle," a written communication.

There is no agreement among interpreters on the question whether the words "as from us," from Paul and his colleagues, are to be taken with only the last term, the last two, or with all three. That they may readily be extended to the last two is obvious, but some feel hesitation about extending them to the first term as well. Those who restrict the reference to the last two terms usually think of the pretended prophecy as uttered by some member of the Thessalonian church. But it seems best to take the expression as covering all three terms, all indicating efforts at claiming apostolic authority for the teaching. This is favored by the use of the same negative (*mēte*) with all three terms; it separated things "which are of the same kind or which are parts of one whole."[7] Either of the first two terms seems incomplete if separated from the defining "as from us." Lenski remarks that "the three form a gradation: spirit is the ultimate means—word or statement the intermediate—letter the direct means."[8] Once introduced, apparently all three means were appealed to by different advocates to gain apostolic sanction for the teaching. But "as from us" (purporting to come from us), marks all such claims as spurious. It is possible that Paul was not certain how the erroneous teaching there had arisen and consequently resorted to this comprehensive denial of any connection with the view. Yet it is quite possible that his denial was evoked by definite information on the matter.

That a spurious letter, claiming apostolic authorship, actually circulated at Thessalonica is not expressly asserted. But in the light of 3:17 this conclusion seems probable. Since Paul thought it necessary to warn them against imposture, this suggests that actual deceit was attempted. Stevens remarks, "The present passage hints at the existence thus early of counterfeit apostolic documents, and shows that the church, very soon after its origin, had to be trained to distinguish between the spurious and the authentic."[9]

Some scholars, like Frame, hold that the reference is to 1 Thessalonians which had been misinterpreted to support the erroneous teaching.[10] But the apostle does not complain of a misapprehension of his former letter but rather disowns entirely the pretended letter. In 1 Corinthians 5:9 we see how Paul did refer to a former letter that had been misinterpreted; there the fact of a former letter is clear, but the expression used is inconsistent with such a view here.

c) NATURE OF THE ERRONEOUS TEACHING (v. 2*b*). The nature of the unsettling teaching is stated in the words rendered "as that the day of the Lord is just at hand." "As that" points to a subjective statement of another's thought without a personal committal to its objective reality. The context makes it clear that the thought is being repudiated.

There is no word in the original for *just*, nor can the rendering "at hand" be accepted as strictly accurate. Of the six occurrences of this verb in the perfect tense in the New Testament it is rendered "at hand" only in this passage. In the perfect tense the verb (*enestēken*) denotes strictly present time and should be rendered "is present" or "has come." In the present tense the verb means "to stand in, to enter," and the perfect, which speaks of completed action in past time with existing result, means "has come and is here." Findlay stresses that the perfect tense "signifies more than *nearness,* more even than *imminence;* it means *to be in place, in course*—not merely approaching but *arrived.*"[11] Milligan points out that "the verb is very common in the papyri and inscriptions with reference to the *current* year."[12] Paul's employment of it in Romans 8:38 and 1 Corinthians 3:22 to express a contrast between the present and the future makes clear the basic meaning of the word. This meaning is recognized by most of our modern versions.*

*A variety of renderings all give this thought: "hath arrived"—Young; "had arrived" —Berkeley; "is present"—Darby; "hath set in"—Rotherham; "is come"—Conybeare; 20th Cent; "has come"—RSV, NASB; "has already come"—Goodspeed, Phillips; "is already here"—Weymouth, Moffatt, Williams; NEB. Only Montgomery retains "at hand" while Way has "is imminent."

The rendering "at hand" is not due to the acknowledged meaning of the word; it is due rather to a doctrinal difficulty felt by the translators. They could not conceive how anyone could really think that "the day of the Lord" had actually arrived.† The supposed doctrinal difficulty lies in the failure to distinguish between the *parousia* and the day of the Lord. The advocates of the false teaching at Thessalonica conceived that the day of the Lord was not merely "at hand," which was true (Ro 13:12), but actually "present," which Paul denied. Such a view denied the believer the hope of the imminent rapture.

"The day of the Lord," a term rooted in the Old Testament, is not a simple concept.[13] It is not a single event but is rather a period associated with the divine judgment upon sin and the deliverance of God's people. Neil remarks that it is "the traditional Jewish expression for the day when God would intervene in history to vindicate His chosen people, destroy their enemies, and establish His kingdom."[14] The Old Testament speaks of that day as a day of darkness and unparalleled judgment, a day of trial to men (cf. Is 13; Joel 2; Amos 5:18). It is a time definitely associated with suffering and the divine judgment upon sin. Walvoord defines the scope of the day as follows:

> It includes the tribulation time preceding the second advent of Christ as well as the whole millennial reign of Christ. It will culminate in the judgment of the great white throne. The Day of the Lord is therefore an extended period of time lasting over one thousand years.[15]

The Thessalonians, undergoing trying persecution, were being told by those promulgating this controverted teaching that they were already in that great and terrible period of anguish and tribulation called "the day of the Lord." The persecutions they were enduring seemed to confirm this view. The natural reaction to this teaching was fear and agitation. The apostle appeals to them in the interest of the very hope of "our gathering together unto him," set forth in the first epistle (4:13-18), not to allow themselves to be shaken and troubled by this unwarranted teaching.

2 Events Which Must Precede (vv. 3-4)

As his corrective to the false teaching, Paul names two events which must occur before the day of the Lord can be truly said to have come. He prefaces his statement with a warning against deception (v. 3a) and names the events (vv. 3b-4).

a) WARNING AGAINST DECEPTION (v. 3a). "Let no man beguile you in any wise" is a sweeping warning intended to assure the safety of the readers

†The KJV rendering, "the day of Christ," follows an inferior reading and is properly replaced with "the day of the Lord."

by putting them on guard against deception. The negative with the aorist tense (*mē exapatēsē*) sharply warns them against the attempt of any one, whoever he may be, to *beguile* them. The preposition prefixed to the verb strengthens its force, "to deceive thoroughly, to delude." Lünemann thinks that the term need not be interpreted to denote "a deceit occurring from wicked intention" but "only the idea of delusion, i.e. of being misled into a false and incorrect mode of contemplation."[16] But Findlay feels that the warning "seems to be directed against a wilful, dishonest deception."[17] Paul knew the persistence of error and realized that these deceptive teachers would not readily cease their efforts to make their view plausible, hence he warns against deception "in any wise," in any other manner than the three already specified. He was aware how readily many are attracted by the new and novel. "It is amazing how gullible some believers can be when a new prophetic fad appears!"[18]

b) EVENTS INDICATED (vv. 3*b*-4). *For* introduces the justification for the warning. The words in italics, *"it will not be,"* are rightly supplied by the translators to complete the sentence which Paul leaves unfinished. Such an ellipsis is natural in the freedom of animated conversation; it suggests that Paul is dictating the letter.

The crucial day of the Lord will not come "except the falling away come first, and the man of sin be revealed." Paul is thinking of two distinct, although related, events. The two designations do not refer to "a single phenomenon" as Moffatt suggests.[19] The two verbs, emphatic by position, serve to distinguish the events. The man of sin is not the personal embodiment of the falling away, nor is he simply the personal culmination of the apostasy. While the two events are clearly related as expressions of enmity towards God, they are yet distinct. The falling away indicates a tragic movement within the sphere of professed Christendom, the treason of the avowed friends of Christ, while the public manifestation of the man of sin in the arena of history marks the personal culmination of the hostility of the avowed enemies of Christ.

The first sign which Paul insists must precede the day of the Lord is "the falling away" (*hē apostasia*), the term from which our English word apostasy is derived. It denotes a deliberate abandonment of a formerly professed position or view, a defection, a rejection of a former allegiance. In classical Greek it was used to denote a political or military rebellion; in the Septuagint it was used of rebellion against God (Josh 22:22); in 1 Maccabees 2:15 it is used of the enforcement of apostasy to paganism. This religious connotation appears in the use of the term in the New Testament (Ac 21:21; 1 Ti 4:1; 2 Ti 3:1-9; 4:3-4; Heb 3:12). Obviously

Paul's sign has reference to apostasy within the circle of the professed Christian church.

Such a defection within the ranks of Christ's followers began early, as indicated in the pastoral epistles. The history of the Christian church has repeatedly shown periods of declension and apostasy from the truth of the gospel. But by his use of the definite article, in "the falling away," Paul clearly points to the well-known apostasy, "the great revolt" (Williams),‡ which will characterize Christendom in the end-time (1 Ti 4:1-3; 2 Ti 3:1-5; 4:3-4; Ja 5:1-8; 2 Pe 2:1-22; 3:3-6; Jude). The expression points to an expected apostasy concerning which Paul knew that the readers were informed (cf. v. 5). No further elaboration of the apostasy is given here.

Within recent times certain evangelical Bible teachers have proposed that *hē apostasia,* following a secondary meaning of the term, should be rendered "the departure," meaning the rapture of the church.[20] But this interpretation is not in harmony with the nature of the rapture. Nowhere else does the Scripture speak of the rapture as "the departure." A departure denotes an act on the part of the individual or company departing. But the rapture is not an act of departure on the part of the saints. In the rapture the church is passive, not active. At the rapture the church is "caught up" or "snatched away," an event wherein the Lord acts to transport believers from earth into His presence (1 Th 4:16-17). Everything that takes place with the believer at the rapture is initiated by the Lord and done by Him. Paul has just referred to the rapture as "our gathering together unto him" (v. 1); why then should he now use this unlikely term to mean the same thing? But to apply the term to the apostasy is to give it its proper meaning, since the apostasy is the action of professed believers. The biblical usage of the term points to something sinful. In Acts 21:21, the only other place where the noun occurs in the New Testament, it definitely asserts an apostasy from Moses. In view of the Old Testament usage of the term, any reader familiar with the Greek Old Testament or the history of the Maccabees would understand the word when thus used by itself to mean an apostasy from the faith.

Paul names a second precursor to the day of the Lord, "and the man of sin be revealed." The verb *revealed,* standing emphatically forward, is in the aorist tense and points to a definite time when the veil will be removed. His revelation will herald the fact that the day of the Lord has actually arrived. The importance of this revelation is shown by the repetition of the verb in verses 6 and 8. His public appearance in the

‡The versions employ a variety of terms: "the revolt"—Rotherham, Way; "the apostasy"—Darby, Lattey, Weymouth; Berkeley, NASB; "the great apostasy"—Montgomery; 20th Cent; "the rebellion"—Moffatt, Goodspeed; RSV; "the final rebellion"—NEB.

arena of human history will disclose his true identity. The verb implies his prior existence on earth, for he will doubtless have been living many years before his manifestation as the man of sin.

Three designations, standing in apposition, serve to identify this personage. He is "the man of sin." It is not a personal name but a characterization of the man, indicating his evil character. Sin has such absolute domination over him that he seems to be the very embodiment of it.

There is uncertainty concerning the true reading here. The rendering, "the man of lawlessness," follows a variant reading (cf. v. 8).§ The evidence is divided and the critical editors are not in full agreement as to the original reading here.|| The two terms are similar in meaning. "Sin," the more general term, has the basic meaning "missing the mark," while "lawlessness" denotes the breaking of law. According to 1 John 3:4 "sin is lawlessness," hence the terms are readily interchangeable.#

The added designation, "the son of perdition,"** indicates his certain doom. The Hebrew idiom "son of" (cf. 1 Th 5:5) points to his characteristic relationship. It marks him as one who "stands in the sort of relation to it that a son does to a father, and who falls under its power and domination."[21] So completely has he fallen under the power of "predition," destruction or ruination, that he may rightly be said to belong to it by nature. *Perdition* (*apōleia*) denotes loss of well-being, not loss of being, extinction. As the very opposite of all that is implied in *salvation*, it points to "an everlasting state of torment and death."[22] It is a "destruction which consists in the loss of eternal life, eternal misery, the lot of those excluded from the kingdom of God."[23]

The further apposition, consisting of two present middle participles under one article, "he that opposeth and exalteth himself against all that is called God or is worshipped," depicts his blasphemous activity. His double activity will establish his true identity.

"He that opposeth" (*ho antikeimenos*) characterizes him as "the opponent" or adversary of Christ. He "keeps up his opposition" (Williams) to "all that is called God or is worshipped." He "embodies not merely an Anti-Christian, but an Anti-theistic revolt."[24] Haughtily he will seek to

§Rotherham, Lattey; RSV; NASB; "the lawless man"—Phillips; "the representative of lawlessness"—Williams; "the embodiment of disobedience"—Goodspeed; "the Incarnation of Wickedness"—20th Cent; "wickedness will be revealed in human form"—NEB.

|| The T.R. reading, "the man of sin," follows the majority of the witnesses. It is accepted by Souter. "The man of lawlessness" is accepted by Westcott and Hort, Nestle, and the Bible Societies text, but with admitted uncertainty.

#Frame points out that the important uncials Aleph and B frequently vary in their use of the two terms ("A Critical and Exegetical Commentary," p. 253).

**The fact that this designation is also applied to Judas Iscariot (John 17:12) offers no valid basis for the assumption that "the man of sin" will be Judas reincarnated. For the view see Oliver B. Greene, *The Epistles of Paul the Apostle to the Thessalonians*, pp. 253-258.

abolish all existing forms of worship by seeking to replace them. Every so-called god will be deposed in favor of himself. He "exalteth himself" by lifting himself above them all.

The expression "called God" shows Paul's natural caution as a Christian, since the designation included not only the true God but also the heathen divinities. The addition, "or that is worshipped," that is, an object of reverence, expands the scope to include every conceivable object connected with man's religious activity. All will fall under the ban of this Antichrist.

"So that he sitteth in the temple of God, setting himself forth as God" brings this picture of self-deification to its awful climax. "So that" introduces the blasphemous result. The original order, which Rotherham fairly reproduces in rendering "So that he within the sanctuary of God shall take his seat," by position makes both *he* and *sitteth* emphatic. *Sitteth* is in the aorist tense and denotes the definite act of taking his seat "in the temple of God," the inner sanctuary of the temple. As contrasted to the Greek term *hieron,* also translated "temple" and denoting the entire temple complex with its courts, the word here, *naos,* when used of a pagan temple, indicated the inner shrine where the image of the god was placed. For a Jew "the temple" (*ton naon*) could only denote the holy place of the Jerusalem temple, that portion into which the priests alone could lawfully go. The construction used (*eis* with the accusative) implies motion toward and indicates that by his impious act the man of sin puts himself "into" God's seat in the inner sanctuary. Ellicott remarks, "His arrogancy rises to such an impious height as to lead to this uttermost act of unholy daring."[25] Paul's use of the definite article and the added definition "of God" excludes any reference to a pagan temple. Whether Paul is referring to a literal temple in Jerusalem or is using the term metaphorically of the church has been much debated. The view adopted will be determined by one's understanding of end-time prophecy. The whole picture seems naturally to suggest an eschatological Jewish temple. This was the view of Irenaeus (*Against Heresies,* V. 30. 4) and other early church Fathers.

"Setting himself forth as God" states the open implication of his act. He not only takes possession of the temple but publicly displays himself in divine dignity, "parading himself as the very Deity" (Way). The present tense marks this display as a course of conduct attending and centering in the taking of his seat in the temple. He makes *himself* the object of the display, showing himself off as absolute and exclusive deity. "This is the climax of human sin; it is self-assertion in its falsest, most impious and defiant form—a colossal, monstrous lie."[26]

An attentive reading of this passage, uninfluenced by theological presuppositions, naturally leads to the conclusion that Paul is describing an actual eschatological individual, not a mere principle, or even a succession of persons. The context plainly places him in the end-time, for he will be personally slain by the returning Christ (v. 8). Throughout the paragraph Paul describes him in terms that suggest a deliberate parallel to Christ. Each has a "coming" (*parousia*)—2:9 and 2:1; each has a "revelation" (*apokalupsis*)—2:3 and 1:7-8; each has his own gospel—"a lie" (2:11) in contrast to "the truth" (2:10, 12). The man of sin claims exclusive homage and worship and will brook no rival (2:4), and in imitation of Christ (Ac 2:22) will support his claim with "all power and signs and lying wonders" (2:9). As Christ, the true Messiah, was empowered by God, so this Antichrist will be empowered by Satan (2:9). Clearly he is Satan's parody of the true Messiah. While imitating Christ, he will be the complete contrast to the character of Christ. The complete opposite of Christ cannot be a spiritual tendency or a principle but must be a person. Clearly we have here the prophetic individual elsewhere spoken of as "*the* Antichrist," a name that well sums up his character and career.

The recognition that Paul is speaking of a definite eschatological person at once helps to clear away some misconceptions concerning "the man of sin." He cannot be regarded merely as the personification of the principle of lawlessness. He is not an abstract power. He is not simply the personification of "the mystery of lawlessness" (v. 7). Paul says that "the mystery of lawlessness doth already work" but this is an eschatological person who will appear at the end-time. He will form the climax to the development of ungodliness. There have been many antichrists but these precursors only serve to prepare the way for the final personal Antichrist.

Neither can this eschatological figure be identified with the line of Roman emperors, as was held by Warfield. It was his opinion that the man of sin must be identified with such Roman emperors as Caligula, Nero, Vespasian, Titus, and Domitian; he felt that every item of Paul's hideous description of the son of perdition "was fulfilled in the terrible story of the emperors of Rome."[27] But the eschatological nature of this personage is an insurmountable obstacle to this view. Then the sign of the revelation of the man of sin as indicative of the presence of the day of the Lord proved false.

The recognition of his eschatological nature also disposes of the popular view that the man of sin is the papacy, a view eagerly seized upon by many leaders of the Reformation. It is quite natural that the Reformers, locked in fierce conflict with the papal forces, should come to this conclusion. This view still has its able defenders, but it is beset with serious difficulties. The papacy does not offer a true fulfillment of Paul's picture.

The popes have never claimed for themselves exclusive divine honor. As Erdman remarks, "No pope 'is called God' nor 'worshipped' as God, but each declares himself to be the 'vicar' of Christ and only as such infallible in matters of religion."[28] Romanism does not oppose all that is called God or is an object of worship, for the adoration of the Virgin Mary and the saints is a leading feature in it. It is also inconsistent with the fact that the man of sin is an eschatological person, since it must regard him as a long succession of persons extending over a period of hundreds of years. Then Paul's teaching that the revelation of this person marked the presence of the day of the Lord has long since ceased to have the significance he attached to it.

3. Reminder of Past Oral Teaching (v. 5)

Paul breaks off his eschatological picture with the reminder that it was nothing new to the readers. "Remember ye not" implies a "yes" answer from them and conveys a mild rebuke. Had they remembered they would not have been so easily disturbed by this unwarranted teaching. Let them recall *that*, "when I was yet with you, I told you these things." *Told* is in the imperfect tense, indicating that on different occasions he had talked to them about "these things," these very eschatological truths. It shows that apocalyptic teaching had a regular place in the apostle's ministry. Clearly Paul did not believe that prophetic teaching should be withheld from new converts. It assures them that he is not contradicting himself or advancing some new position in opposing the teaching that the day of the Lord was already present.

Here for the first time in this epistle Paul uses the singular pronoun. "I told you" pointedly recalls that he himself had given them this information on his own authority. Those who were promulgating a different view were doing so in opposition to his own teaching to them.

B. RESTRAINT UPON THE MYSTERY OF LAWLESSNESS
(vv. 6-7)

From the developed future of lawlessness as manifested in the man of sin, the thought now turns to the restraint upon its present development. Paul notes the purpose of the restraint (v. 6) and mentions the removal of the restrainer (v. 7).

1. Purpose of the Restraint (v. 6)

And marks the continuation of the discussion after the brief interruption of verse 5. "And now ye know that which restraineth." The force and connection of the adverb *now* may be differently understood. It may be connected with *restraineth* as in Rotherham's rendering, "And what now restraineth ye know." Hendriksen holds that the logic of the passage demands this connection.[29] But others connect it with "ye know" and give it a temporal force, their present knowledge of these things as contrasted to the future season appointed to the man of sin. But perhaps it is best simply to regard it as a mere particle of transition to the new aspect of the presentation.

"Ye know that which restraineth" (*to katechon oidate*) places the object emphatically before the subject, indicating that the thought centers on the restraint. The neuter present participle presents this restraint as an impersonal operative force. This restraining force the readers *know*, which may mean that they perceive the meaning of Paul's words from his past oral teaching or that they have personal acquaintance with it.[30]

The verb *restraineth* (*katechō*) quite literally means "to hold down" and three different suggestions as to its force have been advanced: "to hold back, to restrain;" "to hold fast, to retain;" "to hold sway, to rule." Proponents of the last view generally think of some mythical dragon or Satan himself as now holding sway. But this meaning of the verb is not found elsewhere in the New Testament and the view is unacceptable as contrary to the context.

The other two meanings are closely related and can be made to yield practically the same resultant interpretation. But the first meaning seems clearly indicated by the context. The participle is the present active and indicates that this restraining force is now actively at work.

This restraint is now being exercised "to the end that he may be revealed in his own season." The expression "to the end that" again conveys the thought of purpose, but obviously there is in it a blending of purpose and result. The divine purpose in the restraint is that "he," the man of sin mentioned in verse 4, "may be revealed in his own season." The restraint prevents the premature manifestation of the man of sin as the very embodiment of iniquity. The result is that he will be manifested in his "own season," in the time divinely appointed for him, when the time will be ripe for his unveiling. Just as there was a "fulness of the time" for the manifestation of Christ (Gal 4:4), so there will be a "fulness of time" when the man of sin will be revealed. The development of evil is under God's control. "If He allows moral evil to exist in His creatures (and its possibility seems to be inseparable from moral freedom), yet He knows how to control its activity, till the time shall come when its full manifestation will best subserve its overthrow and judgment."[31]

2. Removal of the Restrainer (v. 7)

For introduces explanatory evidence for the statement just made. It explains why the present restraint is needed. The truth is, which by implication explains their present affliction, that "the mystery of lawlessness doth already work." The adverb *already* indicates that even as he is writing this to them the mystery of lawlessness is actively at work, but because of the restraint it has not yet reached its climax. The verb *work* indicates the active operation of some supernatural power. In 1 Thessalonians 2:13 Paul used it of the working of the Word of God in the readers; here it denotes the energetic satanic activity behind the working of lawlessness. Behind the aggressive forces of evil is an aggressive agent, Satan himself. Being now restrained from bringing the man of sin on the scene, the worst he can do is to actively promote the spirit of lawlessness.

In the unusual expression, "the mystery of lawlessness" (*to mustērion . . . tēs anomias*) the flexible Greek separates the genitive from the nominative by placing the adverb and the verb between them, thus giving each an emphasis. The term mystery in the New Testament does not mean something mysterious and unintelligible but rather something which was previously hidden and unknown to man and undiscoverable by mere human search but has now been divinely revealed. Almost invariably Paul uses the term in connection with words which indicate revelation and publication (Ro 16:26; 1 Co 2:6-12; Eph 1:9; 3:3-5; Col 1:25-27). The mystery is disclosed by divine revelation in order that it may be proclaimed. Nowhere in the New Testament does it imply an esoteric teaching intended only for an inner circle of disciples. It is available to all who have the spiritual qualification to understand it.

The mystery is defined by the added genitive, "of lawlessness." Used with the definite article, "the lawlessness," it does not merely denote disorder and violation of law but rather that definite aim of the devil to overthrow the law of God and establish his own rule. Present lawlessness bears an eschatological mark. The expression here connects with "the lawless one" in verse 8. That sinister individual has not yet been revealed, but the spirit that will dominate his career is already operative. So monstrous will be the depths of iniquity plumbed by the man of lawlessness that human thought would never have fully conceived of such depths apart from divine revelation.

As indicated by the italics, the statement, "only *there is* one that restraineth now, until he be taken out of the way," is somewhat irregular. We may accept an ellipsis and supply a verb, as is done in our version. Findlay sees in this another indication that the letter was written by dictation.[32] Or we may adopt the view that there is no ellipsis but rather an unusual word order, holding that the words "one that restraineth now" have been placed before "until" for emphasis and render "only until he that now restraineth be taken out of the way." Under either construction the general idea remains the same.

There is a time limit upon the present restraint of the mystery of lawlessness. The restraint will continue only "until he be taken out of the way." "Be taken" is more literally "became, may come to be." The aorist tense points to a definite event, while the subjunctive mode leaves the time undetermined. The deponent verb does not denote removal by an outside force but rather a voluntary act on the part of the restrainer. He will terminate his restraining function when he is "out of the way," literally, "out of the midst."

Much discussion has been raised by the fact that the neuter participle (*to katechon*) of verse 6 is now replaced with the masculine participle (*ho katechōn*), "the one restraining." The change indicates that a personality stands at the head of the restraining activity. Riggenbach remarks that the identity of this restrainer "is really the darkest point in the whole passage, now that we have no longer the oral interpretation; a proof, what oral tradition would amount to without a written record."[33] Varied indeed have been the identifications proposed:—a Roman emperor or emperors; the Roman empire, or human government generally; the Jewish state; the preaching of the gospel; Paul himself; Satan; Elijah; Michael; the providences of God; the Holy Spirit.

Our identification of the Restrainer must ultimately be determined by the question, What person is able to hold back the efforts of Satan? To effectively counteract and restrain the personal activities of Satan demands a person, and one that is more than human. Only a supernatural person can truly frustrate the supernatural workings of Satan. This would at once rule out human agencies as well as all evil supernatural agents Only a superhuman Restrainer can do the work.

This elimination leaves the attractive suggestion that "the restrainer is God, that which restrains, the countless operations of His providences."[34] But the book of Revelation makes it clear that His providential interventions in the affairs of men will not cease during the days of the Antichrist. The fact that the Restrainer will be "out of the midst" seems rather to speak of one who is now "in the midst." This seems to point clearly to the Holy Spirit who is now here in person as the indweller of the saints. The indwelling Spirit will be "out of the midst" of this present scene when the returning Christ calls His church to Himself. "When the Church is taken away to be with her Lord, then will He be also out of the midst; the Pentecostal dispensation, which began with His descent from heaven, will be at an end with His return to it."[35] Since the removal of the Restrainer takes place before the manifestation of the lawless one, this identification implies a pretribulational rapture.

The usual objection to this identification is that while it is "easy to think of the Spirit as restraining the forces of evil it is impossible to envisage

Him as being 'taken out of the way.' "[36] Ryrie replies that the answer "lies in the difference of meaning between *residence* and *presence*."[37] As a member of the Godhead the Spirit is omnipresent and has always been in the world and He certainly will continue to be present during the great tribulation. But at Pentecost He assumed a special relationship to the church as its Indweller (cf. Jn 14:16-17). After the completion of His work in the church, He will resume the relation to mankind that He had before Pentecost.

In harmony with the identification of the Spirit as the Restrainer, it may be suggested that the neuter of verse 6 is due to the fact that the Greek word for Spirit is neuter, while in verse 7 the masculine is used to make clear the personality of the Restrainer.†† The suggestion that the neuter designation refers to the church or to the saints is precarious in view of the fact that neither of these terms is neuter in the Greek. Clearly the Holy Spirit now works through the church and the individual saints, who are the salt of the earth, but while using them as restraining means, the work of restraining evil is His own.

C. CAREER OF THE LAWLESS ONE (vv. 8-12)

"And then" is emphatic and asserts that the career of the lawless one will run its course following the removal of the Restrainer. After the mention of the present working of lawlessness (vv. 6-7), Paul again turns to the final development of lawlessness, fulfilling the condition set forth in verses 3b-4. He states the termination of the career of the lawless one (v. 8) and describes his deceptive power over the lost (vv. 9-12).

1. His Career Terminated by Jesus (v. 8)

Paul's consolatory aim leads him at once to connect the fearful revelation of the lawless one with his sure fate. With the removal of the Restrainer there "shall be revealed the lawless one." "The lawless one," the personal embodiment and head of open lawlessness, is clearly to be identified with the man of sin in verse 3. The term indicates his connection with "the mystery of lawlessness" (v. 7) which he will bring to its full expression. The designation does not mean that he will be without any law but rather that he will set himself in rebellion against God's law. The passive form of the verb "shall be revealed" points to the agency of Satan behind his unveiling. Satan's efforts toward that end are now being frustrated (v. 7), but with the removal of the restraint he will have free course to realize his purpose. This is the third mention of the revelation of this dread person in the paragraph (vv. 3, 6), indicating its crucial

††See Jn 15:26; 16:13-14; Eph 1:13-14 for the use of the masculine pronoun with the neuter noun "Spirit" to bring out the personality of the Holy Spirit.

significance. It points to his appearing "as of some portentous, unearthly object holding the gazer spell-bound."[38]

The termination of his career is given a vivid double statement, "whom the Lord Jesus shall slay with the breath of his mouth, and bring to nought by the manifestation of his coming." The agent of his destruction is the Lord Jesus.‡‡ The designation identifies "the Lord" acting in judgment with the human "Jesus" to whom the Father has committed all judgment (Jn 5:22). The name *Jesus* serves to bring into clear focus the contrast between the man of God and the man of Satan in this encounter. The true Christ will swiftly terminate the career of the deceiving Antichrist. The two future verbs state the result of Jesus' action against the lawless one but they do not indicate the time interval between the appearing of the Antichrist and his destruction. This uniting of his beginning and end suggests that his career will not be prolonged but rather will be relatively brief and decisively terminated.

This lawless one Jesus "shall slay with the breath of his mouth." The expression implies the ease with which his end will be brought about. No fierce, drawn-out conflict will be necessary. Jesus will *slay*, "take away, destroy, kill," him, thus bringing to a decisive end the career of this usurper.§§ The alternative rendering "shall consume" (KJV) follows a somewhat less adequately supported text; it conveys the picture of destruction by fire (cf. 1:7-8). "With the breath of his mouth" names the instrument of destruction Jesus will employ. The expression may be a metaphor for His word of command, but more probably the reference is directly to His actual breath. The very breathing of the glorified Jesus will slay the lawless one like the blast of a fiery furnace.

The parallel verb, "bring to nought" (*katargēsei*) is a characteristically Pauline term having the basic meaning "to render idle or inoperative, to reduce to inactivity."|| || The lawless one will be rendered inactive by the returning Lord. Not his annihilation but his immobilization is thus indicated.

The two verbs stating the fate of the lawless one are parallel in time but not completely parallel in their impact. "Slay" points to the fate that will befall the lawless one personally, while "bring to nought" seems to indicate what will happen to his program of activities. Thus Williams aptly renders, "The Lord Jesus will destroy him with the breath of His mouth and put a stop to his operations."

The parallel statement of means, "by the manifestation of his coming,"

---

‡‡The *Textus Receptus* omits "Jesus" but the manuscript evidence for it is sufficiently strong to cause the critical editors to admit it, although with acknowledged doubt.

§§The verb is frequently used to designate murder; the end of the lawless one will be as decisive as that of a man who is murdered.

|| ||Twenty-five of its twenty-seven occurrences in the New Testament are found in the letters of Paul.

is quite literally, "by the epiphany of his presence." Neil stamps the combination as "tautological," for both are terms associated with the second advent.[39] The noun *manifestation,* used elsewhere in the New Testament only in the pastoral epistles,## basically means "a shining forth" (our English word epiphany). The term was "often used by the Greeks of a glorious manifestation of the gods, and especially of their advent to help."[40] *Coming* (see discussion under 1 Th 2:19) is a standard term for the second advent, having the basic meaning of "presence." The unique combination of the two terms stresses that the whole Antichristian system will be put out of operation by the conspicuous shining forth of our Lord's presence. The visible encounter with the glorious Lord Jesus will paralyze the daring presumption and arrogant activity of the lawless one.

2. His Power over the Lost (vv. 9-12)

After pointing out the sure fate of the lawless one, Paul now describes his career in more detail. He indicates the nature of his power (vv. 9-10*a*), those who will succumb to his power (v. 10*b*), and the resultant judgment upon the deluded (vv. 11-12).

a) DESCRIPTION OF HIS POWER (vv. 9-10*a*). The italicized words, *even he,* are properly supplied by the translators to show that the reference is to the lawless one, a fact made clear by the context. By using again the word *coming,* Paul seems to set the advent of the lawless one deliberately in arresting contrast to Christ's advent. His coming "is according to the working of Satan." The present tense of the verb *is* sets forth the certainty of his future coming. "According to the working of Satan" indicates that he will act in harmony and agreement with the working that is characteristic of Satan. The man of lawlessness is not Satan himself but he will operate in the power of Satan, the instigator and energizer of the evil that is already aggressively at work in the world (v. 7). The word *working,* used only by Paul in the New Testament, denotes the inward operation of some supernatural power.*** Elsewhere used of God, only here does Paul use it of Satan. Superhuman power will characterize the career of the lawless one. He will operate *with* (*en*), or in the sphere of, "all power and signs and lying wonders." The three terms form a comprehensive description of miracles. *Power,* in the singular here, denotes the cause of the miracle, the inherent power producing it; *signs* point to the significance lying behind the miracles; *wonders* indicates their abnormal nature and the astonishment they produce in the beholders. *All,*

##Of the first advent, 2 Ti 1:10; of the second advent, 1 Ti 6:14; 2 Ti 4:1, 8; Titus 2:13.
***Eph 1:19; 3:7; 4:16; Phil 3:21; Col 1:29; 2 Th 2:9, 11. On the verb, see comments under 1 Th 2:13.

or "every kind of," while agreeing in gender with the nearest term, seems best taken with all three. He will make a display of all manner of power, producing signs which point to the reality of his claims and wonders which hold the spectators spellbound in admiration of him.

These three terms are used to designate the miracles of Christ (Ac 2:22) and the apostolic church (Heb 2:4) as authenticating their ministry. The lawless one will also use his miracles to authenticate his "lying" (*pseudous*) claims, literally, "of falsehood." The genitive stands after the three nouns and applies to all three. It does not assert that the miracles will be fraudulent, the result of trickery and pretense, but rather that they belong to the realm of falsehood, false in their very character. They have the essential nature of the devil himself, who is a liar by nature (Jn 8:44).

"And with all deceit of unrighteousness" draws attention to the subjective side of the working of the lawless one. He will operate *with* (*en*), in the sphere of, "all deceit," every kind of deceit; he will employ every conceivable means of deception "of unrighteousness," every form of deception which unrighteousness can devise to palm itself off as righteousness. Hand in hand with his objective deeds will go a subjective purpose to mislead. Phillips paraphrases, "He will come with evil's undiluted power to deceive."

b) SUBJECTS OF HIS POWER (v. 10*b*). The deceptive workings of the lawless one will be effective "for them that perish" (*tois apollumenois*), "for those perishing." The present articular participle denotes the class, those who have succumbed to the deceptions of the lawless one and are now "in the path that leads to ruin" (Way). The present tense connotes that their perishing has already begun and that "a complete transformation" of these victims would be "required to bring them out of the ruin implicit in their state."[41] As a class they are the very opposite of those now "being saved" (cf. 1 Co 1:18). The path that they are persistently following will inevitably plunge them into "perdition" (see remarks under v. 3 above), for in character and conduct they show themselves to be children of perishing. This stated limitation of the victims of the lawless one was obviously intended as an encouragement to the afflicted readers.

Paul does not imply that those perishing are the unfortunate victims of "predestination unto damnation." The cause for their perishing lies not in God but in themselves, "because they received not the love of the truth, that they might be saved." *Because* (*anth' hōn*), a classical expression occurring only here in the New Testament, is quite literally, "over against, or corresponding to, these things," and conveys the idea of a just requital. Their fate is the just and deserved punishment for their deliberate rejection of the divine offer of salvation. "They received not" (*ouk edexanto*)

The Thessalonian Epistles

looks back to their definite decision not to receive God's salvation; they did not as a voluntary and willing act open their hearts to welcome "the love of the truth." "Their offence was worse than the mere rejection of the truth."[42] Not only did they refuse "the truth" (not truth abstractly but the saving truth of the gospel, as the added clause makes clear), but manifested a disposition of aversion to the truth, showing no desire to seek and possess the saving truth of God. Their unbelief was not so much a matter of the head as of the heart. They revealed that they loved darkness rather than light (Jn 3:19). It is the *love* of the truth, or its absence, that is the real test of a man's true character.[†††] God sought to awaken in them this love of the truth through the message of the gospel but they willfully rejected it and refused to cooperate with it.

"That they might be saved" expresses the divine purpose or intended result for them. God is not a monster who has pleasure in the death of the wicked (Eze 33:11), for He desires and has provided for their salvation (1 Ti 2:4-6). Having no love for the truth, they remained ignorant of the magnitude of the gift being offered them. They displayed a criminal indifference toward their eternal welfare, recognizing neither their danger nor the way of escape.

c) JUDGMENT UPON THE DELUDED (vv. 11-12). *And* marks the connection between their guilt and the judgment befalling them. "For this cause" points back to their distaste for and rejection of the truth. The judgment is not capricious; a cause and effect relationship is operative.

The judgment is divinely inflicted, "God sendeth them a working of error, that they should believe a lie." *God* is emphatic by position; He is the sovereign Judge. As a moral Being, He cannot remain passive toward active evil. Sin must be punished in a moral universe. (See further discussion under 1 Th 1:10).

The tense of the verb *sendeth* has been viewed in two different ways. The present tense may be taken to mean that "this retributive judgment of God is even now in force."[43] This is supported by the fact that reference has just been made to the present working of the mystery of lawlessness (v. 7). But the context suggests that the tense should rather be taken as a prophetic present, stating with assurance that which is being predicted. The primary reference certainly is to the future, the judgment to fall upon the dupes of the Antichrist, but it is true that the principle is already in operation (Ro 1:18-25). "What will take place in those deceived by Antichrist, is seen on a smaller scale every day."[44]

†††"The expression, not receiving the love of the truth, does not imply any higher degree of alienation from the truth than the simpler form of words, 'not receiving the truth'" (Benjamin Jowett, in *The Epistles of St. Paul to the Thessalonians, Galatians, Romans*, 1:167). C. J. Ellicott rightly regards this view of Jowett as "somewhat perverse" (*A Critical and Grammatical Commentary* p. 125).

The divine punishment is inflicted by sending upon them "a working of error," "an inward working of delusion" (Conybeare). It should be noted that God does not send upon them "error" as such but rather an inward working of the inevitable consequences of error. They will fall under the influence of a power working within them which leads them farther and farther away from the truth. Since they deliberately chose falsehood in defiance of the truth of God, God subjects them to the power of the error they chose. God uses their choice of evil as the very instrument to punish their sin. "His own iniquities shall take the wicked, and he shall be holden with the cords of his sin" (Pr 5:22). Modern thinking would prefer to reduce the action of God to the operation of an impersonal law of nature, but Paul clearly sees the activity of God in the operation of the law which He has established.

"That they should believe a lie" states the immediate purpose of God in sending them a working of error, but it also indicates the actual result for the recipients. The tense of the verb *believe* is an effective aorist and points to the time when they actually came to believe and trust in "a lie," literally, "the lie," the opposite of the truth (v. 10). *The* lie is that pictured in verse 4 above, " 'the lie' *par excellence,* the last and crowning deception practiced by Satan in passing off the Lawless One as God."[45] The delusion which Satan had deliberately fostered is now divinely confirmed in them since they voluntarily accepted it and desired it.

The ultimate purpose of God in making them reap the consequences of their own choice of sin is "that they all might be judged who believed not the truth, but had pleasure in unrighteousness." While the Greek word "be judged" is neutral, the context indicates that an adverse verdict will be pronounced upon them. In the original *all* stands before the double participial designation of those judged; it stresses the comprehensiveness of the judgment for the class indicated. The subjects of the judgment are designated both negatively and positively. The one article with the two participles indicates that one class is in view. Negatively, they "believed not the truth," never as a definite act entered into a personal relationship of trust and obedience to "the truth," the gospel revelation. *But,* a strong adversative particle, introduces the damning positive characteristic; they "had pleasure in unrighteousness," "were well-pleased with the unrighteousness," (Rotherham). The deception of the man of sin found a ready response in such men. Their willful rejection of the truth had resulted in the love of evil; evil had become their good. A moral perversion of character had taken place. He who will not accept and obey the truth will inevitably find his delight in unrighteousness.

19

THANKSGIVING AND PRAYER

2:13-17 But we are bound to give thanks to God always for you, brethren beloved of the Lord, for that God chose you from the beginning unto salvation in sanctification of the Spirit and belief of the truth: (14) whereunto he called you through our gospel, to the obtaining of the glory of our Lord Jesus Christ. (15) So then, brethren, stand fast, and hold the traditions which ye were taught, whether by word, or by epistle of ours.

(16) Now our Lord Jesus Christ himself, and God our Father who loved us and gave us eternal comfort and good hope through grace, (17) comfort your hearts and establish them in every good work and word.

THIS BRIEF but weighty section seems best regarded as transitional in position and function. It would seem to serve as an insert between the didactic and hortatory portions of the epistle. The section readily divides into three parts; it contains a thanksgiving for God's choice of the readers (vv. 13-14), a brief exhortation to them because of the choice (v. 15), and a prayer for them as God's chosen (vv. 16-17).

A. THANKSGIVING FOR GOD'S CHOICE OF THEM
(vv. 13-14)

The particle *de,* here rendered "But," may have an adversative force. Those who accept the adversative force here usually find a contrast between *we* and the doomed of the preceding verses. But for the emphatic form to be pertinent, the contrast should rather be between the Thessalonians and the doomed, or the *we* must be expanded in meaning to include all Christians. The context, however, seems more clearly to restrict the first personal pronoun to the writers. More probably the *de* is transitional in force, intended to mark the resumption of the thanksgiving with which the epistle began (1:3). The fact that with slight variations Paul repeats the opening words employed to express their thanksgiving seems intentional to mark the resumption. The transitional force of the particle may be indicated by rendering "Now." The writers state the character of their thanksgiving (v. 13a) and the grounds for their thanksgiving (vv. 13b-14).

320

1. Character of the Thanksgiving (v. 13*a*)

The assertion, "we are bound to give thanks to God always for you," repeats with some rearrangement the opening words of 1:3. Here the separately expressed first personal pronoun (*hēmeis*) makes *we*, Paul and his colleagues, strongly emphatic.* The writers stress that personally they feel a strong obligation to give thanks for the readers. Also the two words rendered "we are bound to give thanks" (*opheilomen eucharistein*) are now written in reverse order. In 1:3 the infinitive, "to give thanks," was placed forward to stress the nature of the duty, while here the verb "we are bound" is placed first to bring out their sense of continued obligation. They *always* give thanks "to God" (*tō theō*), the true God whom the missionaries made known to the Thessalonians. They feel obligated to thank Him because of all that He has wrought in the readers.

Their thanksgiving is specifically "for you," now affectionately addressed by the rich appositional designation, "brethren beloved of the Lord." In 1 Thessalonians 1:4 a nearly identical form of address was used, "brethren beloved of God." There they were designated as the objects of the abiding love of "God," here of "the Lord." That "Lord" here means "the Lord Jesus Christ" is clear from the following verses where He is distinguished from the Father. This change in the person said to love them is evidence that for Paul the two designations were equivalent. The reference to the Lord Jesus (2:8) here as the one loving them seems due to the foregoing picture of Him as the invincible Judge of evil men. Men may hate and persecute them, but they can take courage from the fact that they are the objects of the love of the Lord who will triumph over all evil. Frame holds that this paragraph is specifically designed to encourage the faint-hearted at Thessalonica.[1]

2. Grounds for the Thanksgiving (vv. 13*b*-14)

The conjunction rendered "for that" (*hoti*) may be taken as introducing the subject matter of the thanksgiving or the reason for it. Views as to its force here vary.† That verses 13*b*-14 state the contents of their thanksgiving may be accepted, but the very formulation of the statement conveys weighty reasons for their feeling of obligation to give thanks. The causal meaning is in full harmony with the context.

Their statement, elaborating the writers' assurance concerning the readers, is a beautiful picture of the reality concerning genuine disciples.

---

*Conybeare, Montgomery, and Way limit the reference to Paul by rendering "I", the plural being taken as an editorial "we."

†Our versions have varied renderings: "for that"—Rotherham; "that"—Darby, Young; "for"—20th Cent; "because"—Conybeare, Goodspeed, Lattey, Moffatt, Montgomery, Way, Weymouth, Williams, Berkeley, NEB, NASB, RSV. Phillips does not render the conjunction.

Denney calls it "a system of theology in miniature."[2] It sets forth a salvation that reaches from eternity past into eternity future. The writers are thankful because of the divine choice (v. 13b) and calling (v. 14) of the readers.

a) BECAUSE OF THE DIVINE CHOICE (v. 13b). The writers give thanks because "God chose you from the beginning unto salvation." The entire statement has *God* as it subject, made emphatic by being placed after the verb and the object (*heilato humas ho theos*). The middle voice of the verb, "He chose you for Himself," brings out God's personal interest in the choice, while the aorist indicative states the choice as a past fact. Their salvation is entirely due to the divine initiative. This is the only place where Paul uses this verb (*haireomai*) of divine election. His usual words are *proorizō*, "to mark out beforehand" (Eph 1:5) and *eklegomai*, "to pick out or select for oneself" (Eph 1:4; see the cognate noun in 1 Th 1:4). But since the verb used here occurs in the Septuagint of God's choice of Israel (Deu 26:18; compound form in Deu 7:6-7), Morris well regards its use here as "no more than a stylistic variant."[3] The term used here well brings out "the sovereign pleasure and preference which guided the choice."[4]

God chose them "from the beginning" (*ap' archēs*). Some interpreters, like Findlay, understand the meaning to be from the beginning of the preaching of the gospel at Thessalonica. He holds that in the light of 1 Thessalonians 1:4 their election "practically and to human view" took place when the missionaries preached to them and asserts that "the Apostles speak here in the language of grateful remembrance, not of theological contemplation."[5] Against this view Hogg and Vine point out that "Paul does not elsewhere speak of the election of men unto salvation taking place in time; what takes place in time is God's call, see next verse."[6] If he had meant the beginning of the work at Thessalonica, Paul probably would have added a defining genitive, "of the gospel," as he does in Philippians 4:15. Riggenbach also sees a time problem in this view, for it "would imply that the time, when Paul wrote, was already considerably remote from the time when the church was founded."[7] Neil further opposes the temporal meaning by remarking, "Paul is not here indulging in platitudes, as it would be to take 'in the beginning' as meaning 'in the beginning of the Christian Mission.' He is setting out a theology as profound as that of Rom. viii. 28-30."[8]

The view that "from the beginning" means "from eternity past" is in full accord with Paul's teaching concerning the pretemporal beginning of the program of redemption (1 Co 2:7; Eph 1:4; 2 Ti 1:9; Titus 1:2). The readers are assured that their election was no recent innovation; they were included in God's plan from the dateless past.

The reading "from the beginning" is uncertain; there is strong evidence for reading "firstfruits" (*aparchēn*).‡ This reading makes good sense and would be in harmony with Paul's practice of speaking of the first converts in a province as "the firstfruits" of their countrymen (Ro 16:5; 1 Co 16:15).§ Against this reading is the fact that Paul never elsewhere uses the term in connection with election or choosing. It also labors under the historical difficulty that the Thessalonian believers were not the "firstfruits" of the province of Macedonia. That honor belonged to the Philippians. "Firstfruits" is admittedly the harder reading, and textual criticism may appeal to this as an argument in its favor as the original reading, but it does not suit the context as well as "from the beginning" in the pretemporal sense. It is but logical that those whom God called unto salvation through the preaching of the gospel (v. 14) had been previously chosen by Him.

God chose the Thessalonians "unto salvation," with the purpose that salvation in its fullest meaning might be realized in them. It is deliverance from sin and all its consequences, the very opposite of the doom befalling the lost at Christ's return (2:8-12). (See further discussion under 1 Th 5:9-10).

The salvation unto which they were chosen does not operate automatically; the electing purpose of God is carried out "in sanctification of the Spirit and belief of the truth." None are chosen apart from them. The preposition *in* (*en*) may denote means or sphere. Perhaps its force here may best be conveyed by rendering "in connection with," for the realization of salvation is inseparably connected with "sanctification of the Spirit and belief of the truth." The two aspects are closely connected, being under the government of one preposition.

Sanctification (*hagiasmos*) denotes not the state but the process of being detached from the world to become increasingly conformed to the character of Christ (see comments under 1 Th 4:3). The genitive "of the Spirit" (*pneumatos*) is capable of two different interpretations. It is usually taken as a subjective genitive, meaning that the sanctification is being wrought in them *by* the Holy Spirit. This is in full harmony with the office work of the Spirit (Ro 5:5; 8:2, 9; 1 Co 6:11; Gal 3:3; 5:16). But others, like Lenski, insist that it is objective, meaning that "it is our spirit that is sanctified."[9] Under this view it is assumed rather than stated that the Holy Spirit is the Sanctifier. It is held that if the Holy Spirit were meant, Paul would have prefixed the definite article. But the absence of

---

‡Westcott and Hort, as well as Souter, place this reading in their margin, but Nestle and the Bible Societies' text put it as the accepted reading but with acknowledgment that the other may be the original.
§Our English versions use the plural, but the Greek is always singular.

the definite article does not prove that the Holy Spirit cannot be meant.||
It is held that the objective genitive is supported by the fact that the genitive in the next clause is clearly objective. But Paul's usage of the genitive
does not support the claim that both genitives must be objective. Paul's use
of the genitive is not that regular. Against the objective meaning is the fact
that in 1 Thessalonians 5:23 Paul prays that their whole spirit, soul, and
body may be sanctified, not just their spirit. We accept the statement
as a definite reference to the Holy Spirit. So viewed we have here "all
three Persons of the Trinity: Thanks to the Father for those who are
beloved by the Son and sanctified by the Spirit."[10] But this is not a formal
statement of the doctrine of the Trinity but rather a recognition of the
experiential working of the members of the Trinity in our salvation; the
trinitarian experience gave rise to the formulation of the doctrine.

Closely connected with the divine aspect in the realization of their
salvation is the human, "and belief of the truth" (*kai pistei alētheias*),
"and through your faith in the truth" (Williams). "Truth" is without the
article, denoting that what is believed has the quality of truth, not de-
luding error. This sets them in contrast to those who refused to believe the
truth but loved unrighteousness (v. 12). "Belief" here does not mean the
initial reception of that which is true but rather "that habit of faith by
which one adheres to the truth."[11] The divine choice unto salvation becomes operative through our truth-accepting faith.

Paul's double statement gives recognition to the interaction of the
human and the divine in salvation. Scripture accepts and stresses both.
Concerning this combination of the divine and the human, Denney writes,

> It is impossible to separate these two things, or to define their relation to
> each other. Sometimes the first seems to condition the second; sometimes
> the order is reversed. The two, as it were, interpenetrate each other. If
> the Spirit stood alone, man's mind would be baffled, his moral freedom
> would be taken away; if the reception of the truth were everything, a
> cold, rationalistic type of religion would supplant the ardour of the New
> Testament Christian.[12]

b) Because of the divine call (v. 14). The divine choice of them unto
salvation in the eternal past received its historical commencement in the
lives of the Thessalonian believers by mean's of God's call through the
gospel. "Whereunto" (*eis ho*), "unto which thing," looks back to the entire preceding statement; the call given them was with a view to the
realization of the divine choice. "He called you through our gospel"
records a specific past act of God in the lives of the readers. His call to
them was efficacious; it was accepted by the Thessalonians. It took place
during the preaching of the missionaries at Thessalonica and was effected

|| See 1 Pe 1:2 where "Spirit" is without the article but where the mention of the
Father and the Son makes it clear that the Holy Spirit is intended.

"through our gospel," the good news which the missionaries had appropriated as their own. (Cf. 1 Th 1:5). Their preaching had an essential place in the fulfillment of God's purpose for them (Ro 10:13-15). Paul well knew that the faithful preaching of the gospel was God's means for realizing in time what He had planned in eternity. Let preachers of the Word appreciate the high function committed to them!

This salvation, grounded in the divine choice in the eternal past and initiated in present personal experience through the call of the gospel, looks forward to a glorious culmination, "to the obtaining of the glory of our Lord Jesus Christ." "To" (*eis*) means "with a view to" and designates the end in view, the ultimate goal of the salvation, "the obtaining of the glory." "Obtaining" (*peripoiēsin*) denotes the act of acquiring or taking possession of something, the added genitive, "of the glory," indicating the thing to be obtained. In 1 Thessalonians 5:9 the expression "unto the obtaining of salvation" is synonymous as denoting salvation in its completeness. Their call did not immediately transport them to glory but set them on the way to the obtaining of "the glory of our Lord Jesus Christ." "Glory" is the splendor and honor which now belong to our Lord as exalted at the right hand of God. That glory will be shared with His saints at His return (1:10-12). In 1 Thessalonians 2:12 Paul told the Thessalonians that God was calling them "into his own kingdom and glory," while here he associates that future glory with Christ. This ascription of glory to Christ, which Isaiah 48:11 declares Jehovah will not share with another, is clear testimony to Paul's belief in the deity of Christ. The full confessional title "our Lord Jesus Christ" stresses the character of the one whose glory they will share.

B. EXHORTATION TO THOSE CHOSEN (v. 15)

However lofty the sweep of Paul's thoughts may be, he always brings his readers back to the realities of daily responsibility. "So then" (*ara oun*) draws a logical practical deduction from what has just been said. True believers recognize that the divine choice and calling demand the cooperation of the called. The appeal is directed to those who are accepted as *brethren*.

Two general exhortations are given, "Stand fast and hold the traditions." Both verbs are present imperatives setting forth continuing duties, "continue to stand firm and keep a tight grip on the teachings" (Williams).

"Stand fast" has an intensive force, "stand firm, be steadfast." The positive command looks back to the negative appeal in 2:2 not to be quickly shaken or agitated. The verb *hold* basically means "to exert strength," whether physical or mental. The readers are called upon to take a vigorous hold and keep a firm grip on "the traditions which ye were taught." They already possess these traditions and have the duty to retain them. The command is doubtless given in view of the new teaching concerning the day of the Lord that was exciting them.

The "traditions," literally, "the things handed on," denote the teachings passed on from teacher to pupil. The New Testament makes reference to three kinds of tradition. There were the rabbinical "traditions of the elders" (Mk 7:3-9; Mt 15:2-6), the oral teachings of the Pharisees which had received a monstous and harmful development by the time of Jesus. There was the heretical teaching seeking to invade the Colossian church which Paul castigates as being "after the tradition of men" (Col 2:8), a spurious teaching of purely human origin. Paul's words here refer to the third type of tradition in Scripture, the true God-given gospel message. His reference here is to the varied Christian doctrines which the Thessalonians had been taught, while in 3:6 the term denotes the instructions concerning everyday conduct which they had received. Their conversion had been accompanied by definite doctrinal instruction by the missionaries. Clearly Paul believed in grounding his converts in the faith they had accepted. Bicknell remarks, "There never was a time when Christianity was an undogmatic religion."[13]

Imbedded in the basic meaning of the word tradition lies the thought of the derivative nature of the gospel message. It was a message which Paul had received from the Lord and passed on to his converts (1 Co 15:1-3). The gospel was not the product of his own fertile imagination but was a divine revelation to him. It was the origin of the message they had received that assured its validity. Because the message given them came from God they must cling to it and not allow any other teaching to displace it.

The apostolic message was communicated by two means, "whether by word, or by epistle of ours." The pronoun *ours* qualifies both nouns. Their teaching was given either orally or in writing. They had received the oral teaching while the missionaries were still with them; the mention of "epistle" seems a clear reference to our 1 Thessalonians, although the expression is quite general. Clearly Paul expected the Thessalonians to accept his letters and his oral instructions with equal authority. In 2:2 he warned them against any attempt to misuse his authority through either means.

The Thessalonians possessed apostolic traditions that were both oral and written, but the same is not true today. Today the apostolic teaching is preserved for us in the New Testament. If it could be shown that the spoken traditions of the apostles had come down to us with the same undoubted mark of genuineness as their written traditions, they would be equally authoritative for us today. But by the very nature of things this is impossible. Any supposed apostolic teachings perpetuated on the authority of subsequent ages cannot be accepted as having the authority of their authenticated writings.

C. PRAYER FOR THE CHOSEN (vv. 16-17)

The conjunction *Now* (*de*) is transitional, marking the passing from exhortation to prayer. Paul well knew that if his teaching and exhortation were to be effective they must be accompanied by divine working in the readers.

The indication of the one to whom their prayer is addressed, "our Lord Jesus Christ himself, and God our Father," is similar to that in 1 Thessalonians 3:11. The pronoun translated *himself* (*autos*) again stands emphatically at the head of the sentence and has a similar intensive force, "Now may *he*," the one to whom their petitions are directed, grant their requests. But now the two members of the Godhead addressed are named in reverse order, "our Lord Jesus Christ" standing before "God our Father" (cf. Gal 1:1; 2 Co 13:14). The confessional *our* applied to both the Son and the Father indicates that their prayer is not addressed to a deity strange to them; an experiential relationship existed between them.

The reason for the reverse order here used in the prayer-address is not clear, perhaps because of the prominence given the Son in the preceding paragraph. The variation in the order shows that Paul did not regard the Son as inferior to the Father as touching His Godhood. Milligan notes the order as "another striking example of the equal honour ascribed to the Son with the Father throughout these Epistles."[14]

The designation, "who loved us and gave us eternal comfort and good hope," by its position seems to be limited to "God our Father." But this is not certain since the initial *autos* may also be extended to include the Father and the verbs in verse 17 are in the singular. It seems that the whole construction is intended to stress the unity of the persons in the Godhead. Clearly the two persons are conceived of as one in their action (cf. Jn 10:30; 12:45; 14:9). It is through the Son that the Father has revealed Himself (Mt 11:27). Whether the appositional additional is taken as referring to both the Son and the Father, or to the Father alone, as seems grammatically more probable, under either view the asserted actions were divine in their origin.

"Who loved us and gave us" translates two aorist participles under the government of one article; the two acts are closely related, the second being the outcome of the first. While the aorists may be viewed as constative, simply stating the summary fact, more probably they point back to specific events, those historical manifestations with which the gospel originated. The supreme manifestation of the Father's love was made at the cross, and upon the basis of that event His gifts are bestowed. *Us*, the named objects of the divine love, means both writers and readers and all of God's people. Had Paul merely been thinking of events at Thessalonica in connection with the mission there he would have written *you* instead.

Two of God's tremendous gifts are named, "eternal comfort and good hope." Both nouns are without an article to point out their quality. "Eternal comfort" is the present possession of believers and stands in abiding contrast to the transcient, fleeting "comfort" which this world offers. "Comfort" (see discussion under 1 Th 2:3) here may either mean "consolation, the alleviation of grief," or "encouragement." If the former meaning is accepted here the reference is to the divinely imparted consolation which the trials and sorrows of this world cannot exhaust. But since the gift is "eternal," not limited to this present existence, it seems best to accept the meaning of encouragement. It gives us good courage in the face of present distress. In reality both thoughts are included, "comforting encouragement."

The gift of "good hope" is likewise a present possession but it looks forward to the blessings connected with Christ's return. The hope is well founded because it is based on the sure promises of God. This hope, an essential feature of a well-rounded Christian life (1 Th 1:10), is in its very nature and effect *good*, beneficial in its impact. It cheers and sustains the believer who cherishes it.

"Through grace" connects not with *hope* but rather with *gave* and denotes the sphere or element in which these gifts are realized. They are not given on the basis of human merit but bestowed as wholly undeserved, on the basis of the redemptive work of Christ.

Two prayer requests for the readers are made, "comfort your hearts and establish them." Both verbs are aorist optatives expressing the prayer-wish and are constative in force, summarily stating the blessings requested. The request for their comfort looks back to the alarming excitement concerning the day of the Lord (2:1-2). They pray that their *hearts*, the inner core of their very being (see discussion under 1 Th 2:4), may be comforted and encouraged. They also pray that God may *establish*, make their hearts firm and stable, bringing their whole Christian life to full maturity. This will be reflected "in every good work and word," in deed and speech. The order "work and word" is a reversal of Paul's usual order (Ro 15:18; 2 Co 10:11; Col 3:17) and suggests that in a mature Christian life, practice comes before precept. *Every* stresses the inclusiveness and *good* the beneficial character of these two activities.

The exhortations and prayer requests were broad and general in scope. They well prepare the readers for the more specific exhortations which follow.

20

EXHORTATIONS

3:1-15 Finally, brethren, pray for us, that the word of the Lord may run and be glorified, even as also *it is* with you; (2) and that we may be delivered from unreasonable and evil men; for all have not faith. (3) But the Lord is faithful, who shall establish you, and guard you from the evil *one*. (4) And we have confidence in the Lord touching you, that ye both do and will do the things which we command. (5) And the Lord direct your hearts into the love of God, and into the patience of Christ.

(6) Now we command you, brethren, in the name of our Lord Jesus Christ, that ye withdraw yourselves from every brother that walketh disorderly, and not after the tradition which they received of us. (7) For yourselves know how ye ought to imitate us: for we behaved not ourselves disorderly among you; (8) neither did we eat bread for nought at any man's hand, but in labor and travail, working night and day, that we might not burden any of you: (9) not because we have not the right, but to make ourselves an ensample unto you, that ye should imitate us. (10) For even when we were with you, this we commanded you, if any will not work, neither let them eat. (11) For we hear of some that walk among you disorderly, that work not at all, but are busybodies. (12) Now them that are such we command and exhort in the Lord Jesus Christ, that with quietness they work, and eat their own bread. (13) But ye, brethren, be not weary in well-doing. (14) And if any man obeyeth not our word by this epistle, note that man, that ye have no company with him, to the end that he may be ashamed. (15) And *yet* count him not as an enemy, but admonish him as a brother.

THIS CONCLUDING SECTION of the epistle is hortatory in character. It is introduced with "Finally" (*to loipon*), "as to the rest" (Young), which looks forward to the practical advisory matters that were still on the apostle's mind. Paul uses the expression to introduce practical exhortations, but it does not promise that the letter is about to end. (See comments under 1 Th 4:1). Neither does it imply that what still remains to be said is unimportant. It is quite clear that this chapter deals with one of the primary reasons for writing the letter.

The section falls into three parts. In verses 1-2 the writers request the prayers of the readers, while in verses 3-5 they express their personal confidence in the continued progress of their converts. But clearly these matters form a characteristic Pauline introduction to the important but unpleasant matter of the needed disciplining of the disorderly members in the Thessalonian church (vv. 6-15). This matter is of primary importance and is dealt with forcefully at some length.

A. REQUEST FOR THEIR PRAYERS (vv. 1-2)

The writers state their request for the prayers of the readers (v. 1a) and formulate two petitions to be offered on their behalf (vv. 1b-2).

1. Request Stated (v. 1a)

"Brethren, pray for us" repeats a request already made in 1 Thessalonians 5:25. The verb used here before the address, "brethren," is emphatic by its position in the original. The present tense again calls for continued prayer on their behalf. The order and force of the original may be reproduced in awkward English, "Be praying, brethren, concerning us." "For us" (*peri hēmōn*) urges that the Thessalonians are to center their prayers around the writers, making them the specific subject of their prayers.

Such requests for the prayers of his readers are characteristic of Paul (Ro 15:30-31; Eph 6:18-19; Col 4:3; Phile 22). His reference to the results of such prayers (2 Co 1:11; Phil 1:19) reveal that Paul was deeply convinced of the power of prayer. His strong sense of his continual need for divine empowerment motivated his efforts to enlist the prayers of others on his behalf.

2. Petitions Indicated (vv. 1b-2)

The writers give expression to two prayer requests, each followed by an additional comment.

Their first request is "that the word of the Lord may run and be glorified." "The word of the Lord" (as in 1 Th 1:8) denotes the gospel, Christ's good news. "The Lord," as usual in these epistles, means Jesus Christ. Milligan, in view of its frequent occurrences, remarks that it is "entitled to be regarded as the distinctive Name of these Epistles."[*,1] The title indicates the authoritative nature of "the word," which is here personified by the verbs employed. "Run" and "be glorified" seem to picture it almost as an independent force sweeping victoriously through the land. Both verbs are in the present tense; they are not to ask for a single striking triumph but its continual progress, that it "may be running and gaining glory" (Rotherham). *Run,* apparently a metaphor drawn from the race track, shows Paul's love of athletic figures, but possibly it is

---

*It occurs 22 times with or without the article and "as in the vastly preponderating number of instances it can only apply to the Son, it is better so to refer it throughout" (George Milligan, *St. Paul's Epistles to the Thessalonians,* p. 137).

an "unconscious quotation" of Psalm 147:15.[2] The metaphor points out "the living, active nature of the word in the Apostles' eyes."[3] The thought is that of its swift advance in its onward course, not necessarily meaning a race unencumbered by obstacles.

The second verb, "and be glorified" (*kai doxazētai*), records the result of the first. *And* marks the consecutive relationship. The verb is not middle, "glorifying itself," but passive, "and be extolled" (Weymouth). The Word is "glorified," honored and admired for its inherent qualities, when men see a demonstration of its transforming power in the lives of believers.

The added comment, "even as also it is with you," is a laudatory acknowledgment of the reception that the readers gave the apostolic message. The preaching of the gospel at Thessalonica had produced rapid and arresting results (1 Th 1:5-2:12). "Even as" denotes an exact parallel and implies that events in their own case offer a pattern of what they are to pray for elsewhere. The "also" gently reminds them that similar receptions have taken place elsewhere. "With you" (*pros humas*) suggests that these results were produced at Thessalonica when they were brought face to face with the gospel. This comparative phrase shows that "run" means "move swiftly" rather than "unencumbered by obstacles" since the gospel made a swift advance at Thessalonica but was bitterly opposed. Since Paul writes no verb, as shown by the italics, he may have in mind not only events while he was there but also conditions at the time of writing.

Their second prayer request is, "and that we may be delivered from unreasonable and evil men." The first petition was for the success of the gospel, this for the safety of the messengers. The first was quite impersonal, this is distinctly personal, *we* denoting the writers directly. *And* indicates the relationship between the two requests. That this petition reveals Paul's human instinct of self-preservation need not be denied. Paul was not immune to the natural "shrinking of the flesh from the dangers which awaited him."[4] Nor need we blame him for asking for prayer for deliverance from his enemies. But his motive is not personal ease but the continued proclamation of the gospel. Such deliverance was needed for his effectiveness in diffusing the good news. The request also served to remind the readers that the writers too were facing hardship because of their loyalty to the gospel.

The verb *delivered*, or "rescued," is in the aorist tense and denotes a definite occasion, deliverance from an actually existing peril when their enemies seem to have them in their grip. The writers were in a difficult situation. These enemies are described as "unreasonable and evil men" (*tōn atopōn kai ponērōn anthrōpōn*). The definite article points to a specific, well-known class of assailants characterized by the two adjectives. The first adjective, *unreasonable*, does not denote that they are irrational. Its root meaning is "place-less, out of place," and is usually applied to things. Only here in the New Testament is it applied to people. When used in an ethical sense it denotes that which is "improper," hence, "outrageous, monstrous," and so "unrighteous." In the papyri it is used of outrages against property.[5] When used of people it denotes men capable of wicked, outrageous, harmful conduct. The companion adjective, *evil*, is more than passive badness, but rather active malice. It pictures the vicious, destructive disposition of these enemies. The first adjective describes their conduct, the second their character.

This picture of the enemies seems to point clearly to the fanatical Jewish opponents at Corinth.[6] The Thessalonians had personal experience with such antagonists (Ac 17:5-9); they would readily understand the seriousness of the threat. Paul had further experience with such bitter opponents at Berea (Ac 17:13-15), and even as he was writing this letter the Jews who rejected his message were revealing the same threatening attitude at Corinth. The attack against Paul launched by them as described in Acts 18:12-17 doubtless came later than this letter, but it was simply the open explosion of a hostility that had been gathering force for some time.

"For all have not faith," or "for the faith is not of all" (Young), explains the existence of these enemies. Their hostility is due to their lack of faith in the gospel. There lies the real source of their vicious reaction. The definite article with *faith*, "the faith," denotes the Christian faith. The reference is apparently not to the body of Christian teaching constituting "the faith" but to that attitude of receptivity which the gospel demands. Clearly these enemies are non-Christians. That the faith is not "of all," not possessed by all, is a mournful understatement. The meaning is that there are many who do not accept the faith. "The phrase is a reminder that, however successful the gospel may be at certain places, there are still those who do not accept it."[7]

The comment appended to the first petition spoke of the reception of the gospel; here the comment mournfully acknowledges the fact of its widespread rejection. It is a recognition of the fact that the gospel produces both a positive and a negative reaction when preached in power.

B. CONFIDENCE CONCERNING THEIR PROGRESS
(vv. 3-5)

After the writers' prayer request on their own behalf, their thoughts again revert to their beloved converts. The safety and progress of the readers was a matter of vital concern to them. But their feeling toward them is not one of frustration and confusion but of confidence and assurance. Their confidence is grounded in the Lord's faithfulness toward them (v. 3) and the assurance of the readers' obedience to the commands given them (v. 4). This confidence is undergirded by further prayer for them (v. 5).

1. Faithfulness of the Lord Toward Them (v. 3)

But (*de*) marks the transition to a contrasted truth. From the depressing fact of man's lack of faith the thought turns to the cheering truth that "the Lord is faithful." The abrupt transition is suggested by placing two similar sounding words in juxtaposition in the original: "for not of all the faith [*pistis*]. But faithful [*pistos*] is the Lord." Such a word play is common to Paul. This contrast between faithless men and the faithful Lord assures the readers that in spite of the wicked and pernicious opposition of satanic forces the Lord's purpose and plan will ultimately triumph. Swete comments that "S. Paul ever delights to contrast the Divine perfections with human frailty and sin: comp. Eph. ii. 3, 4; 2 Tim. iv. 16, 17."[8] "The Lord" Jesus, the Ruler and Defender of His people, will always show Himself *faithful*, trustworthy and dependable, in fulfilling His promises and maintaining His covenantal commitments. The reality of His faithfulness is emphasized by the insertion of the verb *is* which might have been omitted (cf. 1 Co 1:9; 10:13; 2 Co 1:18). Paul usually writes "God is faithful" but the change to "the Lord" here is in harmony with his stress on the Lord Jesus in these epistles. Plummer comments, "Fidelity to His word is in O.T. a special attribute of God; Deut. vii. 8, 9; Is. xlix. 7; and it is here transfered to Christ."[9]

A double assurance, based on the Lord's faithfulness, is given the readers, "who shall establish you, and guard you from the evil one." It is gracious encouragement from the pastoral heart of the writers. After the brief mention of their own plight, the thoughts of the writers readily revert to the safety of the readers.

The assurance that the Lord "shall establish" them, make them firm and solid, connects with the prayer in 2:17. What was stated there as a prayer is now expressed as an assurance; the faithful Lord will grant the prayer. Their excited reaction to the teaching that the day of the Lord was present (2:2) made clear their need for such inner stability.

"And guard you from the evil one" continues "the ring of magnificent confidence."[10] Only here are the two verbs "establish" and "guard" joined in the New Testament. The first promises their inward stabilization, while the second assures that they will be protected from outward assault. Both verbs are future and may be accepted as denoting continued action.

It is the constant working of the Lord that secures the inward grounding and outward safety of God's people.

The verb *guard* conveys a military image, implying conflict and armed protection again violent attack. They are promised safety "from the evil one" (*apo tou ponērou*). Grammatically, the expression may be either neuter, "from the evil," or "all that is evil" (Phillips), or masculine, "the evil one," the devil. The context must decide the meaning. The same ambiguity appears in the identical expression in the Lord's Prayer (Mt 6:13). Either makes good sense. If it is neuter, evil is conceived of generally, as one collective mass; if it is masculine, evil is thought of as exhibited in its personal head.

The masculine is more in harmony with the context. It places the victorious Lord in direct antithesis with the evil one. It marks the contrast between the Lord who protects and Satan who seeks to harm. This agrees with the problem pictured in the second chapter, where the conflict unquestionably was personal. Findlay observes, "The conflict of the Church and of the Christian life is not a matter of principles alone and abstract forces; it is a personal encounter, and behind all *forces* there are living wills."[11] The masculine is also more probable here in view of its frequency as over against the neuter in the New Testament. Lightfoot finds that there are only two unquestionable instances of the neuter in the New Testament (Lk 6:45; Ro 12:9) but ten instances where the masculine is certainly employed (Mt 5:37; 13:19, 38, 49; Eph 6:16; 1 Jn 2:13, 14; 3:12; 5:18, 19). The masculine, making evil personal, is in full harmony with the New Testament teaching that evil is not merely an impersonal force but is rather the direct result of the malicious machinations of the devil. Lightfoot further points out that external evidence is strongly in favor of the masculine interpretation.†[12]

2. Confidence in Their Obedience (v. 4)

"And" (*de*) marks the transition to a further point which assures confidence concerning the readers. While they entrust the safety of the flock to the protecting Lord, the writers give tactful recognition to the obedience of the readers. It is another reminder that the work of the Lord in the believer does not leave the believer passive. In the grand plan of man's salvation, divine empowerment and human effort are united.

"We are confident" compliments the readers with the assurance that the writers have a settled persuasion concerning their obedience. It is

†J. B. Lightfoot observes that "among Greek writers there is absolute unanimity on this point," and that "the evidence of early versions and of the Eastern Liturgies points decisively to the masculine rendering." He notes that the Latin Fathers are divided on the point, but points to the influence of Augustine for the wide acceptance of the neuter (*Notes on the Epistles of St. Paul*, p. 126).

another skillful touch intended to win the voluntary compliance of the readers in regard to the difficult matter about to be discussed.

They have this confidence "in the Lord touching you" (*en kuriō eph' humas*). It is possible to connect the word *confidence* with either of these prepositional phrases. If connected with "touching you" the meaning is "we have confidence in you because of your relationship to the Lord." Thus Williams renders, "We have confidence in you through the Lord." But more probably it is to be closely connected with "in the Lord." The word order favors this connection. The writers hold this confidence as those who are "in the Lord," which may be accepted as the equivalent of Paul's favorite expression "in Christ." Their confidence is not in the reliability of human nature but rather in the Lord who will work this willingness in them to obey voluntarily the commands laid upon them. In thus renouncing trust in that which is merely human, Christian confidence "acquires the distinctive assurance of faith."[13] The writers hold this confidence "touching you," the Thessalonians personally. The preposition (*epi* with the accusative) pictures the confidence as directed toward and resting upon them as its object.

The stated substance of the confidence is "that ye both do and will do the things which we command." In the original "the things which we command" stands before the two verbs, "do and will do," thus drawing attention to the point of their obedience. The verb "we command" carries the thought of a message passed on to others from one in authority. (Cf. the cognate noun in 1 Th 4:2 and the verb in 4:11). The reference is not to mere suggestions or helpful advice but to binding orders. The present tense indicates that the reference is not to past injunctions given them. The things being commanded have reference not merely to the charge to pray for them (vv. 1-2) but specifically to the command to discipline the disorderly (vv. 6-15) which the writers already have in view. This forward look of the verb here is verified by the repetition of the very term in verses 6, 10, and 12 below.

This authoritative tone is softened by the gracious acknowledgment "that ye both do and will do" these things. It gives them full credit for their present performance and notes that they confidently expect this to continue. The writers have no occasion to question the loyal obedience of their converts and have no reason to doubt their ready compliance in the future.

3. Prayer for Their Growth (v. 5)

The difficulty of the demand being made causes the writers to break into another spontaneous prayer for the readers. It is the third prayer offered expressly for them in this brief epistle (1:11-12; 2:16-17). The conjunction rendered "And" (*de*) here seems to have a slightly adversative force, "but." It serves to introduce the fact that without the work of the Lord, disposing them to keep the commandments, the apostolic commands would prove quite ineffective.

The prayer is addressed to "the Lord," that is, the Lord Jesus. It is another of the comparatively rare instances of a prayer addressed directly to Jesus in the New Testament (cf. Acts 7:59). This fourth mention of "the Lord" in the first five verses of this section of the epistle underlines Paul's firm conviction of Christ's controlling presence in the lives of the saints in spite of the plots and passions of evil men and the present imperfections of the people of God.

The prayer offered for the readers is that the Lord may "direct your hearts into the love of God, and into the patience of Christ." The verb *direct* conveys the picture of opening up the way by the removal of obstacles so that the desired goal may be reached. Its New Testament usage implies that this is brought about by the divine providential controlling of human action. (See the verb in 1 Th 3:11.) The term implies that the Thessalonians have not yet reached the point which Paul would have them attain. The aorist tense summarily states the prayed-for action without indicating the process involved. Only as they are directed by the supreme guide will the goal be attained.

They pray that their "hearts," their inner being, may be directed "into the love of God, and into the patience of Christ." An experiential realization of this prayer will truly dispose them to carry out the apostolic commands.

In the expression "the love of God," the words "of God" may be interpreted as either an objective or subjective genitive.‡ As an objective genitive it means their love for God. In support of this view Gloag comments, "This love of God is the fulfilment of the Law; and hence the apostle prays that the Thessalonians may be directed into it as the source and essence of all acceptable obedience."[14] But other interpreters hold that in harmony with the prevailing sense of the phrase in Paul's writings, the genitive should be viewed as subjective, God's love for them. Then the prayer means "that they may be led to a fuller appreciation of the divine love as manifested in Christ."[15] But Lightfoot seems to be right when he insists that "the Apostles availed themselves, either consciously or unconsciously, of the vagueness or rather comprehensiveness of language, to express a great spiritual truth," and that both meanings

‡"We have the subjective genitive when the noun in the genitive *produces* the action, being therefore related *as subject* to the verbal idea of the noun modified," and the objective genitive "when the noun in the genitive *receives* the action, being thus related *as object* to the verbal idea contained in the noun modified" (H. E. Dana and Julius R. Mantey, *A Manual Grammar of the Greek New Testament*, pp. 78-79, italics in original).

"are so combined and interwoven, that it is very seldom possible, where the expression occurs, to separate the one from the other."[16] This gives us the comprehensive truth that God's love for us as it is experienced by us produces a reciprocal response of love in our hearts for Him. (Cf. 1 Jn 4:9-10). Only our love for God, produced and stimulated by our experience of His love for us, will motivate us to joyously obey the commandments of God.

They also pray that the readers may be directed "into the patience of Christ." Here again the genitive may be either objective or subjective. If objective, it means the patience which looks to Christ, hence "the patient waiting for Christ" (KJV). It is held that this is in harmony with the fact that "the dominant theme of both Epistles is the Second Coming of Christ. . . . They should learn patience in waiting for the great consummation. The chief purpose of our Epistle is to inculcate patience with that end in view."[17] Hauck, who holds that "the patience of Christ" here means "expectation of the Christ who will come again in glory," recognizes that in most New Testament passages patience "refers to the steadfast endurance of the Christian under the difficulties and tests of the present evil age."[18] Being a compound form, the word rendered "patience" (*hupomonēn*) has the root meaning of "remaining under, standing fast," and thus its prevailing significance is "steadfastness, endurance." This basic significance well suits the interpretation of the genitive as subjective, "the endurance of the Christ" (Rotherham). The use of the definite article with *Christ*, "the Christ" indicates that it is not the historical person Jesus that is thought of but rather the suffering Messiah as foreseen by the prophets and now known to believers. "The endurance of the Christ" thus may mean the endurance which the Messiah displayed (subjective genitive) or the endurance which He inspires in the hearts of His followers (genitive of the author). It seems best to accept that both truths are involved in the prayer here. The steadfast endurance which was displayed by the Master must challenge them to have this same characteristic wrought in their own lives.

C. DISCIPLINING OF THE DISORDERLY (vv. 6-15)

The transitional *de*, rendered "Now," marks the introduction of the topic for which the writers have been skillfully preparing the readers in the preceding verses. The space given to this subject and the peremptory manner of its treatment indicate its importance in the thinking of the writers. The harmony and spiritual welfare of the young church were at stake. Only the doctrinal error concerning the day of the Lord receives a fuller treatment (2:1-12). There is no expressed connection between the doctrinal error and the disorderly conduct of certain members. The doctrinal error apparently did not produce the practical problem, although it may well have stimulated its development. The problem of the disorderly was lightly touched upon in the first epistle (4:11-12; 5:14), but it is clear that the gentle proddings did not produce the desired results. Stronger measures are now required.

The discussion is opened with the express command to withdraw from the disorderly (v. 6) and two facts are cited which support the demand (vv. 7-10). Reference is made to the reports which show the need for the command (v. 11), an explicit order is given concerning the disorderly (v. 12), and instructions are appended to guide the faithful members (vv. 13-15).

1. Command to Withdraw from the Disorderly (v. 6)

The command is stated with a mingled tone of authority and affection, "we command you, brethren, in the name of our Lord Jesus Christ." The statement of the command which follows indicates that *you* is directed specifically to the sober majority who are asked to take disciplinary action against the disturbing minority. The affectionate address, *brethren*, appeals to their sense of duty as members of the spiritual brotherhood; the interests of the entire brotherhood are concerned. But the authoritative verb *command* stresses that what is now asked is not a suggestion which is open to debate or modification on their part, but is a binding order which they are expected to obey. In verse 4 above, the writers expressed their confidence that the Thessalonians were obeying their commands; now a command is given them to be obeyed.

The command is given "in the name of our Lord Jesus Christ." There is a tone of dignified formality, implying the gravity of the command. They speak "in the name of," as the official representatives and with the authority of, "our Lord Jesus Christ." The full confessional title lends dignity to His person, recalling all that believers acknowledge Him to be. Plummer remarks, "Again we have an expression (*in the name of the Lord*) which in the O.T. is used of Jehovah (Exod. v. 23; Lev. xix. 12; Deut. xviii. 22; Jer. xi. 21; etc.) transferred readily to Christ (I Cor. vi. 11; Eph. v. 20; Col. iii. 17, etc.)."[19] The Thessalonians themselves must carry out the disciplinary responsibility as those who acknowledge His lordship.

The specific command is "that ye withdraw yourselves from every brother that walketh disorderly." The treatment demanded here is sterner than that in 1 Thessalonians 5:14. There they were told, "Admonish the disorderly;" now the command is, "Withdraw yourselves from them." Since admonition has failed, social pressure in the form of a limited segregation must now be applied. The command is not to expel or excommunicate them, for it is assumed that the demanded action will make such a final step unnecessary.

The root meaning of the verb *withdraw* (*stellesthai*) was "to set or place," and came to mean "to bring together" as in the furling of sails, and then more generally it meant "to restrain, to check." In the middle voice it means "to draw or shrink back from" anything, whether from fear or some other motive. The present tense denotes that they are to make it their practice to withdraw themselves *from*, personally separate themselves from, the disorderly by withholding fellowship from them. They must continue "to hold aloof from" (Way) the offenders to impress upon them that their undesirable conduct produces a gap between themselves and the other members. This command implies that they were to be refused participation in the love feasts of the congregation as well as the Lord's Supper.

This treatment is to be accorded "every brother that walketh disorderly." The action does not deny that he is a *brother*, but his fault must be censured. "Every brother" indicates that these faulty members were not numerous, one here and one there, but the congregation as a whole was sound. The welfare of the brotherhood demanded that these brothers be subjected to the stern disapproval of the brethren. But no such discipline is to be exercised toward those that are without; it is the duty of the church to discipline its own members (1 Co 5:11-12).

A positive and negative description is given these individuals, every one "that walketh disorderly, and not after the tradition which they received." The present tense of the verb *walketh* denotes that it is a deliberate course of action. Their disorderly conduct is not an occasional lapse but a persistent practice.

In 1 Thessalonians 5:14 the "disorderly" were named with two other classes of individuals, the fainthearted and the weak, as needing brotherly attention. From the usage of the term it appeared that the reference was to individuals who were addicted to deliberate loafing. The context here confirms that significance of the term, but it is clear that more than mere idleness is involved. While neglecting their own daily labors, they were very active as busybodies (v. 11), interfering in the work of others. From verse 12 it is clear that while they did not work for a living, they expected to receive their livelihood from others.

The exact character of these loafers is not quite clear. They may simply be drones who expected the Christian community to support them. But more may be involved. De Boer suggests that they may indeed be would-be teachers in the church who

> had been infected with devious ideas about what constitutes true spirituality and Christian maturity. They had become enthusiasts and fanatics

339

in spiritual matters, laying aside their ordinary earning of a living, and were devoting themselves to prophesying, edifying their fellow Christians, and ministering to the spiritual needs which, according to them, were being neglected. For this they expected to receive support from the congregation.[20]

This may be reading more into the situation than was actually there, but it is clear that they were not just lazy loafers. They were very busy with their own intrusive activities.

The walk of these individuals is also negatively described as "not after the tradition which they received of us." "The tradition" points to the specific teaching which the missionaries had given their converts concerning everyday Christian conduct (cf. discussion under 2:15). They had not been left uninstructed on this important matter. This included not only all the oral teaching given them but also the instructions contained in the first epistle to them. The aorist tense of the verb "they received" simply records the past reception of the teaching without indicating the time element involved. On the basis of the verb used,§ Hogg and Vine suggest that this reception was rather a matter of the outward ear.[21] There is considerable manuscript variation concerning the subject of this verb.‖ The third person plural *they* is clearly a construction according to sense, referring to "every brother" which implies a number. An alternative reading, "ye received," has considerable manuscript support.# But this is probably a scribal change to get rid of the third person plural with the expressed singular subject. It is less likely that a scribe would change the smooth "ye received" to the irregular form used (*paralabosan*). If the original was "ye," meaning the whole Thessalonian church, then "they," the disorderly, also received it. If the true reading is *they*, as seems probable, there is direct reference to the fact that they are not acting in harmony with what they received. Their guilt is that they are not walking *after* (*kata* and the accusative), "down along, according to," the apostolic teaching. Christian conduct must be governed by guidelines set forth in the Word of God.

2. Facts Supporting the Command (vv. 7-10)

"For" introduces an explanatory justification for the command just given. The demand that they discipline the disorderly is warranted in view of the apostolic example (vv. 7-9) as well as the apostolic teaching

§*Paralambanō* rather than *dechomai*. Compare this with the discussion under 1 Th 2:13.

‖ Because of the grammatical discord between the singular "every brother" and the plural verb, a few ancient copyists changed the plural to the singular, "he received" (KJV). It has little manuscript support.

#It is received into their text by Westcott and Hort, also by Nestle; Souter and the Bible Societies text read "they received." All the editors indicate the alternative reading in their margins.

which the Thessalonians have received. It is confirmed by their deed and word.

a) APOSTOLIC EXAMPLE GIVEN THEM (vv. 7-9). In the first epistle the apostolic conduct at Thessalonica was delineated to refute enemy attacks (2:1-12). Now their example is used to support a demand given to their converts. The writers remind the readers of their personal knowledge of that example (v. 7*a*), the nature of the example given them (vv. 7*b*-8*b*), and the twofold purpose behind the example (vv. 8*c*-9).

(1) *Their knowledge of the example* (v. 7*a*). "For yourselves know" is another appeal, characteristic of the former letter (2:1-11; 3:3; 5:2), to the personal knowledge of the readers. Although the statement is addressed to the whole church, it is aimed at the disorderly members. The emphatic "yourselves" (*autoi*) underlines that they did possess the needed knowledge. It was common knowledge at Thessalonica and there could be no plea of ignorance. They really did not need to be told again.

They knew from personal observation "how ye ought to imitate us." In 1 Thessalonians 1:6 the Thessalonians' imitation of the apostolic example was joyfully recognized as a blessed reality; here the demand is for the steady practice of that example. "How" points to the manner of that practice, "by what kind of conduct." Their continued imitation (present tense) of the example set before them Paul does not regard as optional; it is a moral necessity, as indicated by his use of *ought* (*dei*) which is often translated "must." This may seem a daring demand to us but Paul was deeply convinced that the missionaries had left their converts a worthy model for their conduct. They had preached by their lives as well as their sermons. He could confidently say, "Be ye imitators of me, even as I also am of Christ" (1 Co 11:1).

(2) *Nature of the example* (vv. 7*b*-8*b*). "For" introduces the historical justification that their example was a trustworthy model. The essential features are briefly stated, both negatively and positively. This recital is clearly intended to establish the contrast between the missionaries' conduct and that of the disorderly. The negative aspect of their conduct receives a double statement, "we behaved not ourselves disorderly among you; neither did we eat bread for nought at any man's hand." The first is general; the second is particular.

"We behaved not ourselves disorderly among you" is a comprehensive negative assertion concerning the entire period that the missionaries labored at Thessalonica. The aorist with the negative (*ouk etaktēsamen*)**

**The verb *atakteō*, "to be disorderly," occurs only here in the New Testament. It is the practical equivalent of "walk disorderly," v. 11.

states the summary denial, "there was no disorder in our life among you" (Weymouth). It was a modest understatement, for their entire life while at Thessalonica had been a busy one, given to hard labor and willing service. There was no contradiction between their own conduct and what was demanded of their converts.

"Neither did we eat bread for nought at any man's hand" passes to a particular feature of the negative aspect of the example. The aorist tense again states the summary denial. "To eat bread" does not simply mean "to take a meal" but rather "to receive maintenance, to get a living." Paul does not mean that the missionaries never accepted a friendly invitation to a meal with one of their converts, but they did refuse to be dependent upon them for a living. They refused to receive support at any man's hand (*para tinos*), more literally, "from alongside of any one," the owner passing it on to them. They refused support "for nought" (*dōrean*), "as a gift," without cost to themselves. This adverb stands emphatically forward to stress the gratuitous nature of the support rejected. Mason comments, "There is a flavour of scorn in St. Paul's disclaimer of such a parasite's life."[22]

It is clear that the disorderly at Thessalonica did claim such support for themselves (v. 12). But on what basis their claim was advanced is not clear. Was it simply a matter of feeling that, as members of the church, the church owed them a living? Was their self-acclaimed poverty, although it was due to their indolence, advanced as a just claim upon the charitable funds of the church? Or did they claim that their "services," which Paul regarded as nothing but meddlesome activities in other people's affairs (v. 11), merited such support?

The positive aspect of the apostolic example is introduced by the strong adversative *but*, "but in labor and travail, working night and day."†† The words are almost a verbatim repetition of the description of the apostolic labors at Thessalonica in 1 Thessalonians 2:9. This positive portrayal of the apostolic conduct again forms a sharp contrast to the conduct of the disorderly brethren and was intentionally stressed to rebuke them and bring them to their senses.

(3) *Purpose behind the example* (vv. 8c-9). As related to their converts, the missionaries' purpose in providing themselves as an example of diligent self-support had both a negative and a positive aspect. Negatively, their purpose was "that we might not burden any of you." Their self-sacrificing labors were motivated by their personal concern not to put a financial burden upon their converts. In 1 Thessalonians 2:9 this aspect of the missionaries' conduct was recalled as evidence to refute any

††Some ancient manuscripts, instead of the genitive, "by night and by day," here have the accusative which would stress the uninterruptedness of their labor.

charge that their preaching was for personal profit. Here the reminder that they deliberately refrained from making financial demands upon their converts is intended to shame such unjustified demands being made by the disorderly.

But Paul is anxious that their practice of not taking pay for their work of preaching the gospel should not be misunderstood. He at once adds a restriction, "not because we have not the right." "Their working hard was not meant as a protest against the principle that ministers have a claim to maintenance; that principle is just; I Cor. ix. 3-14; I Tim. v. 18."[23] Paul was sensitive about his *right*, moral power or authority, to receive financial support from his missionary labors and insisted that the fact must not be forgotten. He is anxious that his own example shall not be used to deny that right to other workers. They must not make his practice into "a rule for other ministers in the future."[24] But Paul was equally insistent upon the fact that he had voluntarily waived this right. This reminder adds force to the rebuke to the disorderly: the missionaries have the moral right but have deliberately refused to use it, while the disorderly at Thessalonica do not have the legitimate claim yet insist on it.

The strong adversative *but* introduces the contrasting truth that the missionaries also had a positive purpose in working for their livelihood. They had a positive aim of training in mind for their converts, "to make ourselves an ensample unto you, that you should imitate us." They acted the way they did "in order that" (*hina*) "ourselves as an ensample we might hold forth unto you" (Rotherham). "Ourselves" stands emphatically forward to stress the personal nature of the *ensample* or pattern provided them. The singular number of the noun rendered "ensample" (*tupon*) does not prove that "Paul speaks of himself in the plural," as Whedon thinks, but rather indicates that the conduct of the writers was united on the point.[25] Unitedly they gave them an example in industry and independence. The example given "unto you," while they were with them, was costly to the missionaries. "To make ourselves" is literally "in order that we might give ourselves." This gift of self cost them the surrender of their own rights and involved them in hard, self-sacrificing toil (cf. 1 Th. 2:8).

Their costly example had the intention "that ye should imitate us." It gave them a pattern to copy. The present tense indicates the standing desire for them, "to the end ye might be imitating us" (Rotherham). This second reason for not receiving financial support from them is not stated in 1 Thessalonians 2:9, although it is implied in the picture drawn of their relations to their converts (2:8-12). The fact that this training aspect is now insisted upon is less complimentary to the readers. It is made necessary by the conduct of the disorderly brethren among them.

b) PRACTICAL MAXIM TAUGHT THEM (v. 10). "For even" (*kai gar*), "for also," introduces a second historical fact in support of the command given them in verse 6. "For" coordinates with the "for" of verse 7, where the first supporting fact was given, while "even," or "also," marks the additional point being made. The first fact relates to the missionaries' practice, the second to their precept. The two stand side by side. "When we were with you, this we commanded you, If any will not work, neither let him eat." The temporal clause, "when we were with you," covers the entire stay of the missionaries at Thessalonica. "With you" (*pros humas*) denotes a personal face-to-face relationship and reminds them that the teaching was personally given, while "commanded" recalls that the teaching was given as a binding duty. The verb is in the imperfect tense and denotes repeated action. Repeatedly "this," the pithy saying which follows, had been enjoined upon them. The demonstrative pronoun *this* (*touto*) draws attention to the very statement of the teaching given them. This clearly suggests that from the very beginning "the inspired and far-seeing wisdom of the Apostle had detected the seeds of disorder and indolence, even whilst he was yet at Thessalonica."[26] These undesirable tendencies the missionaries had sought to arrest by their repeated teaching, "If any will not work, neither let him eat."

The conditional form of the statement accepted the fact that there were such individuals, persons who "will not work." The point is not their inability but their unwillingness to work. There is no reproach cast on those who cannot work. "To any weakness or incapacity for work, except in himself, St. Paul would be very tender; the vice consists in the defective will."[27] Paul's dictum condemns the idle rich as well as the idle poor. Findlay remarks, "This law . . . makes that a discredit which one hears spoken of as if it were a privilege and the mark of a gentleman,—to 'live upon one's means', to live without settled occupation and service to the community."[28]

For such loafers Paul had a simple remedy, "neither let him eat." The imperative makes it clear that Paul is not stating the platitude that one who does not work will not have anything to eat. He is insisting that such deliberate loafers must not be supported out of a false sense of charity. He is making a stern demand, "If a person refuses to work, he must not be allowed to eat" (Williams). Misguided charity to such loafers only encourages their indolence and degrades them. If they refuse to work, let them go hungry! That will help overcome their indolence. Paul believed in the dignity of human labor and insisted that all those who professed faith in the gospel must engage in honest toil and not be drones. Lenski well remarks, "This dictum abolishes all false asceticism, all unchristian disinclination to work, all fanatic exaltation above work, all self-inflicted pauperism."[29]

There has been considerable guessing as to the source of Paul's maxim. Some regard it as a Jewish proverb based on Genesis 3:19. Others think it was a saying derived from the Greek workshop. Still others think it goes back to some unrecorded saying of Jesus. But clearly it is a common-sense truth of a moral nature and may well have found independent expression in various places. Paul gives it the sanction of Christianity.

3. Information Requiring the Command (v. 11)

For introduces the actual situation which prompted the whole discussion concerning the disorderly. "For we hear of some that walk among you disorderly" frankly states the reason for the concern of the missionaries. "Hear" is in the present tense and seems best taken as denoting repeated action; this information was being received on different occasions. The verb naturally implies oral information, although Frame points out that papyrus usage does not rule out written communications.[30] Clearly the reference is to information received since the sending of the first epistle. The thriving commercial contacts between Corinth and Thessalonica provided varied occasions for travelers to bring the reports to Paul at Corinth. The matter seemingly was common knowledge at Thessalonica and the information received by the writers was explicit and adequate.

They were hearing "of some that walk among you disorderly." The construction used (the accusative after *akouō*) points to the existing situation that is being reported. "Some" implies that the writers knew the identity of the offending individuals but the indefinite term leaves them unnamed. It further indicates that they were not many, but the writers are seriously concerned about them because a few can be a hurtful leaven (1 Co 5:6). They are mentioned as being "among you" (*en humin*), "in your midst," rather than "of you." The expression seems to suggest that their public conduct raised some question as to their true relationship to the church. Their disorderly conduct was setting up a barrier between them and the other members. The present tense points to their persistence in conduct that is disorderly, underlining their guilt.

The character of their conduct is made explicit by the appositional description, "that work not at all, but are busybodies" (*mēden ergazomenous alla periergazomenous*). The word-play in the original, which cannot be adequately reproduced in a literal translation, gives the rebuke a keen edge. Both participles are in the present tense denoting continuing action, "working." The scornful description is produced by the preposition *peri*, "around," prefixed to the second participle, "working around," giving it a bad sense, since that which encircles anything does not belong to the thing itself, but lies outside and beyond it, going beyond its proper limits.[31] This compound verbal form, used only here in the New Testament, thus "denotes a bustling disposition, busy in useless and superfluous things, about which one should not trouble himself."[32] In 1 Timothy 5:13 the cognate adjective is used of persons who are "paying attention to things that do not concern one, meddlesome, curious."[33] The negative designation, "that work not at all," marks their refusal to engage in daily toil, while the positive designation, introduced by the strong adversative *but*, "but are busybodies," sets forth their fussy, meddlesome activity.

Varied attempts have been made to seek to preserve the word-play of the original. Note the following: "At nothing working yet too busily working!" (Rotherham); "Busybodies who do no business" (Conybeare, marg.); "not busy men they, but busybodies" (Way); "busybodies instead of busy" (Moffatt). The German can reproduce the word-play quite well, *keine arbeit treiben, aber sich herumtreiben.*

In precisely what way the activity of these busybodies expressed itself is not said. That they were deliberately intruding into the domestic affairs of other members need not be assumed. But their excited activities were definitely interfering with the work of others. They may simply have been cloaking a disposition to idleness under a mask of feverish activity, perhaps spending on "religious" work the time that should rightly have been given to manual labor. While their activities are not said to be related to the erroneous doctrine about the day of the Lord which was exciting the church (2:2), such a connection is generally assumed. As former Greeks who had never been excited about the dignity of manual labor, the habit of idleness seems to have been a part of the background of some of the Thessalonian church members. The view that the day of the Lord had already set in and that the Lord would return at just any time would naturally stimulate their native tendency to give themselves to excited discussion in preference to dull manual labor. Their meddlesome activities may well have consisted of their excited efforts to convince others of the correctness of the startling news that the prophesied day of the Lord had already begun. "We may picture them," says Lenski, "sitting around for hours in the bazaars and little shops of the other members, making a nuisance of themselves, trying to unsettle the stable members with their fanatical notions."[34] Then returning home without money to buy the needed food, they appealed to other members to meet their needs or pestered the leaders to provide them with money from the charity fund of the church.

4. Command to the Disorderly (v. 12)

With a transitional *de*, rendered "Now," the writers turn to issue their order to these disorderly ones. The same solemn and authoritative manner employed in addressing the church in verse 6 is again used in addressing them. "Now them that are such we command and exhort in the Lord Jesus Christ." They speak to "them that are such" (*tois toioutois*), to all that belong to the class having such characteristics, "to the people of this kind," the "some" of the preceding verse. The form of the address is indirect. Instead of saying, "You busybodies," the command is directed to all who come under this category. It is an appeal to their conscience, asking them to see themselves and acknowledge that they have these undesirable characteristics. The writers are anxious not to condemn but to change them.

The coordinated verbs, "we command and exhort," make clear the attitude of the writers. It is a command in the full sense of the word but at the same time it is a brotherly exhortation, or admonition, to them. They speak "in the Lord Jesus Christ," in virtue of their union with Him.‡‡ The use of the triple name again adds solemnity.

The substance of the command and exhortation is "that with quietness they work, and eat their own bread." The statement of the command contains the intended result that the writers have in view. In 1 Thessalonians 4:11 the duty to work quietly was stated as an earnest exhortation; now it is asserted as a binding command. "With quietness," emphatic by its forward position, points to the quality of mind that is to be associated with their working. It denotes a condition of inward peace and tranquillity reflecting itself in outward calmness; it is the opposite of their fussy activity as busybodies. *Work* translates a present participle and denotes that they are expected to be steadily engaged in regular employment. The solemn preamble, "in the Lord Jesus Christ," raises such daily labor to the rank of Christian service. Such steady working will enable them to "eat their own bread." "Own" is emphatic to mark their "bread" or sustenance as that which they have themselves earned instead of being received gratis from another. Thus they will cease being a nuisance, a source of irritation among the members will be eliminated, and the reproach cast upon the church will be stopped.

5. Instructions to the Faithful Members (vv. 13-15)

With their emphatic "But ye" (*humeis de*) the writers again turn to

‡‡The KJV rendering, "by our Lord Jesus Christ," follows the *Textus Receptus dia*, "by, through," but this reading lacks adequate manuscript support. Modern editors do not accept it. This reading would mean that the writers avail themselves of His name and person to give impressiveness to their command.

those free from blame with some closing instructions. As in verse 6, they are again affectionately addressed as *brethren*. They are urged to continue in well-doing (v. 13) and given further instructions concerning their relations to the disorderly (vv. 14-15).

a) Appeal for continued well-doing (v. 13). The faithful members themselves are urged to "be not weary in well-doing." The negative appeal, "be not weary" (*mē engkakēsēte*), does not mean that they have already succumbed but rather that they must not yield to such a reaction. They must be on guard against the temptation to become "weary," to lose courage, falter, and give up. They "must never grow tired of doing right" (Williams). They must persist in their "well-doing." The compound present participle, found only here in the New Testament, denotes the continued doing of that which is right and noble, honorable and upright. Plummer renders "in your noble course."[35]

The statement of the appeal is quite general. But in view of the context, some interpreters hold to a more restricted meaning. The reference may then be to their continued efforts to bring the disorderly into line. Still others have interpreted the well-doing to mean exercising charity toward the disorderly, to continue to feed them and not let them go hungry (Chrysostom). Calvin held that Paul was warning them that their experience with the idlers who were abusing their liberality should not be allowed to make them uncharitable toward deserving members of the church.[36] While the exhortation to well-doing does not exclude the thought of doing good by alms-giving, it is best to adhere to the broad force of the term.§§

b) Instructions concerning those refusing to obey (vv. 14-15). The translation "And" of the particle *de* gives it a coordinating force here, adding another point in the instructions addressed to the orderly majority. But this would more naturally have been expressed by *kai*, the usual coordinating connective particle. The *de* may here have an adversative force, contrasting their duty toward themselves, as given in the previous verse, with their duty toward those who still refuse to obey. But more probably it should simply be rendered "now" to mark the transition to one further matter in rounding out the discussion concerning the disciplining of the disorderly.

Since the exhortations given in 1 Thessalonians 4:11 and 5:14 have been disregarded by the disorderly members at Thessalonica, Paul recognized the possibility that some might not obey the command now given them. "If any man obeyeth not our word by this epistle" contemplates an actual

§§If the thought were restricted to beneficent, charitable conduct it would more probably have been expressed by *agathopoieō*, rather than *kalopoieō*.

instance of such a refusal to obey. He accordingly suggests the course of action to be adopted by the loyal majority in dealing with such an insubordinate individual. The present tense *obeyeth* is used in accordance with the Greek epistolary idiom, the writer stating the action from the point of time of the readers. The letter will have been read in the assembly and the disorderly will have heard the explicit command directed to them. If any one still "obeyeth not our word," having heard it, still refuses to submit to it, the church is told how to act. Such a continued refusal to obey a command given in the authority of the Lord Jesus Christ (v. 12) would not be a light matter and the church must take firm action against such a one. Moffatt thinks that in saying "by this epistle" Paul indicates that he "has spoken his last word on the subject."[37] He expects compliance with the command. His written word was of equal authority with his oral message which they had accepted during the preaching mission at Thessalonica. "The New Testament writers nowhere betray any consciousness, either on their own part, or on the part of their hearers, that their written teaching was inspired in any higher sense than their oral teaching."[38]

Some interpreters have suggested that "by our epistle," literally, "through the epistle," should be connected with the following verb, "by the epistle note that man." This might be taken to mean, use this epistle to mark or brand the man with your open disapproval. But this is forced and unnatural. A more probable meaning would be that the Thessalonians are asked to mark the man by means of a letter to Paul. But this is contrary to the fact that Paul is asking the Thessalonian church itself to discipline the individual. Having just asked them to deal with the man, he probably would not now ask them to report to him by a letter so that he might pronounce punishment upon the offender. It is unlike Paul to keep the church so dependent upon himself in matters of local discipline. This suggestion is to be rejected that "by our epistle" connects with what follows. It is contrary to the position of the clause, the scope of the context, as well as the use of the definite article in the original, "the epistle." The definite article is often equivalent to a possessive pronoun and when used near the end of a letter seems clearly to refer to the letter being written (Ro 16:22; Col 4:16; 1 Th 5:27).

If such a case of insubordination did develop, the congregation is told how to proceed. "Note that man, that ye have no company with him." "That man" (*touton*), "this one," emphatically points out the offending individual. He has brought himself under the direct attention of the church by his refusal to obey. Him they must *note* (*sēmeiousthe*), quite literally, "mark him out for yourselves," the middle voice indicating their own concern in the matter. Hogg and Vine remark that the continuous action of the present tense suggests "that no hasty conclusion was to be drawn from an act, but that the course and general conduct was to be observed."[39] In what way the congregation is to *note* or mark the individual is not stated. Lenski observes that the verb "does not imply that the congregation had a blackboard on which it wrote the names of its black sheep."[40] It may simply mean that they are to note his disapproval in their own minds, but more probably some form of public censure is implied. Whatever the form of action to impose discipline, for effectiveness it would need to be the united act of the congregation.

"That ye have no company with him" (*mē sunanamigusthai autō*) expresses the contemplated result of their action against the man. The negative infinitive is quite literally, "not to be mixing yourselves up with him" (Rotherham). The simple verb, meaning "to mix, mingle," is prefixed with two prepositions which add the thought of accompaniment (*sun*) and interchange (*ana*). The expressive compound thus has the meaning of intimate association with an individual as a close and acceptable friend. The negative (*mē*) with the present tense demands that such an association must be discontinued. The recalcitrant member is to be put under the pressure of group disapproval through social ostracism. Such a cutting off of fellowship with other Christians in a heathen city would indeed be a serious thing for one who truly knew the saving grace of God. That a formal excommunication is meant, as Calvin held, is improbable.[41] That would follow if he did not respond to the discipline being meted out to him (cf. Mt 18:17).

The discipline to be applied is to be remedial in its aim, "to the end that he may be ashamed" (*hina entrapē*), "so that he will feel ashamed of it" (Williams). "He may be ashamed" renders an ingressive aorist passive verb with the basic meaning "to be turned in upon oneself," which came to mean "to be ashamed." The social pressure applied is to make him keenly aware of the disapproval of the church, turn his thoughts in upon himself so that he will realize the enormity of his rebellion, and be led to repentance. Restoration to full acceptance is held out through the door of repentance. The aim is not exclusion but reformation.

To insure that the majority will maintain a right relationship toward the offender in administering discipline, a further exhortation is added. "And yet count him not as an enemy, but admonish him as a brother." *Yet* has been added by the translators and may properly be omitted. No contrast is involved. *And* is not adversative but rather, as Ellicott observes, "subjoins the previous exhortation a further one that was fully compatible with it, and in fact tended to show the real principle on which the command was given."[42] The appended exhortation gives them guidance as to their own attitude and action toward the individual under discipline.

"Count him not as an enemy" warns against having a wrong attitude toward the man. "Not as an enemy be esteeming him" (Rotherham). "Not as an enemy," standing emphatically forward, urges that no feeling of hostility toward him is to be harbored. To regard him "as an enemy," one personally antagonistic to God and the church, would only hinder the moral result aimed at in the discipline. "Disapproval, as a means of moral discipline, loses all its effect if the offender does not realize its object and reason, or if it is tainted with personal hostility."[43] Such an attitude toward him would probably only evoke sullen persistence in his refusal. The verb *count*, "to consider, account, regard," indicates that their attitude toward him must not be based on their "inner feeling or sentiment, but on the due consideration of external grounds."[44] Aroused feelings must not lead to a wrong evaluation of the man's true character.

"But" (*alla*) sets a strong contrast between the attitude prohibited and the action enjoined, "but admonish him as a brother." With no hostile feelings toward him, they must with brotherly concern and tenderness actively "admonish" him. (On the meaning of this verb, see discussion under 1 Th 5:12). While refusing intimate association with him as though there were nothing amiss, they must not simply neglect him but patiently admonish him, putting him in mind of his duty by calling attention to his failing. They must remonstrate with him "as a brother," because he still is a brother, even though misguided and failing. Paul is concerned about protecting each man's status as a Christian brother and restoring him to usefulness in the brotherhood.

21

CONCLUSION

3:16-18 Now the Lord of peace himself give you peace at all times in all ways. The Lord be with you all.

(17) The salutation of me Paul with mine own hand, which is the token in every epistle: so I write. (18) The grace of our Lord Jesus Christ be with you all.

THE BRIEF CONCLUSION consists of three parts. A concluding prayer is offered for the readers (v. 16), Paul writes the greeting with his own hand as the sign of the authenticity of the letter (v. 17), and adds the final benediction (v. 18).

A. CONCLUDING PRAYER (v. 16)

The epistle is closed with the utterance of a fourth prayer by the writers for the readers (cf. 1:11-12; 2:16-17; 3:5). These repeated, spontaneous prayers reveal the spirit of prayer and supplication which characterized Paul.

The prayer is introduced by the particle *de*, here rendered "Now." This rendering simply makes it transitional in force, marking the passing to the conclusion of the letter. Ellicott holds that it is mildly adversative, "putting in slight antithesis the prayer with the foregoing exhortation."[1] It is another recognition by the writers that their own exhortations apart from the gracious working of the Lord in the readers would be quite ineffectual. With willing hearts they turn from censure to intercession.

"Now the Lord of peace himself" names the recipient of the prayer. The pronoun rendered "himself" (*autos*) again stands emphatically at the head of the statement (cf. 1 Th 3:11; 2 Th 2:16). It is intensive in force. "Now may he, the Lord of peace" turns the thought from their own corrective efforts to the Lord whose peace must pervade and control the readers.

The one petitioned is called "the Lord of peace," a designation used only here in Paul's letters. Elsewhere Paul uses "the God of peace" (Ro 15:33; 16:20; 2 Co 13:11; Phil 4:9; 1 Th 5:23). The two expressions seem to be used quite synonymously. Adeney holds that "Paul does not seem to discriminate between God and Christ in this place."[2] While the distinc-

352

tions in the Godhead may not be in view,* the consistent usage in these epistles strongly favors the view that "the Lord" is the Lord Jesus Christ. The genitive "of peace" has the definite article, "the Lord of the peace," and marks His distinctive relationship to the saints as the true source and bestower of Christian peace. It denotes the peace which He established through His work on the cross (Eph 2:14-16) and now bestows as His gift to believers (Jn 14:27).

The petition is that the Lord of peace may "give you peace." The aorist optative expresses the prayer-wish and summarily states the request for His bestowal of peace upon the readers. This peace can never be acquired by personal effort but must be received as a free gift. *Peace* again has the definite article, "the peace," pointing to that well-known peace which only Christ Jesus can bestow. The peace is objective, the peace received as a gift, but it should not be disassociated from the subjective experience of peace by the believer. The petition is not for relief from persecution, or even the cessation of the internal confusion in the church, but for that inner calm and bliss of soul that come to those who have been reconciled to God through the atoning work of our Lord Jesus Christ.

Two appended prepositional phrases mark the comprehensiveness of the peace requested for the readers, "at all times in all ways." The first relates to the duration, the second to the manner of its experience. "In all ways" (*dia pantos*), "through all" or "continually," points to the unbroken duration of the peace, flowing uninterruptedly. "In all ways" refers to the possession of the peace under the varied circumstances of life, "in every circumstance" (NASB). Outward circumstances, however unpleasant, cannot destroy this deep-seated inner peace of heart.

"The Lord be with you all" is not a further distinct petition but rather a petition pointing to the means whereby the prayer for peace will be accomplished. It is not a gift from afar but is mediated through the personal presence of the Lord with them. The gifts of Christ cannot be separated from the person of Christ. This prayer for His presence is based on His promise (Mt 28:20).

The writers expressly pray for the Lord's peace "with you all," all the believers at Thessalonica, even the disorderly. All alike share their good will and their prayers. All needed the peace-producing presence of the Lord Jesus Christ *with* (*meta*) them, the consciousness of His personal presence in their midst. The Lord is among His people at all times but they are not always aware of the reality of His presence.

*"In a certain sense it may be truthfully said that any one of the three Persons of the Blessed Trinity is 'the God of peace.' When we come to consider the individual office of the Three Blessed Persons we find that (a) The Father is *the source* of all Peace (I Thess. v. 23; Phil. iv. 7, 9). (b) The Son *is* our Peace (Eph. ii. 14). (c) The Holy Spirit *brings this Peace* to man (Gal. v. 22)" (G. W. Garrod, *The Second Epistle to the Thessalonians,* p. 145, Garrod's italics).

B. AUTHENTICATING SALUTATION (v. 17)

This autographic salutation makes it clear that Paul has been dictating the letter but at this point he takes the pen from the amanuensis and adds the closing words with his own hand. A few traces of this method of its composition have been observed. There is evidence that Paul made it a practice to dictate his letters (Ro 16:22; 1 Co 16:21; Col 4:18). Many scholars think that Paul's words in Galatians 6:11 mean that he picked up the pen at this point and wrote the remainder of the epistle himself. But since Paul seems never to use an epistolary aorist when writing only a few concluding words, scholars like Zahn, Lenski, Wuest, and others hold that it is best to assume that Paul wrote all of Galatians with his own hand. (Cf. Phile 19.)

Various conjectures have been made to account for Paul's usual practice of dictating his letters. It has been thought that he used this method because of imperfect eyesight, or that he lacked the ability to write the Greek characters rapidly, or that his work of tentmaking had left his fingers stiff, making writing difficult, or that his hand had been injured in one of the scourgings he had received. All of these suggestions are unconvincing. The real reason is nowhere stated. But obviously it was the very convenience of the method. Competent scribes were readily available and probably there were professional scribes in most of the churches, whom Paul could employ. They could easily take his dictation, perhaps even use a form of shorthand in doing so.† This method released Paul from the laborious mechanics of actual writing and left him free to concentrate on the development of the thought and the precise manner of its expression.

In rendering "The salutation of me Paul with mine own hand," our version obscures the fact that in the original *Paul* stands at the end of the expression, "This greeting is in my own hand, Paul's" (Williams). It is exceptional for him to add his own signature at the end. In the epistolary form of that day the writer gave his name in beginning his letter. Paul here explicitly asserts that the letter is an authentic document from him directly. He is personally responsible for it. Throughout these epistles to the Thessalonians, Silvanus and Timothy are recognized as partners with him, and apparently they shared in the discussion of the contents, yet Paul himself dictated the letters and regarded himself as the responsible author.

Paul at once adds the significance of his autograph, "which is the token in every epistle: so I write." "Which" (*ho*), being in the neuter gender, clearly does not refer directly to the salutation itself but to the fact that it was written by Paul personally. His autograph is the *token* or sign of the genuineness of the letter. It puts the Thessalonians on notice that no

---

†"Roman business men were great letter-writers. They invented three systems of shorthand as aids to business" (James C. Muir, *How Firm a Foundation*, p. 14).

document can claim to have his authority which does not have on it his own manual sign. "In every epistle" need not mean that already a number of letters by him bearing this mark of their authenticity were in circulation. It is generally accepted that 1 and 2 Thessalonians are our first extant letters from the hand of Paul.‡ Paul seems to mean that any further letters which he may write to them can be recognized as written by him from his autograph. This method of authenticating his letters was apparently adopted by Paul to discourage any further attempts to claim his authority for some position advocated on the basis of a spurious letter (cf. 2:2). Since 1 Thessalonians gives no indication that the salutation was added in his own hand, it seems probable that he did not add it personally. The need thus to authenticate his own letters may not have occurred to Paul until he and his colleagues learned that attempts were being made to claim his authority on the basis of documents which he had not written.

Reference to the fact that the salutation is in his own hand is found in only two other Pauline epistles (1 Co 16:21; Col 4:18). But that no further reference is made to this fact does not prove that Paul did not adhere to the practice. In the original, the fact would be readily evident from the difference in the handwriting. He would not need to call attention to it. Deissmann has reproduced an interesting instance of this custom in a papyrus letter written in A.D. 50. The letter is in one hand but the final greeting and date are in another hand, obviously that of the writer himself. Deissmann finds in it clear evidence that "we must not say that St. Paul only finished off with his own hand those letters in which he expressly says that he did."[3]

"So write I" seems to point clearly to the visible and recognizable difference between the handwriting of Paul and that of the scribe. *So* (*houtōs*), "in this manner, thus," calls attention to the distinctive character of his letters. "This is my handwriting" (Williams). Just what made his handwriting distinctive is not stated. In Galatians 6:11 reference is made to the fact that he was writing in an unusually large, bold hand. Bailey suggests that his bold hand was "possibly a natural reflection of his own bold, forthright spirit."[4] Yet the large letters mentioned in Galatians may have been used there for emphasis. How he wrote, rather than what he wrote, seems to provide the mark of authenticity. But there is no need to assume that Paul used some ingenious monogram, difficult of imitation, as the sign. Lünemann holds that this is erroneous because it is "transferring a modern custom into antiquity."[5] Others have thought that the authenticating sign was the greeting which follows in verse 18. But this is improbable. The closing formula of benediction varies considerably in

‡Some scholars, like William Hendriksen ("Exposition of Galatians," *New Testament Commentary*, pp. 14-16), place Galatians earlier than the Thessalonian epistles.

the Pauline epistles. If the reference were to a specific formula, that would not really guarantee the authenticity of the letter since a forger might readily adopt the formula employed. But the distinctiveness of his own handwriting would constitute a reliable sign of authenticity.

C. INCLUSIVE BENEDICTION (v. 18)

The letter closes with the same benediction used in 1 Thessalonians 5:28, except that here, like in verse 16 above, "all" is added. The missionaries have found it necessary to use strong words of censure against the disorderly, but they are anxious to make it clear that all alike have an affectionate place in their prayers and wishes for God's blessings.

Some manuscripts add an "Amen." While it has considerable manuscript support, modern editors are agreed that it is a scribal addition derived from the liturgies.

The subscription, "Written from Athens," found in some manuscripts, is obviously a later scribal comment. It embodies a scribal error based on a misinterpretation of 1 Thessalonians 3:1. Like 1 Thessalonians, this epistle was written from Corinth.

In looking back over these two letters to the church at Thessalonica one is deeply impressed with their timeliness and imperishable value for believers today. "They give us an illuminating, and in some ways a surprising, impression of certain phases of Christian faith and life twenty years after the death and resurrection of Christ."[6] We are reminded anew that apostolic churches were not perfect churches, but the transforming encounter of the members with the living Christ had produced a startling change in their lives and thinking. They had passed from death unto life, and their living faith centered in Jesus Christ as their Saviour and Lord, whose return they eagerly expected. But this hope for the future, which they did not yet fully understand, produced some reactions which the missionaries found it necessary to guide and correct. This eschatological concern caused Paul to give a strong emphasis to this hope in these epistles, rightly called the eschatological group among the Pauline writings. What Schaff said of the Pauline epistles in general is equally true of these two epistles:

> Tracts for the times, they are tracts for all times. Children of the fleeting moment, they contain truths of infinite moment. They compress more ideas in fewer words than any other writings, human or divine, excepting the Gospels. They discuss the highest themes which can challenge an immortal mind. . . . And all this before humble little societies of poor, uncultured artisans, freedmen and slaves! And yet they are of more real and general value to the church than all the systems of theology from Origen to Schleiermacher.[7]

Or, one may add, Barth or Bultmann.

NOTES

CHAPTER 1

1. Edgar J. Goodspeed, *An Introduction to the New Testament*, p. 4.
2. J. B. Lightfoot, *Biblical Essays*, p. 254.
3. Quoted in Lightfoot, p. 255.
4. Everett F. Harrison, *Introduction to the New Testament*, p. 245.
5. Lightfoot, pp. 257-58.
6. James Hope Moulton and George Milligan, *The Vocabulary of the Greek Testament*, p. 525; Lightfoot, p. 256.
7. Moulton and Milligan, and the references there cited; F. F. Bruce, *The Acts of the Apostles*, p. 326-27.
8. Roland Allen, *Missionary Methods, St. Paul's or Ours?*, p. 12.
9. Theodor Zahn, *Introduction to the New Testament*, 1:203.
10. R. C. H. Lenski, *The Interpretation of St. Paul's Epistles to the Colossians, to the Thessalonians, to Timothy, to Titus, and to Philemon*, p. 286.
11. Allen, p. 22.
12. Bruce, *The Books and the Parchments*, pp. 139-140.
13. William Mordaunt Furneaux, *The Acts of the Apostles*, p. 275.
14. Donald Guthrie, *New Testament Introduction, the Pauline Epistles*, p. 179.
15. Ibid., p. 212.
16. James Everett Frame, "A Critical and Exegetical Commentary on the Epistles of St. Paul to the Thessalonians," in *The International Critical Commentary*, p. 7.
17. E. J. Bicknell, "The First and Second Epistles to the Thessalonians," in *Westminster Commentaries*, p. xiii.
18. R. C. H. Lenski, *The Interpretation of the Acts of the Apostles*, p. 688.
19. Richard Belward Rackham, "The Acts of the Apostles," in *Westminster Commentaries*, p. 296.
20. F. W. Beare, "Thessalonians, First Letter to the," in *The Interpreter's Dictionary of the Bible*, 4:622.
21. Ibid., p. 623.
22. P. J. Gloag, "I Thessalonians," in *The Pulpit Commentary*, p. v.
23. Frame, p. 121.
24. W. M. Ramsay, *St. Paul the Traveller and the Roman Citizen*, p. 228.
25. James Moffatt, "The First and Second Epistles of Paul the Apostle to the Thessalonians," in *The Expositor's Greek Testament*, 4:3.
26. Ramsay, p. 230.
27. Ibid., p. 231.
28. Chalmer E. Faw, "On the Writing of First Thessalonians," *Journal of Biblical Literature* 71:217-25.
29. Ibid., p. 248.
30. William Hendriksen, "Exposition of I and II Thessalonians," in *New Testament Commentary*, p. 13.
31. Gloag, p. viii.
32. For the text of the inscription and discussion see F. J. Foakes Jackson and Kirsopp Lake, eds., *The Beginnings of Christianity*, 5:460-64; C. K. Barrett, *The New Testament Background: Selected Documents*, pp. 48-49; Adolf Deissmann, *Paul, A Study in Social and Religious History*, App. I, and Plate I; Jack Finegan, *Handbook of Biblical Chronology*, pp. 316-22; Finegan, *Light from the Ancient Past*, p. 282.
33. Finegan, *Light from the Ancient Past*, p. 282; F. F. Bruce, *The Acts of the Apostles*, p. 346; Werner Keller, *The Bible as History*, p. 386; Merrill F. Unger, *Archaeology and the New Testament*, p. 245.

34. Lenski, *The Interpretation of St. Paul's Epistles*, p. 215.
35. J. H. Harrop, "Gallio," in *The New Bible Dictionary*, p. 451.
36. Lenski, *Interpretation of St. Paul's Epistles*, p. 215.
37. Werner Georg Kümmel, *Introduction to the New Testament*, p. 180.
38. Milligan, *St. Paul's Epistles to the Thessalonians*, p. lxxv.
39. A. Robert and A. Feuillet, *Introduction to the New Testament*, p. 390.

CHAPTER 2

1. Adolf Deissmann, *Bible Studies*, pp. 3-12, 42-49; *Light from the Ancient East*, pp. 217-34.
 2. C. F. D. Moule, "The Epistles of Paul the Apostle to the Colossians and to Philemon," in *Cambridge Greek Testament Commentary*, p. 155.

CHAPTER 4

1. James Fergusson, *An Exposition of the Epistles of Paul*, p. 381.
 2. R. C. H. Lenski, *The Interpretation of St. Paul's Epistles, to the Colossians, to the Thessalonians, to Timothy, to Titus, and to Philemon*, p. 220.
 3. George G. Findlay, "The Epistles to the Thessalonians," in *Cambridge Bible for Schools and Colleges*, p. 46.
 4. Gottlieb Lünemann, "Critical and Exegetical Handbook to the Epistles of St. Paul to the Thessalonians," in *Meyer's Critical and Exegetical Commentary on the New Testament*, p. 18.
 5. John Calvin, "The Epistles of Paul the Apostle to the Romans and to the Thessalonians," in *Calvin's Commentaries*, p. 333.
 6. William Barclay, *The Mind of St. Paul*, p. 238.
 7. *The New English Bible, New Testament*.
 8. Joseph Bryant Rotherham, *The Emphasized New Testament*; J. N. Darby, *The 'Holy Scriptures' A New Translation from the Original Languages*.
 9. James S. Stewart, *A Man in Christ*, p. 307.
10. Findlay, "The Epistles of Paul to the Thessalonians," in *Cambridge Greek Testament*, p. 17.

CHAPTER 5

1. E. J. Bicknell, "The First and Second Epistles to the Thessalonians," in *Westminster Commentaries*, p. 5.
 2. Benjamin Jowett, *The Epistles of St. Paul to Thessalonians, Galatians, Romans*, 1:45; David A. Hubbard, "The First Epistle to the Thessalonians," in *The Wycliffe Bible Commentary*, p. 1349.
 3. Rendered "I" in the versions of Conybeare, Way, Montgomery. See the Bibliography.
 4. W. J. Conybeare, *The Epistle of Paul, A Translation and Notes*, Note 4, pp. 1-2. Conybeare's italics.
 5. George Milligan, *St. Paul's Epistles to the Thessalonians*, pp. 131-32.
 6. Adolf Deissmann, *Light From the Ancient East*, Note 3, pp. 168. See pp. 168-72 for the papyrus letters.
 7. William Hendriksen, "Exposition of I and II Thessalonians," in *New Testament Commentary*, p. 46.
 8. William Neil, "St. Paul's Epistles to the Thessalonians," in *Torch Bible Commentaries*, p. 32.
 9. C. F. Hogg and W. E. Vine, *The Epistle of Paul the Apostle to The Thessalonians*, p. 30.
10. George G. Findlay, "The Epistles of Paul the Apostle to the Thessalonians," in *Cambridge Greek Testament*, p. 19.
11. Milligan, p. 6.
12. Gottlieb Lünemann, "Critical and Exegetical Handbook to the Epistles of St. Paul to the Thessalonians," in *Meyer's Critical and Exegetical Commentary on the New Testament*, p. 21.
13. Charles J. Ellicott, *A Critical and Grammatical Commentary on St. Paul's Epistles to the Thessalonians*, p. 20.

14. John Calvin, "The Epistles of Paul the Apostle to the Romans and to the Thessalonians," in *Calvin's Commentaries*, p. 334.
15. James Everett Frame, "A Critical and Exegetical Commentary on the Epistles of St. Paul to the Thessalonians," in *The International Critical Commentary*, p. 75.
16. For the different Greek words for "love" and the New Testament usage of *agape*, see William Barclay, *New Testament Words*, pp. 17-30.
17. Henry Alford, *The New Testament for English Readers*, p. 1315.
18. Hendriksen, p. 48.
19. J. B. Lightfoot, *Saint Paul's Epistles to the Colossians and to Philemon*, p. 132.
20. G. R. Harding Wood, *St. Paul's First Letter*, p. 19. Wood's italics.
21. Ellicott, p. 22.
22. Lightfoot, *Notes on the Epistles of St. Paul*, p. 12.
23. Jowett, 1:44-45.
24. Milligan, p. xliv.
25. Albert Barnes, *Notes on the New Testament, Explanatory and Practical—Thessalonians, Timothy, Titus and Philemon*, p. 10.
26. Lightfoot, *Notes on the Epistles*, p. 12.
27. Milligan, p. 8.
28. Findlay, p. 21.
29. H. C. G. Moule, "Election," in *The International Standard Bible Encyclopedia*, 2:925.
30. A. J. Mason, "The Epistles of Paul the Apostle to the Thessalonians," in *Ellicott's Commentary on the Whole Bible*, 8:130. Mason's italics.
31. G. W. Garrod, *The First Epistle to the Thessalonians*, p. 55. Garrod's italics.
32. R. C. H. Lenski, *The Interpretation of St. Paul's Epistles to the Colossians, to the Thessalonians, to Timothy, to Titus and to Philemon*, p. 226.
33. William Neil, "The Epistle of Paul to the Thessalonians," in *The Moffatt New Testament Commentary*, p. 15.
34. Leon Morris, "The First and Second Epistles to the Thessalonians," in *The New International Commentary on the New Testament*, p. 55.
35. Joseph Henry Thayer, *A Greek-English Lexicon of the New Testament*, p. 118.
36. John Trapp, *Trapp's Commentary on the New Testament*, p. 622.
37. Lenski, p. 227.
38. F. W. Grant, *The Numerical Bible—Acts to 2 Corinthians*, p. 407.
39. Adam Clarke, *Clarke's Commentary, New Testament*, 2:540.
40. James Denney, "The Epistles to the Thessalonians," in *An Exposition of the Bible*, 6:321.
41. Hermann Cremer, *Biblico-Theological Lexicon of New Testament Greek*, p. 502.
42. Milligan, p. 9.
43. Denney, pp. 321-322.
44. Willis Peter De Boer, *The Imitation of Paul, An Exegetical Study*, p. 110.
45. Edward Headland and Henry Barclay Swete, *The Epistles to the Thessalonians*, p. 40.
46. Ellicott, p. 24.
47. Alford, p. 1316.
48. Charles Augustus Auberlen and C. J. Riggenbach, "The First Epistle of Paul to the Thessalonians," in *Lange's Commentary on the Holy Scriptures*, p. 17.
49. De Boer, p. 124.
50. Bicknell, p. 7.
51. Milligan, p. 138.
52. Ibid., p. 136.
53. Alfred Plummer, *A Commentary on St. Paul's First Epistle to the Thessalonians*, p. 11.
54. John W. Bailey and James W. Clarke, "The First and Second Epistles to the Thessalonians," in *The Interpreter's Bible*, 11:262.
55. Barnes, p. 12.
56. F. F. Bruce, *Are the New Testament Documents Reliable?*, p. 76.
57. Walter Grundmann, *"dechomai,"* in *Theological Dictionary of the New Testament*, 2:54.
58. Morris, p. 59.
59. Neil, "Epistle of Paul to the Thessalonians," pp. 19-20.
60. Findlay, "The Epistles to the Thessalonians," in *Cambridge Bible for Schools and Colleges*, p. 55. Findlay's italics.

61. Neil, p. 19.
62. Denney, p. 322.
63. William Alexander, "Thessalonians," in *The Speaker's Commentary, New Testament*, 3:708.
64. Calvin, p. 338.
65. Plummer, p. 12.
66. Findlay, "Epistles of Paul," p. 25.
67. Ibid., p. 27.
68. Milligan, p. 12.
69. Lightfoot, *Notes on the Epistles of St. Paul*, p. 15.
70. Alexander, 3:708.
71. Morris, p. 61.
72. Barnes, p. 14.
73. William Kelly, *The Epistles of Paul the Apostle to the Thessalonians*, p. 11.
74. Neil, p. 24.
75. Ibid., p. 23.
76. Auberlen, p. 22.
77. Lünemann, p. 36.
78. Alford, *The Greek Testament*, 3:240.
79. R. Mackintosh, "Thessalonians and Corinthians," in *The Westminster New Testament*, p. 39.
80. Clarke, 2:541.
81. Hogg and Vine, p. 44.
82. Quoted in James A. Stewart, *Heaven's Throne Gift*, p. 156.
83. Calvin, p. 339.
84. Frame, p. 88.
85. James Hope Moulton and George Milligan, *The Vocabulary of the Greek Testament*, p. 170.
86. Denney, p. 324.
87. Fergusson, p. 390.
88. Barclay, p. 56.
89. Auberlen, p. 23.
90. Denney, p. 324.
91. Neil, p. 31.
92. Ibid.
93. Morris, p. 64.
94. Findlay, "Epistles of Paul," p. 30.
95. Gloag, p. 4.
96. Plummer, p. 15. Plummer's italics.
97. R. V. G. Tasker, *The Biblical Doctrine of the Wrath of God*, p. 8.
98. John Murray, "The Epistle to the Romans," in *The New International Commentary on the New Testament*, 1:35.
99. Fritz Rienecker, "The Cross and Demythologizing," *Christianity Today*, March 16, 1962, p. 11.
100. Hendriksen, p. 57. Hendriksen's italics.
101. Cf. Tasker, pp. 27-36.
102. Philip Edgcumbe Hughes, "Paul's Second Epistle to the Corinthians," in *The New International Commentary on the New Testament*, p. 205.
103. C. H. Dodd, "The Epistle of Paul to the Romans," in *The Moffatt New Testament Commentary*, p. 23.
104. Barclay, "The Letter to the Romans," in *The Daily Study Bible*, p. 17. Barclay's italics.
105. Fredk. W. Robertson, "Expository Lectures on St. Paul's Epistles to the Corinthians," in *Life, Lectures and Addresses of Fredk. W. Robertson*, p. 614.
106. Morris, *The Biblical Doctrine of Judgment*, p. 70.
107. Milligan, p. 15.

CHAPTER 6

1. Gottlieb Lünemann, "Critical and Exegetical Handbook to the Epistles of St. Paul to the Thessalonians," in *Meyer's Critical and Exegetical Commentary on the New Testament Epistles*, p. 42. Lünemann's italics.

2. James Moffatt, "The First and Second Epistles of Paul the Apostle to the Thessalonians," in *The Expositor's Greek Testament*, p. 6.
3. J. B. Lightfoot, *Notes on the Epistles of St. Paul*, p. 18.
4. William Hendriksen, "Exposition of I and II Thessalonians," in *New Testament Commentary*, p. 60.
5. Leon Morris, "The First and Second Epistles to the Thessalonians," in *The New International Commentary on the New Testament*, p. 68.
6. Albert Barnes, *Notes on the New Testament—Thessalonians*, p. 20.
7. Morris, "The Epistles of Paul to the Thessalonians," in *The Tyndale New Testament Commentaries*, p. 42.
8. D. D. Whedon, *A Popular Commentary on the New Testament*, 4:366.
9. William Neil, "The Epistle of Paul to the Thessalonians," in *The Moffatt New Testament Commentary*, p. 35.
10. Morris, "First and Second Epistles to the Thessalonians," p. 69.
11. Edward Headland and Henry Barclay Swete, *The Epistles to the Thessalonians*, p. 49.
12. R. C. H. Lenski, *The Interpretation of St. Paul's Epistles to the Colossians, to the Thessalonians, to Timothy, to Titus and to Philemon*, p. 244.
13. Neil, p. 35.
14. James Everett Frame, "A Critical and Exegetical Commentary on the Epistles of St. Paul to the Thessalonians," in *The International Critical Commentary*, p. 94.
15. C. F. Hogg and W. E. Vine, *The Epistles of Paul the Apostle to the Thessalonians*, p. 52.
16. John W. Bailey, "The First and Second Epistles to the Thessalonians," in *The Interpreter's Bible*, 11:267.
17. William Arnold Stevens, "Commentary on the Epistles to the Thessalonians," in *An American Commentary*, p. 28.
18. Bailey, p. 270.
19. William Alexander, "I Thessalonians," in *The Speaker's Commentary, New Testament*, 3:710. Alexander's italics.
20. Charles J. Ellicott, *A Critical and Grammatical Commentary on St. Paul's Epistles to the Thessalonians*, p. 32.
21. Stevens, p. 28.
22. George G. Findlay, "The Epistles to the Thessalonians," in *Cambridge Bible for Schools and Colleges*, p. 63.
23. James Denney, "The Epistles to the Thessalonians," in *An Exposition of the Bible*, 6:326.
24. Lightfoot, pp. 20-21.
25. Frame, p. 95.
26. Bailey, pp. 269-270.
27. Morris, "First and Second Epistles to the Thessalonians," p. 71, note 7.
28. Lightfoot, p. 20.
29. Findlay, "The Epistles of Paul the Apostle to the Thessalonians," in *Cambridge Greek Testament*, p. 37.
30. Lenski, p. 246; Hendriksen, p. 62.
31. Moffatt, p. 26.
32. Alexander, p. 710.
33. George Milligan, *St. Paul's Epistles to the Thessalonians*, p. 18.
34. Richard Chenevix Trench, *Synonyms of the New Testament*, p. 281.
35. Hogg and Vine, p. 55.
36. James Hope Moulton and George Milligan, *The Vocabulary of the Greek Testament*, p. 75.
37. Johannes Behm, "*kardia*," in *Theological Dictionary of the New Testament*, 3:611.
38. Frame, pp. 97-98.
39. William Barclay, "The Letters to the Philippians, Colossians, and Thessalonians," in *The Daily Study Bible*, p. 221.
40. Findlay, "Epistles to the Thessalonians," p. 65.
41. Findlay points out that the change "to the participial construction distinguishes the third vice as a *practice* rather than a disposition." ("Epistles of Paul," p. 40.)
42. Quoted in Findlay, "Epistles to the Thessalonians," p. 65.

43. Hogg and Vine, p. 58.
44. Frame, p. 99.
45. Findlay, "Epistles to the Thessalonians," p. 66.
46. Findlay, "Epistles of Paul," p. 40.
47. Ibid., p. 27.
48. Morris, "First and Second Epistles to the Thessalonians," p. 70.
49. Lightfoot, pp. 24-25.
50. Brooke Foss Westcott and Fenton John Anthony Hort, "Notes on Select Readings," in *The New Testament in the Original Greek*, 2:128.
51. Quoted in Milligan, p. 21.
52. E. J. Bicknell, "The First and Second Epistles to the Thessalonians," in *Westminster Commentaries*, p. 25.
53. Bruce M. Metzgar, *The Text of the New Testament*, p. 232.
54. Walter F. Adeney, "Thessalonians and Galatians," in *The Century Bible*, p. 168; Metzgar, pp. 232-233.
55. Moffatt, p. 27.
56. C. A. Auberlen and C. J. Riggenbach, "The First Epistle of Paul to the Thessalonians," in *Lange's Commentary on the Holy Scriptures*, p. 30.
57. Milligan, p. 22.
58. Quoted in Milligan, p. 22.
59. Lenski, p. 252.
60. Lünemann, p. 55; Ellicott, p. 37; Lenski, p. 253; Frame, p. 102.
61. Ellicott, p. 37. Ellicott's italics.
62. Lightfoot, p. 26.
63. Lünemann, p. 55.
64. W. M. Ramsay, *The Church in the Roman Empire*, p. 85, note.
65. F. F. Bruce, *The Dawn of Christianity*, p. 12.
66. Hogg and Vine, p. 63.
67. Lightfoot, p. 27.
68. Trench, p. 329.
69. Findlay, "Epistles to the Thessalonians," p. 70.
70. James A. Stewart, *Pastures of Tender Grass*, p. 59.
71. Lightfoot, p. 28.
72. Lünemann, p. 58.
73. David Lipscomb and J. W. Shepherd, A Commentary on the New Testament Epistles, 5:29.
74. Neil, p. 43.
75. Hogg and Vine, pp. 65-66.
76. John Calvin, "The Epistles of Paul the Apostle to the Romans and to the Thessalonians," in *Calvin's Commentaries*, p. 345.
77. Findlay, "Epistles of Paul," p. 47.
78. Neil, p. 43.
79. James Hope Moulton, *A Grammar of New Testament Greek*, 1:219.
80. Morris, "First and Second Epistles to the Thessalonians," p. 85.
81. A. J. Mason, "The Epistles of Paul the Apostle to the Thessalonians," in *Ellicott's Commentary on the Whole Bible*, 8:133.
82. Adeney, p. 169.
83. Bicknell, p. 26.
84. Henry Alford, *The New Testament for English Readers*, p. 1320.
85. Findlay, "Epistles of Paul," pp. 50-51.
86. Frame, p. 106.
87. Lenski, p. 262.
88. Benjamin Jowett, *The Epistles of St. Paul to the Thessalonians, Galatians, Romans*, 1:59.
89. Frame, p. 106.
90. Lünemann, p. 63.
91. J. Rendel Harris, "A Study in Letter-writing," *The Expositor*, 8(Sep, 1898): 161-180.
92. T. C. Hammond, *The One Hundred Texts*, p. 441.
93. Edward Headland and Henry Barclay Swete, *The Epistles to the Thessalonians*, pp. 55-56.
94. Stevens, "Commentary on the Epistles to the Thessalonians" in *An American Commentary*, p. 34.

95. Moffatt, 4:28.
96. Lightfoot, p. 31.
97. Bicknell, pp. 26-27.
98. R. Mackintosh, "Thessalonians and Corinthians," in *The Westminster New Testament*, p. 44.
99. Neil, p. 48.
100. Calvin, p. 348.
101. Lünemann, p. 66.
102. Hogg and Vine, p. 74.
103. Lightfoot, p. 32.
104. Findlay, "Epistles of Paul," p. 53.
105. Neil, p. 50.
106. Bailey, 11:280.
107. H. Rolston, "Thessalonians, Timothy, Titus, Philemon," in *The Layman's Bible Commentaries*, p. 23.
108. Neil, "St. Paul's Epistles to the Thessalonians," in *Torch Bible Commentaries*, p. 53.
109. Moffatt, 4:29.
110. Denney, 6:330.
111. Findlay, "Epistles of Paul," p. 53.
112. Hogg and Vine, p. 76.
113. Neil, "Epistle of Paul to the Thessalonians," p. 51.
114. Lenski, p. 272.
115. Ibid., p. 273; Boyce W. Blackwelder, *Toward Understanding Thessalonians*, p. 82.
116. Ellicott, p. 45.
117. Ibid.
118. A. T. Robertson and W. Hersey Davis, *A New Short Grammar of the Greek Testament*, p. 340.
119. Alfred Plummer, *A Commentary on St. Paul's First Epistle to the Thessalonians*, p. 34.
120. G. W. Garrod, *The First Epistle to the Thessalonians*, p. 79.
121. Calvin, p. 349.
122. R. V. G. Tasker, *The Biblical Doctrine of the Wrath of God*, p. 43.
123. Lenski, pp. 273-74.
124. Marvin R. Vincent, "The Thessalonian Epistles," in *Word Studies in the New Testament*, 4:29.
125. Morris, "First and Second Epistles to the Thessalonians," p. 92; Headland and Swete, p. 58.
126. Frame, p. 114.
127. Lünemann, p. 73. Lünemann's italics.

CHAPTER 7

1. Quoted by W. O. Kloppenstein, "The First and Second Epistles of Paul to the Thessalonians," in *The Wesleyan Bible Commentary*, 5:525.
2. Alfred Plummer, *A Commentary on St. Paul's First Epistle to the Thessalonians*, pp. 36-37.
3. Gottlieb Lünemann, "Critical and Exegetical Handbook to the Epistles of St. Paul to the Thessalonians," in *Meyer's Critical and Exegetical Commentary on the New Testament*, p. 77.
4. Charles Augustus Auberlen, "The First Epistle of Paul to the Thessalonians," in *Lange's Commentary on the Holy Scriptures*, p. 47.
5. Leon Morris, "The First and Second Epistles to the Thessalonians," in *The New International Commentary*, p. 94.
6. J. B. Lightfoot, *Notes on the Epistles of St. Paul*, p. 37.
7. James Everett Frame, "A Critical and Exegetical Commentary on the Epistles of St. Paul to the Thessalonians," in *International Critical Commentary*, p. 119.
8. William F. Arndt and F. Wilbur Gingrich, *A Greek-English Lexicon of the New Testament and other Early Christian Literature*, p. 145.
9. Joseph Henry Thayer, *A Greek-English Lexicon of the New Testament*, p. 286.
10. George Milligan, *St. Paul's Epistles to the Thessalonians*, p. 34.

11. William Hendriksen, "Exposition of I and II Thessalonians," in *New Testament Commentary*, p. 75.
12. Morris, p. 94.
13. Frame, p. 120.
14. Edward Headland and Henry Barclay Swete, *The Epistles to the Thessalonians*, p. 66; Theodor Zahn, *Introduction to the New Testament*, 1:204-205; G. W. Garrod, *The First Epistle to the Thessalonians*, p. 81; Morris, p. 95, note 54; William Neil, "The Epistle of Paul to the Thessalonians," in *Moffatt New Testament Commentary*, p. 57.
15. Headland and Swete, p. 66.
16. W. M. Ramsay, *St. Paul the Traveller and the Roman Citizen*, p. 231.
17. John Calvin, *Calvin's Commentaries*, p. 351.
18. G. G. Findlay, "The Epistles of Paul the Apostle to the Thessalonians," in *Cambridge Greek Testament*, p. 59; Charles J. Ellicott, *A Critical and Grammatical Commentary on St. Paul's Epistles to the Thessalonians*, p. 49.
19. C. F. Hogg and W. E. Vine, *The Epistles of Paul the Apostle to the Thessalonians*, p. 84 .
20. Milligan, p. 35.
21. Ibid.
22. R. C. H. Lenski, *The Interpretation of St. Paul's Epistles to the Colossians, to the Thessalonians, to Timothy, to Titus and to Philemon*, p. 283.
23. Hendriksen, p. 76; John F. Walvoord, "New Testament Words for the Lord's Coming," in *Bibliotheca Sacra*, 101(Jul, 1944) p. 286; Hogg and Vine, p. 88.
24. Morris, p. 99.
25. Lenski, p. 286; Plummer, p. 43.
26. Milligan, pp. 131-132.
27. Headland and Swete, p. 67.
28. Lünemann, p. 85.
29. Lightfoot, p. 40.
30. Plummer, p. 43.
31. Lenski, p. 287.
32. Lightfoot, p. 40.
33. James Moffatt, "The First and Second Epistles of Paul the Apostle to the Thessalonians," in *Expositor's Greek Testament*, 4:31.
34. James Denney, "The Epistles to the Thessalonians," in *An Exposition of the Bible*, 6:333-334.
35. Lenski, p. 286.
36. Headland and Swete, p. 69.
37. Findlay, p. 65. Findlay's italics.
38. Lünemann, p. 87.
39. Calvin, p. 352; Lenski, p. 287; Plummer, p. 44 note.
40. A. J. Mason, "The Epistles of Paul the Apostle to the Thessalonians," in *Ellicott's Commentary on the Whole Bible*, 8:135.
41. Milligan, p. 38.
42. Ellicott, p. 52.
43. Milligan, p. 38.
44. Frame, p. 128.
45. Ibid.
46. Lenski, pp. 289-290.
47. Quoted from Wordsworth in Headland and Swete, p. 70.
48. Calvin, p. 353.
49. Mason 8:135. Mason's italics.
50. Hendriksen, p. 86.
51. Findlay, "The Epistles to the Thessalonians," in *Cambridge Bible for Schools and Colleges*, p. 86.
52. Lünemann, p. 93.
53. Neil, p. 67.
54. Denney, 6:334.
55. Calvin, p. 354.
56. Ibid.
57. Headland and Swete, p. 71.
58. Findlay, "Epistles of Paul," p. 71.

59. Ibid. Findlay's italics.
60. M. F. Sadler, *The Epistles of St. Paul to the Colossians, Thessalonians, and Timothy*, p. 108.
61. Findlay, "Epistles of Paul," p. 73.
62. Hogg and Vine, p. 100.
63. Frame, pp. 133-134.
64. Garrod, p. 89.
65. Findlay, "Epistles of Paul," p. 73.
66. Calvin, p. 355.
67. Moffatt, 4:32.
68. Sadler, p. 108.
69. Denney, 6:336.
70. Ellicott, p. 59.
71. Neil, p. 72.
72. Headland and Swete, p. 73.
73. Walter F. Adeney, "Thessalonians and Galatians," in *The Century Bible*, p. 183.
74. Findlay, "Epistles to the Thessalonians," p. 89.
75. Lenski, p. 304.
76. Otto Procksch, *"hagiōsunē,"* in *Theological Dictionary of the New Testament*, 1:114-115.
77. Neil, p. 73.
78. David A. Hubbard, "The First Epistle to the Thessalonians," in *The Wycliffe Bible Commentary*, p. 1352.

CHAPTER 8

1. William Neil, "The Epistle of Paul to the Thessalonians," in *Moffatt New Testament Commentary*, p. 75.
2. William Arnold Stevens, "Commentary on the Epistles to the Thessalonians," in *An American Commentary*, p. 44.
3. G. G. Findlay, "The Epistles of Paul the Apostle to the Thessalonians," in *Cambridge Greek Testament*, p. 80; John W. Bailey and James W. Clarke, "The First and Second Epistles to the Thessalonians," in *The Interpreter's Bible*, 11:293; George Milligan, *St. Paul's Epistles to the Thessalonians*, p. 46. Milligan's italics.
4. Findlay, p. 80.
5. M. F. Sadler, *The Epistles of St. Paul to the Colossians, Thessalonians, and Timothy*, p. 110.
6. Leon Morris, "The First and Second Epistles to the Thessalonians," in *The New International Commentary*, p. 118.
7. Gottlieb Lünemann, "Critical and Exegetical Handbook to the Epistles of St. Paul to the Thessalonians," in *Meyer's Critical and Exegetical Commentary on the New Testament*, p. 103.
8. R. C. H. Lenski, *The Interpretation of St. Paul's Epistles to the Colossians, to the Thessalonians, to Timothy, to Titus, and to Philemon*, p. 311.
9. E. J. Bicknell, "The First and Second Epistles to the Thessalonians," in *Westminster Commentaries*, p. 37.
10. William Alexander, "The First Epistle of Paul the Apostle to the Thessalonians," in *The Speaker's Commentary, New Testament*, 3:719. Alexander's italics.
11. William Barclay, "The Letters To Philippians, Colossians and Thessalonians," in *The Daily Study Bible*, p. 232.
12. J. B. Lightfoot, *Notes on the Epistles of St. Paul*, p. 53.
13. James Hope Moulton and George Milligan, *"ktaomai,"* in *The Vocabulary of the Greek Testament*, pp. 361-362.
14. Lünemann, p. 109.
15. G. W. Garrod, *The First Epistle to the Thessalonians*, p. 101.
16. Alfred Plummer, *A Commentary on St. Paul's First Epistle to the Thessalonians*, p. 60.
17. James Everett Frame, "A Critical and Exegetical Commentary on the Epistles of St. Paul to the Thessalonians," in *International Critical Commentary*, pp. 146-150.
18. Richard Chenevix Trench, *Synonyms of the New Testament*, p. 324.

19. John Calvin, "The Epistles of Paul the Apostle to the Romans and to the Thessalonians," in *Calvin's Commentaries*, p. 359.
20. Milligan, p. 49.
21. Frame, p. 151.
22. C. F. Hogg and W. E. Vine, *The Epistles of Paul the Apostle to the Thessalonians*, p. 118; Lightfoot, p. 57; Stevens, p. 48; Charles Augustus Auberlen and C. J. Riggenbach, "The First Epistles of Paul to the Thessalonians," in *Lange's Commentary on the Holy Scriptures*, p. 63.
23. Lenski, p. 321.
24. Ibid., p. 319.
25. Milligan, p. 50.
26. Ibid.
27. James Moffatt, "The First and Second Epistles of Paul the Apostle to the Thessalonians," in *Expositor's Greek Testament*, 4:34.
28. Morris, p. 126.
29. Plummer, p. 62.
30. Calvin, p. 360.
31. Lightfoot, p. 58.
32. Milligan, p. 52.
33. Plummer, p. 63.
34. Ibid., p. 64.
35. William Hendriksen, "Exposition of I and II Thessalonians," in *New Testament Commentary*, p. 103.
36. Calvin, p. 361.
37. Alexander, 3:721.
38. Charles J. Ellicott, *A Critical and Grammatical Commentary on St. Paul's Epistles to the Thessalonians*, p. 70.
39. Lünemann, p. 122.
40. Neil, p. 86.
41. Auberlen and Riggenbach, p. 69.
42. Findlay, p. 92. Findlay's italics.
43. Calvin, p. 361.
44. Plummer, p. 66.
45. James Denney, "The Epistles to the Thessalonians," in *An Exposition of the Bible*, 6:342.
46. Lenski, p. 327.
47. Ellicott, p. 71.
48. Frame, p. 162.
49. Neil, pp. 87-88.
50. Lünemann, p. 124.
51. Walter F. Adeney, "Thessalonians and Galatians," in *The Century Bible*, pp. 194-195.

CHAPTER 9

1. R. C. H. Lenski, *The Interpretation of St. Paul's Epistles to the Colossians, to the Thessalonians, to Timothy, to Titus and to Philemon*, p. 330; E. J. Bicknell, "The First and Second Epistles to the Thessalonians," in *Westminster Commentaries*, p. 43.
2. William Alexander, "Thessalonians," in *The Speaker's Commentary, New Testament*, 3:722.
3. William Hendriksen, "Exposition of I and II Thessalonians," in *New Testament Commentary*, p. 109.
4. Alfred Plummer, *A Commentary on St. Paul's First Epistle to the Thessalonians*, p. 69.
5. George Milligan, *St. Paul's Epistles to the Thessalonians*, p. 55.
6. Leon Morris, "The First and Second Epistles to the Thessalonians," in *New International Commentary*, p. 137.
7. Lenski, p. 332.
8. George G. Findlay, "The Epistles of Paul the Apostle to the Thessalonians," in *Cambridge Greek Testament*, p. 96. Findlay's italics.

9. W. J. Conybeare and J. S. Howson, *The Life and Epistles of Saint Paul*, p. 286.
10. J. B. Lightfoot, *Notes on the Epistles of St. Paul*, p. 63.
11. Bicknell, p. 44.
12. J. Sidlow Baxter, *Awake, My Heart*, p. 137.
13. H. Rolston, "Thessalonians, Timothy, Titus, Philemon," in *The Layman's Bible Commentaries*, p. 32.
14. P. J. Gloag, "I Thessalonians," in *The Pulpit Commentary*, p. 76.
15. Walter F. Adeney, "Thessalonians and Galatians," in *The Century Bible*, p. 197.
16. Gottlieb Lünemann, "Critical and Exegetical Handbook to the Epistles of St. Paul to the Thessalonians," in *Meyer's Critical and Exegetical Commentary on the New Testament*, p. 130. Lünemann's italics.
17. George Smeaton, *The Apostles' Doctrine of the Atonement*, p. 315.
18. Charles J. Ellicott, *A Critical and Grammatical Commentary on St. Paul's Epistles to the Thessalonians*, p. 74.
19. Morris, p. 141; Milligan, p. 58.
20. John Calvin, "The Epistles of Paul the Apostle to the Romans and to the Thessalonians," in *Calvin's Commentaries*, p. 364-365.
21. Plummer, p. 74.
22. Ellicott, p. 76.
23. Edward Headland and Henry Barclay Swete, *The Epistles to the Thessalonians*, p. 98.
24. Findlay, p. 100.
25. C. F. Hogg and W. E. Vine, *The Epistles of Paul the Apostle to the Thessalonians*, p. 143.
26. Hendriksen, p. 116.
27. Charles Augustus Auberlen and C. J. Riggenbach, "The First Epistle of Paul to the Thessalonians," in *Lange's Commentary on the Holy Scriptures*, p. 75.
28. Gerald B. Stanton, *Kept From the Hour*, p. 23.
29. Ibid., pp. 192-198.
30. John F. Walvoord, *The Church in Prophecy*, pp. 80-81; E. Schuyler English, *Re-Thinking the Rapture*, Ch. 4.
31. Bicknell, p. 46.
32. Erich Sauer, *The Triumph of the Crucified*, p. 107.
33. Plummer, p. 77.
34. Lightfoot, p. 68.
35. Findlay, p. 102.
36. Plummer, p. 77.
37. James Hope Moulton and George Milligan, *The Vocabulary of the New Testament*, p. 53.
38. Hogg and Vine, p. 146.
39. Stanton, pp. 253-256.
40. Kenneth S. Wuest, *The Practical Use of the Greek New Testament*, p. 98.
41. Hogg and Vine, p. 146.
42. Morris, p. 146.
43. James Everett Frame, "A Critical and Exegetical Commentary on the Epistles of St. Paul to the Thessalonians," in *International Critical Commentary*, p. 176.
44. Ellicott, p. 79.
45. Bornemann, quoted in Findlay, p. 103.
46. Adolf Deissmann, *Light From the Ancient East*, p. 164.
47. See Herman A. Hoyt, *The End Times*, ch. 5–7; and J. Dwight Pentecost, *Things to Come, A Study in Biblical Eschatology*, ch. XI–XIII. See also English, *Re-Thinking the Rapture;* John F. Walvoord, *The Rapture Question;* Leon J. Wood, *Is the Rapture Next?*
48. See Oliver J. Buswell, Jr., *A Systematic Theology of the Christian Religion*, Vol. 2; Norman B. Harrison, *The End: Re-thinking the Revelation.*
49. See George E. Ladd, *The Blessed Hope*; Norman Spurgeon McPherson, *Triumph Through Tribulation*; Harold J. Ockenga, *The Church in God*; Alexander Reese, *The Approaching Advent of Christ.*
50. Walvoord, p. 148.
51. Ladd, p. 165.
52. Wood, p. 115.
53. Cf. Walvoord, pp. 153-155.

CHAPTER 10

1. Charles Augustus Auberlen and C. J. Riggenbach, "The First Epistle of Paul to the Thessalonians," in *Lange's Commentary on the Holy Scriptures*, p. 82.
2. D. D. Whedon, *A Popular Commentary on the New Testament*, 4:381.
3. Walter F. Adeney, "Thessalonians and Galatians," in *The Century Bible*, p. 204.
4. George Milligan, *St. Paul's Epistles to the Thessalonians*, p. 64.
5. George G. Findlay, "The Epistles of Paul the Apostle to the Thessalonians," in *Cambridge Greek Testament*, p. 108. Findlay's italics.
6. Alfred Plummer, *A Commentary on St. Paul's First Epistle to the Thessalonians*, pp. 82-83.
7. William Neil, "The Epistle of Paul to the Thessalonians," in *The Moffatt New Testament Commentary*, p. 109.
8. William Barclay, *The Letters to the Philippians, Colossians, and Thessalonians*, p. 237.
9. Edward Headland and Henry Barclay Swete, *The Epistles to the Thessalonians*, p. 103.
10. W. O. Klopfensteine, "The First and Second Epistles of Paul to the Thessalonians," in *The Wesleyan Bible Commentary*, 5:537.
11. Charles J. Ellicott, *A Critical and Grammatical Commentary on St. Paul's Epistles to the Thessalonians*, p. 81.
12. C. F. Hogg and W. E. Vine, *The Epistles of Paul the Apostle to the Thessalonians*, p. 155.
13. Milligan, p. 65.
14. Albert Barnes, *Notes on the New Testament Explanatory and Practical, Thessalonians, Timothy, Titus, and Philemon*, p. 53.
15. Findlay, p. 110.
16. Milligan, p. 66; R. C. H. Lenski, *The Interpretation of St. Paul's Epistles to the Colossians, to the Thessalonians, to Timothy, to Titus and to Philemon*, p. 350; Hogg and Vine, p. 156; Findlay, p. 110; Headland and Swete, p. 103; Gottlieb Lünemann, "Critical and Exegetical Handbook to the Epistles of St. Paul to the Thessalonians," in *Meyer's Critical and Exegetical Commentary on the New Testament*, p. 146.
17. William Kelly, *The Epistles of Paul the Apostle to the Thessalonians*, p. 58.
18. Findlay, p. 107.
19. Ellicott, p. 82.
20. Milligan, p. 66. Milligan's italics.
21. J. B. Lightfoot, *Notes on the Epistles of St. Paul*, pp. 73, 24-25.
22. Findlay, p. 111. Findlay's italics.
23. Leon Morris, "The First and Second Epistles to the Thessalonians," in *New International Commentary*, p. 155, note 15.
24. Hogg and Vine, p. 160.
25. Neil, p. 113.
26. Lightfoot, p. 74.
27. Lenski, p. 351.
28. Ibid., p. 352.
29. Hogg and Vine, p. 161.
30. William Arnold Stevens, "Commentary on the Epistles to the Thessalonians," in *An American Commentary*, p. 60.
31. John Trapp, *Trapp's Commentary on the New Testament*, p. 628.
32. James Moffatt, "The First and Second Epistles of Paul the Apostle to the Thessalonians," in *The Expositor's Greek Testament*, 4:40.
33. Findlay, p. 115.
34. Whedon, 4:383.
35. Lightfoot, p. 76.
36. Findlay, p. 117.
37. Plummer, p. 88.
38. James Denney, "The Epistles to the Thessalonians," in *An Exposition of the Bible*, 6:348.
39. A. T. Robertson, *The Minister and His Greek New Testament*, Ch. 3.
40. Hogg and Vine, pp. 171-172.
41. Lünemann, pp. 151-152.

42. James Paton, *The Glory and Joy of the Resurrection*, p. 61.
43. Ellicott, p. 85.
44. John S. Howson, *The Metaphors of St. Paul and Companions of St. Paul*, p. 27.
45. Neil, p. 119.
46. Moffatt, pp. 40-41.
47. Adeney, p. 210.

CHAPTER 11

1. E. J. Bicknell, "The First and Second Epistles to the Thessalonians," in *Westminster Commentaries*, p. 58.
2. James Hope Moulton and George Milligan, *The Vocabulary of the Greek Testament*, p. 440.
3. C. F. Hogg and W. E. Vine, *The Epistles of Paul the Apostle to the Thessalonians*, p. 177.
4. H. Rolston, "Thessalonians, Timothy, Titus, Philemon," in *The Layman's Bible Commentary*, p. 36.
5. John Calvin, "The Epistles of Paul the Apostle to the Romans and to the Thessalonians," in *Calvin's Commentaries*, p. 371.
6. Moulton and Milligan, p. 541.
7. George G. Findlay, "The Epistles of Paul the Apostle to the Thessalonians," in *Cambridge Greek Testament*, p. 122.
8. Leon Morris, "The First and Second Epistles to the Thessalonians," in *The New International Commentary*, p. 166.
9. Ibid.
10. P. J. Gloag, "I Thessalonians," in *The Pulpit Commentary*, p. 104.
11. G. W. Garrod, *The First Epistle to the Thessalonians*, p. 135.
12. J. B. Lightfoot, *Notes on the Epistles of St. Paul*, p. 80.
13. Hogg and Vine, p. 181.
14. George Milligan, *St. Paul's Epistles to the Thessalonians*, note "G", pp. 152-154.
15. Moulton and Milligan, p. 89.
16. Milligan, p. 154.
17. William Neil, "The Epistles of Paul to the Thessalonians," in *The Moffatt New Testament Commentary*, pp. 124-125.
18. Hogg and Vine, p. 183.
19. William Hendriksen, "Exposition of I and II Thessalonians," in *New Testament Commentary*, p. 136.
20. Hogg and Vine, p. 184.
21. Alfred Plummer, *A Commentary on St. Paul's First Epistle to the Thessalonians*, p. 95.
22. James Everett Frame, "A Critical and Exegetical Commentary on the Epistles of St. Paul to the Thessalonians," in *International Critical Commentary*, p. 199.
23. Calvin, p. 374.
24. Hogg and Vine, p. 185.
25. Milligan, p. 74.
26. Neil, "St. Paul's Epistles to the Thessalonians," in *Torch Bible Commentaries*, p. 114.

CHAPTER 12

1. James Moffatt, "The First and Second Epistles of Paul the Apostle to the Thessalonians," in *The Expositor's Greek Testament*, 4:41.
2. George G. Findlay, "The Epistles of Paul the Apostle to the Thessalonians," in *Cambridge Greek Testament*, p. 126.
3. P. J. Gloag, "I Thessalonians," in *The Pulpit Commentary*, p. 105.
4. A. J. Mason, "The Epistles of Paul the Apostle to the Thessalonians," in *Ellicott's Commentary on the Whole Bible*, 8:145.
5. J. B. Lightfoot, *Notes on the Epistles of St. Paul*, p. 81.
6. M. F. Sadler, *The Epistles of St. Paul to the Colossians, Thessalonians, and Timothy*, p. 128.
7. George Milligan, *St. Paul's Epistles to the Thessalonians*, p. 75.
8. C. F. Hogg and W. E. Vine, *The Epistles of Paul the Apostle to the Thessalonians*, p. 190.

9. Charles J. Ellicott, *A Critical and Grammatical Commentary on St. Paul's Epistles*, p. 91.
10. Walter F. Adeney, "Thessalonians and Galatians," in *The Century Bible*, p. 215.
11. Findlay, p. 127.
12. D. D. Whedon, *A Popular Commentary on the New Testament*, 4:385.
13. Findlay, p. 127.
14. Findlay, "The Epistles to the Thessalonians," in *Cambridge Bible for Schools*, p. 121.
15. James Everett Frame, "A Critical and Exegetical Commentary on the Epistles of St. Paul to the Thessalonians," in *International Critical Commentary*, p. 204.
16. Leon Morris, "The First and Second Epistles to the Thessalonians," in *New International Commentary*, p. 176.
17. Lightfoot, p. 84.
18. Ellicott, p. 93.
19. Findlay, "Epistles of Paul the Apostle," p. 129.
20. Alfred Plummer, *A Commentary on St. Paul's First Epistle to the Thessalonians*, p. 100.
21. Richard Chenevix Trench, *Synonyms of the New Testament*, pp. 315-317.
22. R. C. H. Lenski, *The Interpretation of St. Paul's Epistles to the Colossians, to the Thessalonians, to Timothy, to Titus and to Philemon*, pp. 370-371.
23. R. Mackintosh, "Thessalonians and Corinthians," in *The Westminster New Testament*, p. 65.
24. W. O. Klopfenstein, "The First and Second Epistles of Paul to the Thessalonians," in *The Wesleyan Bible Commentary*, 5:542.
25. Mason, p. 146.
26. Klopfenstein, pp. 542-543.
27. Lenski, p. 372.
28. Findlay, "Epistles of Paul the Apostle," p. 132.
29. Trench, p. 74.
30. See the listing in Hogg and Vine, pp. 204-207.
31. Benjamin Jowett, *The Epistles of St. Paul to the Thessalonians, Galatians, Romans*, 1:105.
32. Ellicott, p. 95.
33. Hogg and Vine, p. 209.
34. Joseph Henry Thayer, *A Greek-English Lexicon of the New Testament*, p. 32.
35. Milligan, p. 79.
36. Quoted in William Alexander, "Thessalonians," in *The Speaker's Commentary, New Testament*, 3:730.
37. William Neil, "St. Paul's Epistles to the Thessalonians," in *Torch Bible Commentaries*, pp. 119-120.
38. Milligan, p. 79.

Chapter 13

1. William Kelly, *The Epistles of Paul the Apostle to the Thessalonians*, p. 74.
2. Clay Cooper, *Nothing to Win But the World*, p. 82.
3. Alfred Plummer, *A Commentary on St. Paul's First Epistle to the Thessalonians*, p. 105.
4. C. F. Hogg and W. E. Vine, *The Epistles of Paul the Apostle to the Thessalonians*, p. 214.
5. J. Alfred Faulkner, "Salutations," in Hasting's *Dictionary of the Apostolic Church*, 2:443.
6. Alfred Plummer, "A Critical and Exegetical Commentary on the Second Epistle of St. Paul to the Corinthians," in *International Critical Commentary*, p. 381.
7. Faulkner, 2:443.
8. J. B. Lightfoot, *Notes on the Epistles of St. Paul*, p. 91.
9. James Hope Moulton and George Milligan, *The Vocabulary of the Greek Testament*, p. 31.
10. Lightfoot, p. 91.
11. Walter F. Adeney, "Thessalonians and Galatians," in *The Century Bible*, p. 220.

CHAPTER 14

1. George Milligan, St. Paul's Epistles to the Thessalonians, p. lxxvi.
2. Ibid., p. lxxvii.
3. Alfred Wikenhauser, *New Testament Introduction*, p. 369.
4. Quoted in Milligan, p. lxxxvi, note 1.
5. Edgar J. Goodspeed, *An Introduction to the New Testament*, p. 19.
6. W. Graham Scroggie, *Know Your Bible, A Brief Introduction to the Scriptures, Volume II, The New Testament*, p. 114.
7. Kirsopp C. Lake, "The Authenticity of 2 Thessalonians," in *Contemporary Thinking About Paul. An Anthology*, comp. Kepler, p. 235.
8. Theodor Zahn, *Introduction to the New Testament*, 1:250.
9. James Everett Frame, "A Critical and Exegetical Commentary on the Epistles of St. Paul to the Thessalonians," in *The International Critical Commentary*, p. 35.
10. Goodspeed, p. 21.
11. James Moffatt, *An Introduction to the Literature of the New Testament*, p. 79.
12. Lake, p. 237.
13. Donald Guthrie, *New Testament Introduction, The Pauline Epistles*, pp. 189-190.
14. T. W. Manson, *Studies in the Gospels and Epistles*, p. 267.
15. Ibid., p. 273.
16. Ibid., p. 272.
17. R. Gregson, "A Solution to the Problems of the Thessalonian Epistles," *The Evangelical Quarterly*, 38(April-June, 1966) 80.
18. Ibid., p. 77.
19. Manson, pp. 274-277.
20. William Hendriksen, "Exposition of I and II Thessalonians," in *New Testament Commentary*, pp. 16-17.
21. William Neil, "The Epistle of Paul to the Thessalonians," in *Moffatt New Testament Commentary*, p. xx.
22. A. H. McNeile, *An Introduction to the Study of the New Testament*, p. 113.
23. Graafen, mentioned in Wikenhauser, p. 371.
24. John Bird Sumner, *A Practical Exposition of St. Paul's Epistles to the Thessalonians, to Timothy, Titus, Philemon, and to the Hebrews*, p. 73. (He does, however, accept both epistles as written from Corinth.)
25. D. D. Whedon, *A Popular Commentary on the New Testament*, 4:404; Wilbur Fields, "Thinking Through Thessalonians," in *Bible Study Textbook*, p. 232.

CHAPTER 16

1. George G. Findlay, "The Epistles of Paul the Apostle to the Thessalonians," in *Cambridge Greek Testament*, p. 139.
2. Alfred Plummer, *A Commentary on St. Paul's Second Epistle to the Thessalonians*, p. 83.

CHAPTER 17

1. Alfred Plummer, *A Commentary on St. Paul's Second Epistle to the Thessalonians*, p. 8.
2. William Hendriksen, "Exposition of I and II Thessalonians," in *New Testament Commentary*, p. 154.
3. William Neil, "The Epistle of Paul to the Thessalonians," in *Moffatt New Testament Commentary*, p. 141.
4. E. J. Bicknell, "The First and Second Epistles to the Thessalonians," in *Westminster Commentaries*, p. 68.
5. Gottlieb Lünemann, "Critical and Exegetical Handbook to the Epistles of St. Paul to the Thessalonians," in *Meyer's Critical and Exegetical Commentary on the New Testament*, p. 185.
6. William Arnold Stevens, "Commentary on the Epistles to the Thessalonians," in *An American Commentary*, p. 75.
7. J. B. Lightfoot, *Notes on the Epistles of St. Paul*, p. 98.
8. Stevens, p. 76.
9. Edward Headland and Henry Barclay Swete, *The Epistles to the Thessalonians*, p. 132.

10. Ibid., p. 133.
11. Lünemann, p. 188.
12. James Everett Frame, "A Critical and Exegetical Commentary on the Epistles of St. Paul to the Thessalonians," in *International Critical Commentary*, p. 226.
13. George G. Findlay, "The Epistles of Paul the Apostle to the Thessalonians," in *Cambridge Greek Testament*, p. 144.
14. For the papyrus evidence, see James Hope Moulton and George Milligan, *The Vocabulary of the Greek Testament*, pp. 330-331.
15. Leon Morris, "The Epistles of Paul to the Thessalonians," in *The Tyndale New Testament Commentaries*, p. 116.
16. Findlay, p. 144.
17. Stevens, p. 77.
18. Lünemann, p. 191.
19. Headland and Swete, p. 136.
20. Von Dobschütz, quoted in Frame, p. 229.
21. Findlay, p. 146.
22. William Kelly, *The Epistles of Paul the Apostle to the Thessalonians*, p. 89.
23. George Milligan, *St. Paul's Epistles to the Thessalonians*, p. 90.
24. Plummer, p. 23.
25. Morris, "The First and Second Epistles to the Thessalonians," in the *New International Commentary*, p. 204.
26. C. F. Hogg and W. E. Vine, *The Epistles of Paul the Apostle to the Thessalonians*, pp. 231-232.
27. Lünemann, p. 194.
28. C. J. Riggenbach, "The Second Epistle of Paul to the Thessalonians," in *Lange's Commentary on the Holy Scriptures*, pp. 117-118.
29. Wm. Alexander, "II Thessalonians," in *The Speaker's Commentary*, New Testament, 3:732-733. Alexander's italics.
30. Findlay, p. 149.
31. Frame, p. 235.
32. Joseph Henry Thayer, *A Greek-English Lexicon of the New Testament*, p. 21.
33. Headland and Swete, p. 137.
34. Charles J. Ellicott, *A Critical and Grammatical Commentary on St. Paul's Epistles to the Thessalonians*, p. 110. Ellicott's italics.
35. Findlay, "The Epistles to the Thessalonians," in *Cambridge Bible for Schools and Colleges*, p. 134. Findlay's italics.
36. Neil, p. 149.
37. Bicknell, p. 70.
38. Headland and Swete, p. 140.
39. Neil, p. 151.
40. Milligan, p. 92.
41. Brooke Foss Westcott and Fenton John Anthony Hort, "Notes on Selected Readings," in *The New Testament in the Original Greek*, 2:128.
42. Findlay, "Epistles of Paul the Apostle," p. 152.
43. Ibid., p. 153.
44. James Moffatt, "The First and Second Epistles of Paul the Apostle to the Thessalonians," in *The Expositor's Greek Testament*, 4:46.
45. Neil, p. 152.
46. Walter F. Adeney, "Thessalonians and Galatians," in *The Century Bible*, p. 233.
47. Findlay, "Epistles of Paul the Apostle," p. 156.
48. R. C. H. Lenski, *The Interpretation of St. Paul's Epistles to the Colossians, to the Thessalonians, to Timothy, to Titus and to Philemon*, p. 408.

CHAPTER 18

1. William Neil, "St. Paul's Epistles to the Thessalonians," in *Torch Bible Commentaries*, p. 132.
2. Leon Morris, "The First and Second Epistles to the Thessalonians," in *New International Commentary*, p. 213.
3. G. W. Garrod, *The Second Epistle to the Thessalonians*, p. 81. Garrod's italics.
4. Charles J. Ellicott, *A Critical and Grammatical Commentary on St. Paul's Epistles to the Thessalonians*, p. 115.

5. William Kelly, *The Epistles of Paul the Apostle to the Thessalonians*, p. 105.
6. C. F. Hogg and W. E.Vine, *The Epistles of Paul the Apostle to the Thessalonians*, p. 243.
7. Joseph Henry Thayer, *A Greek-English Lexicon of the New Testament*, p. 413.
8. R. C. H. Lenski, *The Interpretation of St. Paul's Epistles to the Colossians, to the Thessalonians, to Timothy and to Philemon*, p. 412.
9. William Arnold Stevens, "Commentary on the Epistles to the Thessalonians," in *An American Commentary*, p. 82.
10. James Everett Frame, "A Critical and Exegetical Commentary on the Epistles of St. Paul to the Thessalonians," in *International Critical Commentary*, p. 246.
11. George G. Findlay, "The Epistles of Paul the Apostle to the Thessalonians," in *Cambridge Greek Testament*, p. 166. Findlay's italics.
12. George Milligan, *St. Paul's Epistles to the Thessalonians*, p. 97. Milligan's italics.
13. See J. Dwight Pentecost, *Things to Come*, pp. 229-232; Gerald B. Stanton, *Kept From the Hour*, ch. 4; Clarence E. Mason, Jr., "The Day of Our Lord Jesus Christ," *Bibliotheca Sacra*, 125 (Oct-Dec, 1968) 352-359.
14. Neil, "The Epistle of Paul to the Thessalonians," in *The Moffatt New Testament Commentary*, p. 109.
15. John F. Walvoord, *The Thessalonian Epistles*, p. 117.
16. Gottlieb Lünemann, "Critical and Exegetical Handbook to the Epistles of St. Paul to the Thessalonians," in *Meyer's Critical and Exegetical Commentary on the New Testament*, p. 208.
17. Findlay, p. 166.
18. Charles M. Horne, *The Epistles to the Thessalonians*, in Shield Bible Study series, p. 64.
19. James Moffatt, "The First and Second Epistles of Paul the Apostle to the Thessalonians," in *Expositor's Greek Testament*, 4:48. Thus Moffatt's translation reads, "till the Rebellion takes place first of all, with the revealing of the Lawless One." (The NEB is similar.)
20. E. Schuyler English, *Re-Thinking the Rapture*, pp. 67-71; John R. Rice, *The Coming Kingdom of Christ*, pp. 188-191; Kenneth S. Wuest, *Prophetic Light in the Present Darkness*, pp. 38-41.
21. Ellicott, p. 118.
22. Albrecht Oepke, "*apōleia*," in *Theological Dictionary of the New Testament*, 1:397.
23. Thayer, p. 71.
24. Findlay, "The Epistles to the Thessalonians," in *Cambridge Bible for Schools and Colleges*, p. 144.
25. Ellicott, pp. 119-120.
26. Stevens, p. 87.
27. Benjamin Breckinridge Warfield, *Biblical and Theological Studies*, pp. 472-473.
28. Charles R. Erdman, *The Epistles of Paul to the Thessalonians*, p. 89.
29. William Hendriksen, "Exposition of I and II Thessalonians," in *New Testament Commentary*, pp. 179-180.
30. Hogg and Vine, p. 254; Alfred Plummer, *A Commentary on St. Paul's Second Epistle to the Thessalonians*, p. 56.
31. Findlay, "Epistles to the Thessalonians," p. 147.
32. Findlay, "Epistles of Paul the Apostle," p. 177.
33. C. J. Riggenbach, "The Second Epistle of Paul to the Thessalonians," in *Lange's Commentary on the Holy Scriptures*, p. 130.
34. Hogg and Vine, p. 259.
35. F. W. Grant, "Acts to 2 Corinthians," in *The Numerical Bible*, p. 438.
36. Morris, p. 229.
37. Charles Caldwell Ryrie, *First and Second Thessalonians*, p. 113.
38. Findlay, "Epistles of Paul the Apostle," p. 179.
39. Neil, "Epistle of Paul to the Thessalonians," p. 173.
40. Thayer, p. 245.
41. James Hope Moulton, *A Grammar of New Testament Greek*, I:114-115.
42. Garrod, p. 111.
43. Hogg and Vine, p. 266.

44. Findlay, "Epistles to the Thessalonians," p. 152.
45. Findlay, "Epistles of Paul the Apostle," p. 185.

CHAPTER 19

1. James Everett Frame, "A Critical and Exegetical Commentary on the Epistles of St. Paul to the Thessalonians," in *International Critical Commentary*, pp. 276-277.
2. James Denney, "The Epistles to the Thessalonians," in *An Exposition of the Bible*, 6:372.
3. Leon Morris, "The First and Second Epistles to the Thessalonians," in *New International Commentary*, pp. 237-238.
4. Edward Headland and Henry Barclay Swete, *The Epistles to the Thessalonians*, p. 166.
5. George G. Findlay, "The Epistles of Paul the Apostle to the Thessalonians," in *Cambridge Greek Testament*, p. 189.
6. C. F. Hogg and W. E. Vine, *The Epistle of Paul to the Thessalonians*, p. 271.
7. C. J. Riggenbach, "The Second Epistle of Paul to the Thessalonians," in *Lange's Commentary on the Holy Scriptures*, p. 145.
8. William Neil, "The Epistle of Paul to the Thessalonians," in *Moffatt New Testament Commentary*, p. 181.
9. R. C. H. Lenski, *The Interpretation of St. Paul's Epistles to the Colossians, to the Thessalonians, to Timothy, to Titus and to Philemon*, p. 450.
10. Alfred Plummer, *A Commentary on St. Paul's Second Epistle to the Thessalonians*, p. 76.
11. Findlay, p. 190.
12. Denney, p. 373.
13. E. J. Bicknell, "The First and Second Epistles to the Thessalonians," in *Westminster Commentaries*, p. 82.
14. George Milligan, *St. Paul's Epistles to the Thessalonians*, p. 108.

CHAPTER 20

1. George Milligan, *St. Paul's Epistles to the Thessalonians*, p. 136.
2. G. W. Garrod, *The Second Epistle to the Thessalonians*, p. 127.
3. Milligan, p. 109.
4. Benjamin Jowett, *The Epistles of St. Paul to the Thessalonians, Galatians, Romans*, 1:171.
5. James Hope Moulton and George Milligan, *The Vocabulary of the Greek Testament*, p. 90.
6. For the view of Calvin that "Paul is referring to unprincipled and treacherous individuals who were lurking in the Church under the name of Christians," which does not suit the context, see John Calvin, *The Epistles of Paul the Apostle to the Romans and to Thessalonians*, p. 413.
7. Walter F. Adeney, "Thessalonians and Galatians," in *The Century Bible*, pp. 249-250.
8. Edward Headland and Henry Barclay Swete, *The Epistles to the Thessalonians*, p. 171.
9. Alfred Plummer, *A Commentary on St. Paul's Second Epistle to the Thessalonians*, p. 89.
10. Ibid.
11. George G. Findlay, "The Epistles to the Thessalonians," in *Cambridge Bible for Schools and Colleges*, p. 160. Findlay's italics.
12. J. B. Lightfoot, *Notes on the Epistles of St. Paul*, p. 126.
13. Rudolf Bultmann, *"peithō"* in *Theological Dictionary of the New Testament*, 6:6.
14. P. J. Gloag, "II Thessalonians," in *The Pulpit Commentary*, p. 63.
15. E. J. Bicknell, "The First and Second Epistles to the Thessalonians," in *Westminster Commentaries*, p. 92.
16. Lightfoot, pp. 127-128.
17. Adeney, p. 251.
18. F. Hauck, *"hupomenō, hupomonē,"* in *Theological Dictionary of the Bible*, 4:586.
19. Plummer, pp. 95-96.
20. Willis De Boer, *The Imitation of Paul. An Exegetical Study*, p. 133.

21. C. F. Hogg and W. E. Vine, *The Epistles of Paul the Apostle to the Thessalonians*, p. 286.
22. A. J. Mason, "The Epistles of Paul the Apostle to the Thessalonians," in *Ellicott's Commentary on the Whole Bible*, 8:163.
23. Plummer, p. 100.
24. Calvin, p. 418.
25. D. D. Whedon, *A Popular Commentary on the New Testament*, 4:405.
26. Headland and Swete, p. 181.
27. Mason, 8:163.
28. Findlay, p. 165.
29. R. C. H. Lenski, *The Interpretation of St. Paul's Epistles to the Thessalonians, to Titus and to Philemon*, p. 472.
30. James Everett Frame, "A Critical and Exegetical Commentary on the Epistles of St. Paul to the Thessalonians," in *International Critical Commentary*, p. 306.
31. Wm. Alexander, "The Second Epistle of Paul the Apostle to the Thessalonians," in *The Speaker's Commentary, New Testament*, 3:745.
32. Gottlieb Lünemann, "Critical and Exegetical Handbook to the Epistles of St. Paul to the Thessalonians," in *Meyer's Critical and Exegetical Commentary on the New Testament*, p. 250.
33. William F. Arndt and F. Wilbur Gingrich, *A Greek-English Lexicon of the New Testament*, p. 652.
34. Lenski, p. 473.
35. Plummer, p. 105.
36. Calvin, p. 420.
37. James Moffatt, "The First and Second Epistles of Paul the Apostle to the Thessalonians," in *Expositor's Greek Testament*, 4:53.
38. Lightfoot, p. 133.
39. Hogg and Vine, p. 291.
40. Lenski, p. 477.
41. Calvin, p. 421.
42. Charles J. Ellicott, *A Critical and Grammatical Commentary on St. Paul's Epistles to the Thessalonians*, p. 141.
43. Moffatt, 4:53.
44. Joseph Henry Thayer, *A Greek-English Lexicon of the New Testament*, p. 276.

CHAPTER 21

1. Charles J. Ellicott, *A Critical and Grammatical Commentary on St. Paul's Epistles to the Thessalonians*, p. 141.
2. Walter F. Adeney, "Thessalonians and Galatians," in *The Century Bible*, p. 255.
3. Adolf Deissmann, *Light From the Ancient East*, p. 158. For the letter, see Fig. 19 and pp. 157-159.
4. John W. Bailey and James W. Clarke, "The First and Second Epistles to the Thessalonians," in *The Interpreter's Bible*, p. 338.
5. Gottlieb Lünemann, "Critical and Exegetical Handbook to the Epistles of St. Paul to the Thessalonians," in *Meyer's Critical and Exegetical Commentary on the New Testament*, p. 254.
6. F. F. Bruce, "Thessalonians, Epistles to the," in *The New Bible Dictionary*, p. 1272.
7. Philip Schaff, *History of the Christian Church*, 1:741.

BIBLIOGRAPHY

TEXT OF 1 AND 2 THESSALONIANS

GREEK

Aland, Kurt; Black, Matthew; Metzger, Bruce M.; and Wikgren, Allen. *The Greek New Testament.* American Bible Society; British and Foreign Bible Society; National Bible Society of Scotland; Netherlands Bible Society; Württemberg Bible Society, 1966. (Referred to as the Bible Societies' text)

Nestle, Erwin; and Aland, Kurt; *Novum Testamentum Graece.* 24th ed. Stuttgart: Privileg. Württ. Bibleanstalt. (Nestle)

Scrivener, F. H. *Hē Kainē Diathēkē Novum Testamentum, Textus Stephanici A.D. 1550.* London: Whittaker et Soc: Bell et Daldy, 1867. (*Textus Receptus*)

Souter, Alexander. *Novum Testamentum Graece.* 1910. Reprint. Oxford: Clarendon, 1962.

Westcott, Brooke Foss; and Hort, Fenton John Anthony. *The New Testament in the Original Greek.* Reprint. New York: Macmillan, 1935.

ENGLISH VERSIONS

Conybeare, W. J. *The Epistles of Paul, A Translation and Notes.* Reprint from W. J. Conybeare and J. S. Howson, *The Life and Epistles of Saint Paul,* 1902. Grand Rapids: Baker, 1958.

Darby, J. N. *The 'Holy Scriptures' A New Translation from the Original Languages.* Reprint. Kingston-on-Thames, Eng.: Stow Hill, 1949.

Goodspeed, Edgar J. *The New Testament, An American Translation.* Reprint. Chicago: U. of Chicago, 1923.

The Holy Bible containing the Old and New Testaments. Cambridge: U. Press, 1885. (KJV)

Lattey, Cuthbert, S. J. *The New Testament in the Westminster Version of the Sacred Scriptures.* London: Sands, 1947.

Moffatt, James. *The New Testament, A New Translation.* Rev. ed. Reprint. New York: Harper, 1935.

Montgomery, Helen Barrett. *The New Testament in Modern English.* 1924. Reprint. Philadelphia: Judson, 1946.

New American Standard Bible, New Testament. Nashville: Broadman, 1963. (NASB)

New English Bible, New Testament. Oxford: U. Press, 1961. (NEB)

Phillips, J. B. *The New Testament in Modern English.* New York: Macmillan, 1962.

Revised Standard Version, The Holy Bible. Philadelphia: A. J. Holman, 1962. (RSV)

Rotherham, Joseph Bryant. *The Emphasized New Testament.* Reprint. Grand Rapids: Kregel, 1959.

Twentieth Century New Testament: A Translation into Modern English. Reprint. Chicago: Moody, n.d.

Verkuyl, Gerrit, ed. *The Holy Bible: The Berkeley Version in Modern English.* Grand Rapids: Zondervan, 1945.

Way, Arthur S. *The Letters of St. Paul.* London: Macmillan, 1926.

Weymouth, Richard Francis. *The New Testament in Modern Speech.* 1902. 5th rev. ed. Reprint. New York: Harper, n.d.

Williams, Charles B. *The New Testament: A Private Translation in the Language of the People.* 1937. Reprint. Chicago: Moody, n.d.

Young, Robert. *The Holy Bible, Translated according to the Letter and Idioms of the Original Languages.* 1862. Rev. ed. London: Pickering & Inglis, n.d.

BOOKS ON 1 AND 2 THESSALONIANS

Adeney, Walter F. "Thessalonians and Galatians." In *The Century Bible.* Edinburgh: T. C. and E. C. Jack, n.d.

Alexander, Wm. "Thessalonians." In *The Speaker's Commentary: New Testament,* vol. 3. London: John Murray, 1881.

Alford, Henry. *The Greek Testament.* Vol. 3. 2nd ed. London: Rivingtons, 1857.

———. *The New Testament for English Readers.* Reprint. Chicago: Moody, n.d.

Auberlen, Charles Augustus; and Riggenbach, C. J. "The First Epistle to the Thessalonians." In *Lange's Commentary on the Holy Scriptures.* Trans. and ed. Philip Schaff. Reprint. Grand Rapids: Zondervan, n.d.

Bailey, John W.; and Clarke, James W. "The First and Second Epistles to the Thessalonians." In *The Interpreter's Bible,* vol. 11. Nashville: Abingdon, 1955.

Barclay, William. "The Letters to the Philippians, Colossians and Thessalonians." In *The Daily Study Bible.* Edinburgh: Saint Andrew, 1959.

Barnes, Albert. *Notes on the New Testament Explanatory and Practical—Thessalonians, Timothy, Titus and Philemon.* Reprint. Grand Rapids: Baker, 1949.

Bicknell, E. J. "The First and Second Epistles to the Thessalonians." In *Westminster Commentaries.* London: Methuen, 1932.

Blackwelder, Boyce W. *Toward Understanding Thessalonians.* Anderson, Ind.: Warner, 1965.

Calvin, John. "The Epistles of Paul the Apostle to the Romans and to the Thessalonians." In *Calvin's Commentaries.* Trans. Ross Mackenzie. Grand Rapids: Eerdmans, 1961.

Clarke, Adam. *Clarke's Commentary, New Testament.* Vol. 2. Reprint. New York: Carlton, n.d.

Denney, James. "The Epistles to the Thessalonians." In *An Exposition of The Bible,* vol. 6. Hartford, Conn.: S. S. Scranton, 1903.

Ellicott, Charles J. *A Critical and Grammatical Commentary on St. Paul's Epistles to the Thessalonians.* Andover: Warren F. Draper, 1864.

Erdman, Charles R. *The Epistles of Paul to the Thessalonians.* Philadelphia: Westminster, 1935.

Fergusson, James. *An Exposition of the Epistles of Paul.* Reprint. Evansville, Ind.: Sovereign Grace, n.d.

Fields, Wilbur. *Thinking Through Thessalonians.* Bible Study Textbook series. Joplin, Mo.: College Press, 1963.

Findlay, George G. "The Epistles of Paul the Apostle to the Thessalonians." In *Cambridge Greek Testament.* Cambridge: U. Press, 1904.

————. "The Epistles to the Thessalonians." In *Cambridge Bible for Schools and Colleges.* 1891. Reprint. Cambridge: U. Press, 1898.

Frame, James Everett. "A Critical and Exegetical Commentary on the Epistles of St. Paul to the Thessalonians." In *The International Critical Commentary.* New York: Scribner, 1912.

Garrod, G. W. *The First Epistle to the Thessalonians.* London: Macmillan, 1899.

————. *The Second Epistle to the Thessalonians.* London: Macmillan, 1900.

Gloag, P. J. "I Thessalonians and "II Thessalonians." In *The Pulpit Commentary.* Ed. H. D. M. Spence, and Joseph S. Excell. Reprint. Chicago: Wilcox and Follett, n.d.

Grant, F. W. *The Numerical Bible—Acts to 2 Corinthians.* Reprint. New York: Loizeaux, n.d.

Greene, Oliver B. *The Epistles of Paul the Apostle to the Thessalonians.* Greenville, S. C.: Gospel Hour, 1964.

Headland, Edward, and Swete, Henry Barclay. *The Epistles to the Thessalonians.* London: Hatchard, 1863.

Hendriksen, William. "Exposition of I and II Thessalonians." In *New Testament Commentary.* Grand Rapids: Baker, 1955.

Hogg, C. F.; and Vine, W. E. *The Epistles of Paul the Apostle to the Thessalonians.* Reprint. Grand Rapids: Kregel, 1959.

Horne, Charles M. *The Epistles to the Thessalonians.* In Shield Bible Study series. Grand Rapids: Baker, 1961.

Hubbard, David A. "The First Epistle to the Thessalonians." In *The Wycliffe Bible Commentary.* Ed. Charles F. Pfeiffer and Everett F. Harrison. Chicago: Moody, 1962.

Jowett, Benjamin. *The Epistles of St. Paul to the Thessalonians, Galatians, Romans.* Vol. 1. London: John Murray, 1859.

Kelly, William. *The Epistles of Paul the Apostle to the Thessalonians.* 3rd ed. London: C. A. Hammond, 1953.

Kloppenstein, W. O. "The First and Second Epistles of Paul to the Thessalonians." In *The Wesleyan Bible Commentary,* vol. 5. Grand Rapids: Eerdmans, 1965.

Lenski, R. C. H. *The Interpretation of St. Paul's Epistles to the Colossians, to the Thessalonians, to Timothy, to Titus and to Philemon.* Columbus, O.: Lutheran Book Concern, 1937.

Lightfoot, J. B. *Notes on the Epistles of St. Paul.* Reprint. Grand Rapids: Zondervan, 1957.

Lipscomb, David. *A Commentary on the New Testament Epistles.* Vol. 5. Ed. J. W. Shepherd. Nashville: Gospel Advocate, 1942.

Lünemann, Gottlieb. "Critical and Exegetical Handbook to the Epistles of St. Paul to the Thessalonians." In *Meyer's Critical and Exegetical Commentary on the New Testament.* Edinburgh: T. & T. Clark, 1884.

Mackintosh, R. "Thessalonians and Corinthians." In *The Westminster New Testament*. New York: Revell, n.d.

Mason, A. J. "The Epistles of Paul the Apostle to the Thessalonians." In *Ellicott's Commentary on the Whole Bible*, vol. 8. Reprint. Grand Rapids: Zondervan, n.d.

Milligan, George. *St. Paul's Epistles to the Thessalonians*. Reprint. Grand Rapids: Eerdmans, 1952.

Moffatt, James. "The First and Second Epistles of Paul the Apostle to the Thessalonians." In *The Expositor's Greek Testament*, vol. 4. Ed. W. Robertson Nicoll. Reprint. Grand Rapids: Eerdmans, n.d.

Morris, Leon. "The Epistles of Paul to the Thessalonians." In *The Tyndale New Testament Commentaries*. Grand Rapids: Eerdmans, 1957.

———. "The First and Second Epistles to the Thessalonians." In *The New International Commentary on the New Testament*. Grand Rapids: Eerdmans, 1959.

Neil, William. "The Epistle of Paul to the Thessalonians." In *Moffatt New Testament Commentaries*. London: Hodder & Stoughton, 1950.

———. "St. Paul's Epistles to the Thessalonians." In *Torch Bible Commentaries*. Naperville, Ill.: Allenson, 1957.

Ockenga, Harold J. *The Church In God. Expository Values in Thessalonians*. Westwood, N. J.: Revell, 1956.

Plummer, Alfred. *A Commentary on St. Paul's First Epistle to the Thessalonians*. London: Robert Scott, 1918.

———. *A Commentary on St. Paul's Second Epistle to the Thessalonians*. London: Robert Scott, 1918.

Riggenbach, J. C. "The Second Epistle of Paul to the Thessalonians." In *Lange's Commentary on the Holy Scriptures*. Reprint. Grand Rapids: Zondervan, n.d.

Rolston, H. "Thessalonians, Timothy, Titus, Philemon." In *The Layman's Bible Commentaries*. Richmond, Va.: Knox, 1963.

Ryrie, Charles Caldwell. *First and Second Thessalonians*. Chicago: Moody, 1959.

Sadler, M. F. *The Epistles of St. Paul to the Colossians, Thessalonians, and Timothy*. London: George Bell & Sons, 1899.

Stevens, William Arnold. "Commentary on the Epistles to the Thessalonians." In *An American Commentary on the New Testament*. 1890. Reprint. Philadelphia: Amer. Bapt. Pub. Soc., n.d.

Sumner, John Bird. *A Practical Exposition of St. Paul's Epistles to the Thessalonians, To Timothy, Titus, Philemon, and to the Hebrews*. London: Thomas Hatchard, 1851.

Trapp, John. *Trapp's Commentary on the New Testament*. Reprint. Evansville, Ind.: Sovereign Grace, 1958.

Vincent, Marvin R. "The Thessalonian Epistles." In *Word Studies in the New Testament*, vol. 4. 1900. Reprint. Grand Rapids: Eerdmans, 1946.

Walvoord, John R. *The Thessalonian Epistles*. Findlay, O.: Dunham, 1955.

Whedon, D. D. *A popular Commentary on the New Testament*. Volume IV, *I Corinthians–II Timothy*. London: Hodder & Stoughton, 1876.

Wood, G. R. Harding. *St. Paul's First Letter*. London: Henry W. Walter, 1952.

OTHER BOOKS

Allen, Roland. *Missionary Methods, St. Paul's or Ours?* London: Robert Scott, 1913.

Arndt, William F., and Gingrich, F. Wilbur. *A Greek-English Lexicon of the New Testament and Other Early Christian Literature.* Chicago: U. of Chicago, 1957.

Barclay, William. "The Letter to the Romans." In *The Daily Study Bible.* 2nd ed. Edinburgh: Saint Andrew, 1962.

———. *The Mind of St. Paul.* New York: Harper, 1958.

———. *New Testament Words.* London: SCM Press, 1964.

Barrett, C. K. *The New Testament Background: Selected Documents.* New York: Harper & Row, 1961.

Baxter, J. Sidlow. *Awake, My Heart.* Grand Rapids: Zondervan, 1960.

Bruce, F. F. *The Acts of the Apostles.* London: Tyndale Press, 1951.

———. *Are the New Testament Documents Reliable?* 2nd ed. Chicago: Inter-Varsity, 1948.

———. *The Books and the Parchments.* London: Pickering & Inglis, 1950.

———. *The Dawn of Christianity.* Grand Rapids: Eerdmans, 1950.

Buswell, J. Oliver, Jr. *A Systematic Theology of the Christian Religion.* Vol. 2. Grand Rapids: Zondervan, 1954.

Conybeare, W. J.; and Howson, J. S. *The Life and Epistles of Saint Paul.* People's Edition. Hartford, Conn.: S. S. Scranton, 1902.

Cooper, Clay. *Nothing to Win but the World.* Grand Rapids: Zondervan, 1965.

Cremer, Herman. *Biblico-Theological Lexicon of New Testament Greek.* Trans. William Urwick. Reprint. Edinburgh: T. & T. Clark, 1954.

Dana, H. E.; and Mantey, Julius R. *A Manual Grammar of the Greek New Testament.* New York: Macmillan, 1927.

De Boer, Willis Peter. *The Imitation of Paul. An Exegetical Study.* Kampen: J. H. Kok, 1962.

Deissmann, G. Adolf. *Bible Studies.* 2nd ed. Edinburgh: T. & T. Clark, 1909.

———. *Light From the Ancient East.* Trans. Lionel R. M. Strachan. London: Hodder & Stoughton, 1910.

———. *Paul, A Study in Social and Religious History.* Trans. William E. Wilson. Reprint. New York: Harper & Row. Torchbooks, 1957.

Dodd, C. H. "The Epistle of Paul to the Romans." In *The Moffatt New Testament Commentaries.* New York: Long & Richard R. Smith, 1932.

English, E. Schuyler. *Re-Thinking the Rapture.* Travelers Rest, S. C.: Southern Bible, 1954.

Finegan, Jack. *Handbook of Biblical Chronology.* Princeton, N. J.: Princeton U., 1964.

———. *Light From the Ancient Past.* Princeton: Princeton U. Press, 1946.

Furneaux, William Mordaunt. *The Acts of the Apostles.* Oxford: Clarendon, 1912.

Goodspeed, Edgar J. *An Introduction to the New Testament.* Chicago: U. of Chicago, 1937.

Guthrie, Donald. *New Testament Introduction, The Pauline Epistles.* Chicago: Inter-Varsity, 1961.

Hammond, T. C. *The One Hundred Texts of the Society for Irish Church Missions.* 4th ed. London: Irish Church Missions, 1954.

Harrison, Everett F. *Introduction to the New Testament.* Grand Rapids: Eerdmans, 1964.

Harrison, Norman B. *The End: Rethinking the Revelation.* Minneapolis: Harrison, 1941.

Hendriksen, William. "Exposition of Galatians." In *New Testament Commentary.* Grand Rapids: Baker, 1968.

Hiebert, D. Edmond. *An Introduction to the Pauline Epistles.* Chicago: Moody, 1954.

Howson, John S. *The Metaphors of St. Paul and Companions of St. Paul.* Boston: American Tract Soc., 1872.

Hoyt, Herman A. *The End Times.* Chicago: Moody, 1969.

Hughes, Philip Edgcumbe. "Paul's Second Epistle to the Corinthians." In *The New International Commentary on the New Testament.* Ed. F. F. Bruce. Grand Rapids: Eerdmans, 1962.

Jackson, F. J. Foakes; and Lake, Kirsopp, eds. *The Beginnings of Christianity.* Vol. 5. Reprint. Grand Rapids: Baker, 1966.

Keller, Werner. *The Bible As History.* New York: William Morrow, 1956.

Kepler, Thomas S., comp. *Contemporary Thinking About Paul. An Anthology.* New York: Abingdon-Cokesbury, 1950.

Kümmel, Werner Georg. *Introduction to the New Testament.* Trans. A. J. Mattill, Jr. Nashville: Abingdon, 1966.

Ladd, George Eldon. *The Blessed Hope.* Grand Rapids: Eerdmans, 1956.

Lenski, R. C. H. *The Interpretation of the Acts of the Apostles.* Columbus, O.: Lutheran Book Concern, 1934.

Lightfoot, J. B. *Biblical Essays.* London: Macmillan, 1893.

———. *Saint Paul's Epistles to the Colossians and to Philemon.* Reprint. London: Macmillan, 1900.

McNeile, A. H. *An Introduction to the Study of the New Testament.* Oxford: Clarendon, 1927.

McPherson, Norman Spurgeon. *Triumph Through Tribulation.* Otego, N. Y.: Author, 1944.

Manson, T. W. *Studies in the Gospels and Epistles.* Philadelphia: Westminster, 1962.

Metzger, Bruce M. *The Text of the New Testament.* New York and London: Oxford U., 1964.

Moffatt, James. "An Introduction to the Literature of the New Testament." In *International Theological Library.* Reprint. Edinburgh: T. & T. Clark, 1949.

Morris, Leon. *The Biblical Doctrine of Judgment.* Grand Rapids: Eerdmans, 1960.

Moule, C. F. D. "The Epistles of Paul the Apostle to the Colossians and to Philemon." In *Cambridge Greek Testament Commentary.* Cambridge: U. Press, 1957.

Moulton, James Hope. *A Grammar of New Testament Greek.* Vol. I, *Prolegomena.* Edinburgh: T. & T. Clark, 1908.

Moulton, James Hope; and Milligan, George. *The Vocabulary of the Greek Testament.* Reprint. London: Hodder & Stoughton, 1952.

Muir, James C. *How Firm a Foundation.* Philadelphia: National, 1941.

Murray, John. "The Epistle to the Romans." In *The New International Commentary,* vol. 1. Grand Rapids: Eerdmans, 1959.

Paton, James. *The Glory and Joy of the Resurrection.* London: Hodder & Stoughton, 1902.

Pentecost, J. Dwight. *Things to Come. A Study in Biblical Eschatology.* Findlay, O.: Dunham, 1958.

Plummer, Alfred. "A Critical and Exegetical Commentary on the Second Epistle of St. Paul to the Corinthians." In *The International Critical Commentary.* 1915. Reprint. Edinburgh: T. & T. Clark, 1951.

Rackham, Richard Belward. "The Acts of the Apostles." In *Westminster Commentaries.* 9th ed. London: Methuen, 1922.

Ramsay, W. M. *The Church in the Roman Empire Before A.D. 170.* Reprint. Grand Rapids: Baker, 1954.

———. *St. Paul the Traveller and the Roman Citizen.* New York: Putnam, 1896.

Reese, Alexander. *The Approaching Advent of Christ.* London: Marshall, Morgan, & Scott, n.d.

Rice, John R. *The Coming Kingdom of Christ.* Wheaton, Ill.: Sword of the Lord, 1945.

Robert, A., and Feuillet, A. *Introduction to the New Testament.* New York: Descelle, 1965.

Robertson, A. T. *The Minister and His Greek New Testament.* London: Hodder & Stoughton, 1923.

Robertson, A. T.; and Davis, W. Hersey. *A New Short Grammar of the Greek Testament.* New York: Harper, 1935.

Robertson, Fredk. W. *Life, Letters, Lectures, and Addresses of Fredk. W. Robertson.* New York: Harper, n.d.

Sauer, Erich. *The Triumph of the Crucified.* Grand Rapids: Eerdmans, 1952.

Schaff, Philip. *History of the Christian Church.* Vol. 1. 3rd rev. New York: Scribner, 1910.

Scroggie, W. Graham. *Know Your Bible. A Brief Introduction to the Scriptures.* Volume II, *The New Testament.* London: Pickering & Inglis, n.d.

Smeaton, George. *The Apostles' Doctrine of the Atonement.* 1870. Reprint. Grand Rapids: Zondervan, 1957.

Stanton, Gerald B. *Kept From the Hour.* Grand Rapids: Zondervan, 1956.

Stewart, James A. *Heaven's Throne Gift.* Asheville, N. C.: Revival Lit., n.d.

———. *Pastures of Tender Grass.* Philadelphia: Revival Lit., 1962.

Stewart, James S. *A Man in Christ.* New York: Harper, n.d.

Strong, Augustus Hopkins. *Systematic Theology.* 1907. Reprint. Philadelphia: Judson, 1946.

Tasker, R. V. G. *The Biblical Doctrine of the Wrath of God.* London: Tyndale Press, 1951.

Thayer, Joseph Henry. *A Greek-English Lexicon of the New Testament.* Reprint. New York: Amer. Book, 1889.

Trench, Richard Chenevix. *Synonyms of the New Testament.* Reprint. Grand Rapids: Eerdmans, 1947.

Unger, Merrill F. *Archaeology and the New Testament.* Grand Rapids: Zondervan, 1962.

Walvoord, John F. *The Church in Prophecy.* Grand Rapids: Zondervan, 1964.

———. *The Rapture Question.* Findlay, O.: Dunham, 1957.

Warfield, Benjamin Breckinridge. *Biblical and Theological Studies.* Ed. Samuel G. Craig. Philadelphia: Presb. Ref., 1952.

Westcott, Brooke Foss; and Hort, Fenton John Anthony. Introduction and Appendix to *The New Testament in the Original Greek*, vol. 2. London: Macmillan, 1907.

Wikenhauser, Alfred. *New Testament Introduction*. New York: Herder & Herder, 1958.

Wood, Leon J. *Is the Rapture Next? An Answer to the Question: Will the Church Escape the Tribulation?* Grand Rapids: Zondervan, 1956.

Wuest, Kenneth S. *The Practical Use of the Greek New Testament*. Chicago: Moody, 1946.

————. *Prophetic Light in the Present Darkness*. Grand Rapids: Eerdmans, 1955.

Zahn, Theodor. *Introduction to the New Testament*. Vol. 1. Edinburgh: T. & T. Clark, 1909.

DICTIONARY AND ENCYCLOPEDIA ARTICLES

Beare, F. W. "Thessalonians, First Letter to the." In *The Interpreter's Dictionary of the Bible*, vol. 4. Nashville: Abingdon, 1962.

Behm, Johannes. "*kardia.*" In *Theological Dictionary of the New Testament*, vol. 3. Ed. Gerhard Kittel, trans. and ed. Geoffrey W. Bromiley. Grand Rapids: Eerdmans, 1964-68.

Bruce, F. F. "Thessalonians, Epistles to the." *The New Bible Dictionary*. Ed. J. D. Douglas. Grand Rapids: Eerdmans, 1962.

Bultmann, Rudolf. "*peithō.*" In *Theological Dictionary of the New Testament*, vol. 6.

Faulkner, J. Alfred. "Salutations." In *Dictionary of the Apostolic Church*. Ed. James Hastings. 2:442-444. Edinburgh: T. & T. Clark, 1918.

Grundmann, Walter. "*dechomai.*" In *Theological Dictionary of the New Testament*, vol. 2.

Harrop, J. H. "Gallio." In *The New Bible Dictionary*. Ed. J. D. Douglas. Grand Rapids: Eerdmans, 1962.

Hauck, F. "*hupomenō, hupomonē.*" In *Theological Dictionary of the New Testament*, vol. 4.

Moule, H. C. G. "Election." In *The International Standard Bible Encyclopedia*, vol. 2. Ed. James Orr. Grand Rapids: Eerdmans, 1939.

Oepke, Albrecht. "*apōleia.*" In *Theological Dictionary of the New Testament*, vol. 1.

Procksch, Otto. "*hagiōsunē.*" In *Theological Dictionary of the New Testament* vol. 1.

MAGAZINE ARTICLES

Faw, Chalmer E. "On the Writing of First Thessalonians." *Journal of Biblical Literature* 71(Dec. 1952):217-232.

Gregson, R. "A Solution to the Problems of the Thessalonian Epistles." *The Evangelical Quarterly* 38:2 (April-June 1966):76-80.

Harris, J. Rendel. "A Study in Letter-writing." *The Expositor*, 5th ser. 8(Sept. 1898):161-180.

Mason, Clarence E. Jr. "The Day of Our Lord Jesus Christ." *Bibliotheca Sacra* 125:500 (Oct.-Dec. 1968):352-359.

Rienecker, Fritz. "The Cross and Demythologizing." *Christianity Today* 6, no. 12 (March 16, 1962):9-12.

Walvoord, John F. "New Testament Words for the Lord's Coming." *Bibliotheca Sacra* 101:403 (July-Sept. 1944):283-289.